# A Synoptic History of
# Classical Rhetoric

Continuing its tradition of providing students with a thorough review of ancient
Greek and Roman rhetorical theory and practices, *A Synoptic History of Classical
Rhetoric* is the premier text for undergraduate courses and graduate seminars in the
history of rhetoric. Offering vivid examples of each classical rhetor, rhetorical period,
and source text, students are led to understand rhetoric's role in the exchange of
knowledge and ideas. Completely updated throughout, Part I of this new edition inte-
grates new research and expanded notes and bibliographies for students to develop
their own scholarship. Part II offers six classical texts for reading, study, and criticism,
and includes keys to the text in Part I.

# A Synoptic History of Classical Rhetoric

## Fourth Edition

James J. Murphy,
Richard A. Katula, and
Michael Hoppmann

 Routledge
Taylor & Francis Group

NEW YORK AND LONDON

Fourth edition published 2014
by Routledge
711 Third Avenue, New York, NY 10017

Simultaneously published in the UK
by Routledge
2 Park Square, Milton Park, Abingdon, Oxon OX14 4RN

*Routledge is an imprint of the Taylor & Francis Group, an informa business*

© 2014 Taylor & Francis

The right of James J. Murphy, Richard A. Katula, and Michael Hoppmann to be identified as authors of this work has been asserted by them in accordance with sections 77 and 78 of the Copyright, Designs and Patents Act 1988.

First edition published by Lawrence Erlbaum Associates 1983
Third edition published by Lawrence Erlbaum Associates 2003

*Library of Congress Cataloging-in-Publication Data*
Murphy, James Jerome.
A synoptic history of classical rhetoric / by James J. Murphy, Richard A. Katula, Michael Hoppmann. — 4th edition.
   pages cm
1. Rhetoric, Ancient. 2. Classical literature—History and criticism—Theory, etc. I. Katula, Richard A. II. Hoppmann, Michael J. III. Title.
PA3265.M8 2013
808'.00937—dc23                                          2013000536

ISBN: 978-0-415-53240-2 (hbk)
ISBN: 978-0-415-53241-9 (pbk)
ISBN: 978-0-203-11484-1 (ebk)

Typeset in Sabon
by Cenveo Publisher Services

SFI® Certified Sourcing
www.sfiprogram.org
SFI-00453

Printed and bound in the United States of America
by Edwards Brothers, Inc.

# Contents

# About the Authors

**James J. "Jerry" Murphy** (Ph.D., Stanford University, 1957) is Emeritus Professor at the University of California, Davis. He is the author or editor of 21 books and more than 70 scholarly articles. His book *Rhetoric in the Middle Ages* was acknowledged with the 1975 Speech Communication Association Book Award. He is a Fellow of the Medieval Academy of America, and a Fellow of the Rhetoric Society of America. He was the founding Editor (1983–1988) of *Rhetorica*, journal of the International Society for the History of Rhetoric. He was until 1995 the publisher of Hermagoras Press, devoted to publishing books related to language use. Hermagoras Press is now an imprint of Routledge Publishers. His most recent edited book is *A Short History of Writing Instruction from Ancient Greece to Contemporary America* (Routledge, 2012). His professional motto is a line from Thomas Aquinas: "Teachers don't teach, learners learn."

**Richard A. Katula** (Ph.D., University of Illinois, C-U, 1974) is a Professor in the Department of Communication Studies at Northeastern University. Professor Katula has authored *Principles and Patterns of Public Speaking* (1987) and *The Eloquence of Edward Everett* (2010). He has also co-authored two books, *Communication: Writing and Speaking* and *A Synoptic History of Classical Rhetoric, 3rd edn* (2003). Professor Katula's documentary video on *The Gettysburg Address: A Speech for the Ages* (2000) was awarded the Eastern Communication Association's Everett Lee Hunt prize for scholarship. Professor Katula is the Director of "The Lyceum and Public Culture: the Rhetoric of Idealism, Opportunity, and Abolition," sponsored by the National Endowment for the Humanities. He directs a "Dialogue of Civilizations" program to Greece every summer, and is fond of the expression, "Respect speaks when spoken to."

**Michael Hoppmann** (Ph.D., University of Tübingen) is a lecturer in the Department of Communication Studies at Northeastern University. He has authored *Argumentative Verteidigung (Argumentive Defense)* and co-authored four books on applied argumentation, debate, and rhetoric in German. In addition, he has contributed numerous articles on classical rhetoric and modern argumentation theory to German and English publications, including a number of entries to two of the largest rhetorical lexica, the *Historisches Wörterbuch der Rhetorik (Historical Lexicon of Rhetoric)* and the *Handbuch der Sprach- und Kommunikationswissens* *chaft (Handbook of Linguistics and Communication Science)*. Before coming to the United States, Dr. Hoppmann worked at the University of Tübingen (Germany) where he wrote his dissertation on stasis theory under the supervision of Joachim Knape and Frans van Eemeren. He teaches courses in argument, debate, and public speaking.

# Introduction

Ideal voices, the beloved voices
of those who have died or of those who are
lost to us as if they were dead.

Sometimes they speak to us in dreams;
sometimes, in thought, the mind hears them,

And with their sounds for a moment return
sounds from our life's first poetry –
like music at night, far off, fading out.
                    Excerpt from C. P. Cavafy, *Voices*

In this passage the celebrated modern Greek poet Cavafy praises the ancient writers of Greece and Rome whose ideas live on even though they themselves are gone. They were, indeed, the first "poets" of our world, the world of western civilization. Today their words revive in us the culture of classicism, a body of ideas that has penetrated American and European society even though at times their voices seem to us like quiet music in the night, far off and fading out.

We seldom recognize that so much of what we observe around us—our art, architecture, literature, our political system, even our alphabet—derives from ancient Greece and Rome, where, during brilliant flashes of insight and transformation, western culture was created. Guided by no deity, the ancient Greeks constructed their own society, one uniquely human in its origin. It is from this body of knowledge, in fact, that we get the word "Humanities." Some of these thinkers, Plato and Aristotle, for instance, stand today beside the great minds of other periods in our history—Aquinas, Locke, Hegel, Jefferson, Einstein, to name a few. Moreover, their ideas survive as the seminal principles of all democratic societies. And why? As G. W. Bowersock writes, "The main reason that classicism survives in America and elsewhere is precisely that it is so porous and multiform. It can instruct and delight according to many different moral and political systems" (*New Republic*, November 4, 2002, p. 31).

Representative democracy did not spring full blown from the heavens. It is a system for governing human relations that evolved out of the experience of the Greeks as they settled the islands and coastal areas around the Mediterranean, Aegean, and Ionian seas particularly from the 8th century BCE until the 4th century BCE. Democratic forms such as laws, and democratic institutions such as assemblies and courtrooms, all of which we take for granted today, arose from the age-old fact that people, when living together in complex societies, quarrel with one another. Such disputes must be resolved in order that the society may remain stable. When we observe our judicial, legislative, and executive branches engaged in the difficult task of resolving human disputes in accord with the wishes of the public, we see in them a reflection of the model devised for this purpose by the ancient Greeks. For instance, even as early as Homer's *Iliad* (8th century BCE), we find passages in which judgments about disputes are made by a king or by the elders of the tribe, but always with the consent of the public gathered together and serving as the conscience of the community. It was this deliberative principle which ultimately led them to invent democracy, and by the end of the 8th century there had emerged the idea of the *polis*, the city-state, as the principal form of social organization, with its centerpiece the urban center and with its culmination in the 5th century BCE in the full-blown democracy of Athens.

Enlightened thinkers in every age since, from Thomas Aquinas to Abraham Lincoln, have looked to the classical world for guidance as they crafted the essential ideas upon which the societies of the world would govern themselves. America's most essential documents, the Declaration of Independence, the Constitution, and the Gettysburg Address, were written by students of the Classical Age. In its formative period in the early 19th century, America's first intellectuals brought classicism from Europe to the American university to be studied, not as abstract philosophy or philology, but as a practical model for culture and civilization. The ideals of ancient Greece, the ones Cavafy romanticizes about, were the source of the original ideals upon which America was built. Students in 18th and 19th century America and Europe studied Greek and Latin as a regular part of their education, and they recited the orations of Greek and Roman statesmen as a way of developing their own public speaking. In fact, the study of language and expression that is so central a part of our educational system today is modeled after the schools in ancient Athens and Rome. Once they have a chance to read them, university students today remain drawn to classic texts such as Pericles' *Funeral Oration*, Socrates' *Apology*, and Cicero's *Catalinian Orations*, not only because they capture moments of supreme human drama, but also because they evoke universal ideas and images that speak to us even today.

History tells us that the impulse toward self-government was driven by the emergence of a rhetorical self-consciousness. It was through the arts of expression, both spoken and written, that democratic and republican forms of government were nurtured. As far as one may judge from surviving evidence, the Greeks were the first people of the ancient world who endeavored to analyze the ways in which human beings communicate with each other, the *logos*. Greece is, therefore, the birthplace of the arts of discourse, which includes not only rhetoric but also logic, grammar, and poetry. Although many other ancient civilizations produced literature, only the Greeks produced analytic, expository treatises, and attempted to discover the bases of human communication. Written treatises for the purpose of teaching argument and persuasion led to the formation of a body of precepts that guided speakers for centuries thereafter. This body of principles forms the basis of the rhetorical theory that explains the art of human discourse.

Nevertheless it is also true that each age is threatened by the entropic forces of inarticulate and coarsened speech, or sloppy and hackneyed writing. Slippage into linguistic babble remains but one generation away. As always, to maintain the precision in language that advanced civilizations require, we turn to the Classical Age. As the philosopher Karl Jaspers reminds us:

> each great uplift of selfhood has been brought about by a fresh contact with the classical world. When that world has been forgotten, a barbarism has always revived. Just as a boat cut loose from its moorings drifts aimlessly hither and thither, at the mercy of the winds and waves, so do we drift when we lose touch with antiquity. Our primary foundation, changeable though it may be, is invariably the classical world.

It has been frequently observed that our modern epoch seems detached from its roots. Decisions we make about our society and our own lives often seem based upon fads or trends, upon what is socially or politically correct or current at the moment. An ordered knowledge seems to elude us. Concepts such as freedom, heroism, justice, happiness, and persuasion lose their meanings as they are detached from the times in which they were forged on the twin anvils of individual thought and public debate. Through the study of classical rhetoric we revive and sharpen the meaning of these foundational notions, learn how to find common ground, and discover the way forward.

*A Synoptic History of Classical Rhetoric* thus provides a clear understanding of the classical roots of rhetoric. While no single volume can account for every idea developed in ancient Greece and Rome, it does concentrate on the key concepts that have shaped the field for centuries. The book begins with a chapter providing an overview of the historical context in which the study of rhetoric emerged, including the contributions of women and the Presocratics.

Chapter 2 provides an extensive review of the rise of the "sophists," those first teachers of the art of speaking and writing persuasively. The lives and ideas of important sophists are reviewed, and the chapter describes and evaluates the debate that raged in the 5th century BCE between the sophists and their indefatigable critic Socrates.

Chapter 3 provides a thorough review of the most important rhetorical treatise of the Classical Age, Aristotle's *Rhetoric*. It also introduces the concept of "metarhetoric," that is, the set of knowledges Aristotle demands of his speaker (*rhetor*). This chapter has been revised from the third edition with a more readable format, more extensive commentary on key concepts such as the *Enthymeme* and the *Topics*, and a more consistent and detailed development of Aristotle's 28 common forms of argument. The chapter includes boxed presentations of key concepts for more focused reading. Finally, while retaining much of the material that has made this chapter so successful with teachers and students for four decades, the revised chapter incorporates new ideas about Aristotle's theory of rhetoric published in recent years.

Chapter 4 provides an introduction to standardized Roman rhetoric, with synopses of three pragmatic handbooks. It has also has been extensively revised to include fuller development of two important topics: *stasis* theory and *figures of speech* (*Topos* and *Figura*). With regard to Figures of Speech and Figures of Thought first found in Book IV of the *Rhetorica ad Herennium* (c.87 BCE), the authors have focused on those figures most commonly used in ancient and modern oratory in an effort to balance the focus of this chapter between theory and pedagogy.

Chapter 5 provides synopses of six major treatises on rhetoric composed during the era of the Roman republic by Marcus Tullius Cicero, one of the most influential orators and rhetoricians of the ancient world. Roman rhetoric and its educational background is studied further in Chapter 6, a comprehensive review of the life of Quintilian and his educational and rhetorical theory as developed in his 12-volume *Institutio oratoria* (*The Education of the Orator*). This chapter also notes the influence of the *Institutio oratoria* down through the ages.

We welcome Michael Hoppmann as a co-author of this fourth edition. Michael brings his knowledge of *stasis* theory to the text as well as his broad European education in the classics.

We have many people to thank for this fourth edition. First, all of you who used the preceding editions of *Synoptic* and sent us your comments and criticisms. They have made the text much stronger. We thank Linda Bathgate, the publisher at Routledge, for her guidance and support throughout this process. We thank our respective institutions for their support in completing this work.

On a more somber note, we lament the passing of Forbes I. Hill and Donovan J. Ochs, each of whom contributed so much to previous editions of this book.

We return, then, to ancient Greece and Rome, to discover the roots of our civilization and to review the first investigations into the art of public discourse—rhetoric—to keep alive the "Voices" Cavafy so loved, and to keep, as Jaspers put it so well, "our boats moored."

# Theories of Rhetoric

# Chapter 1

# The Origins of Rhetoric in the Democracy of Ancient Greece

Whoever does not study rhetoric will be a victim of it.

Ancient Greek wall inscription

## Introduction: The Urge to Study Rhetoric in Ancient Greece

It may be said that rhetoric is the handmaiden of democracy. Whether in the courtroom, the legislature, or the public forum, free and intelligent speaking and writing are the lubricants that keep the gears of democracy running smoothly. Instruction in the arts of discourse affords each one of us the opportunity to participate in the public debate and thus to feel invested in the decisions that are made. In his treatise *On Rhetoric*, Aristotle notes four advantages to studying this practical art for citizens living in a democracy: (1) to help truth prevail in the world of human affairs; (2) to help us understand how people are moved to action through speech; (3) to help us see both sides of an issue; and (4) to help us defend ourselves against the arguments of others. To understand democracy, then, as a lively exchange of ideas among the people living in it, one must understand rhetoric; and to understand rhetoric, one must understand democracy. This chapter details how democracy emerged as a form of government and how the art of rhetoric facilitated the practices that allowed it to flourish in ancient times, especially in Athens.

## The Rise of Democracy in Athens

The transformation of institutions of government into democratic forms created the need for expertise in speaking and writing. Prior to the 8th century before the Common Era (BCE),[1] ancient Greece was predominantly an oral culture.[2] Although forms of writing with symbols (rather than with pictures such as in hieroglyphic writing) known as Linear A and Linear B existed in Minoan and Mycenaean times, the emergence of alphabetic writing on papyrus during the Homeric Age in the late 8th century triggered a significant advance in literacy, especially in Athens, the most progressive of the Greek city-states. By the 5th century, Athens had evolved from a *mythic* society created, ordered, and governed by gods into an oral *and* written culture characterized by its focus on *logos*, or the search for order in the universe through speech and rational argument.[3] It was during this time that language came to be categorized and studied as a body of principles. Speaking and writing lessons soon became accessible to ordinary citizens in Athens, giving them the practical skills they would need to participate more effectively in the public institutions they had created. These two parallel developments, democracy and literacy in both spoken and written forms, created the need for, and the possibility of, an artful and strategic theory of communication: the art of rhetoric.

Democracy (from the Greek words *demos*, "the people," and *kratein*, "to rule") emerged as a response to changing conditions among the Greek people in the Attic, or southeastern, region of that country. During the period between approximately 3,000 and 850 BCE, kings such as King Minos in Crete and King Theseus in Athens ruled the various tribes throughout Greece. The king was considered a descendant of God, usually Zeus, and he ruled with omniscience. As Botsford notes:

> His honor [the King] was from Zeus, lord of counsel, who cherished him, granted him glory, and furnished him even with thoughts. His sceptre, the sign of his power, was made in heaven, and given by a god to the founder of his dynasty. The people, therefore, prayed and hearkened to him as a god.[4]

*Figure 1.1* Ancient Greece hand drawn set

Kings were commanders on the battlefield. Although during Minoan times there were long periods of peace, war remained a constant threat during these centuries, and kings were needed to order the troops into battle and to lead the defense of the villages when outside forces invaded. Thus, while the throne was inherited, kings remained in place to the extent that they were successful in preserving the peace and defending the tribe against enemies.

During these early periods encompassing the Minoan and Mycenaean Ages, people settled their disputes in various ways. According to the poet Homer in his *Iliad* and *Odyssey*, it was common for two men or two families to meet in a field and fight to settle a land dispute or a domestic feud, perhaps over a seduction or a property dispute. But the early Greeks also often preferred to talk out their differences, and they often consulted a third party who represented the voice of the community to sit in judgment of their arguments. These "*istors*" or "knowers" were the kings. Thus it was that kings became judges, because it was accepted that they alone knew what was right and they alone who could find the truth in competing stories.[5] Rather than laws as we might think about them today, there emerged a "code" of customs and traditions rooted in myth, tribal history, and kingly decrees that provided guidance for daily living. While the king might consult tribal elders during his deliberations over disputes, his was the first and last word. Since writing had not advanced to the linear alphabetic script used by Homer, records were kept on clay tablets or walls when they were kept at all, and justice was often a capricious undertaking since precedents did not accumulate on record. Justice at the hands of a king was often justice denied.

**BCE**

| | |
|---|---|
| 3000–1400 | The Minoan Age |
| 1600–1150 | The Mycenaean Age |
| 900–700 | Age of Homer |
| 700ca | Unification of Athens and the Attica region |
| 650–500 | Oligarchies overthrown by Tyrants |
| 630 | Dracon establishes written code of laws—The Laws of Blood |
| 593 | Solon reforms legal code |
| 492–479 | Persian wars |
| | Defeat of Persians at Marathon, 490 |
| | Defeat of Persians at Salamis, 480 |
| | Defeat of Persians at Plataea, 479 |
| 462–429 | Periclean Age, Golden Age of Athenian Democracy |
| 462–322 | The Classical Age |
| 431–404 | Peloponnesian War |
| | Sparta destroys Athenian navy, 405 |
| 404–371 | Spartan dominance of Greece |
| 403 | Democracy restored to Athens |
| 377 | Second Athenian Confederacy |
| | Athens defeats Spartan navy, 376 |
| 359–336 | Reign of Philip of Macedon |
| 336–323 | Reign of Alexander the Great |
| 323–276 | The Hellenic Age; last flowering of Athenian culture |
| 276 | The Roman Age; Greece conquered by the Roman Empire |

*Figure 1.2* The rise and decline of democracy in Athens: a chronological timeline

In civil affairs, the king was also supreme ruler. But during the Homeric Age councils emerged to administer the daily activities of the people and the king often deferred to the council in civil matters. The idea of the "state" began at this time as a crude institution. There were no administrators (bureaucrats) and the council of elders worked through the monarchy to maintain civil order. In matters of civil dispute, the king would often defer to an appointed magistrate. Legislative issues were usually discussed by a council of elders that submitted its decisions to the king for his approval or disapproval. Because the state did not function as an official intermediary in civil affairs, the family was the usual source of strength and support for the individual.

As groups of people settled into culturally distinct tribes and began to develop more involved forms of interaction with one another, civil affairs became more complex and kings by necessity were forced to heed the voice of their councils. Indeed, wise kings began to call councils into session regularly to seek their advice and respond to their needs. Some monarchies were actually close to aristocracies with a ruling class often holding sway in civil and military decisions, particularly when the king was weak. In matters of dispute, it became common for one of the disputants to make a speech in the presence of others, appealing for justice, we might say, by swaying public opinion. As MacDowell notes:

> Appealing to public opinion is something different from appealing to the king. A king may have special expertise as a judge, from talent or experience or divine inspiration. The general public can hardly be said to have such special expertise. But what they do have, if they care to use it, is power.[6]

This power is the power to influence the decision-makers, even if with no other means than their "cheers" or "boos" for the speakers or the verdicts of the judges.

Monarchies eventually gave way to more popular modes of decision-making, councils became more dominant in civil affairs so that by the late 8th century a transition began to aristocratic forms of government, oligarchies. Oligarchies were either powerful families or groups of powerful individuals who seized control of a city by wresting power from the king. Oligarchies were not always oppressive, but they served predominantly the needs of those in power. Oligarchies began to fail during the later years of the 7th century because they began making political decisions on a purely economic basis; that is, those individuals who could make a contribution to the treasury were favored.

Considering the state of affairs during the Homeric Period, it is clear to see why the urge for democracy arose. Those who fought the battles desired a greater voice in military decisions. In matters of state, magistrates too often used customs and traditions for personal benefit. Even a shift from a pure monarchy to an oligarchy or an aristocracy resulted in an abuse of power. Oligarchies were soon replaced with tyrannies; that is, forms of government where one powerful person ruled with the power of the military. Tyrannies differed from monarchies because the tyrant ruled not by the divine grace of the gods, but by his own political and military power.

The Homeric Age witnessed, then, an evolution in forms of government from monarchy to oligarchy to tyranny, and shortly thereafter, as we will see, to democracy. These changes, while both subtle and complex, can be seen most clearly in the light of human nature; that is, the natural desire human beings have for freedom, justice, peace, and community.

As noted earlier, and especially from the Mycenaean Age forward, warfare was a constant reality for the villages and cities of Greece. The most famous of these wars was the ten-year-long Trojan War (the war fought over Helen of Troy) thought by archaeologists to have been waged during the 12th century. It was common, indeed, for city-states to be at war for years at a time until one either retreated or was conquered. Since the penalty for military failure was enslavement or death, governments existed principally to insure victory in war. Democracy, in fact, arose first in the Attic region when it became a form of government capable of insuring domestic tranquility through triumph on the battlefield. Its value as a mode of associated living among people, as we shall see, is a later occurrence.

It was during the waning years of the Mycenaean Age that Attica was unified. The powerful King Theseus brought the tribes that inhabited the area under one kingdom so that by 700 Attica was one nation with the city of Athens as its center. About the year 700, the last dynasty to rule Attica, the Medontidae, was deposed for failure to lead successful military campaigns. In its place, an *Archon* (usually an ordinary citizen) was appointed to lead the nation in war. The Archon ruled with the aid of magistrates, the Areopagus, originally appointed to ten-year terms by the Archon, but later, around 683, to appointments of one year, and beginning in 487 through yearly election. Later, the term of the Archon was reduced to ten years. Thus, by the middle of the 7th century Attica was ruled by an Archon who served for ten years and an annually appointed council of magistrates. The final transition from oligarchic to representative government occurred near the end of the 6th century with the fall of the tyrant Hippias (510) and the democratic reforms of his successor Cleisthenes who reorganized the citizenry of Athens into villages (*demes*), thus breaking up the territorial domains of the oligarchs and creating a representative assembly of 500 citizens, 50 from each of the ten demes.[7]

While the Archon's chief function was military and the council of magistrates' chief function was civil, a group of six magistrates chosen from the noble classes, the *Thesmothetae*, served as judges in matters of civil offense. As the Thesmothetae evolved, it soon became an institution in itself taking on the role of managing the courts and administering justice in all its forms. There were now three branches of government: the Archon serving as the Executive primarily in charge of foreign affairs but also involved in some civil matters; the Areopagus or Council of Magistrates serving as the Legislative branch; and the Thesmothetae serving as the Judicial branch of government.

During this same period, essential reform became necessary in the military. Increasing warfare with neighboring city-states and increasing costs for military operations required the rulers of Athens to appeal to all classes of citizens for money and service. One group in particular, the hoplites or footsoldiers, came to bear much of the burden of battle. As Athens succeeded in her military ventures, the hoplites and later the naucraries (sailors) began making demands for more personal and political power.[8]

In the year 630, the last Archon to serve as tyrant of Athens, Cylon (or Kylon), seized the Acropolis, the seat of government in Athens, and established himself as the ruler of all Attica. His reign was short-lived for within weeks he was deposed by the citizenry in an uprising led by farmers and the hoplites. Cylon's followers were stoned or butchered in the center of Athens; only a few escaped to the hills around the city. Frightened by this occurrence, the nobles in Athens realized that their security lay in the hands of the citizenry. Athenian democracy was born in this violent turn of events.

## Establishment of the Athenian Court System and Legislature

In 621, following the overthrow of Cylon, the citizens of Athens commissioned Dracon (Draco), an elder citizen considered to be the wisest of the Greeks, as "thesmothete with extraordinary power." His task was to transform the oral code of customs and traditions into a body of written "laws" (*nomos*). By writing down the laws, Dracon gave them a new permanence in language, making them accessible to all citizens and less subject to self-interested interpretation and abuse by those in power. Dracon was concerned only with criminal offenses, which until this time had been settled through blood feud or rulings by the king or Archon. He used what had been places of sanctuary in Athens for the establishment of tribunals or courts complete with magistrates drawn from the ruling classes or from the council to hear cases of homicide, assault, and robbery. By regularizing the code for criminal offenses, Dracon began the tradition of justice, where complaints are resolved through clearly enunciated crimes and where laws are applied equally to all.[9]

The Code of Dracon served the Athenians well, and it constituted a surge in the evolution of democracy from which there would be no retreat. Dracon was revered by the people of Athens. His laws were later to become known as the "Laws of Blood," however, since the penalty for almost any offense was death, whether the crime was murder or theft, even of an apple or a cabbage. Though Dracon was simply transcribing the existing oral code into written form and was thus not responsible for the penalties incurred, his name has become synonymous with harsh or severe treatment; i.e., "draconian."

In 594, the wise man, poet, and legislator Solon was appointed as Chief Magistrate to reform the Code of Dracon. Solon had earned the trust of all Athenians, and his legal reforms would be adopted and used in Athens for the succeeding three centuries. Solon's chief accomplishment was to abolish existing debts secured with personal freedom, thus saving many Athenians from slavery or certain exile. He also restored all mortgaged land to the original owners. While Dracon had relied on magistrates chosen from the upper classes to administer his system of justice, Solon reformed the court system to allow for juries numbering between 501 and 2,000 citizens chosen by lot to hear all cases except those involving homicide and certain religious offenses (these were heard by the Council of the Areopagus composed of all former Archons). The emergence of the concept of a "trial by a jury of one's peers" is a critical step in the evolution of democratic forms of government, because, as we learn from the *Athenaion Politeia*, the most frequently cited ancient text on the matter of laws, "when the people control the vote, it controls the constitution."[10]

Solon's Code was written onto a wooden wheel that was placed in the center of the marketplace (*Agora*) so that everyone had access to the laws. Solon also established courts throughout Athens, many of them outdoors. Here is a list of some of those courts and the crimes for which they were established:

The Areopagus—Cases of Bloodshed and Religious Offenses
The Palladion—Involuntary Homicide
The Delphinion—Homicide Involving Justification
The Phraetto—Exiled Citizens Later Accused of Murder
The Prytaneion—Creatures or Objects Condemned for Crimes
The Heliaea—All Other Cases Except Arson and Bloodshed

The courts soon became the social center of Athenian life as citizens came to enjoy the drama of the courtrooms (*agồn*). Jurors heard litigation on a complete range of offenses, both criminal and civil. Citizens delivered their own speeches, one to present the case and one to rebut the other person's. Witnesses were also allowed to testify in most cases. A waterclock was used to time the speeches, and jurors voted by placing a clay ballot in a voting box, one ballot signifying innocent and one signifying guilty. Cases were usually decided by a simple majority. Passions often ran high, and to come before the court was, Freeman tells us, "Like addressing a public meeting."[11] As we shall see in the next chapter, the institution of the courts created the need for training in rhetoric as a citizen's very freedom often depended on his ability to speak persuasively.

*Figure 1.3* Ancient Greek waterclock

*Figure 1.4* Ballots

Through his legal reforms, Solon introduced the first form of popular democracy into Athens, and his judicial system remained relatively intact for the next 200 years. Solon's courts became the model for the Romans and centuries later for England and America. The Code of Solon was frequently challenged and occasionally reformed; however, its essential ingredients were never altered. Solon's reforms mark the unalterable impulse toward popular government in western civilization.

The period of democratization included legislative as well as judicial reform. Reforms in the military that gave social power to the hoplites and naucraries were also responsible for reform in the assembly. As noted earlier, the legislative branch of government had evolved from a king's council, to a decennial council of appointed members who had some power independent of the king, to an annual council of 500 citizens appointed by lot. During the period between the demise of Cylon and the reforms of Solon, the military took on much greater power and became themselves an assembly for the election of magistrates and for other business. Soon, the military assembly became an official body of 401 "councillors," representing the tribes that made up the Attic nation. The Council of Areopagus now became the aristocratic council denuded of its political power while the Council of 400 became a more popular assembly, a Senate and House of Representatives to use contemporary terminology.

For the rest of the 6th century, from a few decades following Solon's reforms in 594 to the year 510 Athens was ruled by the Archon Peisistratus, himself from 560 to 527, and then until 514 by his two sons, Hippias and Hipparchus. The reign of the *Peisistratidae* ended in 510 following which Athens was ruled by the benevolent Archons Cleisthenes and Themistocles and by democratic assemblies such as the Council of Areopagus. In the year 492, a war erupted with Persia that would last until the Athenians achieved victory in the year 479. The victory over the Persians would change forever the character of ancient Athens.

## Cultural and Intellectual Traditions in Athens: Writing, Self-Restraint and the Golden Mean, the Place of Women, and Slavery

Before turning to the period following the Persian War, it is important to review the cultural and intellectual awakening occasioned by, and running parallel to, the political evolution just discussed.

### The Evolution of Reason and Rationality as Guides to Understanding the Universe

Ancient Greece, beginning in the 6th century, is distinguished in western thought for being the first culture to speculate about the universe from a purely human perspective. Early Greek thinkers such as Thales, Anaximander, and Anaximenes ushered into history a new way of thinking about the world around them. Prior to these thinkers, and the speculations of other "Presocratics" as they are known, it was accepted belief that the gods controlled the universe, and that human life was dominated, somewhat capriciously, by the actions of the gods. In other words, it was the *mythology*, first of Mother Earth and then of the Gods of Olympus, through which people sought to understand and see order in the world around them.

Presocratic thinkers asserted that the world can be understood and comprehended by the human mind alone, through rational thought and argumentation about that world (*logos*). In assigning what had been the functions of the gods to natural phenomena such as air, water, fire, and other forms of energy (*dynamis*), Presocratic thinkers began to shift the answers given to questions such as "What is the nature of reality?" "Where do human beings fit into the nature of things?" and "How does that peculiarly human gift of rationality guide us to the truth of things?" Moreover, they began to think of the universe as a place of balance and harmony. As Waterfield writes:

> The Greeks had long believed, except in their more pessimistic moments, that there was a law of compensation in human affairs – that the gods would, sooner or later, belittle a man who rose too high or too fast, but Anaximander extended this law to the world at large, making it a cosmic principle – and, importantly, one that was governed by "necessity," an abstract and unchanging force, not a bunch of fickle gods. His vision of a universe ordered by cosmic justice was potent, and soon took hold of the Greek imagination.[12]

From ideas such as these a paradigm shift in human thought followed, one that led gradually to the first "self-reflective" society, governed by *logos* or reasoning through speech, and accessible to the human mind of even the most common peasant. Of course, belief in the gods remained popular, and we must think of the Presocratic shift in thinking as a slow but gradual evolution of ideas, at times existing parallel to traditional thought, but slowly gaining preeminence, especially in the intellectual world that would come to Athens during the time of Pericles. Presocratic thinking would provide the philosophical foundations for the urge toward democracy and the preeminence of rhetoric as the appropriate vehicle for moving that society forward. In the next chapter, we will see how Presocratic thinking catalyzed the rise of the sophists, those first teachers of speech and rhetoric who dominated education and political life in Athens during its Golden Age.

### The Development of Writing and Prose

In addition to the revolution of thought about the nature of the universe, it was largely due to advances in the technology and the teaching of writing that Greek culture established both permanence and continuity. Through the technology of writing, it became possible to keep records of civil, military, and legal matters. Richard Leo Enos notes, for instance, that,

> As democracy stabilized political procedures in Athens, the need for writers to record specific events of oral and civic functions increased. Writing was also helpful in recording the oral deliberations necessary in the operations of the *polis*; it was used to record events that had immediate and pragmatic impact.[13]

Writing also made possible the development of a tradition in literature and art, and a systematic approach to commerce. Writing for the purpose of performing Homeric literature and for inscriptions on works of art became a significant means through which Greek culture would become self-reflective. As Gomperz notes, through the development of scrolls from the pulp of the papyrus shrub in the 7th century,

> The circulation of thought was accelerated, the commerce of intellect enlarged, and the continuity of culture guaranteed, in a degree which can well-nigh be compared with that which marked the invention of the printing press at the dawn of modern history.[14]

The various tribes in the Attic region adopted a simple alphabet in the late 8th century and they began immediately to establish a literary tradition and a history of themselves as a people. It was principally through the epic poems of Homer, *The Iliad* and *The Odyssey*, that people in the Attic region began to see themselves as a community. Through their struggles, defeats, and victories as chronicled by Homer, and in succeeding centuries by the rhapsodists who performed Homeric literature in the villages and city-states throughout Greece, heroes and villains were celebrated and vilified, forms and styles of expression in poetry and oratory were ensconced in theory and practice, and appropriate modes of interaction such as between the individual and the gods and between the sexes were established. When such a history is present in drama and writing, it is more easily passed from generation to generation, thus becoming part of the dialogue between people and between generations that is, in fact, culture. As we will see in the next chapter, writing also played a critical role in the development of rhetoric, both as practiced in the courtrooms, legislatures, and in public ceremonies, and as studied on a more theoretical basis in the schools.

## The Ideal of Harmony, Proportion, and Balance: Preference for the Mean

As noted earlier, even in Presocratic times Greeks believed that there was harmony and balance in the universe. In the Attic region, Greeks also developed a penchant for self-restraint, living as they did in a pluralistic society composed of numerous tribes, aliens, slaves, and temporary visitors. This traditional mode of behavior would be transformed into a philosophy of moderation and balance in living that would later become a hallmark of their society, expressed most clearly, although centuries later, in Pericles' "Funeral Oration," and in Aristotle's philosophy of the Golden Mean (described in his treatise, *Nichomachean Ethics*).

For the Greeks, a beautiful spirit was expressed in a beautiful body. The Olympic Games, held at Olympia beginning in 776, were a celebration not just of athletic ability but of the mental discipline that athletic prowess represented. Contests such as wrestling were often conducted in the courtyards of temples and they were surrounded with festivals featuring music, dance, and poetry. This balance between the physical and the aesthetic became the ideal to which Greeks aspired. As Dickinson notes:

> Body and soul, it is clear, are regarded as aspects of a single whole, so that a blemish in the one indicates and involves a blemish in the other. The training of the body is thus, in a sense, the training of the soul, and gymnastic and music, as Plato puts it, serve the same end, the production of a harmonious temperament.[15]

Similarly, Greek tradition favored moderation in food and drink, and in most social activities. "Nothing in excess" was a motto inscribed above the entrance to the Temple of Apollo at Delphi, and the proper citizen aimed at this ideal, often giving in to temptation, but always remaining faithfully devoted to the pursuit of the ideal. It is this ideal of harmony, balance, and proportion in all things that we see in Greek literature, art, and architecture that prepared the way in later centuries for Athenians to debate both sides of an issue and to assimilate opposing ideas into their decision-making. The rhetorical admonition to consider your opponent's arguments as carefully as your own was, then, consistent with other cultural practices in Athens.

### Women in Classical Times and in the Rhetorical Tradition

From Homeric times to the middle of the 5th century, a male person was a citizen if his father was a citizen. The mother did not have to be Greek. This law was changed in 451 at the request of the Athenian Archon Pericles (who, ironically, had a foreign mother), and henceforth all persons claiming citizenship had to prove that both the mother and father were Greek.[16]

The "idea" of citizenship, as opposed to the "ideals" of citizenship that we will discuss shortly, evolved with the establishment of the laws and the courts. Citizenship under Solon's Code determined who had rights, both legal and political. The women of Athens were not given legal rights, but they were given some political rights. While they could not serve on the legislative council or the juries, they were protected by the laws and they had religious privileges. As a result, women did not play a public role in Athenian society as it embraced democracy, but they were fully vested in its existence and preservation.

The role of women in Athenian society was to produce children and run the household. We should not conclude from these roles, however, that women were depreciated in the classical period in Athens since bearing children was considered a sacred duty, and managing a household meant supervising domestic slaves and often a large holding of land and property.

Greek society during the period of the rise of democracy and the study of rhetoric in Athens had a clear image of the ideal woman. She was a private person engaged in the domestic affairs of Greek family life, devoted to her husband (he could have an affair, for instance, while she could not), and valued for her appearance. Ideal images of women were represented in female goddesses such as Aphrodite (goddess of love), Artemis (goddess of the hunt and protector of young women), and Athena, after whom was named the city of Athens and who symbolized victory in war, civilization, wisdom, strength, and justice. The same Greek society also had negative stereotypes of women, as in Plato's *Republic* where women are variously seen as nagging, weaker,

*Figure 1.5* Diotima

purely sexual creatures, and prone to gossip. Female goddesses also represented negative qualities such as temperament (Demeter) and jealousy (Hera).

Because they were excluded from the public sphere, women did not engage in public speaking. Thus, women had no need to study or use rhetoric. Or did they? If we think of rhetoric strictly as the study of speaking in public such as in the courtrooms or assemblies, it is true that women did not speak in these public forums. But they did engage in persuasive discourse and study *logos* or reasoning through speech. Aristotle, for instance, in his seminal treatise on rhetoric that we shall study in Chapter 3, uses examples from the 6th century female poet, Sappho, in his development of *epideictic* or ceremonial rhetoric in Book I, and in his explanation of *arguments from induction* or *from previous judgments* in Book II.[17] In addition, females such as Pericles' wife Aspasia were highly regarded students of rhetoric, and it has been asserted that Aspasia wrote Pericles' most famous speech, "The Funeral Oration."[18] Further evidence of the contribution of women to the study of speech or *logos* occurs in the Platonic Dialogue "Symposium." In this treatise on love, Socrates recounts a conversation he had with a priestess, Diotima of Mantinea, from which he claims he learned the real meaning of love. Love, according to Diotima, is the culmination of a searching between two human beings for a spiritual (as opposed to a purely physical) connection or communion. Each stage of this awakening to the power of love is guided by speech,

*Figure 1.6* Aspasia

beautiful speech that brings the lovers to the essence of this most aesthetic experience: love. As Johnstone tells us, the erotic process as explained by Diotima, "centers on the uniqueness of the souls who seek fusion with one another through dialogue."[19]

Such examples lead to the conclusion that Aristotle and Plato/Socrates considered that rhetoric was not limited only to males engaged in public speaking, but to other forms of discourse such as dialogue and narration. Women engaged in such rhetorical activities, and thus studied the art of speaking in order to master it. Women may also have been involved in the study of writing, and the revolution in literacy that it produced.[20] It is important to note that in our world women need to understand the art of rhetoric and learn the skill of public speaking as much as men, and that female scholars are engaged in the study of rhetoric equally with male scholars. In ancient Greece, we can say with surety that women studied philosophy, wrote poetry, and engaged in verbal discourse in notable ways.

Not all of the traditions regarding women as passed down from the Homeric Period to the end of the Persian War in 479 are laudable, at least by today's standards. Relations between the sexes, for instance, begin in Homer as idealistic and romantic. Men go off to war and the women wait faithfully at home. Men are wounded and battered and women come to their rescue, bathing them and nursing them back to health. As Dickinson writes:

> Readers of the *Iliad* and the *Odyssey* will find depicted there, amid all the barbarity of an age of rapine and war, relations between men and women so tender, faithful, and beautiful, that they may almost stand as universal types of the ultimate human ideal.[21]

During the 6th and 5th centuries, this view is replaced with one that often sees women as equal to children and slaves, confined to the home and with few legal rights. We could even say that marriage relations were subordinated to the ideal of consenting romantic relations between adult men and younger boys. While some dramatists such as Euripedes and some sophists such as Gorgias defended women through accurate depictions of their struggles, the status of women in Athens during the 6th and 5th centuries was generally inferior to male citizens.

### The Institution and Tradition of Slavery

Ancient Greek civilization is often criticized in our times for its practice of slavery. Slavery was an accepted institution throughout ancient Greece, and in Athens slaves made up approximately 50–75 percent of the population during the 6th and 5th centuries (200,000 free persons and 200,000–400,000 enslaved persons). Slaves were mostly non-Greeks who were acquired through war, kidnapping, and purchase. Slave labor was used in the fields and mines in order to free citizens to participate in civic affairs or wars. Slaves were also used for most domestic activities such as shopping and housekeeping. Slaves were sometimes treated poorly such as in the mining operations around Athens, but other slaves were treated with kindness and legal protections were established for domestic slaves to prevent their being abused. In Athens, slaves were sometimes manumitted (freed for a fee) to the status of foreign alien (*metic*) and slaves who practiced a skilled trade such as carpentry or pottery were usually allowed to keep a proportion of their earnings.[22] During the Age of Pericles, when Athens flowered into the greatest civilization yet known to history, slaves played a minor role in the construction and industrialization of the city, and many of those who were impressed were treated as regular laborers.[23]

Today we look with condemnation at the institution of slavery. By the traditions of the time of ancient Greece, however, slavery was a common and accepted practice.

## The Emergence of the Humanities in Greek Culture Through Rhetoric

As with any culture, the developing Athenian culture was a mixture of good and bad. By the end of the 7th century, Athenian culture had produced great art, literature, music, philosophy, and science—hallmarks of advanced civilizations. On the other hand, it was burdened by war, and a growing *hubris* (arrogance of pride) occasioned by its successes. As the first truly self-reflective society, however, Athenian citizens were the first to scrutinize themselves, to engage in debate and discussion about themselves, and to evolve into a better society through their reflections.

The ancient Greeks were the first civilization to invent a society through the search for a purely human wisdom rather than through the study of received wisdom in texts such as the Bible or mythology. When we say that in ancient Greek civilization, particularly Athenian society, lies the foundation of what we think of as the "humanities," we mean that it was the ancient Greeks who constructed their world through their own purely human meditations about it. Johnstone calls this the search for "wisdom," both practical (*phronesis*) and theoretical (*sophia*) through speech. "Human wisdom," he writes,

> involves a kind of knowing ... Wisdom is both a grasping of the "way things are" – of the patterns and regularities in human experience and of how these fit into the *kosmos* – and an appreciation of the truths thus grasped ... It is generated by apprehensions of the truths of human nature, by one's realization and understanding of how humanness "fits into" the nature of things.[24]

It was through their inventiveness, self-restraint, and reflective nature that Athenians of the 5th century BCE reached a point in their development where they would flower into a great civilization. We turn now to that period, the Age of Pericles.

## The Persian Wars and the Reign of Pericles

The war with Persia lasted for 13 years from 492 to 479. Persia was an oriental nation bent on the conquest of the territory to its west, that is, Greece. Citizens of the many Greek city-states that had been developing along with Athens during the previous centuries understood the Persian aggression as no less than a struggle for their very existence. The city-states united in their defense of Greece, and led by Athens they secured victory. The Battle of Marathon (490) was the first and one of the most important military victories of the Persian Wars. This victory over the Persian invaders gave the Greek city-states confidence in their ability to defend themselves and the conviction that theirs was the superior culture. The battle is considered a defining

**Athenian Empire
Fifth Century, B.C.E.**

*Figure 1.7* Athenian Empire

moment in the development of western culture. Ten years later, at the decisive battles of Thermopylae (480) Salamis (480) and Plataea (479) the Persian forces would be driven for the final time off the Greek mainland back to Asia Minor, where they would not challenge Greek hegemony for the next 100 years.

For the next several years, the struggle would be for supremacy of the mainland itself, a struggle chiefly between the Spartans and the Athenians. Due to its naval superiority and its cultural dynamism, Athens would achieve the status of an empire with allied states as far away as Egypt and Sicily. The Spartans, masters of fighting on land, would also establish an empire with allies across the Greek mainland and its islands. In the years following the Persian Wars, and because of its invincible navy, Athens would become the more powerful of the two city-states, and the Persian Wars would prepare the way for the emergence of the greatest of all the Greek leaders, the Athenian general Pericles.

The historian Thucydides tells us that Pericles was the most brilliant man of his time, the ablest ever to lead the Athenian democracy. He was a brilliant political strategist, but perhaps even more importantly, he was the foremost orator in Greece, a man able to persuade others to accept his policies through the polish of his public speaking. Pericles spoke directly to the Athenian people once each week from the hill of the Pnyx near the Acropolis. His teacher, Anaxagoras, tells us that Pericles had,

> a lofty spirit and an elevated mode of speech, free from the vulgar and knavish tricks of mob-orators, but also a composed countenance that never gave way to laughter, a dignity of carriage and restraint in the arrangement of his clothing which no emotion was allowed to disturb while he was speaking, a voice that was evenly controlled, and all the other characteristics of this sort which so impressed his hearers.[25]

Pericles' rhetorical skills endeared him to the masses and the aristocrats. He won election every year for three decades, making him one of the most successful politicians of his or any time.

It was during the reign of Pericles that Athens achieved its greatest glory. From his ascendance to power in 462 to his death from the plague in 429 Pericles oversaw the establishment of a vast military empire, the maturation of a pure democracy the likes of which the world had never seen, and the flowering of all the arts and sciences that we know today as the basis of western civilization. No 30-year period in history can compare to it.

Pericles constructed his empire principally on two complementary policies: imperialism and popular democracy. About 478 at the conclusion of the Persian Wars, the city-states in the Aegean region formed a confederacy, the Delian League, to repel further invasion by Persian forces. Upon taking control of Athens, Pericles seized the leadership of the League by superior military might, and he coerced the surrounding city-states to a tax to pay for military protection from the Persians. Athens now became a protectorate for neighboring states that were required to lay down their arms and to rely on Athens for their defense.

At the same time, Pericles installed a direct democracy to maintain popular support, both at home in Athens and in the city-states he had subdued. Solon's judicial reforms had extended civil rights, but the reforms had not completely enfranchised all citizens. Pericles liberalized the judicial system to include popular juries chosen by lot, a system he supported with grants to the poorer citizens so that they could serve. By running for office each year, Pericles eliminated fears of a tyranny. He also established a popular legislative assembly, the Five Hundred, which reviewed on a yearly basis all laws established by the Thesmothetes. In addition, any citizen could propose or oppose a law during the time of the assembly. Grants were provided to the Five Hundred so that they could serve in the assembly, thus completing Pericles' reform of Athens into a pure democracy.

Pericles instituted laws to protect artists and craftsmen from sanctions on their work; they were now allowed to write, speak, or build freely. He brought jobs to Athenians in the form of shipbuilding and produced the largest navy of the time. He established colonies as far away as Sicily, Egypt, and Spain, an accomplishment leading to increased trade, commercial relationships, and the movement of talented people to and from Athens. Pericles also provided price supports to the farmers so that food could be purchased inexpensively in the marketplace. These and other initiatives created the conditions through which Athens thrived with commerce and creativity.

In 458 Pericles concluded the construction of a massive "long walls" project begun by Themistocles and intended to connect the central city of Athens to the coastal area, the Peiraeus, thus insuring a route to the sea and trading lines with western colonies. The walls ran parallel to one another about four and a half miles in length and 550 feet apart. The construction of the long walls provided jobs for the Athenian working class and for soldiers who were idle between military engagements.

Pericles initiated numerous other construction projects, most notably many of the temples that still mark the Athenian landscape today. The Parthenon, for instance, was begun in 447 and soon thereafter the Areopagus court was constructed. Shrines and palaces dedicated to the gods were built throughout the city, as were schools, theatres, courts, and marketplaces. Such a massive number of projects kept stonemasons, architects, and miners immersed in work, thus assuring domestic tranquility.

Athens soon became the crossroads of the world, a place where ideas flourished and discussion thrived. Citizens flocked to the *Agora*, the civic center and marketplace to attend court sessions, legislative assemblies, theatres, sporting events, and festivals. Rhapsodists played music and recited poetry, and dramatists presented their plays, both celebrating Athenian life and lampooning its excesses. Religious festivals such as the January and March festivals of Dionysus, one of the gods most revered by the peasants, were the occasion for musical celebrations and poetic compositions. Dancing was a favorite activity and dancing floors were built around many of the temples. Athens was the center of western civilization, noted for the life of leisure and elegance, of refined amusements, privacy, and reflection. As Smith notes:

> All these aspects of civilization had been anticipated in the Greek cities of the sixth century and before, in the developments of archaic art and architecture, of the festivals and games, of lyric poetry, and of Ionian philosophy. But except for the public buildings and the festivals, they had been chiefly for the aristocrats. The economic development of Athens and the exploitation of her empire now afforded a modicum of wealth and leisure to a middle class of perhaps twenty thousand of Athens' citizens, their wives, and families. These, concentrated in the one city, created a new sort of demand for a more economical elegance and for the cheaper luxuries, including individualism and reflective thought.[26]

Athens, it must be remembered, became a community in which the freedoms granted by Pericles to artists, philosophers, and ordinary citizens were directed toward the maintenance of the state. Athenian society, while protecting individual freedom, placed the state above the individual. Individuals were expected to subordinate their interests to the interests of the community, or, perhaps more precisely, to accommodate and fulfill their needs within the rights and responsibilities granted to them as citizens. To a citizen of Athens the state was more than a political machine or a bureaucracy; it was a spiritual bond. Dickinson concludes that, "In the Greek view, to be a citizen did not merely imply the payment of taxes, and the possession of a vote; it implied a direct and active cooperation in all the functions of civil and military life."[27] During Pericles' reign, approximately 500,000 people lived in Attica, most of them in Athens. Of the inhabitants, 30,000 were male citizens vested with the power to vote and serve as jurors, another 30,000 were women, and perhaps double that number, or 120,000, were children. The rest of the population was composed of approximately 15,000 foreign aliens (*metics*) and 200,000 slaves. Citizens were expected to arm themselves for battle and at times to arm an entire naval vessel or infantry unit. Eligible citizens were expected to serve on juries and in the legislature; they were also expected to speak and vote on all the critical issues of the time. Civic virtue, then, was more than an ideal; it was a practical necessity and a requirement in this pure democracy.

It should be emphasized that the Greeks saw no contradiction between individual freedom and the needs of the state; the two concepts were not opposites; rather, they were seen in harmonious balance, a symbiosis. Preparing one's self fully, developing one's body and spirit, was to prepare one's self to participate in the activities of the state. The philosopher Aristotle would later define the state as "an association of similar persons for the attainment of the best life possible."[28] The clearest expression of the relationship between the individual and the state comes from Pericles himself in his "Funeral Oration": "We do not say that a man who takes no interest in politics is a man who minds his own business; we say that he has no business here at all." Individualism was later to become a problem for Athens, a source of the breakdown of traditional values and unity in time of war, but during the time of Pericles it was the liberation of the individual spirit to create and express that defined the Age.

## The Peloponnesian War

The Age of Pericles continued until his death from a plague in 429. From 431 to 404, Athens would be engaged in the Peloponnesian War, a devastating struggle between Athens and its allies and the city-states of Lacedaemon led by Sparta. The war, undertaken reluctantly by Pericles (who died after the first year of the conflict), led to the fall of the Athenian empire. There were intermittent truces during the war and shifting alliances that would lead at one point to cooperation with Sparta and at another point to war. It was a period of intrigue, betrayal, heroism, and suffering, relieved infrequently by brief respites of peace. Athens fell to a cabal of oligarchs (the Council of 400) in 411, and was ultimately conquered by the Spartans in 404 although in 403 self-rule was restored. In 399, as revenge for his life's work and for his actions during the war, Socrates was put to trial for atheism and for corrupting the youth of Athens. He was found guilty, and was put to death by drinking poison hemlock.

In the ensuing decades, Athens would rise and fall as her military and political fortunes dictated. At one point, in 387, Persia regained a foothold on the Greek mainland and controlled the governments of the city-states. Statesmen such as Isocrates would plead for unity among the city-states against the encroaching Macedonians from the north, and for the peace that had so long eluded Greece. In ensuing decades, orators such as Demosthenes would attempt to rally Athenian citizens to arm themselves against those he considered enemies, primarily Philip of Macedon. Throughout this period, Athenians would continue to produce great works of art, philosophy, literature, science, and engineering. By this time, however, the city-states were exhausted by their enmities, and their hatreds were of such long duration that any chance for a union of the "Hellenes" (all those bound together by Greek culture) was doomed by history. The decades of the 370s and 360s were marked by warfare as one city-state sought to impose its rule on the other. In 362, all the forces of Hellas engaged in a pitched battle at Mantinea, a final bloodletting to gain ultimate control of Greece. No army was victorious. The world of Greece was forever sundered. As Botsford concludes, "It was inevitable that the chaos should last long and wreak manifold injury upon the Greek world."[29] So weakened were the city-states by the decades of war that aggressors saw their chance to conquer the Athenian empire. In 359, Philip of Macedon mounted the throne of the Macedonian kingdom and began his conquest of the world.

## The Reign of Philip of Macedon

Philip of Macedon (located in northeastern Greece) was a man of extraordinary physical and mental power. He had been educated in Greece and he had assimilated Greek ideals. As he attained power, Philip began a lifetime of conquest, plundering surrounding territories and gathering up the gold and other precious possessions of those he conquered. With his newly amassed wealth and his military genius, he set out to conquer the world. He organized a huge army, the largest ever conceived of at that time, and struck out for the city-states to the south. Between diplomatic ventures and military might, he gradually gained victory. In 349–348, Philip engaged the city-states of the Olynthian Confederacy, of which Athens was not a member. The Olynthians asked Athens for help, and the orator Demosthenes presented the third of his memorable series of orations, "the Philippics," urging Athens to respond to the call. His pleas went unheeded as many Athenians welcomed Philip to their soil, and soon he had a foothold in the southern part of Greece. Athens would now fight Philip on its own, a losing battle from the start. In 346, Athens proposed peace with Philip (the Treaty of Philocrates), a peace he accepted but never intended to keep. In the ensuing years, as the peace of Philocrates brought down the Athenian guard, Philip crept closer to Athens. Those who had bartered the Treaty were brought to trial, often prosecuted by Demosthenes. Demosthenes' oratorical genius almost kept Athens and her neighbors united against Philip, but ultimately the Macedonian general prevailed and Athens became a part of the Macedonian empire following Philip's victory at the Battle of Chaeronea in 338.

Philip of Macedon died by assassination in the year 336. He was a philanderer who married a new woman in each city he conquered. This practice was eventually to catch up with him as one of his wives, Olympias, plotted successfully to have him killed during a festival. It fell to Philip's son, Alexander the Great, to complete his empire.

## The Reign of Alexander the Great

Alexander the Great set out in the year 334 to complete the Macedonian conquest of the world. Alexander, who had been educated by the Athenian philosopher Aristotle and raised on the heroic tales of Achilles in the *Iliad*, would come to believe that he was the son of the god, Zeus. He moved first through Greece, and then through what is today Iraq (Persia), Iran (Mesopotamia), Egypt, Syria, and India. He settled in the Egyptian city of Alexandria and there he oversaw his vast empire. Before his thirtieth birthday, Alexander the Great controlled most of the known world.

In Greece, although Alexander's appointees controlled the city-states, some such as Athens were allowed to continue living according to their traditions. In fact, because he had been educated as a Greek by Aristotle and raised on the exploits of Athenian warriors and gods, Alexander sought to assimilate Athenian ways into his entire empire, forcing many of his subjects to speak Greek and to study Greek ideas. What Pericles had produced with his money and patronage, Alexander disseminated with his conquests. In an ironic way, by conquering Athens, Alexander assured the historical and cultural legacy of the Athenian empire by spreading its ideas throughout the entire known world.

As Alexander pursued new victories while maintaining his hold over already conquered peoples, he became aloof and arrogant. Having proclaimed himself a god, Alexander forced those who approached him to prostrate themselves at his feet. Such behavior undermined his support. In addition, he was given to drinking and carousing to excess, and soon he was unable to fight in his campaigns. He died from a fever in the year 322 at the age of 33, ruler of all he surveyed but hated by most and spent by his own indulgences.

Upon Alexander's death, Athens aligned itself with many of the other city-states to regain her freedom from Macedon, but in 322 Athens was subdued by the Macedonian general, Antipater. Many of her citizens were imprisoned, enslaved, or expatriated. During the next 20 years Athenian generals would regain and then lose control of the city, but the last vestiges of Athenian military hegemony were crushed.

## The Enduring Athenian Empire

It is often thought that Athenian preeminence terminates with its defeat by the Macedonians in the Lamian War in 322. In another sense, however, the next two centuries are an age of dissemination and assimilation of Athenian culture equal to the Age of Pericles in importance for western civilization. Philip conquered Athens only in the military sense; his son, Alexander, deferred to Athens in all matters of culture. Rather than destroying the ideals of the Athenian empire, he sought to assimilate them into his empire; in fact, to spread them throughout the world. Connor asserts that:

> It was not the weakness of Greece that drew Philip, but the strength of a culture he could not help but admire. The combination of sensuosity and intellect, of individual freedom and corporate order, of beauty and manliness which Pericles praised ... converted one of its earliest and one of its most important devotees in Philip of Macedon.[30]

The demise of Athens as the political center of the universe was a prelude to the ascendancy of its cultural forms to the place they hold yet today; that is, as the fountainhead of western civilization.

---

*Perhaps the most important ideal deriving from the Classical Age is the ideal of freedom of expression. As we shall see in the next chapter, Athenians were taught to believe that the power of persuasion through speech, the logos, is the most enduring force in a culture, one that must not and cannot be stifled. It is the ideal upon which individualism is founded, the ideal upon which civilized communal action is founded, and the ideal upon which justice is founded. Throughout the Classical Age and the ensuing 100 years after Pericles' death Athenians studied rhetoric, and rhetoric played a critical role in Athenian social and political life. From the patriotic orations of generals and statesmen, to the pathetic appeals of the courtrooms, to the political pamphleteering of patriots such as Isocrates, rhetoric served as the handmaiden of democracy. Now that we understand the broad context of the times, we can turn to an examination of this important and practical art, the art of rhetoric. We will learn how it was taught and practiced in Athens, and how it was advanced through the invention and assimilation of writing into the educational system. We will explore in particular the controversies resulting from the arrival of the first teachers of rhetoric, the sophists.*

Chapter 2

# Rhetorical Consciousness and the Rise of the Sophists

Man is the measure of all things, of things that are as to how they are, and of things that are not as to how they are not.

Protagoras

## The Growth of Rhetorical Consciousness

By the term "rhetorical consciousness" we mean an awareness of language as a strategic tool, providing the speaker or writer choices through which to communicate an idea to others. We all use language somewhat instinctively, but with the ancient Athenians we see the first attempts to study and understand language itself as an objective phenomenon, a tool, so to speak, capable of being exploited to achieve the ends of clarity, beauty, and persuasiveness. Persuasive speaking and writing were both historically and socially grounded in Greek culture when Pericles ascended to power in Athens in 461 BCE. As we have read, speaking to influence public opinion, whether in the marketplace or the courtroom, had for centuries become a common alternative

Figure 2.1 Socrates

Figure 2.2 Protagoras

to fighting, and Homer's *Iliad* and *Odyssey* contain numerous persuasive speeches from parties on both sides of the controversy. In addition, early Greek drama was distinguished by the chorus, a group of singers or dancers who responded to the actors, usually antithetically, so that the audience was able to feel the tension of the moral dilemmas faced by the characters. This consciousness of antithesis as it was played out on the Greek stage is a significant prelude to the establishment of a rhetorical consciousness among the Greeks. "With the Greeks," writes Dobson, "oratory was instinctive; in the earliest semi-historical records that we possess, eloquence is found to be a gift prized not less highly than valor in battle."[1]

Even the Athenians' beliefs in deity prepared the way for a rhetorical world-view. For them, gods were essentially like humans, superior to them not so much in their wisdom or moral attributes but in their strength, grace, and beauty. The gods were capricious beings, fighting among themselves and seeking to impose their wills on humanity, often in ways contradictory to one another. Gods did know what was going to happen; they did know truth, but they were not disposed to implant it in the souls or minds of the living. Rather, it was for the Greek citizen to beseech the gods to help him in his quest for a happy life. As Dickinson notes, "In the midst of a crowd of deities, capricious and conflicting in their wills, he had to find his way as best he could."[2] He did this by consulting oracles, by praying to gods, and in all ways by seeking to find the truth known to the gods by persuading them to speak.

Thus, the seeds of a rhetorical consciousness were embedded in 5th century Athenian culture as a function of Greek literature, politics, and religion since the time of Homer. So central had oratory become to the Athenian way that the historian Thucydides, whose extensive chronicles form the basis for much of what we know about the Classical Age, particularly the years of the Peloponnesian War, 431–404 BCE, devoted a large part of his work to orations given by citizens in the public forum. The orations are often given in pairs representing the opposing views on military matters or matters of public concern. Thucydides thought that by doing so he was best able to characterize the entire period about which he was writing.[3] Ancient rhetorical theory, then, as Kennedy notes, was a "continuous, evolving tradition" by the end of the Persian Wars and the subsequent rise to power of Pericles.[4]

In the pure democracy instituted by Pericles, however, the practical need for skill in rhetoric among ordinary citizens reached new and dramatic proportions. Athenians now found themselves immersed in a world of public discourse. Each citizen soon realized that his very future often depended on his ability to speak or write persuasively. Courtrooms bristled with litigation as citizens sought to protect their families, properties, and businesses. Husbands defended themselves for murdering wifely seducers, veterans wounded in wars sought to keep their pensions, and farmers defended their lands from encroachment by others. With large juries now selected by lot among the entire populace of citizens, skill in persuasion required great attention to one's audience since the local butcher, baker, or tradesman was now entrusted with the scepter of justice.

Popular assemblies, the quorum for which was 6,000 citizens, were charged with reviewing and instituting laws on a yearly basis. Each year, the laws were posted in the marketplace, discussed among the citizenry, and debated in the councils of government. A vote one way or the other could mean war or peace, poverty or prosperity,

*Table 2.1*  The Classical Age of rhetoric

*A chronological timeline*

**B.C.E.**

| | |
|---|---|
| 461–429 | Reign of Pericles–flowering of Athens |
| 485–336 | Rise of the Sophists |
| | Gorgias (485–380) |
| | Protagoras (485?–410) |
| | Antiphon (480–411) |
| | Isocrates (436–338) |
| | Lysias (440–370s) |
| | Demosthenes (384–322) |
| 469–399 | Life of Socrates |
| 429–347 | Life of Plato |
| 384–322 | Life of Aristotle |
| 322–150 | Hellenistic Period |
| 106–43 | Life of Cicero |
| 86 | *De Inventione* |
| 55 | *De Oratore* |
| 56 | *Brutus Orator, De Optimo Genere Oratorum* |
| 45 | *The Partitione Oratoria* |
| 44 | *Topica* |

**C.E.**

| | |
|---|---|
| 30?–96? | Life of Quintilian |
| 95–43 | *Institutes of Oratory* |
| 340–430 | Life of St. Augustine |
| 426 | *De Doctrina Christiana* |

or the loss of freedom. Those elected to the assembly were responsible for speaking on behalf of their constituents, and for these legislators, in particular, rhetoric was an essential tool.

In addition to the courts and the assemblies, a variety of festivals and ceremonial events had evolved, each of which called for an orator to address the citizenry. One distinct type of performance was the *epideixis* or public display lecture. Kerford writes that:

> Hippias gave such performances regularly at the Panhellenic games at Olympia in the sacred precinct where he offered to speak on any one of a prepared list of subjects, and to answer any questions. And it appears that this may have been a regular feature there. Gorgias offered to speak on any subject whatsoever in the theatre at Athens and he spoke also at Olympia and at the Pythian games at Delphi.[5]

We will soon learn more about some of these famous speakers.

To the oral forms of discourse was now added the invention of prose writing as a common means for addressing the public. The great teacher Isocrates, for instance, preferred to compose his "orations" as political pamphlets that were then distributed throughout the city and sometimes read in public. And citizens accused of crimes began to resort more frequently to delivering speeches in the courtroom written for them by a new professional class, the "*logographers.*" Enos tells us that writing in the service of public speaking was one of the distinguishing features of this Golden Age.[6] Whether in oral or written form, then, Athens had become a city of words. In fact, intellectuals of this period came to see that language was itself a material phenomenon, separate and distinct from the thoughts or events it represented. This realization and the resulting inquiries into the workings of language mark a turning point in western civilization, one with both good and bad consequences.

## The Rise of the Sophists

To meet the need for skill in public discourse, a group of men emerged in Athens whose profession was the study and practice of rhetoric. These were the "sophists," a word derived from the Greek word "*sophos,*" which means "wise." Sophists were "wisdom bearers," and while the term originally applied to any wise person, it soon came to denote those who engaged in the art of rhetoric in the courts, the legislature, and/or the public forum.[7]

Three distinct types of sophistry were practiced in Athens. Some sophists taught persuasive speaking and writing in schools they founded for this purpose. Others, the previously mentioned "*logographers,*" wrote speeches for litigants in the courtrooms. The last type of sophist was the professional orator who traveled around the city giving lively philosophical discourses on all manner of topics. Of course, sophists often engaged in two or more of these practices. The sophists were soon to dominate the public scene in Athens to the point that training in rhetoric was deemed an essential part of every citizen's education. Indeed, as George Kennedy notes:

> It is not too much to say that rhetoric played the central role in ancient education. In Hellenistic times it constituted the curriculum of what we would regard as the secondary schools and it acquired an important place in advanced education.[8]

## The First Writers on Rhetoric: Corax and Tisias

According to an ancient tradition reflected in Aristotle, Cicero, and Quintilian, the formal study of rhetoric as an art (*techne*) began about the year 476 BCE by Corax, a resident of the Athenian colony of Syracuse in Sicily, and transmitted to mainland Greece by his pupil, Tisias. The main tradition states that Corax devised a systematic approach to argument when it became necessary to settle lawsuits over property confiscated by tyrants. According to another version, Corax used his new skill in political assemblies, not in law courts. Whatever the origin of the tradition, Corax is best known for his "doctrine of general probability."

Argument from probability is based upon the idea that, of two propositions, one is *more likely* to be true than the other one. In the ancient tradition, the classic example of probability is that of the little man accused of beating a larger man: "It is not likely [probable] that I would do so," he would argue, "for the bigger man is stronger than I am and would defeat me. Since I would know that, I would not anger him by hitting him." The standard rebuttal, of course, is also based on argument from probability: "The little man knows people would think it unlikely that he would hit me," the bigger man responds, "so he felt safe in hitting me." Notice that neither of these arguments is founded on evidence: both are based on likelihood alone.

An ancient story concerning a lawsuit between Corax and Tisias also illustrates the general probability method. Corax sues Tisias for his fee for teaching him, and each man argues as follows:

CORAX: You must pay if you win the case, because that would prove the worth of my lessons. If you lose the case you must pay me also, for the court will force you to do so. In either case you pay.

TISIAS: I will pay nothing, because if I lose the case it would prove that your instruction was worthless. If I win, however, the court will absolve me from paying. In either case, I will not pay.

Tradition holds that the court postponed its decision indefinitely, although Kennedy asserts that the court turned them out with the epithet, "A bad egg from a bad crow."[9]

Whatever we may think of such legendary tales, we may conclude that Corax and Tisias did make a significant contribution toward the systematic collection of rhetorical precepts; however, none of their works has survived. Certainly by 470 BCE, it had become clear that the objective of a speaker was persuasion, that a given speech might be analyzed as to its parts (*prooemium* or introduction, *agon* arguments including narration, and *epilogue* or conclusion), and that an audience would sometimes accept probability as supporting proof when deciding whether or not to believe a speaker. It must be remembered, though, that Corax and Tisias lived on the island of Sicily hundreds of miles west of mainland Greece. We have it only on legend that Tisias ever left Sicily for Athens. Meanwhile, as we have noted, the cultural development of major Greek cities was proceeding rapidly. The Sicilian ambassador, Gorgias, who opened a school of rhetoric in Athens in 431 BCE, succeeded at least in part because Athenians were already deeply interested in persuasive discourse.

## The Practice of Rhetoric in Athens

Sophists differed from one another in their approach to teaching rhetoric. Some such as Protagoras and Antiphon taught their students to debate both sides of a case as a practical exercise in learning to persuade. Some like Gorgias were concerned with the beauty and rhythm of language, and they focused their teaching on the stylistic aspects of speech and writing. Others such as Thrasymachus focused on audiences and the pathetic or emotional appeals most likely to sway them. Opportunistic sophists opened schools that trained students mainly in the art of delivery. Most schools were a mixture of these elements. All understood, however, that rhetoric was aimed at persuasion, and persuasion at a particular moment in time. Debates in the law courts, assemblies, and at festivals came to be seen, one could say, as competitive events almost in the same way that Athenians viewed athletic contests. Exercises in the schools of the sophists were devoted to winning the argument through the giving of "good reasons" to an audience of citizens charged with choosing one side or the other.

Sophistry proved a useful and effective art in the courts and assemblies of Athens. In such situations, truth is elusive. People see past events differently, according to their

*Figure 2.3* The dicast's ticket into court

interests and their recollections, and decisions about policies that will shape the future can only be based on what is "probably" the best course of action. In such public affairs, where exigencies of the situation make each decision unique, rhetoric proved to be an effective method for deciding the appropriate course of action; that is, each person with a position on the matter at hand gave his speech and decisions were based upon which speech seemed most accurate, persuasive, appropriate at the moment. In an uncertain world, there is no better alternative to civil living.

Public speaking as it was practiced in the Athenian courtrooms and assemblies often strayed significantly from the ideal of reasoned argument. While some speeches emphasized the facts and the application of those facts to the law, others were characterized by personal attacks on one's opponent, and emotional excess—passionate outbursts, beating one's breast, even bringing one's children into the arena to appeal to the jury for sympathy. An egregious flaw in the court system, at least by today's standards, was the occasional practice of torturing slaves to testify. Litigants and legislators alike were singularly concerned with winning the case since losing often brought severe consequences, in many cases death. Thus, as practiced by the masses now enjoying the freedom that a pure democracy brings, the art of composing highly probable arguments was sometimes transformed into the art of hoodwinking the audience in any manner possible. Flashy delivery and emotional groveling too often carried the day with the generally uneducated juries (the *dicasteria*).

For many observers of the Athenian judicial system, rhetoric as *practiced*, not necessarily as *taught* by the sophists, was less a path to justice and more a means for making the worse cause appear the better. Skill in argument often allowed the guilty to go free, and rhetoric was often used in the cause of vengeance against one's political opponents. With the courts having now become the social center of Athenian life, rhetoric as practiced there was soon considered the norm for all types of interactions, and the typical Athenian juror (an elderly male) was soon seen as an easy target for the skillful rhetorician.

## The Attack on the Sophists

Because of the rhetorical excesses witnessed in Athens, critics soon assailed the sophists as corruptors of public morals. Questions were raised: What exactly does the sophist know? What is his subject matter and on what is he an expert? Was it satisfactory that wrongdoing might go unpunished simply because wrongdoers had enough money to afford lessons in public speaking? Was it good that someone should have a semblance of wisdom because he was able to buy a speech from a sophist? Were the teachings of the sophists leading Athens to a better society?

These and other questions caused skepticism among Athenian intellectuals about sophistry, especially when some of the prominent sophists were charging large sums of money for their seminars (up to the equivalent of 100 minas for a ten-lecture seminar of 20 students, or approximately $7,800).[10]

The most serious indictment of the sophistic school of thought was leveled against its basic premise. This premise, phrased most succinctly by the first renowned sophist, Protagoras, states that "man is the measure of all things, of things that are as to how they are, and of things that are not as to how they are not." This idea asserts that each one of us sees the world differently, and thus each one of us forms our own beliefs about the world around us. There are immutable truths and there is an objective world, but we are not given truth as individuals; as individuals we have only our individual perceptions of what is and what is not. The world is a relative place constructed by arguments each one of us makes for our perceptions and based on our ability to persuade others that our perceptions are more accurate than our opponent's. We see in this precept the influence of the Presocratic thinkers who we discussed in Chapter 1.

In the law courts and the assembly, and even in ceremonial events such as festivals, the notion that each one of us sees the world subjectively is a useful one because it cautions us to avoid being trapped into seeing our perceptions as truth. We understand that others will see the same events differently, and that for us to be persuasive we must understand their perceptions as well as ours. As we will see in the profiles of the sophists that follow this discussion, a sophistic education required students to argue both sides of the topic as a way of helping them see the many facets of an issue. For the Athenian citizen, immersed as he was in a world of politics and litigation, understanding Protagoras' dictum was a key to success.

When the "man-measure" doctrine was applied to moral and philosophical affairs, however, it raised difficult questions. Rhetoric was criticized as a method for discussing moral behavior, for instance, since it assumed that there were no moral absolutes. Athenians had long believed that there were absolute truths in the world; that the purpose of the Athenian citizen's life was to pursue these truths through the oracles, through reasoning, or through beseeching the gods, and that even though this was a difficult process, it was worth the effort since the result would be a virtuous life. To abandon the notion that there was one true morality was to sink into skepticism, even atheism or hedonism, where what was right was whatever one decided was most advantageous at the moment. For many intellectuals of the day, this rampant individualism was reducing traditional Athenian society to chaos. As Smith notes:

> By their studies of rhetoric, argument (whence logic), and grammar, the sophists laid the basis for Greek higher education, from which was to come the mediaeval university program. By their immediate teaching, however, they—intentionally or unintentionally—obscured the traditional patterns of Greek morality and raised up a generation of skeptics prepared to argue for any action which seemed to be in their own interest.[11]

## Plato's *Gorgias* and *Phaedrus*: Socrates' Arguments Against the Sophists

The sophistic tradition was attacked by many prominent Athenian intellectuals, especially the aristocrats whose observations of the daily spectacles in the Athenian courtrooms convinced them that the masses were little more than a bleating herd of sheep, unable to govern themselves, much less a nation.[12] The playwright Aristophanes, for instance, lampooned the sophists as unscrupulous charlatans in his popular play of the time, "The Clouds." And the prominent historian Xenophon wrote that, "The sophists talk to deceive and write for their own gain and are of no benefit to anyone; for none of them is wise or ever became so; but it is enough for each one of them to be called a sophist, which is an insult at least to men of sound understanding."[13] The most direct and influential attack on the sophists, however, was leveled by the philosopher Socrates (470–399 BCE) in the writings of his most famous pupil, Plato.

Plato (427–347 BCE) is one of the most influential thinkers in the western world. His translator, Benjamin Jowett, once remarked that, "The germs of all ideas are to be found in Plato," and the 19th century writer Samuel Taylor Coleridge declared that, "every man is either a Platonist or an Aristotelian." Plato's *Republic*, a description of an ideal state governed by philosopher-kings, is often termed the first major treatise on political science, while his 25 "dialogues" cover a wide variety of subjects, including love, virtue, psychology, rhetoric, logic, and the nature of reality.

Plato's dialogues use Socrates as the major character, the antagonist. Socrates' words, then, are frequently expressions of Plato's own views so that it is sometimes impossible to determine whether the ideas were initially Socrates' or Plato's. For this reason, the ideas are usually called "Platonic" even though Socrates is the character in the dialogue who expresses them.

Plato taught at Athens in a grove called the Academus. His academy attracted many notable students, among them Aristotle who was also to make lasting contributions to philosophy, natural science, logic, and rhetoric (as we shall see in the next chapter). Plato's academy ultimately became a formal school that lasted for 900 years until the Roman emperor Justinian closed it in 529 CE.

Plato's dialogues are of interest to us because they represent a method of discourse, the question-and-answer-based mode of conversation, or Socratic method, and because they contain two divergent views on the value of rhetoric.

The "Socratic dialogue" or the "Platonic dialogue" usually begins with Socrates professing ignorance of the subject matter. He asks questions of the other characters, the result being a fuller understanding of the subject. The dialogues are usually named after the key person interrogated by Socrates, as in *Protagoras* where this famous sophist is questioned about his views on rhetoric. The dialogue has obvious relations to both the dramatic form of a play as well as the form of a debate. In the dialogues, the characters speak in ways appropriate not only to their own views, but to their speaking styles as well. Lane Cooper points out four elements of the dialogues: the plot or movement of the conversation, the agents in their moral aspect (*ethos*), the reasoning of the agents (*dianoia*), and their style or diction (*lexis*).[14]

The dialogues are also a form of "dialectical" reasoning, a branch of logic focusing on reasoning in philosophical matters where absolute certainty may be unattainable but where truth is pursued to a high degree of probability. The dialectical method is based on the use of antithesis, the pairing of contradictions to display the necessity of choice between them. Plato himself recognized that the dialectical method could easily be used for merely "argument for argument's sake" and he comments in several places in his works that reasonable people should be warned that the training they have received in such methods could make them overly disputatious (*eristic*). It should be noted that since dialectic involves opinions, conclusions drawn from them can be no better than the responses of the participants.

Socrates' scrutiny of the practice of rhetoric is most clearly revealed in two of Plato's dialogues, *Gorgias* and *Phaedrus*. We may use these two dialogues to summarize Plato's views on rhetoric since they are scattered throughout his writings.

In *Gorgias*, Socrates' arguments against the sophistic tradition are as follows:

1. That rhetoric has no subject matter of its own, as, for instance, medicine or sculpture does.
2. That since it has no subject matter of its own, rhetoric is speech about appearances, like cooking or cosmetics.
3. That rhetoric is not good for the individual because it often allows the wrongdoer to go unpunished simply because he is better at using words. It is better for the individual to suffer punishment for wrongdoing than it is for his words to absolve him of punishment so that the evil is still embedded in his soul.
4. That rhetoric is not good for society because it does not lead to truth, only persuasion, and only to pleasure for the individual who is persuasive. Rhetoric is not necessarily good for the society that must often suffer because wrong ideas have been advanced through persuasion. Rhetoric is, then, the tool of the skeptic and the hedonist.[15]

As the dialogue proceeds, each one of these arguments is drawn out in full detail and the characters engage one another in questioning and answering. Of course, in the end, Socrates claims that the politician, the one who uses rhetoric most, is simply a flatterer who does not believe that there is truth in the world and so does not know toward what end he is persuading people. The politician, then, is engaged in practices that will bring Athenian society to a fatal downfall. Socrates, on the other hand, has chosen to spend his life in the pursuit of truth and justice—the philosophical life—so that when he speaks he is a true statesman who tells people not what they want to hear or what might be politically expedient, but what they need to hear in order to lead a good life.

We see in *Gorgias* a fundamental cleavage between two irreconcilable ways of viewing the world.[16] On the one hand, Socrates is arguing for a world where absolute truths must be pursued, principally through the dialectical struggle for precise definitions of things and through inductive reasoning. Socrates did not believe that the common man (the man whom Pericles had now bestowed with the power to govern) was capable of attaining such knowledge because the common man was not willing to devote his life to the struggle for knowledge, but was more interested in getting his way by any means possible, chiefly the art of persuasion. Thus, giving this common man lessons in an art that would only feed his penchant for the easy way is of little value because in the long run this man's life will lead to nothing more than the tyranny of the masses. For Socrates, the virtuous life was a life spent in the solitary and meditative pursuit of truth.

On the other hand, the four characters Socrates challenges in the dialogue—Gorgias, Polus, Callicles, and Chaerephon—were among the most important figures of their day, celebrities who stood for the Periclean ideal of successful engagement in civic life. As opposed to the ascetic and individual pursuit of knowledge, men like these were charged with involving themselves in the everyday challenges brought on by democratic life. They did not have time to search for the "ultimate truths" in the world; they had decisions to make about war, about guilt or innocence, about how best to govern themselves in a fast-paced and confusing world. In their view, the ideal citizen did not have to be a master of metaphysics; he simply needed to possess a modicum of reason, the *logos*, and through this power of reasoning to know right from wrong. Using his natural ability to reason, which Athenians believed was given them by their birth as social animals, the common man could give sufficient consideration to the rights of others to constitute a civilized community.[17]

As in so many of the dialogues, the questions raised about rhetoric are not completely answered. It may well be, however, that the questions are more important than the answers since they invite further discussion by future generations. As for Socrates, in the dialogue *Phaedrus*, his views on rhetoric are softened, even deferential to this practical art. In this dialogue, Socrates sees a place for rhetorical training as an accompaniment to the man who has acquired knowledge so that he might frame his ideas carefully to insure comprehension and persuasion in his listeners. Socrates allows that he has treated the study of rhetoric rather roughly in earlier dialogues. He admits that the precepts laid down by the sophists have not, after all, forced anyone to use them unwisely or for evil purposes. Rhetoric is a neutral art, Socrates now concludes. The person who uses it determines its veracity, and it may, therefore, be used for ill or for good. Thus, it is not the precepts of the rhetorical art that raise concern; indeed, wise persons will learn these precepts. Rather, it is the use of the art by the ignorant or evil that must be condemned. While now admitting training in rhetoric into the education of the statesman, Socrates allows for the value of its existence even if only in the hands of the philosopher.

Plato's conclusions about rhetoric in *Phaedrus* are worthy of note since it has been asserted by the modern scholar of rhetoric, Everett Lee Hunt, that Aristotle's *Rhetoric*, the significant work reviewed in the next chapter, is virtually an expanded *Phaedrus*. These principles may be categorized as follows:

1. Disgrace lies in speaking badly, not in the act of speaking itself.
2. Knowledge of the subject matter is essential to the speaker.
3. Rhetoric is most useful in doubtful matters, where the outcome is unclear.
4. The true art depends upon:

   A. The speaker's knowledge of nature
   B. The speaker's knowledge of the soul
      i.   The genus and species of souls
      ii.  How the soul acts or is acted upon
      iii. How causes affect the soul
   C. The speaker's ability to enchant the soul.

5. A discourse has a bodily structure, and therefore, has parts (proem, narrative, testimony, evidence, probabilities, and recapitulation).
6. Rhetoric is a difficult art, but worth practicing.[18]

The summaries of the dialogues given here do not attempt to capture in full detail the broad range of philosophical questions raised. Entire books have been written to interpret the ideas in them, and students interested in an advanced understanding of the debate over sophistry are encouraged to read the dialogues in their entirety. It was Aristotle's great contribution in the *Rhetoric* to assimilate and synthesize the opposing views of Plato and the sophists, seeing rhetoric as a practical art but one that must emphasize the use of reason over emotion, and of factual argument over stylistic flourish in either words or delivery. It should also be noted that the sophists continued teaching throughout this period of criticism, acknowledging but ignoring critics such as Socrates and Plato.

## An Evaluation of the Sophists

What can we conclude from the debate about the sophists, that cadre of men who dominated Athens with their teaching and rhetorical practices for more than 150 years? First, and most importantly, we must remember that there were many, many people called "sophists," and just as there are good carpenters and bad carpenters, there were also good sophists and bad sophists; that is, there were teachers of rhetoric who focused on reasoned discourse, and there were those who taught the art of sheer display and appearance. Thus, we must treat the sophists as a group only to the extent that they shared the fundamental belief that truth is subjective and relative to the situation, the "man-measure" doctrine. We must evaluate sophists as individuals from that point forward, praising those who taught logic, writing, and speaking as a way of helping others frame their arguments most persuasively, and criticizing those who taught the charlatan's art.[19] The historian B. A. G. Fuller captures this sentiment best in the following passage from his *History of Greek Philosophy*:

> The earlier and better representatives of this class were men not only of intellectual ability and distinction but also of upright and honest character. As time went on, however, there also sprang up in increasing numbers a small fry, who, like the corrupt lawyer, the cheap orator, and the "crooked" boss or lobbyist of today, were a discredit to their profession. This cheaper crowd was concerned only with the success at all costs of their pupils and clients, and to attain it they were ready to descend to any means of doubtful propriety. They were prepared to give instruction in the dirtier tricks of the trade and the most improved methods of fooling the people, and they had little scruple about taking shady cases and silly or unjust measures and cooking them up with unsound arguments spiced with flashy oratory ... It is to this smaller and later fry with their inferior standards that we owe much of the opprobrium which already attached to the word "sophist," in antiquity, and makes it today along with "sophistry," "sophism," and the like, a term of disparagement ... In contemporary evidence there is no slur upon the integrity of such men as Protagoras and Gorgias, who were at the head of the profession in Athens in the Fifth Century, and no suggestion that their characters were not held in the highest respect.[20]

The sophists of ancient Greece had their finger on the public pulse; they understood that each one of us clings tenaciously to our own point of view, and they understood that we may find good reasons for almost any human activity, especially our own. Their teaching did lead to skepticism in some cases, perhaps even a healthy skepticism, and they did give wing to an individualism that in some cases became a sort of "me first" approach to life, a belief that cut against the basic premise of Athenian life that placed the state before the individual. But the sophists also raised important questions about language: about its origins, its connection to thought, and the proper way to use it to be persuasive. Perhaps most importantly, they gave to the common citizen a voice in public affairs. Some of the sophists suffered because they were aristocrats during times of heightened democratic urges, and others suffered because they were on the wrong political side at the moment. But that they had a major impact on their times and western civilization is indisputable.

With regard to the spread of democracy, the sophists are responsible for the spread of the Athenian empire in the 5th century BCE. Enos tell us, for instance, that, "Athens built her base of power in the West through subject allies, using sophists and rhetoric as tools for democratic security and expansion."[21] Greek colonies in Sicily and southern Italy evolved into democratic enclaves, thriving on the democratic principle of self-government. From these successful beginnings, Athenian culture found its way to Rome through the early expansion of the Roman empire. The influence of Greece was thus permanently ensconced in Western Europe through the expansion of the Roman empire. As Enos writes:

> Roman interaction with the landed tribes and Greek cities of Italy and Sicily greatly Hellenized Roman culture. Not only were Romans influenced by the century-long domination of the Hellenized Etruscans, but Roman interaction with Greek sites in southern Italy and Sicily over the centuries influenced her law, art, politics, religion and (eventually) the Roman acceptance of rhetoric.[22]

Regardless of how one evaluates the sophists, it is important to emphasize that while intellectuals debated the propriety of sophistic education in this new democracy, rhetoric itself continued throughout the Periclean Age and for the next century as the defining characteristic of life in Athens. Dobson concludes that oratorical training and practice ended at about the same time as the Athenian empire fell for the last time—322 BCE, signaling the end of the Classical Age and the beginning of the Hellenistic. After that, the rhetorical arts entered a less public, less dynamic, but equally important period of codification and systematization as we will learn in Chapter 4 of this text, and from that period, as we have seen, rhetoric was revitalized during the time of the Roman Republic. The legacy of speaking and writing from the previous 150 years would belong to the ages.[23] Rhetoric as taught and practiced in Athens during the time we have covered is still the model for us today, leading us to our best and sometimes worst actions, and providing a medium for public discussion of the principles upon which we are governed.

During the century following the Classical Age, Aristophanes of Byzantium (c.257–c.180 BCE) and Aristarchus of Samothrace (220?–c.145 BCE?), two Greek scholars living in Alexandria, compiled a treatise called *The Alexandrian Canon* in which they listed the ten Attic Orators considered to be the greatest rhetoricians (teachers, orators, and logographers) of the Classical Age.[24] At this point, we will review the lives and ideas of four of these prominent sophists, Antiphon, Lysias, Isocrates, and Demosthenes, learning who they were, what they believed about the art of rhetoric, and how they either taught or practiced the art. We will begin, however, with profiles of two other sophists, Protagoras and Gorgias, since they were the first and most successful sophists to come to Athens, and since their ideas form so much of what we study in the rhetorical arts today.

## Protagoras (485–410 BCE)

The first of the sophists to have a significant impact in Athens was Protagoras. Protagoras was born in Abdera, a Greek colony, and thus he was in the prime of his life during the reign of Pericles. Protagoras was a vain person, but talented and provocative in his thought. His father was a prominent Thracian who curried the favor of the Persian King Xerxes, and thus secured for his son a Persian education. Protagoras was soon considered to be a genius by his contemporaries in the Greek world and he traveled throughout the Greek colonies delivering lectures and orations to adoring masses. For these presentations, he charged large sums of money and soon he was rich and famous.

During the mid-440s, Protagoras journeyed to Athens where he became the acquaintance of Pericles. Pericles was enthralled with Protagoras' brilliance and accompanied him frequently to various civic events. In 444 BCE, Pericles requested that Protagoras travel to the Greek colony of Thurii in Sicily to draft the democratic constitution. Protagoras would make subsequent visits to Athens, one in 432 BCE and again in 421 BCE. The last record of Protagoras in Athens occurs in 411 BCE where he was on trial for supporting the oligarchy against the democratic forces. He escaped Athens prior to the trial by securing a small ship; however, during the flight the ship was wrecked and he perished.[25]

Protagoras was a man of education and aristocratic roots. He was not a proponent of democracy, believing the common man to be unsuited to the task of self-government. But his philosophical beliefs are also largely responsible for the sophistic movement in Athenian culture and for his particular brand of sophistic education. Let us turn, then, to a consideration of his four most important ideas.

Protagoras taught that *"man is the measure of all things, of things that are as to how they are, and of things that are not as to how they are not."* He probably received this idea, which borders on atheism and is thus decidedly not Greek, from the Persians who educated him. For Protagoras, knowledge was subjective: things are what the individual believes them to be. This idea does not assert that things in the world have no objective reality, or that they do not exist as concrete facts; rather, it means that our individual sensations of these things are all we can know of them. Thus, each one of us, not necessarily human beings in the collective, decides what something means to us.[26]

In the Platonic dialogue, *Theaetetus*, we get Socrates' understanding of the "man-measure" doctrine. "Now doesn't he say," says Socrates to Theaetetus,

> that as each thing appears to me, so it is for me, and as each thing appears to you, so in turn it is for you, you being a man and I, too? Isn't it true that at times, when

the same wind is blowing, one of us will be cold and the other will not, or the one slightly colder and the other extremely so? In that case, shall we say that the wind is cold in itself or not cold, or shall we agree with Protagoras that it is cold to the man who feels it to be cold but not so to the other? ... Appearance and perception, then are equivalent when one is speaking of warmth or anything of that sort.

Socrates likes this explanation and concludes, "I'm quite delighted with his statement that what appears to each man also *is*."[27]

Protagoras taught, second, *that for every idea, there is a corresponding contrary idea*.[28] This notion suggests that there are at least two sides to every dispute, two equally reasonable sides. The purpose of speech is to put forth arguments for and against a proposition, seeking to persuade the audience of one or the other side. Protagoras required his pupils to debate both sides of an issue, one side in the morning and the other in the afternoon, to drive home his point that they could, with equal rationality, argue both for and against a proposition. The idea that there are at least two sides to every issue is at the heart of the rhetorical consciousness of Greece and at the heart of the sophistic school of thought. It is a quite controversial but brilliant idea.

For Greeks of the time, speech was thought to be the verbal representation of what one believed to be the truth. Protagoras' idea of speech, his concept of logos, challenged this notion by asserting that a person could make any statement with conviction, even statements that the person did not believe. Protagoras' idea shattered the traditional notion that there was an inherent correspondence between a person's words and the truth (at least what that person thought was the truth). Kerford notes that what emerged from Protagoras' teaching was a realization that the relationship between speech and what is the case is far from simple. While it is likely that 5th century thinkers all were prepared to accept that there is and must always be a relationship between the two, there was a growing understanding that what is very often involved is not simply a *presentation* in words of what is the case, but rather a *representation*, involving a considerable degree of reorganization in the process. It is this awakening of what has been called a "rhetorical self-consciousness" that is a feature both of contemporary literature and of theoretic discussion in the 5th century.[29] We will trace this discussion further in the profiles of Gorgias and Antiphon that follow.

The widening gulf between speech and reality caused great skepticism among Greek intellectuals about the entire sophistic movement. The movement challenged their firmly held belief that truth existed, that to "know thyself," as the Delphic oracle challenged people of the time, was to search for the truth.[30] Protagoras was now apparently asserting that there was no truth, only opposing ideas and moral equivalencies between which one chose as a guide to decision-making, whether in the court, the assembly, or one's life.

Protagoras' third profound idea was that *the worse cause may always be made to appear to be the better cause*. This idea asserts that when a weak argument (or thought) appears to us, we have the ability through speech to make a stronger argument for a more rational solution to whatever problem we have confronted. For instance, suppose that a person is sick in the stomach. To that person, even tasty and healthy food will appear unappetizing, while that same food to a healthy person will appear sumptuous. Protagoras believed that the sick person has the power to see that food as healthy and appetizing by the power of rationality.[31] Through the powers of reason, the person can tell him or her self that the reason he or she thinks the food is sour is because he or she is sick. This understanding of *logos*, the power of words and reasoning, is a valuable insight into the rhetorical world in which we operate, and it made Protagoras' school one of the most successful in Athens.

Protagoras' school of rhetoric was controversial because he taught the concept of relativism in public affairs. In fact, Protagoras was mainly concerned with the world of politics and public affairs and his students were often wealthy citizens who had taken prominent places in Athenian or Greek political life. Protagoras asserted in the Socratic dialogue named after him that his students would improve on a daily basis. "He will learn," Protagoras said, "what he came to learn, and that is prudence in affairs private as well as public; he will learn to order his own house in the best manner and he will be able to speak and act for the best in the affairs of the state."[32]

Beyond the healthy skepticism he taught his students in order to open their minds to opposing ideas, Protagoras also preached agnosticism in religious affairs. In fact, the fourth idea of this brilliant thinker is his most infamous: "*Concerning the gods, I am unable to know, whether they exist or whether they do not exist, or what they are like in form.*"[33] For this idea, Protagoras was eventually charged with teaching atheism and disrespect for the gods, and he would have been put to death had he not escaped Athens before his trial.

Protagoras' assertion of agnosticism is less controversial to us today, but to Athenians it was blasphemy. Protagoras did not intend to blaspheme the Greek deity, but to point out that such speculations result in endless metaphysical arguments. He believed that, in practical terms, it matters little whether the gods exist or not. In everyday public affairs, what matters most is the reason one is able to muster for a particular point of view. Invoking the gods for one's cause might be a persuasive argument if it works with a particular audience; however, one's opponent may make the same invocation. Asserting that god is on one's side is not a reasonable argument since it does not stem from the matter itself, but is an appeal to some external force that one cannot control. So, Protagoras believed, why spend time on hopeless and irrelevant appeals; better to spend time on making clear arguments for and against a proposal.

Protagoras taught his students to speak in clear language. He believed in the use of aphorisms; that is, the use of precise and pithy phrases that captured the essence of an idea in a few words. "Love is what is left when the passion subsides" is an example of an aphorism. Such statements capture self-evident "truisms" in memorable phrases, the result being that as the audience thinks about the aphorism, it begins to "unpack" itself, revealing its cogency with greater and greater lucidity.

Protagoras also required his students to study grammar and to make themselves masters of prose discourse in all ways possible. He compiled a list of "proper" words as distinct from metaphors; that is, denotative words rather than connotative.[34] He also studied gender and mood as grammatical principles that add precision to one's speech. Protagoras was the first person to distinguish parts of speech, about which he wrote in a treatise entitled, "On Correct Speech." He was particularly concerned with teaching his students the rules of grammar through which they could be more accurate in their speaking.[35]

Cicero writes about Protagoras' use of "commonplaces," or *communes loci*, standard arguments that can be used in any speech to support a position or weaken it.[36] For instance, it is possible to have an example developed to show that if one can do the more difficult of two things, one can do the easier. When a debate calls for such an argument, it is ready-made for insertion into the speech. By having such commonplace arguments available to him, the orator can discourse on any topic at any given time or place. Such rhetorical devices can become building blocks in the composition of an argument, allowing for a more extemporaneous sounding speech.

In Protagoras' teaching, we find the central ideas of the sophistic movement, the only ideas that seem to connect one sophist to another. Protagoras was controversial throughout his life, in both his ideas and his politics. But he was a consistent thinker, a man whose ideas held together to form the essence of what we think of as a rhetorical consciousness. Protagoras taught that each individual receives the world differently through the senses, and then organizes those sensations into knowledge through an internal argument about the meaning of those sensations. He taught that knowledge was the result of this internal struggle, and that this knowledge is then challenged in public discourse as it confronts the knowledge others have attained through their own internal struggle with their own sense experiences. He believed that virtue was a part of knowledge, something that was learned just as other things are learned; virtue was not received through lineage or heritage. For all his ideas, he became both famous and infamous, celebrated and vilified, adored by the masses and ultimately condemned by them to death.

## Gorgias (485–380 BCE)

Perhaps the most remarkable feature about the sophist Gorgias is that he lived to be at least 105 years old, depending on when one fixes his birth.[37] Gorgias' life spans the era of the Periclean Age, the wars with Persia, Sparta, and the beginning of the downfall of the Athenian empire. But Gorgias is most remembered not for his age, but because Plato uses him as the central character in the dialogue in which Socrates most severely attacks the sophistic art. Because *Gorgias* is the most commonly referenced work used to assail the art of rhetoric as practiced in Athens, and because in that dialogue the character Gorgias asserts that he can speak eloquently about any matter, even those about which he is not an expert, Gorgias' name has become synonymous with speech that is flowery and pleasing but that has little substance.[38] The reputation is undeserved.

Gorgias' ideas are far more complex and original than Plato represents them, and his practice of rhetoric is more substantive than simply pleasing speech. While he was a stylist, a man whose words were often so poetic they could charm an audience into adulation but who was also given to rhetorical excess, he had good reasons for his style and manner of delivery.

Gorgias was born in Leontini, in the Greek colony of Sicily. He was educated by leading philosophers and scientists of the time. There is evidence that he studied with Empedocles, the man credited by Aristotle with having "invented" rhetoric.[39] Gorgias arrived in Athens in 427 BCE to seek the Athenians' help in resisting an attack by Syracuse against Leontini. His oratory was deemed a sensation, but Athens refused, nevertheless, to help Leontini, and it was destroyed. Gorgias, however, soon became an orator of great repute, traveling from city to city charming audiences with his new brand of prose, a rhythmic, almost poetic speech that was laden with rhetorical figures and flourishes. At various points in his career, Gorgias was invited to both Delphi and Olympia to participate with the Greeks in celebrating their festivals of religion and sport, and he delivered speeches with great success at both, being awarded the Golden Statue at Delphi.

Gorgias soon became a teacher of the art of rhetoric, and he attracted a following of the most brilliant students in Athens. Gorgias believed that success in rhetoric was important for young people because it taught them to persuade and to be persuaded. His lessons included exercises in argumentation, elocution, and declamation. Philostratus, a Greek sophist of the Roman period, credits Gorgias with having invented "extemporaneous" speaking; that is, speaking without notes on any topic suggested by the audience. Gorgias also taught the use of rhetorical figures such as those used in poetry. Gorgias is known to have written a number of speeches and essays, including an epistemological treatise called *Helen*, and a *Funeral Oration*, as well as his Olympic Orations. He may also have written a book on the art of rhetoric, and his instruction was equally devoted to writing and oral discourse. In fact, Gorgias' focus on reasoning through writing and speaking may have influenced his pupil Isocrates to emphasize writing as the gateway to critical thinking.

Gorgias' longevity is due to his ability to resist all temptation. He was a man of great discipline who avoided excess in all its forms (except speech), whether in food, drink, or sport. He did not marry. Untersteiner tells us that his death was serene, that he simply fell into a deep slumber and died slowly from exhaustion.[40] During his life, Gorgias made important contributions to western civilization, as he wrestled with the most vexing problems facing those who saw a brave new world arising, where, because of the enormous growth of knowledge about the physical universe and the mind's appropriation of it, things no longer always were what they appeared.

Gorgias' most serious philosophical work is *On Not-Being or On Nature* (sometimes referred to as *On the Nonexistent*). In this essay, Gorgias examines what is actual and what is simply appearance. He argues three propositions: first, *that nothing exists*; second, *that even if it exists, it is inapprehensible to man*; and third, *that even if it is apprehensible, it is still incapable of being expressed or explained to the next person.*[41] Gorgias' development of these propositions is complex, far beyond the scope of this text. We are able to see in them, however, the essential ideas that illuminate his thinking about rhetoric: that we do not experience reality directly, only through the words we use to call that reality into existence, and that since each one of us experiences the world uniquely and chooses our words differently, it is impossible to communicate perfectly with others. Even the phrase "nothing exists" can be understood in opposite ways depending on which word we emphasize, and how many times we say it.

Gorgias' ideas are the result of his lifelong struggle to resolve apparent contradictions in the world. Specifically, part of his education had taught him that the world was a potentially beautiful, harmonious place where all conflict could be resolved through expressions of universal truths that countenanced all experience. He learned this principle through his study of the poet Pindar. On the other hand, he also studied the tragic poets of the age, who believed that there were insoluble conflicts caused by the mind's ability to perceive opposites in everything, and which thus created a situation of permanent and impending tragedy.[42] Gorgias believed that unifying experiences do not exist as such for the individual, and he sought to resolve this conflict by seizing upon the power of speech.

Gorgias held that opposites do exist, but that they could be held together in harmonious balance through the power of words. Poets, who are the masters of words, can weave together the intimate connections between seemingly apparent contradictions. In fact, it is the poet's responsibility, Gorgias believed, to help others understand the harmony in polarities. For example, let us take an apparent contradiction such as "We two are one." Our first reaction is that two of us cannot be one person. But as we think on the matter, we can avail ourselves of the concept of "love," as a way of explaining how two hearts can be joined together in mutual concern and sharing for one another, and thus become one in spirit even though their physical bodies are still separate. It is this power of words, which, when mastered, can overcome life's contradictions. It is the power of words that allows the poet Wordsworth to proclaim that "The child is father of the man" ("My Heart Leaps Up") or that allows the Welsh poet Dylan Thomas to speak of leaves "undying" as they fall from the trees in the autumn to become nutrients for future growth ("Author's Prologue"). When we employ the power of speech, Gorgias believed, we can accommodate life's paradoxes even if we cannot know truth.

Gorgias believed that the speech of the poet could arouse in us feelings of universal humanity, experienced in our souls.[43] The poetic experience in words culminates when the individual rises to a humane vision capable of feeling and understanding the sorrows of others. By so doing, we overcome the tragic moments of life and rise above them. When particular emotions of others become for us a personal experience, there is in some way a confluence of our egos, the empathic moment. The act of empathizing with another is the ultimate artistic experience for the human being because it is the most difficult journey we can make; that is, into the soul of another person. Gorgias' great idea, then, is that the power of speech can resolve conflicts between the beautiful and the tragic, between the ideal and the real, between any opposing concepts.

At the same time, Gorgias realized that speech could be used to deceive as well as reveal and resolve. He felt that speech "has the power to put an end to fear, to remove grief, to instill joy, and increase pity."[44] But even when it is deceptive, speech can create happiness in others, if in simply the sheer delight of the sounds of the words or the laughter words can provoke.[45] Speech can soothe as when we offer a slightly exaggerated compliment to someone else because they are feeling down and we want to lift their spirits. Speech conditions the mind, Gorgias believed, in the same way that medicine conditions the body.[46] We know that speech is deceptive, Gorgias taught, because in the law courts we can hear two people speak on the same matter in two completely contradictory but reasonable ways. So while speech has the power to reduce opposites to a unity, to create harmony in our world, it also can be used to deceive and unravel, "to bewitch the soul with a kind of evil persuasion."[47] In fact, Gorgias believed that it is not experience that counts as much as the words that are used to recreate them. Given these realities about speech, it falls to oratory—rhetoric—to persuade others; because speech does not always reveal truth, persuasion is what we have left. With this pronouncement, Gorgias helped Athenians cope with one of the pressing dilemmas of their new civilization: that there is a difference between thought and speech; that thought is a *representation* and speech is a *presentation*. Fact and truth, in the world of human affairs, must give way to a rhetorical self-consciousness.[48]

Gorgias' rhetoric is notable for its emphasis on style. His style, which involves an excessive use of figures, was typical of Sicilian oratory, and to some extent Gorgias was simply following the teaching of Empedocles. For followers of Empedocles, words were a form of knowledge in what they believed was an essentially nonrational, divinely inspired world.[49]

Gorgias defines rhetoric as the "psychagogic art," the art of guiding and winning souls. To reach the soul, oratory must borrow rhetorical figures from the language of poetry to appeal to the audience's emotions. Figures of speech are artful deviations either from the structure of ordinary language as in parallel phrasing or from the meaning of words such as occurs in metaphor. It is understandable, given his concern with overcoming opposites, that he would use figures of speech such as parallel phrasing and antithesis since these figures, by juxtaposing ideas, particularly contrasting ideas, cast them in a dramatic light where their apparent contrariness can be resolved in the mind or at least accommodated as the natural ambiguity of reality.

In his own oratory and in his teaching, Gorgias used figurative expressions to excess, the result often being a strange sounding and strained style. Diodorus Siculus tells us that:

> He was the first to make use of figures of speech which were far-fetched and distinguished by artificiality: antithesis, isocolon, parison, homoeoteleuton, and others of that sort which then, because of the novelty of the devices, were thought worthy of praise, but now seem labored and ridiculous when used to excess.[50]

He also delivered his speeches with great flourish, almost like a musical composition with cadences and crescendos. Gorgias provided his pupils with exercises in the use of these figures, and he assigned them to be used in composing theoretical arguments that might be used in the courts, the legislature, and in ceremonial speeches (he is said by Dobson to have originated the "epideictic" or ceremonial style of oratory, although that is conjectural).[51] It was this high oratorical style that he felt would be most persuasive because it was most like the speech of the poets, except in prose form and adapted to rhetorical situations.

Gorgias' theory of rhetoric, when applied to actual oratory, can appear as pure bombast, sheer display with little substance. It is difficult to capture the often pompous and exaggerated style of Gorgias in English so as to compare it, for instance, to the plain style of Lysias that we will read about shortly. A typical example of his style is in the "Encomium to Helen," which begins as follows:

> A fair thing for a city is having good men, for a body is beauty, for a soul wisdom, for a deed virtue ... (and) for a discourse is truth. And the opposite of this is foul. For a man and a woman and a discourse and a deed and a city it is necessary to honor the deed worthy of praise with praise ... and for the unworthy, to attach blame. For it is equal error and ignorance to praise the blameworthy and to blame the praiseworthy.

The following figures of speech are identifiable in this passage:

1. Isocolon—members of equal length
2. Parison—exact syntactical parallelism
3. Paromoeon—alliteration

4. Homoeoteleuton—words in corresponding places in clauses with like endings
5. Polyptoton (traduction)—repetition of words with the same root but different inflectional endings
6. Chiasmus—reciprocal change of words in a sentence
7. Zeugma (juncture)—one word linking together several members
8. Maxim (sententia)—generalized statement of a widely accepted or significant premise.

Although most of the Gorgianic effects depend on various kinds of parallelism, Gorgias also makes strong use of antithesis, pairing of matched opposing expressions in order to indicate their contrariety. For instance, in the "Encomium to Helen," Helen is contrasted to her abductor:

> But if by violence she was defeated and unlawfully she was treated, and to her justice was meted, clearly her violator was importunate, while she, translated and violated, was unfortunate. Therefore, the barbarian who legally, verbally, actually attempted the barbarous attempt, should meet with verbal accusation, legal reprobation and actual condemnation. For Helen, who was violated and from her fatherland separated, and from her friends segregated, should justly meet with commiseration rather than with defamation. For he was the victor and she the victim. It is just, therefore, to sympathize with the latter and to anathematize the former.[52]

As you can see, Gorgias fails to achieve variety. The constant recurrence of the same patterns becomes monotonous, and as the last example shows, straining to produce the desired effect often results in a tortuous twisting of language. Nevertheless, Gorgias' conscious attempt to use sound to manipulate his hearers' reactions marks a new point in the developing Greek consciousness about discourse and the power of words.

It is little wonder, now that we have seen Gorgias' philosophy applied to his rhetorical theory, that Socrates would ridicule him. For Socrates, the emphasis was on the search for absolute truths (rationality), and certainly rhetorical excesses such as those engaged in and taught by Gorgias had the potential for trickery, deceit, and expediency. Socrates favored the dialectical search for definitive answers to the problems confronting humanity; Gorgias, like so many of his counterparts, was a more practical man, assigning to persuasion the task of leading minds to answers in a world where answers were more accessible than truth.[53]

For some Greeks of the time, Gorgias was little more than an entertaining orator, while for others he was a man of great philosophical mind and a man of letters. At the very least, Gorgias' life is more worthy than the caricature of him portrayed in the dialogues of Plato. In fact, beneath a statue erected in his honor at Olympia by his grand-nephew Eumolpus, an inscription reads, "None of the mortals invented a finer art to steel the souls of men for works of virtue."[54] He is a central figure in the development of sophistic thought, and while his own rhetorical excesses cannot be completely excused, when seen in the light of his ideas, they are at least understandable.

## Antiphon (480 to 470–411 BCE)

Classical scholars have debated whether there was one Antiphon, known as Antiphon of Rhamnus, or a second Antiphon called Antiphon the Sophist. Untersteiner, for instance, asserts that two Antiphons must be distinguished,[55] while Kerford argues that the differences in style and political leaning are resolvable within one person named Antiphon.[56] We shall focus on Antiphon as one person, following Kerford, and review his ideas on philosophy and rhetoric.

Antiphon was born between 480 and 470 BCE. He took no part in public affairs in his early years, most likely because he was an aristocrat who disdained the Periclean democracy in which he spent much of his adult life.[57] In his later years, he wrote speeches and consulted with many of his anti-democratic friends, and he was thought to be the primary thinker behind the overthrow of the democracy in Athens in 411 BCE by the Council of 400. When that oligarchy was banished shortly after its rise to power, Antiphon was impeached and brought to trial for treason. At his trial, this man who had spent his life behind the scenes delivered a most brilliant oration in defense of himself, one that the historian Thucydides called "the finest speech of its kind ever heard up to that time."[58] Unfortunately, Athenians viewed Antiphon and his co-conspirators with such anger that he was condemned and executed, being denied even a decent burial in his native Athenian soil.

During his lifetime, Antiphon wrote a number of philosophical treatises, the most important of which are *On Truth* (two books), *On Concord*, a *Politicus*, and *On the Interpretation of Dreams*. Antiphon wrote numerous speeches for others and he opened a school of sophistry to train his aristocratic friends in the art of public speaking. He is considered to be the first professional speechwriter, or "logographer," and he is regarded as the first Athenian to lay down definite rules and principles for oratory. He was a contemporary of two other renowned sophists, Gorgias and Protagoras, and he engaged with them in debate about the philosophical issues surrounding the sophistic movement; that is, issues such as the nature of experience, the possibility of overcoming opposites, the place of probability in rational discourse, etc. In addition, Antiphon was interested in physical science, astronomical problems, and mathematics.

Kerford tells us that Antiphon was an advice-giver of sorts, setting up a counseling bureau in the marketplace near Corinth to help people solve problems that were distressing them.[59]

Antiphon was a practical psychologist, a sort of ancient version of today's advice columnists and talk-show counselors. He taught his clients to anticipate problems before they occurred as a way of avoiding the crises they occasioned. Antiphon believed that words could soothe and encourage. He also believed that dreams were to be interpreted, not taken literally, a precept that helped others to avoid acting unwisely on their premonitions and superstitions.

Antiphon was a man who engaged in both the intellectual and political life of his time. We shall look at his ideas briefly and then at his teachings about rhetoric.

Antiphon's philosophy is most clearly expressed in two extant treatises, *On Truth* and *On Concord*. His beliefs stem largely from his reactions to Protagoras and Gorgias, particularly the latter. Antiphon believed that experiences were real—that they formed the basis for what one knew. Words were intended to capture those real experiences. One could not, Antiphon believed, speak about experiences that one did not have, either concretely or intellectually. Experiences do have a reality of their own and they come before the words used to describe them. For example, we react to a STOP sign based upon our past experiences with STOP signs and our knowledge of them. If we were to simply deny all of our past experiences with STOP signs or create our own meaning in a willful rejection of those past experiences, we would surely meet with tragedy sooner or later. Experience gives unity to what we know and past experience becomes our guide for future decision-making.

As with Gorgias, then, Antiphon believed that words could describe or deceive, soothe or anger, because they were, indeed, independent of experience. But at the same time, if the words are concordant with people's experience and knowledge of what the words are representing, they will ultimately be persuasive because they will be consistent with our collective experiences.

Antiphon believed that justice and politics are artistic expressions, not inherent in human nature itself. The political art and the juridical arts are at their best when they seek a concordance between human experience—the unwritten laws we learn through the ages—and the written laws in force at the present time, which are temporal codifications of these unwritten laws. We all have a sense of what is right and just for all people, argued Antiphon, but we also have our own selfish interests which sometimes conflict with what is good for the community. The best politics are those which seek to attenuate self-interest with community interest; that is the best expression of our human nature. Deceptive politics are practiced by those who seek to impose laws that do not accommodate the needs of the individual with the needs of the community. Persuasion by such deceptive politicians (or litigants) is unethical and must be countered with true persuasion. True persuasion provides evidence of the good of one's proposition, evidence that is drawn from experience or knowledge.

Education, Antiphon believed, had as its primary goal helping students find harmony between their private and public lives. "Every relationship must be regulated by concord," Antiphon writes, "where the intellectual attitude of the individual becomes decisive for his relations with the surrounding world, relations which must assume a joyful tone capable of binding the ethic of the individual and of society into a unity."[60] Thus, Antiphon raised education to the highest rank of human affairs.[61]

Antiphon's method of teaching was to take an imaginary case and prepare two speeches for the prosecution and two for the defense, and then require students to deliver the speeches on both sides of the case. Three of these compositions, known as "tetralogies," still survive. In addition, Antiphon wrote speeches for others for a fee. Three of these speeches survive, all of which are written for cases involving homicide. The point of the tetralogies was to teach students that it is possible to find reason on all sides of a matter, but also to teach them how to succeed in the Athenian courtroom, a much more practical matter.

Antiphon composed his speeches for the courts in the traditional structure: a standard preface composed of commonplaces, an introduction describing and criticizing the circumstances, the facts presented as a narrative, followed by arguments and proofs, and concluding with a peroration or appeal to the jury. Antiphon's tetralogies contain only preface, argument, and peroration.[62] Thus, Antiphon organized his speeches to fit the situation for which they were intended.

Antiphon composed speeches in the grand style of Attic prose, compared to the other celebrated logographer, Lysias, who wrote in clear, plain language. "Atticism" was a style that urged the use of the language and rhythm of the classical period; thus, Antiphon wrote in an elevated, flowery prose, using frequent parallelisms and numerous periodic sentences (sentences that use a series of phrases or clauses that lead to a climax).[63] His speeches seem poetical and somewhat unnatural because Antiphon would often choose the less frequently used word rather than the common term for something he was discussing.

Antiphon favored the excessive use of commonplaces; that is, stock phrases and arguments that were expected by the Athenian jurors. For instance, they enjoyed hearing litigants grovel before them, apologizing in advance for sounding literate and expressing deep appreciation to them for listening. Such flattery was expected, and Antiphon did not disappoint as we can see in the following excerpt:

> I could wish, Gentlemen, that I possessed a capacity for speaking and an experience of the world on a scale corresponding to the misfortunes and sufferings that have befallen me; as it is, my experience in the latter is as much beyond my deserts as my deficiency in the former falls short of my requirements.[64]

We can almost hear Antiphon's disdain for the jurors in this example of a commonplace written in the form of a periodic sentence.

Antiphon's speeches are laced with commonplace appeals to religious deities and to the laws of the democracy, even though he thought them hopeless. Antiphon knew how to please and this combination of the high style and the use of commonplaces made his speeches extremely popular with audiences.[65]

In the following excerpt from his speech of defense "On the Murder of Herodes," Antiphon's formal style can be seen most clearly. In this excerpt, Helus, a Mitylenaean, having been accused of the murder of Herodes, who had mysteriously disappeared from the boat in which the two had embarked together, defends himself with the following words:

> Now, gentlemen, if my conscience were guilty, I should never have come into this city. But I did come—with an abiding faith in the justice of my cause, and strong in conscious innocence. For not once alone has a clear conscience raised up and supported a failing body in the hour of trial and tribulation. A guilty conscience, on the other hand, is a source of weakness to the strongest body. The confidence, therefore, with which I appear before you, is the confidence of innocence. To conclude, gentlemen, I have only to say that I am not surprised that my accusers slander me. That is their part; yours is not to credit their slander. If, on the one hand, you listen to me, you can afterwards repent, if you like, and punish me by way of remedy, but, if you listen to my accusers, and do what they wish, no remedy will then be admissible. Moreover, no long time will intervene before you can decide unlawfully. Matters like these require not haste, but deliberation. On the present occasion, then, take a survey of the case; on the next, sit in judgment on the witnesses; form, now, an opinion; later, decide the facts. It is very easy, indeed, to testify falsely against a man charged with murder. For, if he be immediately condemned to death, his false accusers have nothing to fear, since all

danger of retribution is removed on the day of execution. And, even if the friends of the condemned man cared to exact satisfaction for malicious prosecution, of what advantage would it be to him after his death? Acquit me, then, on this issue, and compel my accusers to indict me according to law. Your judgment will then be strictly legal, and, if condemned, I cannot complain that it was contrary to law. This request I make of you with due regard to your conscience as well as to my own right. For upon your oath depends my safety. By whichever of these considerations you are influenced, you must acquit me.

We can see in this excerpt the use of parallel phrasing, periodicity in sentence structure, commonplaces in terms of flattering the jurors, and many of the figures common to the grand style: alliteration, isocolon, maxim, and asyndeton. It was also the case in this speech on the murder of Herodes that Antiphon uses predominantly argument from general probability rather than evidence despite his previously noted belief in the value of concrete experience and concordance between words and events themselves. Perhaps he could not offer any credible evidence in this situation, or perhaps he felt that the jurors were more easily persuaded with general reasoning. It is a general criticism of Antiphon that he seldom used direct evidence or witnesses' testimony to prove his case.[66]

Dobson notes that Antiphon's style is similar in all his ghostwritten speeches, even those presented by ordinary people.[67] This inability to write in the language of the person for whom the speech is intended is a defect, and it may only be excused by the fact that Antiphon was among the first to ply his trade and he had no models or mentors to help him develop his craft. Despite his highly formal style and his inability at characterization, a speech composed by Antiphon was greatly anticipated by the citizens of Athens who knew that the speech would be flattering and persuasive. Freeman sums it up this way: "The style inclines to stiffness and an over-elaborate balancing of phrases; but the argumentation is brilliant, and the language, always subtle, sometimes rises to a kind of austere poetry, in the best Attic manner."[68]

Antiphon was one of the three most important sophists of his time. With Protagoras and Gorgias, Antiphon wrote many of the rules for rhetoric and he developed many of the methods for teaching it. He had a profound influence on his age and while he was not a convert to Pericles' democracy in his political life, he contributed much to it through his school of sophistry and his speeches written for the courts.

## Lysias (444–370s BCE)

Lysias lived during a period of great turmoil in Athens. He was born in the coastal town of Piraeus, one of two sons of a wealthy arms merchant, Cephalus, who had been invited to live in Athens by Pericles. Around the year 440 BCE, after his father's death, Lysias moved with his brother, Polemarchus, to the Athenian colony of Thurii in Sicily where he was educated under the noted rhetorician Tisias. When the Athenian democracy was overthrown in Sicily in 411 BCE, Lysias and Polemarchus were banished to Athens.

Between 411 and 404 BCE, when Sparta gained control of the Athenian mainland, foreign-born aliens (metics) were considered enemies of the state. Lysias and Polemarchus were sought out to be put to death. Lysias escaped but Polemarchus was imprisoned and forced to drink the poison hemlock. In 403 BCE, democracy returned to Athens when the Athenian general, Thrasybulus, drove out the tyrant Critias. Lysias was allowed to prosecute the murderer of his brother Polemarchus, a man named Eratosthenes. His brilliant speech, "Against Eratosthenes," brought him much fame in Athens and launched his career as a speech writer for the next two decades.

During his first eight years in Athens, Lysias continued his study of rhetoric under the sophist Protagoras. Lysias' study with Tisias had taught him the art of beautiful diction, the value of clear and pointed expression. Under Protagoras, Lysias learned the power of argument, the art of making the weaker cause appear the stronger. In his speech writing, Lysias combined what he had learned from Tisias and Protagoras to become the most celebrated speech writer in the history of the Athenian court.

From the time of his speech against Eratosthenes in 403 BCE, Lysias wrote between 200 and 400 speeches for litigants in the Athenian courts, 23 of which have survived in entirety. The courts were filled during this period with suits to recover land confiscated during the war with Sparta, with requests for pensions from veterans wounded in combat, and with criminal offenses related to the overthrow of the tyrannical Thirty, the despotic government headed by Critias. In the humorous complaint that Lysias puts into the mouth of a wealthy client, matters had come to such a pass that even the unborn children of Athenians shuddered to think of the litigation in prospect for them when they should come into the world.[69] With all this activity, Lysias was a busy man.

Lysias was noted for his ability to grasp the client's circumstances and to write speeches that seemed to be coming from his client's mouths as they declaimed to the jury. He expressed in his speeches the feeling, manner, and language of his clients. Lysias is distinguished among logographers for embodying the concept of "*ethopoeia*."

*Ethopoeia* is the ability to capture the ideas, words, and style of delivery suited to the person for whom the address is written. Even more so, *ethopoeia* involves adapting the speech to the exact conditions under which it is to be spoken. Finally, *ethopoeia* is the art of discovering the exact lines of argument that will turn the case against the opponent. Thus, in style and in invention of argument, Lysias mastered the art of forensic rhetoric as practiced by ordinary Athenians in the courtrooms of his day.

Lysias was noted for his plain style. He seldom used elaborate figures of speech, which at that time and because of the influence of sophists such as Gorgias was considered essential to success. His speeches are straightforward narratives of the events that brought the complaint and the arguments that support his clients. There are few metaphors or other standard stylistic devices such as those used by the ancients and even by orators today. Lysias did frequently use parallel phrasing, although less an ornamental use of language than as a strategy for juxtaposing various positions in dramatic tension so that the jury, as was the case then, might see the arguments in their starkest opposition. In the speech against Eratosthenes, for instance, Lysias uses numerous antithetical parallels such as in the following excerpt:

> When our lives depended upon your cabal, you opposed the opinion of those who sought our death; but when the life of Polemarchus depended on yourself alone, you imprisoned and murdered him! And now you dare expect favor for what

you advised without effect, rather than dread punishment for what you actually committed.

Lysias wrote speeches to be persuasive at the moment they were delivered. He understood that in forensic oratory the vote immediately following the speech is the one that counts; thus, his speeches exemplify rhetoric that is suited to the available means of persuasion in the particular situation. One of Lysias' clients is said to have read his speech for the first time and marveled at its brilliance, but then to have taken it home and read it a few more times at which point he began to notice flaws in it. He complained to Lysias for writing a poor speech, to which Lysias replied, "but the jury will only hear it once." Legend has it that the client went away pleased.[70]

Lysias organized his speeches into four parts: proem or introduction, narrative, proof, and exordium or conclusion. This natural progression served the speaker well in the courtroom where the speech would be delivered just once. Jebb concludes that Lysias' arrangement of his speeches distinguished him from all other Greek orators by a uniform simplicity.[71]

In his use of words and phrases, Lysias developed a prose style that was to become the standard for purity and grace in expression. Kennedy describes this style as "unadorned yet never bald, unenlivened yet never dull."[72] Lysias had the ability to capture thoughts in terms that were proper and in current usage. He used a loose, free sentence structure that strikes the listener as the speech of the marketplace, the idiomatic speech of the average citizen elevated to the situation of the courtroom. This plain style was so admired by later ages that Cicero would refer to Lysias as the complete orator and compare him to Cato; one of the most influential orators of Cicero's time.[73]

In Lysias' writing, then, we have an example of the plain style: writing that fits the person and the situation exactly. Lysias' rhetoric shows the sophistication to depart from traditional forms and to develop forms that fit the person for whom the address is written. *Ethopoeia* remains today a valuable concept in the art of rhetoric.

Lysias became rich and famous for his speechwriting ability, and he delivered at least one speech at Olympia, an honor reserved for only the most distinguished speakers in Greece. Jebb concluded his study of Lysias with the following words:

> His real strength, as far as can be judged, lay in his singular literary tact. A fine perception of character in all sorts of men, and a faculty for dramatizing it, aided by a sense of humor, always under control; a certain pervading gracefulness and flexibility of mind; rhetorical skill, masterly in a sense hardly dreamed of at that day, since it could conceal itself—these were his most distinctive qualities and powers ... He was a man of warm nature, impulsive, hospitable, attached to his friends, fond of pleasure, and freely indulging in it but, like Sophocles at the Chian supper party described by Ion, carrying into social life the same intellectual quality which marks his best work—the grace and the temperate brightness of a thoroughly Athenian mind.[74]

## Isocrates (436–338 BCE)

Isocrates, whom the poet John Milton called "Old Man Eloquent," lived to be almost 100 years of age. His life spans the end of the reign of Pericles to the conquest of

Athens by Philip of Macedon. Born to a wealthy family of flute manufacturers, Isocrates was raised during the years of the Peloponnesian War, 431–404 BCE, a war that ruined his family financially and that had a deep influence on his life and teaching. Although he condemned the sophistry he so often witnessed in Athens, he was himself a teacher of rhetoric and he wrote a number of important speeches (21 survive). Interestingly, due to his weak voice and speech anxiety, Isocrates never delivered the speeches he wrote. Thus, his orations were meant as compositions to be studied by his students in his school, as speeches to be delivered by others, or as political pamphlets for sale in Athens. Although he was not a politician by election, his life was devoted to the task of uniting the Greek city-states against the "barbarians" to the east, a movement known as Panhellenism. According to legend (which some scholars such as Dobson dispute), Isocrates died by starving himself to death. Most likely, he died from the infirmities of old age.

Isocrates wrote profusely about all matters, both internal and external, facing the Greek people during his lifetime. Among his most important works are the *Philippus*, the *Panathenaicus*, *Against the Sophists*, the *Areopagiticus*, *On the Antidosis*, the *Panegyricus*, the *Nicocles*, and *On the Peace*. His school opened sometime around 390 BCE, and he trained some of the most influential citizens of Greece; in fact, Cicero noted that from Isocrates' school, "as from the Trojan horse, none but real heroes proceeded."[75] His ideas, then, are important because they cover the range of issues facing his nation, and because they influenced those who ruled Greece during many of its critical periods. His ideas on politics and education were equally important to succeeding ages, especially the Roman period, the Middle Ages, and the Renaissance.

Isocrates believed that rhetoric must be devoted not only to training for the law courts but to training statesmen who will speak for the benefit of the entire Greek culture. In particular, he believed there was a common intellectual culture of the Greek race which when activated through speech and writing could transform the world into an ideal place.[76] Isocrates' emphasis on Greek hegemony, led by Athens, came in the aftermath of the Pelopponesian Wars when the city-states had turned on one another, leaving the entire culture vulnerable to attack from foreign enemies. This central theme is known as "Panhellenism," and it is most forcefully developed in his composition *Panegyricus* written for the Olympic festival in 380 BCE.

Isocrates expressed his views on patriotism and Greek unity throughout the second half of his life. In addition to *Panegyricus*, and following the Peace of Philocrates in 346 BCE, Isocrates wrote to Philip congratulating him for his victories in the Hellenes and praising him for what Isocrates thought was a final opportunity to unite Greece, especially since Philip had shown such deference to Athenian culture. Even though Philip most likely never read the letter, and even though the letter was ill-advised since Philip was at heart a despot, it shows the unifying idea of Isocrates' thought throughout his political lifetime—that Greek culture must be unified to fulfill its destiny.[77]

Isocrates' ideas about knowledge and education are a creative mixture of two of his most significant teachers, Gorgias and Socrates.

From Gorgias, Isocrates accepted the notion that abstract truth is elusive and that the unending search for absolute definitions advocated by Socrates is futile. He believed, then, in persuasion and rhetorical technique as the keys to the social-political process. Isocrates adopted from Socrates his critical attitude toward Athenian democracy, his criticism of the sophistic excesses in the courtrooms of Athens, his focus on ideas as prefatory to rhetorical technique, and his belief that education should develop moral virtue above all else. Isocrates is, then, a practical man who believes that rational discourse is possible while accepting other forms of nonrational discourse such as poetry and myth as legitimate modes of persuasion.[78]

Isocrates' school is largely responsible for making rhetoric the accepted basis of education in Greece and later in Rome.[79] He defines rhetoric as "the artificer of persuasion." The rhetorical act, however, is simply the final phase of a total process of personal growth and development. In his curriculum, Isocrates favored a balanced approach to training the mind and the body. "Philosophy is for the soul what gymnastic is for the body," he writes.[80] Thus, Isocrates taught his students science, mathematics, geometry, philosophy, and rhetoric. In addition, his students were schooled in the arts and in gymnastics. Thus, when the student spoke, he was utilizing his mind and body completely in the speech.

We can notice Isocrates' influence today in our own school systems, where the ideal curriculum is one that trains the mind and the body, and one that emphasizes moral virtue as well as knowledge. We recognize today that our speaking, indeed, the entire art of interacting with others, is a manifestation of our thinking, our values, our confidence, and our discipline. Isocrates is the first of the sophists, then, to devise a curriculum of instruction aimed at preparing the total person to speak and write persuasively.

Hubbell tells us that an understanding of Isocrates' instruction must begin with his teaching of rhetoric.[81] Isocrates was educated by the most celebrated sophists of his day, among them Prodicus, Gorgias, Tisias, and Theramenes.[82] Thus, he was steeped in the traditions of sophistry from an early age. Perhaps because of his own shortcomings as an orator, Isocrates preached that there were three prerequisites for success in oratory: natural aptitude, theoretical training, and practical experience.[83] Isocrates believed that no amount of education could make everyone an orator. "We cannot make all men orators," he says, "but we can give them culture."[84]

Due partly to his belief in natural ability, Isocrates attacked those sophists who accepted anyone into their classes and promised them skill in oratory. In his treatises, *Against the Sophists* and *Antidosis*, Isocrates condemned those who claimed to teach wisdom to their students strictly through training in public speaking. For Isocrates, moral virtue and knowledge were a prerequisite to instruction in rhetoric; speech training was a way to activate virtue not a way to acquire it. In *Against the Sophists*, Isocrates says:

> We cannot help hating and despising the professors of contentious argument (eristic) who, while claiming to seek for Truth, introduce falsehood at the very beginning of their pretensions. They profess in a way to read the future, a power, which Homer denied even to the gods; for they prophesy for their pupils a full knowledge of right conduct, and promise them happiness in consequence ... They profess to teach all virtue; but it is notable that pupils, before they are admitted to the course, have to give security for the payment of their fees.[85]

As noted in the earlier discussion of the sophist Gorgias, Isocrates' school is principally responsible for the advancement of writing, and for the shift in Athens from an oral culture to a "literate" culture where speaking and writing were emphasized equally.[86]

While other sophists taught writing as a practical skill, i.e., as an aid to speaking, Isocrates viewed writing as an intellectual pursuit. Students were taught that writing was a medium through which they learned about themselves (heuristic) and through which they could develop their ideas fully before presenting them in social or political circumstances. Isocrates would outline for the pupil the "principles" or general rules of oratory, and then drill him in writing and practicing speeches modeled on the ones made in court and the legislature. Enos concludes that:

> In terms of writing instruction, Isocrates was the educator behind Athens' literate revolution, the educator who established the importance of writing in the classical curriculum. Of all the educators of the Classical Period, Isocrates is credited as the first to realize the full potential for writing instruction; that is, as a method for facilitating thought and expression in higher education.[87]

Isocrates' approach to style is distinctive. Unlike Gorgias, who believed that the orator must appropriate the language of the poet, Isocrates believed that speech has its own rhythms and meters. As Kennedy notes:

> The diction is pure, the expression full in the extreme, rhythmical, highly antithetical, but the jingling excesses of Gorgias are avoided. Isocrates particularly disliked hiatus, the clash resulting from ending a word with a vowel and beginning the next word with a vowel.[88]

Isocrates is known for his smooth or florid style of speech composition, sometimes departing from the natural order of language but not in the extreme as with Gorgias.

Isocrates' style is particularly characterized by the use of the periodic sentence, a style still recommended today as a means to achieve emphasis. Periodic sentences are formed by a series of clauses that build to the main clause leading to a climactic effect. Here is an example of the periodic sentence from Isocrates' political treatise, *Panegyricus*:

> For when that greatest of wars broke out and a multitude of dangers presented themselves at one and the same time, when our enemies regarded themselves as irresistible because of their numbers and our allies thought themselves endowed with a courage which could not be excelled, we outdid them both in the way appropriate to each.

The following selection from *Panegyricus* illustrates a second, less common, type of periodic sentence, one that withholds only the verb phrase until the end:

> Philosophy, moreover, which has helped to discover and establish all these institutions, which has educated us for public life, and made us gentle toward each other, which has distinguished between the misfortunes that are due to ignorance and those which spring from necessity and taught us to guard against the former and to bear the latter nobly—philosophy, I say, was given to the world by our city.

The purpose of this periodic style is to match the sound pattern expectancy with the logical expectancy of the audience. By giving bits of information in several preliminary single clauses without revealing the sense of the whole sentence, Isocrates hopes to create a double suspense. Just as the repetition of similar sound patterns creates an expectancy that some break in the aural pattern will occur in order to relieve the psychological tension, the accumulation of ideas also creates an expectation that there will be a final logical resolution. This stylistic blending of sound and sense became popular with orators in both Greece and Rome (notably Cicero), since each was an oral society whose members were accustomed to following intricate vocal patterns.

Isocrates also favored the use of parallel clauses, especially the antithetical clause. As with many of the other sophists, this rhetorical figure was the best way to capture the polarities in issues they were addressing. In the following excerpt from the *Areopagiticus*, we can see a typical example of this common figure:

> For we should find that, starting from that which seems to be worse, things generally improve; while, as the result of that which is apparently better, they usually deteriorate.

In addition to the elements already mentioned, Isocrates' style is characterized by the use of ordinary words used to achieve their greatest effect on the audience, by the use of synonyms, and by the use of consonance—similar sounding consonants used in succession. These elements of style are difficult to exemplify in translation, but they are elements worth remembering in our own speaking.

Since most of Isocrates' rhetorical theory is scattered throughout *Against the Sophists* and *Antidosis*, his basic theories are summarized here:

1. Speech distinguishes men from animals, and makes possible all of civilization.
2. Rhetoric is an art, not a science.
3. A speaker's education should be extensive, not specialized, and should include a study of philosophy.
4. Morals cannot be taught, but study of political discourse will encourage the emulation of good citizens.
5. Orators who discourse on the general welfare are better even than law-givers, for the former have the highest task.
6. Speeches of orators should emphasize justice and virtue.
7. Public opinion can be swayed by the speaker; it does not of itself always tend toward virtue or justice.
8. Natural aptitude is essential to an orator; a man without natural aptitude can become an adequate speaker, but not a great one.
9. Some untaught men have become good orators, but the best orators are those who combine natural ability with training.
10. Both man's physical and mental facilities ought to be developed. Furthermore, they should be developed by the same methods; thus, practical exercises in speaking are necessary to achieve artistry.
11. Voice and assurance are necessary to success in oratory.
12. Students must learn every kind of discourse, not merely one specialized one.

13. Each speech and its parts must be suited to the particular occasion; the same speech might not suit another man.
14. There are as many kinds of prose as there are kinds of poetry.
15. Political discourse cannot be learned by rote, but must be learned and practiced as an art.

Like Gorgias and the other sophists, Isocrates believed preeminently in the power of speech. Words for him were powerful. They could be used to persuade, deceive, praise, or blame. Isocrates' philosophy of speech and rhetoric is perhaps best summed up in the following statement from his treatise, *Nicocles*:

> In most of our abilities we differ not at all from the animals; we are in fact behind many in swiftness and strength and other resources. But because there is born in us the power to persuade each other and to show ourselves whatever we wish, we not only have escaped from living as brutes, but also by coming together have founded cities and set up laws and invented arts, and speech has helped us attain practically all of the things we have devised. For it is speech that has made laws about justice and injustice and honor and disgrace, without which provisions we should not be able to live together. By speech we refute the wicked and praise the good. By speech we educate the ignorant and inform the wise. We regard the ability to speak properly as the best sign of intelligence, and truthful, legal, and just speech is the reflection of a good and trustworthy soul. With speech we contest about disputes and investigate what is unknown. We use the same arguments in public councils as we use in persuading private individuals. We call orators those who are able to discourse before a crowd and sages those who discourse best among themselves. If I must sum up on this subject, we shall find that nothing done with intelligence is done without speech, but speech is the marshal of all actions and of thoughts, and those most use it who have the greatest wisdom.

Isocrates was influential both as a political thinker and educator.[89] As a thinker, Isocrates hewed to the conservative philosophy of "a few laws, wisely administered," and to the notion of Greek hegemony in a world otherwise peopled with barbarians. As an educator, he broadened the notion of persuasion to include moral virtue as a prerequisite to rhetorical technique. He established writing as an essential component of education, equal to training in speech. His prescriptions for composition are worthy of note even today. He is, then, one of the profound thinkers of the Classical Period, a man whose writings rival those of Socrates in their influence on his own times and later ages.

## Demosthenes (384–322 BCE)

Demosthenes was born in Athens in 384 BCE. He was left an orphan by his father, a wealthy manufacturer of swords and furniture, at the age of seven years old. When Demosthenes became a young man, he prosecuted his guardians for embezzling his estate. He sued each of them for a penalty of ten talents (perhaps $3,000,000 by today's standards) and convicted them. He did not recover all of his inheritance, but he did gain public attention as a skillful orator. This notoriety led him to a new career as a logographer and he soon began to write speeches on a variety of different kinds of cases, winning on almost every occasion. From this auspicious beginning, and during the course of his life he would become the greatest orator in the history of Greece, both in the courtroom and in his public orations urging his countrymen to fight for their democracy. The final years of his life are clouded in scandals including bribery (unproved), and he escaped into exile, returning just prior to the final defeat of the Athenians in 322 BCE, by Antipater. At this time, Demosthenes was condemned to death, and rather than face execution he committed suicide by drinking poison.

Demosthenes' early career was devoted mainly to private suits. His most notable speech, written during the early period of his life, was written on behalf of one of the richest men in Athens, the banker Phormio. Phormio had been sued by Apollodorus for mishandling his father's estate over which Phormio had been given custody. Demosthenes' speech was actually delivered by a supporter of Phormio, an unusual deviation from the rule that each man had to speak for himself, but a decision that was based upon Phormio's poor Greek (he was originally a slave who was freed for his service to the bank) or his advanced age.[90] The address was a pointed and devastating attack on the character of Apollodorus and a defense of Phormio's reputation as a man who had given much to the community and was now besieged by a "sycophant," meaning one who seeks to gain the money of a rich person by any means. Sycophancy, we should note, was a crime in Athens at this time. In a conclusion that has become much cited in discussions of Demosthenes' judicial oratory, he says:

> Don't be taken in by his shameless bawling, but be careful to keep in mind what we have told you. If you do, you will be keeping your own oath and you will justly acquit Phormion. He deserves it, by Zeus and by all the gods! I don't know why I need say any more. I think you have understood everything that has been said. Pour out the water!

This last remark was a reference to the water clock that was used to time the speeches, and by gesturing toward it as he speaks, the orator implies that his case is so strong he does not even need the time allotted to prove Phormio innocent. MacDowell tells us that the speech was so moving that Phormio gained four-fifths of the jurors' votes, and that the jurors "refused to listen to the other side and took the unusual step of voting immediately for Phormio."[91]

Legend has it that while he was a young man, Demosthenes confined himself to a den or cave, and there studied his orations. He is said to have shaved half of his head so that, in order to avoid ridicule, he might not be tempted to leave the cave. Demosthenes' name lives in the annals of oratory for his peculiar habits of perfecting his skill in oratory. Plutarch addresses these habits this way:

> And for that he could not very well pronounce the letter R, he accustomed himself very much to that, that he might master it if possible; and likewise because he made an unseemly motion of his shoulder when he spoke at any time, he remedied that by a spit (or, as some say, a sword) stuck in the ceiling just over his shoulder, that the fear of being pricked with it might break him of that indecent gesture. They report of him further that, when he could declaim pretty well, he had a sort

of mirror made as big as himself, and used always in declaiming to look in that, to the end that he might see and correct what was amiss. He used likewise at some certain times to go down to the shore at Phalerum, to the end that, being accustomed to the surges and noise of the waves, he might not be daunted by the clamours of the people, when he should at any time declaim in public. And being naturally short-winded, he gave Neoptolemus, a player [actor], ten thousand drachmas to teach him to pronounce long sentences in one breath.[92]

Demosthenes was soon the most influential orator in Athens, his enemies fearing his rhetorical powers. He wrote and delivered 60 speeches during his career, and he also wrote essays and letters that remain available today. He was first and foremost a practitioner of rhetoric rather than a theorist, but he is said to have answered the question, "What is the essence of great oratory?" with one word: "Action." His speeches are filled with this idea of action, giving them an energy and passion that sometimes drove his opponents from the courtroom. Indeed, legend has it that his powers of persuasion were so great that, after delivering his most famous speeches, the four *Philippics*, in which he urged the people of Athens to fight and defend themselves against the encroachments of Philip of Macedon into Attica, Philip himself said that, "if he had heard him, he should have chosen him general in the war against himself."

The *Philippics* and the *Olynthiacs* provide us with the clearest idea of Demosthenes' theory of rhetoric in practice. As opposed to Isocrates who, as we have read, courted the arrival of Philip of Macedon believing that Philip would once again unite the Greeks against the forces of the east, Demosthenes feared that Philip would conquer Athens and destroy its culture and its cherished traditions of democracy. The *Olynthiac* orations are aimed at convincing the Athenians to aid the city-state of Olynthia against the incursions of Philip. The *Philippic* orations are also intended to rouse the Athenians to defend their own city-state against Philip. In both series of orations, Demosthenes failed, but in them we see the consummate patriotic address, perhaps "nationalistic" is a better term, filled with passionate pleas for action underscored by expediency but moreso by love of country. Demosthenes feared that in Philip's aggressive drive to the south lay the end of the Athenian empire, an empire Demosthenes believed was the grandest ever produced.

We have reproduced the *First Philippic* oration in Part II of this book with a brief history and context to set the stage for the text. Also included is a review of the key ideas in the speech and the brilliant use Demosthenes makes of stylistic devices that bring energy and emphasis to his ideas: maxims, metaphors, antithesis, and flowing periodic sentences. George Kennedy best sums up the rhetorical intensity of the address:

New vigor appears in the *first Philippic*, unlike anything in Greek oratory since the sharply focused speeches in Thucydides. There is no question of weighing the relative expediency of courses of action and of attributing to them justice and honor. It is assumed that Philip acts in his own interest, and Athens must act in hers. Territory in the north is the prize of war. The property of the careless belongs to those willing to run a risk. Demosthenes so focuses Athenian interests that the question seems not one of advantage, but of necessity, not the choice of a course of action, but the pursuit of the only possibility. His major point is that success is possible. All other rhetorical arguments arguments are only accessory: Athens' failure to act will bring on her the deepest disgrace and will allow Philip to go unpunished, but no honor is promised Athens for action, and disinterested justice is not involved. It seems that Demosthenes' patience has been suddenly exhausted; the futility of expecting right to triumph in the course of nature has overwhelmed him.[93]

This characteristic passion in addressing his audience is typical of Demosthenes' other three *Philippic* addresses, and of his other celebrated oratorical triumph, *On the Crown*. Following a courageous but losing battle by a combined force of the armies of many Greek city-states at Chaeronea (just north of Attica) against Philip of Macedon in 338 BCE, it became clear that Athens was doomed. Nevertheless, an ally of Demosthenes by the name of Ctesiphon proposed that Demosthenes receive a crown in recognition of his service to Athens throughout his entire career. A crown was a simple medallion often awarded to honor patriotism or service to the city. The proposal was not debated until eight years later, at which time another noted orator, Aeschines, challenged the legality (and the wisdom) of the proposal, but also used the moment to condemn Demosthenes for his failed appeals to stop Philip. Aeschines' oratory carried the day and demanded a response. Ctesiphon, however, did not respond and deferred instead to Demosthenes. Demosthenes rose to defend his life on the public stage, and his devotion to the Athenian tradition. He pleads with the audience: what else could I have done? What else would any patriot have done? Even had he known that his nation would fall, would that justify abandoning the Athenian democracy and way of life? No, Demosthenes pleads, in that moment the patriot rises: "I showed myself, then," says the orator, "this one, on that day, I."

Here is the argument that dooms Aeschines. Demosthenes has based his defense on the cherished Athenian tradition of free speech, an argument known as an "enthymeme" (see Chapter 3) His actions are within the highest political traditions of the grand but now crumbling democracy. While he may have been wrong, ultimately, Demosthenes can rightly ask why Aeschines did not challenge him then, before the outcome of Philip's assault on Attica was known? As Kennedy notes, "Demosthenes appeals to the very fabric of the Greek democracy as he says that the statesman declares his judgment before the event, and accepts responsibility, while the charlatan holds his peace when he ought to speak and then gloats over any untoward result."[94]

The jury hearing the case of awarding a crown to Demosthenes was so overwhelmed with his logic and his passionate oratory that, MacDowell tells us, Aeschines was fined and sent into exile.[95] The oration *On the Crown* was Demosthenes' greatest oratorical triumph, although it was his last. After learning of his death by suicide, the people of Athens erected a statue in brass to honor this most patriotic Greek. On the base of the statue was engraved the inscription, "Had you for Greece been strong, as wise you were, the Macedonian had not conquered her."

---

*The most fundamental question facing the orators of the Classical Age is one that still puzzles us today: why is that some speakers succeed while others do not? As we have seen, some Greeks like Gorgias sought to persuade with poetic language and musical sound patterns, while others like Protagoras believed in the process of antithesis, of knowing one's opponent's argument as well as one's own; others like Lysias favored a plain style as a means of identifying with one's audience; and Isocrates taught that success lay in mastering the art of oral prose while defending one's country. For Demosthenes persuasion required passion. Plato demanded truth of the speaker. Each of these approaches has its own values, of course, though the question remains whether any one of them is the complete answer.*

*The sophistic movement is thus responsible for the first theories of rhetoric. The sophists are responsible for a maturing rhetorical self-consciousness among the Greeks—an understanding that language, speech, and writing may be studied as phenomena in and of themselves. The sophists taught Athenians that there are better ways than others to say something: more strategic ways, more stylish ways, more reasonable ways. They are responsible for a curriculum in speaking and writing that would become the centerpiece of an Athenian citizen's education, and that itself would be emulated by other great societies throughout the ages. There did remain throughout this period a good deal of skepticism about sophistry, and the ideas of the sophists continued to be compared to the ideas of Socrates as written about in Plato's dialogues. The main point is that ancient Greeks were willing to look at differing views about how oratory succeeds or does not succeed. It was an exciting time of experimentation and the basic elements were there, and all that was needed was someone to pull the disparate parts together into a unified whole.*

*Toward the middle of the 4th century BCE, an intellectual giant would emerge, a man whose writings would synthesize the views of the sophists and of Socrates into one coherent theory of rhetoric, perhaps the most influential theory of rhetoric ever composed. We turn now to that theory and the author of it, Aristotle.*

# Chapter 3

# Aristotle's Rhetorical Theory[1]

> There are only two parts of a speech. You make a statement and you prove it.
>
> Aristotle, III.13 (1414a$_{30}$)

With Aristotle (384–322 BCE) we see for the first time a conception of rhetoric that is based on the entire range of human behavior—mental, social, political, logical, ethical, and psychological—utilizing scientific methods that today would be called sociological and anthropological.

His actual progress toward writing about rhetoric is simple to describe. Aristotle was born on the Macedonian frontier, the son of a physician—from whom he inherited an interest in empirical observation—but at age 18 he came to study with Plato at Athens. This residence at the Platonic Academy was clearly the formative period of his thought; he never entirely lost his Platonism including a certain disdain for most of the sophists and their works. But in the second period of his life, the so-called years of traveling, he gathered up the sophists' writings on rhetoric, his famous collection of the arts (*synagoge technon*) (now lost). In the last third of his adult life he returned for a second residence in Athens, and it was during this period that he composed his lectures on rhetoric, eventually pulled together by his editors into three books on the subject. He is believed to have started lecturing from a framework centered on Plato's dialogues, which were highly critical of practical rhetoric. In response to the dialogues he projected three books that refute the doctrines of the *Gorgias* and develop the prescriptions of the *Phaedrus* (see Chapter 2) almost beyond recognition.

But this bare narrative is premature if it gives the impression that rhetoric was Aristotle's only interest. In his short life he composed a remarkable range of books—35 have survived—which taken together reveal a profound world-view which must be considered in any evaluation of his views on the rhetoric which he saw finally as a necessary and integral element in human life. These include his *Metaphysics* (13 sections or "books") about First Principles, and *On Interpretation*, on the nature of language. In the field of natural science are *Physics* (eight books), *On the Heavens* (four books), *On Beginning and Perishing* (two books), *Parts of Animals* (four books), *Generation* (five books), *On Plants* (two books), and *On the Soul* (three books). In the field of ethics (moral behavior of individuals), *Nichomachean Ethics* (ten books), and politics (behavior of men in groups), *Politics* (eight books). In logic (known collectively as *organon* or "tool"), *Prior Analytics* (two books), *Posterior Analytics* (two books), *On Sophistical Refutations* and *Topics* (eight books). Finally, in the field of applied language, *Poetics* (incomplete) and *Rhetoric* (three books).[2]

What kind of approach to rhetoric could we expect from a writer who had studied so many different fields?

## The Metarhetoric[3] of Aristotle

Aristotle uses a hybrid word (meta-physics) to name his discussion of what he calls "first principles." Thus his title *Metaphysics* combines *meta* meaning "beyond" and *physiké* meaning "nature." It deals with the first principles of nature. It is a study of that which one needs to understand before it is possible to understand anything else.

This same concept can be applied to our efforts to understand his *Rhetoric*. What is it that one needs to know in order to become rhetorical? What is Aristotle's metarhetoric? What, in his view, does a rhetor need to know before he uses language to effect persuasion? Or, to put it another way, which fields of study must the rhetor master?

We can read the *Rhetoric* without knowing the complete answers to these questions, but it is worthwhile to seek the answers because they relate to us, the readers, as future users of rhetoric. We can start by using a sort of reverse engineering, working backwards from the text to re-create at each step what must have been Aristotle's expectations about the knowledge of his readers. By taking notes as he or she goes along, the reader can begin to grasp the totality of Aristotle's understanding of the place he sees for rhetoric in human life. There are many clues for the reader. For example he cites his own book, *Topics*, nine times in the *Rhetoric*; he refers the reader to his *Poetics* for a better discussion of metaphor; he refers to his *Prior Analytics* for a definition of the enthymeme; his discussion of constitutions echoes his same discussion in his *Politics*; and his extensive treatment of emotions relies on his analyses in his *Psychology*. Examples could be multiplied, but the important point is that the modern reader should be aware throughout the reading that he or she is looking at an analysis of rhetoric based on the world-view of one of history's most important thinkers. Even a partial understanding of his metarhetoric can bring to the reader an enhanced appreciation of Aristotle's prodigious effort to grasp the manifold elements involved in human persuasion.

The ultimate search for the answers, perhaps reserved for the serious and determined scholar, is to study each of Aristotle's published works to identify the patterns that led him inexorably to the conclusion that rhetoric is both natural in man and necessary to his public existence. This study has not yet been conducted, and, perhaps, never will be, due to the enormous complexity of ideas Aristotle gleaned from his lifelong study of the way things are. So in the last analysis we have to read the text we have.

The *Rhetoric*, as we have it today, is highly structured, and the parts are joined with careful transitions. Ancient editors may be responsible for some of these transitions; they may also bear responsibility for the division into books and almost certainly for that into chapters. We believe this because certain of the divisions seem to be fairly arbitrary: the division between Book I and Book II, for example, and the long transition and internal summary that goes with it. The division between Book II and Book III, on the other hand, is more organic: the first two books are about invention, and the third about the other departments of the art of rhetoric. Some inconsistencies between the different parts of the *Rhetoric* have led to an extensive scholarly debate about the process of its creation. There is little doubt today that Aristotle composed and revised the *Rhetoric* over a larger period of time and not necessarily in the order in which we read it today. Accordingly it is not easy to date the work as a whole. The latest date referenced in the second book is 336 BCE; namely, the peace following the battle at Chaironea. The latest date referred to in Book III, however, is ten years earlier: 346 BCE. It is generally assumed now that Book III is based on older material and that the work was revised a number of times and in its current form probably not meant for publication but rather as a lecture script for Aristotle himself.[4]

One important thing to remember in looking at these difficulties is that Aristotle apparently did not finish the *Rhetoric* during his lifetime. Therefore modern editors are justifiably concerned about the state of the text as it has come down to us.

But another interpretation of this fact is our realization that even one of the most capable and reflective minds in all of western culture was unable to provide us with a taxonomic description of all the factors in rhetoric, and their relation to each other. Contrast this with the complete, self-sufficient systems he offers in other human-related books like his *Politics* or *Nichomachean Ethics*. It is possible to conclude that rhetoric deals with human inter-relationships involving so many variables that not even an Aristotle can devise a "system" to describe it scientifically.

It is not surprising, then, to find that the uncompleted *Rhetoric* as we have it is very complex. Many of the parts do double and even triple duty because they are cross-referenced to the other parts of the treatise. For example, a reader consulting the section dealing with lines of argument for showing a person to be noble ($I_9$) is referred to the section on *ethos* ($II_1$) where it is stated that the speaker shows his integrity by arguing from the same premises that are used to praise others. The reader is also referred to the list of goods ($I_{5-6}$) because noble qualities are also goods. Since such sections perform multiple functions, it is difficult to provide a simple overview of the *Rhetoric*. The turn-of-the-century scheme, which stated that Book I is devoted principally to the speaker, Book II to the audience, and Book III to the speech, misrepresents the structure of the *Rhetoric*.

Book I, for example, contains all of the value systems shared by the auditors and the speaker, as well as the proofs from outside the art of rhetoric; however, these are related to the arguments made in the speech. Book II covers the *ethos* of the speaker as well as various forms of arguments that are clearly part of the speech. The following outline is also an oversimplification of a complex structure, but it can serve as a guide for an initial study of the *Rhetoric*.

## Outline of the *Rhetoric*

The main sections indicated in this outline (Roman numerals and capital letters) do not reflect traditional editions of the *Rhetoric*, but rather are intended as a substantial division for the benefit of the reader. Traditional editions contain a division into three books with 15 to 26 chapters each (e.g., $II_{26}$: second book, chapter 26) as well as page numbers of the Bekker edition for more precise referencing (e.g., $1355b_{26}$ for Aristotle's definition of rhetoric in the second chapter of the first book). All scholarly editions of the *Rhetoric* include a book, chapter, and Bekker page count.

**Rhetoric, Book I**

I.  **Introduction** ($I_{1-3}$)

    A.  The place of rhetoric as an art ($I_1$)
    B.  The uses of rhetoric ($I_1$)
    C.  The definition of rhetoric ($I_2$)
    D.  Artistic and inartistic proofs ($I_2$)
    E.  Artistic proofs: *ethos*, *pathos*, and *logoi* ($I_2$)
    F.  Preview of the instruments of proof: enthymeme and example ($I_2$)
    G.  Common and specialized *topoi* ($I_2$)
    H.  The three kinds of discourses: forensic, deliberative, and epideictic ($I_3$)

II.  ***Topoi* for Invention of Arguments in the Specialized Subjects** ($I_4$–$II_{17}$)

    A.  Specialized *topoi* for the three kinds of discourses ($I_{4-15}$)
        1.  For deliberative speeches ($I_{4-8}$)
        2.  For epideictic speeches ($I_9$)
        3.  For forensic speeches ($I_{10-15}$)
        4.  For interpreting inartistic proofs ($I_{15}$)

**Rhetoric, Book II**

    B.  Specialized *topoi* for establishing the speaker's good character ($II_1$) (handled by cross-reference)
    C.  Specialized *topoi* for leading the audience into certain states of feeling ($II_{2-11}$)
    D.  Choice of *topoi* as affected by the several ages and fortunes of the auditors—materials for portrayal of the characters of humans ($II_{12-17}$)

III.  ***Topoi* for Invention of Arguments Common to all Subjects and Kinds of Discourses** ($II_{18-19}$)

    A.  For proving what is possible or impossible ($II_{19}$)
    B.  For establishing the probability that certain events have occurred in the past ($II_{19}$)
    C.  For predicting the probability that certain events will occur in the future ($II_{19}$)
    D.  For proving what is more or what is less ($II_{19}$)

IV.  **Forms of Enthymemes and Related Proofs** ($II_{20-26}$)

    A.  The example ($II_{20}$)
    B.  The maxim ($II_{21}$)
    C.  The enthymeme ($II_{22}$)
    D.  A catalogue of typical forms for enthymemes ($II_{23}$)
    E.  A catalogue of typical forms for fallacious enthymemes ($II_{24}$)
    F.  Refutation of enthymemes and examples ($II_{25-26}$)

**Rhetoric, Book III**

V.  **The Language of the Discourse—Style** ($III_{1-12}$)

    A.  Suggestions for a treatise on delivery ($III_1$)
    B.  Qualities of style ($III_{2-7}$)

## Synopses of Aristotle's *Rhetoric* by Sections

The following synopses cover each division of the preceding outline. Each synopsis is followed by a short commentary. Again, as we have noted several times before, the reader must be aware that no synopsis can be a substitute for reading the actual text.

## BOOK I

## I. Introduction

*Argument (the enthymeme) is the essential body of proof—1354a$_{15}$.*

### A. The Place of Rhetoric as an Art (I$_1$)

Rhetoric is the mirror image of dialectic, for both deal with subjects common to all people to know rather than those within the bounds of a specialized science. Whether speakers perform using methods they have learned, or speak spontaneously, rhetoricians can inquire about why they succeed or why they failed; such inquiry is the function of an art, and rhetoric is that art. The arts of the sophists are flawed: they have been interested almost solely in pleasure, pain, and the emotional states of the auditors, and so they have given disproportionate emphasis to speaking in the law courts where using the emotional states is crucial to winning an action for a client. Indeed, having written much that is, strictly speaking, irrelevant to making a case, they have ended up neglecting to consider argument (the enthymeme)—the essential body of proof.

### B. The Uses of Rhetoric (I$_1$)

Rhetoric is useful (1) to uphold truth and justice (since these would always triumph if it were not for their advocates' lack of skill); (2) to inform ordinary people (since instruction by demonstration is impossible for them); (3) to make sure that no argument escapes us (since rhetoric canvasses both sides of any question); and (4) to defend oneself from unjust attack (since not defending oneself would be as shameful as not fighting back when physically attacked). Just as medicine cannot be said to fail if all appropriate remedies are used but the patient dies, so rhetoric is not a failure if all the available means of persuasion are used but some audiences remain unpersuaded.

## C. The Definition of Rhetoric (I₂)

Let this be our definition of rhetoric: the capacity (*dynamis*) to observe in regard to any subject the available means of persuasion. Since rhetoric can be applied to any subject, it has no subject matter of its own.

## D. Artistic and Inartistic Proofs (I₂)

Rhetorical proofs are either artistic (intrinsic) or inartistic (extrinsic); the former must be constructed by the speaker, the latter are preexisting data that one must discover.

## E. Artistic Proofs: Ethos, Pathos, and Logoi

The artistic proofs are of three kinds: those that pledge the speaker's good character (*ethos*) to establish his credibility; those that bring the audience into a certain state of feeling (*pathos*) favorable to accepting the arguments made in the speech; and the arguments themselves (*logoi*) as they appear to prove or disprove the speaker's conclusions. From this division we see that the art of rhetoric is connected on the one hand to the study of probable proofs or dialectic; on the other to the study of human character and the character of society, i.e., ethics and politics.

## F. Preview of the Enthymeme and Example (I₂)

The instruments of proof within the speech are the enthymeme and the example. The enthymeme is an argument from premises that are probable principles, or from signs. When the speaker states the argument, he usually omits one or more of its parts. Signs are either infallible or fallible; that is, they either will or will not make enthymemes that can be formed as valid syllogisms. The example is an argument from one particular to another, working from the premise that if a statement is true about one group of persons or events, it will be true of another that falls within the same general class.

## G. Common and Specialized Topoi (I₂)

There is another grand division of enthymemes: some proceed from basic assumptions common to all subjects; such an assumption is called a common *topos* (plural: *topoi*). Others are drawn from basic principles within one of the specialized fields, like physics or politics; such principles are called special *topoi*.[5] Strictly speaking, only the common *topoi* lie within the art of rhetoric, but since many enthymemes used in discourses are based on *topoi* from the specialized fields, these will be considered next, beginning with those basic to composing the three traditional kinds of rhetorical discourses.

## H. Three Kinds of Rhetorical Discourses (I₃)

Discourses are based on materials from three sources: the speaker [writer, author], the subject matter presented, and the people to whom it is presented. This latter is the audience; it is the end (*telos*), the reason for making the discourse. Now the audience consists of either spectators or decision-makers. If an auditor is a decision-maker, he either decides about events that are past or those that are in the future: the one who decides on the future is a deliberator [legislator]; the one who decides on the past is a juror, but the spectator, who considers how the speaker uses the art, works primarily in the present. Because the kind of auditor and the time of the subject determine the kinds of discourses, there must be these three kinds: deliberative, forensic, and epideictic.

### Ends and Means

The means for deliberation are persuasion and dissuasion, for forensic speaking accusation and defense, and for epideictic praise and blame. The end, or *telos*, of each of the separate kinds is also different: to the deliberator the end is what is advantageous or disadvantageous, the other issues are beside the point; to the litigant the *telos* is what is just or unjust, and for the ceremonial orator what is noble or shameful.

Aristotle opens with a section designed to distinguish his treatise on rhetoric from those of earlier rhetoricians. His treatise is about argument rather than the unrestricted use of the emotions, and his treatise constitutes a real art, a *techne*, one that can assign causes to its prescriptions for success as opposed to just giving "rules of thumb."

Aristotle starts bluntly: "Rhetoric is the mirror-image of dialectic." Why not the mirror image of poetics (the art of writing fiction), or of politics (the study of statecraft)? These are the branches of knowledge that most obviously have close relations to rhetoric. But dialectic is chosen because it is one branch of the study of logic, what Aristotle calls analytics, and Aristotle wants to establish rhetoric as another of the branches of this discipline.

Dialectic can be characterized as the study of logic as it is used in interpersonal exchanges such as those represented by the dialogues of Plato; that is, discussions about abstract values such as love, honor, peace, nobility, etc. The counterparts of dialectic and rhetoric are the treatises on scientific reasoning, the *Prior Analytics* and the *Posterior Analytics*. Elsewhere, Aristotle calls these four taken together the methodical studies (*ta methodika*). Later followers of his called them the tool subjects: in Greek, the *organon*; when these followers composed a curriculum, they kept rhetoric as a branch of the *organon*.

Dialectic works from propositions that are admitted by the participants in the dialogue to general conclusions about human affairs. For example, from the statements that Kallias only acts when he has something to gain, and likewise Hipponikos and Xenophon act this way, to the conclusion that people in general only act when they perceive there is something to be gained. But rhetoric works in the opposite direction; from the generalization that people only act when there is something to be gained to the conclusion that people like this defendant, who could not possibly have thought that he would gain from such actions, did not commit a crime such as this. Hence rhetoric is the mirror image of dialectic.

There is an important corollary to this placement of rhetoric as one of the methodical studies. Like the other branches of the *organon* it can be used to reason about any subject, but particularly if it is in the realm of human affairs. In principle, rhetoric can be used to popularize physics or metaphysics, though considering the specialized nature of the audiences for these subjects, such a treatment is unlikely. But though rhetoric can be applied to any subject, it is said to have no specific subject matter of its own ($1355b_{32-34}$).

Here is another corollary: rhetoric contains in itself no specified moral position other than the general one that conclusions established by reasoning from principles approximating truth are superior to those produced by reasoning tainted with overuse of the emotions. When statements about ethics and politics are used to illustrate the inventory of premises to be used by rhetors, they are treated dialectically; that is, they are assumed as true for the purposes of illustration. These statements may not be entirely compatible, and reasoning from them often will lead to opposite conclusions. Rhetoric and dialectic are the only subjects which require their students to reason indifferently to opposite conclusions: one conclusion is in principle as good as another (1355a). And that is why they can take no specified moral positions.[6]

It has sometimes been said that no one knows whether or not Aristotle intended his *Rhetoric* to be used as a guide to criticism. John Randall calls it a book on how to make a speech,[7] and Edwin Black[8] doubts that Aristotle ever intended to found a school of Aristotelian criticism. The text, however, is explicit in treating criticism as central to rhetoric; Aristotle makes the critical function a major premise of his argument that rhetoric is an art, in Greek a *techne*. The context of this argument is Plato's characterization in the *Gorgias* of rhetoric as a knack, the counterpart of cookery (Gorg. 462bff.); like that activity it cannot be held to certain rules. Aristotle takes the opposite position: though all men construct arguments and refute them, some do this from natural inclination, others by becoming habituated to sound practices, but in either case one can inquire why they succeed and why they fail, and this is surely the function of an art. Inquiring why some arguments succeed and some fail is, of course, a shorthand description of what is now called rhetorical criticism. Aristotle says that it is the critical function of rhetoric that makes it an art; obviously he intended his art to constitute the basis for criticism.

Previous writers, according to Aristotle, have given incomplete treatments of rhetoric because they have neglected proofs in favor of peripheral features. Indeed, they said nothing about enthymemes (in English, defeasible rule-using arguments, i.e., arguments that do not follow with logical certainty but that can be defeated even if properly applied), which are the body of proofs (1354a). In the new art of rhetoric, as Aristotle and his followers construe it, the other proofs operate through enthymemes. Even inartistic proofs, like documents, which are not within the art of rhetoric, require interpretation through arguments. Likewise, the credibility of speakers and the emotional states of auditors are largely produced through arguments. One of the earlier modern commentators on the *Rhetoric*, Ernest Havet, wrote the summary judgment, "Aristotle reduces rhetoric to argumentation."[9] Most commentators since Havet's time would approve the gist of that judgment, while, perhaps, considering the phrasing a little too sweeping.

Aristotle's position that the art of rhetoric in itself takes no moral position but impartially looks at the arguments on both sides of any question is related to his definition of rhetoric: "the capacity for observing in regard to any subject the available means of persuasion." The key word, "observing" (in Greek *theoresai*) implies "being a spectator at." Aristotle's rhetorician is a person who examines the subject before him and makes an inventory of the possibilities, especially those appropriate to his audience in the given situation. As long as they are making inventories of the possibilities, rhetoricians can act without moral involvement; rhetors in actual situations, of course, must make moral choices, something they do according to their understanding of ethics and politics, which are, above all, the disciplines that rhetoric serves. This approach to rhetoric as an observatory art also explains why Aristotle spends very little time on delivery and even matters of style as compared to his complex and extensive treatment of the enthymeme.

It is common to make his definition relate to the "particular case" or the "individual situation." This is not quite Aristotle's meaning when he talks about particulars as distinct from universals. As he states here and elsewhere, there is no art or science of the individual: like medicine. Rhetoric is not about Socrates or Kallias, but about classes of people who are represented by these individuals ($1356b_{30-38}$). Orators deal with Kallias, but rhetoricians when examining the inventory of proofs deal with the class of people who are like Kallias. Therefore, it is better to make the definition read "the capacity for observing in regard to any subject," i.e., any treatment of classes of individuals.

Rhetorical proofs, as opposed to scientific proofs, can be thought of as factors that lead one to trust a rhetor's conclusion: in Greek they are called *pisteis* from the verb *pistevo*, to trust. Accordingly, translating the Greek *pisteis* as "proofs" might be slightly misleading to the modern reader. A more accurate, but stylistically awkward, translation would be "that which supports the claim in question" or simply "means of persuasion." The art of rhetoric seeks to establish the good character of the speaker, *ethos*, those factors that bring the auditors into an appropriate emotional state, the right *pathos*, and those that make arguments for or against the question to be decided by the auditors. In Greek these last could be called the *logoi*, although Aristotle himself does not use that term. The shorthand version of the text is that the artistic proofs are *ethos*, *pathos*, and *logos*.

Since Aristotle considers rhetoric to be a defined art, he clearly means to delineate with this distinction what lies within the scope of the art and what lies outside of it. Proofs (*pisteis*) that lie within the art are artistic, or perhaps intrinsic is better; those outside are inartistic, or extrinsic. The inartistic proofs are the raw data of experience; Aristotle states that they must be discovered, not invented. Those within the art, the intrinsic proofs, must be invented, i.e., they are the product of arguments that interpret the raw data of experience. Aristotle takes notice of five extrinsic proofs: laws, contracts, witnesses, tortures, and oaths.

It is worth noting that while today the distinction between artistic (intrinsic) and inartistic (extrinsic) means of persuasion seems a little counterintuitive, this was not the case during Aristotle's time. In a forensic speech in front of the court, laws, contracts, testimonies, and the like would not be included in the orator's speech but rather be read out by a clerk of the court. It is easy to see then why Aristotle would treat them as separate from those techniques that are included in the speech itself.[10] If he lived today, he would, no doubt, eliminate the section on tortures and include photographs, statistical surveys, reports of experiments, and various kinds of government documents among the extrinsic proofs. None of these speak for themselves; they require interpretation to make them convincing as documentation in the cases that auditors must decide.

Enthymeme is Aristotle's technical term for rhetorical arguments from premises and rules. It is contrasted with the *paradeigma*, or example, which does not use any rule but reasons directly from an individual incident to a particular case. Aristotle defines the enthymeme as a "kind of *syllogismos*" (1355b$_8$). This definition has for centuries led to considerable confusion in the interpretation of the Aristotelian enthymeme. The main problem in this interpretation arose from an identification of *syllogismos* (reasoning) with the later technical *syllogism*. A syllogism is a term from early formal logic, describing a particular kind of reasoning that, if performed accurately and in valid modes, produces logically valid infallible conclusion. The most famous schoolbook example of such a syllogism is:

> All humans are mortal.
> All Greeks are humans.
> (Therefore) All Greeks are mortal.

Taking this formal syllogism as a starting point has led many interpreters of Aristotle to the erroneous conclusion that an enthymeme is just such a syllogism with the only distinguishing criterion that one of the three elements (major premise, minor premise, or conclusion) is suppressed and must be supplied by the audience. This *syllogismus truncatus* definition of the enthymeme can still be found in some modern textbooks, but it is not a faithful interpretation of Aristotle's concept of the enthymeme. Any careful reading of the *Rhetoric* shows that neither the definitions Aristotle gives, nor his examples, support this interpretation. The enthymeme is not a truncated form of a logical syllogism; indeed, it is not any form of the logical syllogism, but instead it is the rhetorical form of *syllogismos*—defeasible reasoning. Accordingly *any* argument that uses any kind of rule (or deduction in the widest sense) is an enthymeme. Enthymemes *can* contain suppressed premises, and indeed usually do so to avoid the impression of redundancy, but they do not have to. What distinguishes the enthymeme from logical deduction is not its truncated form, but its defeasible nature. A valid logical deduction produces truth, but even a good and valid argument (enthymeme) produces, not truth, but a probable or plausible claim. The enthymeme is the centerpiece of the entire *Rhetoric*. Although hierarchically positioned at a subordinate place, it is defined as the most important aspect of persuasion and Aristotle explains it in detail at many central places in the *Rhetoric*. Even his extensive treatment of the *topoi* in the second book is just an extension of the enthymeme.[11]

Figure 3.1 shows an overview over Aristotle's main division of means of persuasion. The enthymeme and the example are further subdivided in Book II of the *Rhetoric*.

The usual settings for speeches in ancient Hellas were the assembly, the law court, and the stadium on the occasions of festivals and games. The traditional names for discourses prepared for these locales were: deliberative, forensic, and epideictic. Other places where it would seem to us that speeches might be given are not among the three; temples, for example, were not much used for public discourse since the religion of the time centered around ritual. Likewise, Aristotle seems deliberately to exclude the lecture space, perhaps because education was for him more of a one-to-one activity, and also because following the lead of Plato's *Gorgias*, he believed that instruction is carried on by scientific demonstration and not by rhetoric.

From the sophists, Aristotle inherited names and places. Following his characteristic method of dealing with traditional materials, he developed a rationale for why these must necessarily describe the only three kinds of discourses: influencing the auditor is

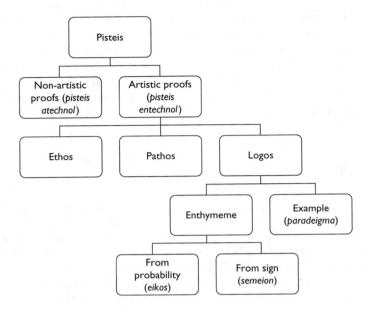

*Figure 3.1*

the end (*telos*) of all rhetorical discourse. Now it is evident that audiences can be divided into spectators or decision-makers about either past or future, and from this division it follows deductively that there must be three kinds of speeches with appropriate locales, ends, and means.[12] The Aristotelian schema can be conveniently summarized in Table 3.1.

The classification of discourses occurs at this point in the *Rhetoric* because each kind is to be associated with a set of specialized *topoi* about a certain subject: government, personal ethics, and criminal behavior. This classification follows immediately upon the division of *topoi* into those that are specific to certain fields of knowledge and those that are common to all fields.

The specific *topoi* are dealt with first. At times, Aristole seems to regard them as an inventory of premises used as parts of enthymemes; he then calls them specific premises (see note 1). At other times he treats them as general headings out of which whole groups of premises are generated, as when he states that, "the deeds of men being

*Table 3.1*

| Kind of Discourse | Kind of Auditor | Time | Ends | Means |
|---|---|---|---|---|
| Forensic | Decision-maker | Past | The just and unjust | Accusation and Defense |
| Deliberative | Decision-maker | Future | The advantageous and disadvantageous | Persuasion and Dissuasion |
| Epideictic | Observer/spectator | Present | The noble and shameful | Praise and Blame |

praised should be connected to the *topos* of virtue." On the other hand, the common *topoi* (*koina*) are always general headings, as are the basic forms of enthymemes in Book II, chaps. 23 and 24, and are also referred to as *topoi*. These last two kinds of *topoi* are the ones that Aristotle thinks belong to the art of rhetoric proper; the specific *topoi* lie on the borderline between rhetoric and the specialized studies.

The foregoing classification introduces us to a long inventory of *topoi* and premises specific to various subjects and uses. First, come those primarily associated with each of the three kinds of discourses, then those used for establishing the speaker's credibility (*ethos*), and then those for bringing the auditors into one or more of the states of feeling (*pathe*). Later ($II_{18-26}$) Aristotle returns to the *topoi* common to all kinds of discourses and fields of study, and the basic forms for making enthymemes. Deliberative discourse has first place in the inventory since Aristotle regards it as the most important kind of speaking.

## II. *Topoi* for Invention of Arguments in the Specialized Subjects

### A. Specialized *Topoi* for the Three Kinds of Discourse ($I_4$–$I_{15}$)

#### 1. For Deliberative Speeches ($I_4$)

The end of deliberative discourse is the advantageous.

A speaker does not give advice about everything; whatever happens of necessity [like a law of physics] is not subject to debate, nor is whatever happens entirely at random. Speakers advise about matters where human choice makes a difference; these are ways and means, war and peace, national defense, imports and exports, and general legislation. Some *topoi* for those subjects will be set forth, though a complete scientific treatment of them is unnecessary; indeed to the extent that one successfully makes such a treatment he assigns to the discipline of rhetoric more than properly belongs to it.

#### Subjects of Deliberation ($I_4$)

To advise about ways and means one must know the sources of revenue and the necessary expenses of the state; for war and peace, the resources of his own and neighboring states, their similarities and differences; for national defense, the size and deployment of military resources; for commerce, those articles that can be produced at home and those that must be imported; for general legislation, the kinds of government and their goals and the hazards of each. A speaker gains this knowledge from histories and accounts of travels.

#### Definitions of Happiness ($I_5$)

Since the end (*telos*) of deliberation is the advantageous, let it be remarked that what is to the advantage of both the individual and the state is universally described by the term happiness [*eudaimonia*]. Happiness is the chief good, the one for the sake of which other goods are chosen. Though everyone shares this term, different people define happiness in slightly different ways. A speaker may find it useful to define happiness as acting successfully while pursuing moral excellence; or he may say that it is a self-sufficient life; or he may hold that it is the most pleasant life that can be had with security, or that it is a flourishing state of households and possessions with the capacity to preserve and increase them.

### Topoi *for Enthymemes to Prove Some Policies Conducive to* Happiness (I₅)

Not only can one argue that the course of action being debated leads to happiness, as defined in one of these ways, he may state that it will result in any of the various goods that are constituent parts of happiness: internal goods of the mind (like the ability to speak or be an artist) or of the body (like health, strength, and beauty) or external goods (like wealth and fame); also goods such as a healthy old age, having many and excellent friends, and even good luck.

### Definitions of Good (I₆)

The various goods are also advantageous. A good may be defined as what is chosen for its own sake and that for the sake of which we choose other things, or the end that everything with sensation or intelligence aims at or would aim at if it became intelligent. Also what intelligence would grant to each individual and what it actually has granted is the good for that individual, and whatever because it is present causes someone to survive well and even self-sufficiently, and self-sufficiency per se. Also whatever preserves or produces what has been defined as good, and what is logically entailed by these definitions, and whatever prevents or is destructive of the opposites of what has been defined as good [i.e., the various kinds of evils].

### Topoi *for Enthymemes to Prove That Some Policies Lead* to Achieving Goods (I₆)

Obviously, getting a greater good is better than getting a lesser one, whereas getting a lesser evil is better than getting a greater one. Goods are divided into those that are admitted universally and those that are disputed. Admitted goods are the various moral excellences, the constituents of happiness, pleasure, goods of the mind and body, honor and reputation, and, of course, life itself. Disputed goods include: the opposite of what is evil, the opposite of what is good for our enemies, what our enemies praise [i.e., reluctant testimony], what is not excessive (for whatever is in excess is evil). And above all, people think that succeeding in the very thing that defines their character is good [e.g., athletes think it the very best thing to win a game; mathematicians to solve an unsolved problem]. And in general we believe things to be good which the multitude pursues or which distinguished persons choose.

### For Enthymemes Proving That Some Policies Lead to Greater or Lesser Goods (I₇)

Deliberations often turn on the better of two goods or the best of several, also the more expedient course of action or the most expedient of several courses of action.

Better and more expedient can often be expressed in quantities; hence one argues that a greater number of goods is better than a smaller number, or what is more common (like sunshine) is better than what is rarer, since it produces more goods, and obviously what produces more goods is better than what produces fewer. (But conversely, the rarer thing is better than the more common because it requires more effort to find or produce.) From the principle that what produces more goods is better, it follows that the causes of goods are better than the effects, for a cause can operate again to produce more goods. But one may also hold the opposite: since the last steps toward a goal are often thought to be more important, and they are necessarily effects of prior causes, effects are better than causes. And of two causes, the one that is a first principle is better than the one that is not. But usually ends are better than means, even though logically further removed from first principles; and the means to better ends are better than the means to ends that are not so good. Finally, what is chosen by superior persons or prudent persons is better than what is chosen by ordinary ones.

### For Showing That a Course of Action Is Appropriate to the Goals of the Kinds of Government (I₈)

The most authoritative means of persuasion come from understanding the constitutions of the various states and the customs and laws entailed by each of them; for what is advantageous to each kind of state is precisely what preserves these laws and customs. Democracy, oligarchy, aristocracy, and monarchy are the four kinds of constitutions. The goals of the first three are freedom, wealth, and discipline or respect for law, but monarchies must be divided into two species: either they are constitutional or tyrannical; the goal of tyrannical monarchy is security of the monarch. The citizens of these states acquire a distinctive character appropriate to inhabiting their kind of state; a speaker should adapt his *ethos* to this character to be persuasive when advising them.

Aristotle begins the preceding inventory of *topoi* for producing enthymemes to be used in discourses about policy with a list of the necessary subjects of public deliberation. The list culminates with general legislation. This category is really about basic law as opposed to routine temporary decrees about taxes or exports. It might better be translated "constitution-making." Aristotle almost contradicts himself here: he advises that citizens acting as constitution-makers should have studied previous constitutions of a number of states; in the preceding breath he reminded us that if the rhetor's studies are so thorough as to comprehend the first principles of politics, he ceases to think rhetorically, i.e., ceases to keep in mind that the popular audience is the *telos* of rhetorical discourse. He becomes a professor of political science or some related substantive field. Rhetoric at its best reasons from statements that are like first principles—statements that are universally probable, as opposed to those universally certain.

Aristotle's term for the *telos* of human action is *eudaimonia*, translated always as happiness. In the *Rhetoric* the advantageous, though it is the *telos* of deliberative speaking, is treated as what leads to *eudaimonia*, that is, it is not the ultimate *telos*. The advantageous could easily be understood differently; a modern utilitarian, for example, would define it as a calculus of pleasures and pains. We are reminded that the charge brought against rhetoric in the *Gorgias* was that it aims solely at immediate gratification. Probably with the dialogue in mind, Aristotle carefully distinguishes between happiness and pleasure; it is happiness that constitutes the end for humankind. The several definitions he gives of happiness have this in common: they are about a life of habitual activity, a life of harmony and balance. Pleasure, on the other hand, is a single movement of the soul into a state of equilibrium; it is retained by Aristotle as the motive of crime.

The definitions of *eudaimonia* provide our first example of Aristotle's dialectical depiction of the inventory of proofs. By dialectical we mean that he surveys each subject without committing himself to any particular moral or philosophical position. The definitions here are so different that they are almost incompatible: the first, acting successfully while pursuing moral excellence, is quite close to that of the *Nicomachean Ethics*, an activity of the soul in accordance with moral excellence. It emphasizes the ethical basis for happy living. The second, a self-sufficient life, is also reminiscent of the ethical treatises, but it emphasizes independence of external coercion and implies the concomitant of liberty of person. The third, the most pleasant life that can be had with security, is a modified hedonist view, putting the emphasis not so much on achieving a moment of pleasure as on preserving a way of life filled with pleasant moments. The fourth is a materialist's definition that emphasizes not simply enjoyment of material things but the accumulation and preservation of wealth.

The definitions are not totally incompatible, of course: the person who acts according to moral excellence may prudently acquire and preserve a measure of wealth. No preference is here evinced for one definition over the others: that is what makes this passage a prototype of dialectical method. One may choose to argue a position from one definition or another as the need arises. What semblance of truth may come of this in the end arises from the running debate—from the dialectical process.

Foremost among the constituents of happiness are the various kinds of goods. The definitions of good emphasize rational choice. The good is not what an animal aims at, but what an intelligent being chooses as his target. Rational choice is one of the key concepts in Aristotle's ethical works; his insistence that it is also important for rhetoric, like his concept of the enthymeme as the body of the proof, gives evidence of his commitment to a conception of rhetoric where intellectual processes are central. In the next sections, the virtues and pleasures are also treated as objects of reasoned choice.[13]

Aristotle seems to have arrived at his list of goods that are admitted by everyone from systematizing and rationalizing the value system of the educated class in the various city-states. The goods are closely related to happiness as the end of human life: the constituents of happiness are the prime goods, but so are necessary conditions for happiness, like life itself, since one can hardly achieve happiness, however it is defined, without living. Health, too, is a necessary condition, and moral excellence, which may be viewed as a kind of moral health, and also various kinds of talents and abilities.

Aristotle assumes that this hierarchy of goods applies universally, that is, wherever humans make rational choices. He does not take any account of cultural or religious differences except in the section on the constitutions of the various states where he shows an awareness that a person educated in an oligarchic or monarchic state thinks about the subjects of deliberation differently than one educated in a democratic state. If some contemporary of his believed that virtue is an end in itself unrelated to happiness, or that the end of existence is the cessation of the life of desire, or perhaps that it is salvation of the immortal soul, Aristotle has not heard about it, or, just possibly, he might consider anyone who thinks in these ways to be a nonrational being. A narrowness of view limits somewhat the utility of Aristotle's treatise as a guide to modern rhetorical *praxis*; modern rhetors must deal with culturally diverse audiences.

Having set out the *topoi* for enthymemes appropriate to deliberative rhetoric, Aristotle now takes up epideictic and forensic discourse.

### 2. Topoi *for Epideictic Speeches (I₉)*

Since the ends of epideictic discourse are the noble and the disgraceful, the noble must be defined: it is whatever being chosen for its own sake is also praiseworthy, or perhaps whatever being good is also pleasant precisely because it is good. Moral excellence (*arete*), then, is necessarily noble, for it is good and also praiseworthy. This excellence is the capacity to produce and preserve the various goods (such as health, strength, or wealth), or the capacity for performing many significant actions well: at best for acting well in relation to everything.

### The Kinds of Arete *(I₉)*

The kinds of moral excellence are justice, courage, self-control, magnificence, magnanimity, liberality, common sense, and wisdom. Since excellence has been defined in relation to production and preservation of the goods, those who are just and also the courageous are seen to be especially excellent: the latter because their character is crucial to the state in time of war, the former because of their contributions to both peace and war. What produces moral excellence is noble, and deeds that result from moral excellence are noble. The signs of virtue are noble (e.g., a calm demeanor is the sign of self-control). Actions performed unselfishly are among the things that are obviously noble, as are also the opposites of disgraceful actions.

### Making Enthymemes From the Aretai

Qualities bordering on moral excellences may be taken as excellent and those close to the vices as disgraceful, e.g., an irascible and excitable person may be called straightforward or a prudent person may be called cold and designing. A rash person can be made courageous by a spurious argument *a fortiori*: if someone goes into dangers unnecessarily, how much more likely will he be to do so in a good cause. Look, too, at where you are speaking [e.g., it is easier to praise free spirits in a democracy]. Accidental actions should be attributed to rational choice; this makes them noble.

Epideictic speaking is closely related to deliberative speaking, both deal with rational choice in relation to accepted values: if a speaker changes "is good" to "should do" he changes the kind of discourse from epideictic to deliberative. The most valuable means for making an epideictic discourse is amplification; the facts are accepted on trust, but they must be amplified to show the subject's nobility or shamefulness.

### 3. Topoi *for Forensic Speeches (I₁₀₋₁₅)*

Crime is voluntary harm contrary to law. Speeches of accusation (*kategoria*) and defense (*apologia*) are about wrongdoing; that is, in legal terminology, crime. To accuse or defend someone adequately a speaker must have an adequate definition of crime, and also know its motives, and the states of mind of criminals, and what is the usual character of crime victims. Crime may be defined as doing voluntary harm contrary to law. Laws are either those written by the legislature of a specific state or those general moral conceptions that are common to all civilized states, e.g., such rules as respect for the gods, and care for the lives of innocent people such as young children.

### Voluntary and Involuntary Action (I₁₀)

Harm is said to be involuntary if it is due to chance, compulsion, or nature, but it is voluntary if due to reasoned choice, habit, anger, and even to irrational desire. These, then, are the seven causes of human action. A person makes a reasoned choice to commit a crime because of the particular moral flaw of his type of character, e.g., the spendthrift to get money and the coward to avoid danger. This follows from what was said about moral excellence and its opposite ($I_9$). Anger will be treated as one of the *pathe* ($II_2$).

All persons act voluntarily to achieve goods and apparent goods or pleasures and apparent pleasures. Goods have been considered in relation to deliberative discourse ($I_6$); what is pleasurable remains to be analyzed.

### Topoi *for Establishing Motive:* Hedone *(I₁₁)*

Pleasure (*hedone*) is a kind of motion of the soul, a sudden and perceptible settling into its natural equilibrium; pain is the opposite. Since what causes a person to move into this state of equilibrium is pleasant, what causes him to move into disequilibrium is painful. Habit is acquired equilibrium, and since acquired states are close to natural ones, it is also pleasant, but what is done because of coercion is painful, since coercion works against nature. Whatever people long for is pleasant, whether their appetite is irrational or reasoned, for longing is desire for pleasure. And since imagination (*phantasia*) is only a fainter version of what is perceptible, anticipations of pleasures to come are pleasant and also memories of events that are past, even those unpleasant when they occurred, if the outcomes were noble and good. Revenge involves imagination, so it is pleasant.

Victory, honor, having friends, and giving or receiving benefits are also among the pleasures. And laughter and the laughable are highly pleasurable. Also doing the things at which a person excels; indeed, repeated activities in general are pleasant, but, conversely, so is change. Above all, learning and wondering are sources of pleasure.

### Topoi *for Establishing a Criminal State of Mind (I₁₂)*

People act criminally when they think the act is possible, and it is possible for them, and when they think they can escape detection, or if detected they will not suffer punishment, or if punished their penalty will be less than the gains to themselves or their confederates. It follows that persons who are powerful or well-connected are likely to commit crimes, as are those who are shameless, and people with various kinds of skills, especially those who are skilled in speaking. To the contrary, however, those who are badly in need and who have nothing to lose are also likely to commit crimes. From these considerations it is obvious that there are numerous special circumstances in which people think that they can commit crimes, such as when their appearance is not like that of people who have previously committed this kind of crime, or when they believe that the penalty will be small now but their gain will be considerable and long-lasting in the future.

### Topoi *for Establishing That Complainants Are Probable Victims (I₁₂)*

Among the likely victims of crime are persons who have what the criminal needs and also helpless persons like the weak and lonely. People living far away and also those near at hand can be said to be equally likely victims: the former because revenge will be slow, the latter because the gain is immediate. Crimes are often committed against the meek, easygoing, or unskillful, and against persons not on their guard; also against victims who are unpopular or hated by nearly everyone, and especially those who have committed crimes of the same kind now committed against them, for such a crime may appear to be almost an act of poetic justice.

### Topoi *for Showing That Situations Are Conducive to Crime (I₁₂)*

People do criminal things that all or most other people are in the habit of doing [in our time a stock case would be violating minor traffic regulations]. They steal what is easy to hide or quickly consumed (e.g., edibles, or what can be changed in shape or color or can easily be mixed with other objects). They also often act wrongfully against victims within their own households: women and others who might be ashamed to reveal the crimes.

   Laws have already been divided into those specific to a given people and those common to all, for some principles about justice and injustice seem to be true by nature (e.g., God left no one a slave; all are born free). Specific laws are either about harm to the individual or to the community as a whole: a violent assault harms the individual, but avoiding military service harms the state.

### Topoi *for Showing That an Act Is Contrary to Law (I₁₃)*

Since criminal action must be voluntary, it is always done knowingly; ignorant action is involuntary. Voluntary and knowing action results from anger or from reasoned choice. Choice, as related to goods and pleasures and to characters of criminals and victims, has just been covered. But to secure a conviction an act must be shown to be contrary to law, for often a defendant will admit to the act but deny the crime (e.g., he took something but did not steal; he struck first but did not commit violent assault; he had sex with someone but did not commit adultery). These acts must be defined: what is stealing? what is assault? and what is adultery? The issue involved in these definitions is the intentional choice, for in the wrongful intent lies the crime. Crimes must be defined according to unwritten law or the law that has been written for this state.

### Topoi *for Showing That the Letter of the Law Should Be Modified by Equity (I₁₃)*

Unwritten laws are of two kinds. There are those that involve extreme acts of virtue and vice (e.g., being grateful to persons who have aided you, or at least not acting treacherously toward them). And there are those that temper the operation of written laws (e.g., stroking someone with a knife meets the technical definition of assault with a weapon but should not be so defined in many cases). This is called equity or fairness; because of the rule of equity what we think is pardonable should not be considered such a serious crime, and often, too, we should look to the intent of the legislator to modify the letter of the law.

### Topoi *for Showing That Crimes Are More Serious or Less (I14)*

Crimes that spring from a more unjust intention are greater (a person who defrauds a religious institution of even a paltry sum has committed a heinous crime). The opposite is true of just deeds: an insignificant action from a good intention is still insignificant. Actions that result in more serious injuries or that have more notoriety, or are more brutal, are greater, as are those that involve more premeditation or are more shameful, e.g., an act against a benefactor. A crime also seems greater if the speaker can divide it into several crimes. The speaker may argue that a crime is more serious if it is against unwritten law, but conversely also if it is against the written law of this state.

### 4. Topoi *for Interpreting Inartistic Proofs (I15) – For Laws*

*Topoi* drawn from proofs extrinsic to the art are also the specifics of forensic discourse: the proofs are laws, witnesses, contracts, tortures, and oaths. When dealing with laws one should use *topoi* such as: if the written law is against a speaker's case, he should appeal to unwritten law, especially to equity; or he should find an ambiguity in the law or a conflict with some other law. On the other hand, if the law is for the speaker, he should argue that a law disregarded might just as well not have been made.

### For Witnesses

Witnesses can be ancient or contemporary. Ancient witnesses are poets or historical figures; contemporary witnesses are those whose sworn depositions are introduced in court. It can be said that the ancients are more trustworthy since they cannot be bribed. If an advocate has no witnesses, he argues that probabilities are more trustworthy; if he has witnesses, that probabilities are speculative. Contemporary witnesses can give testimony either to the facts or to character.

### For Contracts

If contracts are on his side an advocate argues that relations between people would be impossible if the obligation of contract were impaired; if contracts work against his case, he holds that they are contrary to equity or to some written law or that they are ambiguous or obtained by coercion or fraud. Many of the arguments about laws are applicable also to contracts.

### For Tortures

Slaves who are tortured are the kind of witnesses whose testimony seems trustworthy because of the necessity involved. If testimony is favorable to one's case, he makes this point about necessity; if against him, he holds that a person will say anything to be relieved of the pain, and he points to some well-known examples of false testimony given under torture. Indeed, many stupid persons and also those of excellent character will hold out against great force, while cowards will speak falsely before actually seeing the instruments of torture. So much for the trustworthiness of this kind of testimony.

### For Oaths

If a litigant swears an oath to the truth of his claim, he should argue that this shows he has confidence in his case; if he refuses the oath, he should state that any dishonest person would swear at once. If the advocate asks his opponent to swear, he states that it is pious to leave the decision to the gods and impious to refuse to swear when the jurors are expected to decide the case under oath. Such arguments as these may be made for any combination of offering or taking oaths.

All these chapters on the *topoi* for the three kinds of discourses are closely related. The noble and disgraceful, as ends of epideictic speaking, are defined in relation to the goods, which were previously described as the ends of deliberative speaking. Like the good, the noble is chosen for its own sake, but it is also praiseworthy or pleasant or both. What is disgraceful is assumed to be the opposite of the noble; certainly it is not praiseworthy. But there is an additional way in which the opposite of noble is developed; some of the repeated vocabulary makes this plain: disgrace or shame is among the *pathe* and is treated in detail in $II_6$ where a number of shameful actions and situations are listed. Foremost among the qualities that are productive of goods and praiseworthy is moral excellence (*arete*), the subject of most of the rest of the chapter.

The usual translation of *arete* is virtue, but this is misleading because modern readers understand that word as implying a Victorian moral rectitude, some combination of thrift, industriousness, and sexual abstinence. It is to be noted that none of these kinds of virtue are among the constituents listed by Aristotle. The *arete* of anything is its ability to perform its function well, e.g., the *arete* of a knife is that it cuts cleanly. The political *arete*, the subject of a Platonic dialogue named after the sophist *Protagoras*, is the ability of a person to contribute to the community effectively: to treat other citizens equitably, to donate the services requested by the city-state, to hold office willingly in peace, and to fight bravely with the armed forces in war. That conception is best expressed by moral excellence, though perhaps we might be better off just adopting the word *arete* into English, since no translation expresses it adequately. The question raised in the *Protagoras* was, can the political *arete* be taught? Like the great sophist, Aristotle gives a resounding affirmative answer; it is, indeed, one of his celebrated doctrines that the political *arete* is a habit acquired by right education from infancy through adolescence and, perhaps, even in adulthood.

In the *Rhetoric* the *aretai* are defined in a practical way; each is a capacity for producing and preserving goods. Some commentators (e.g., Cope) believe that the conception of *arete* in the *Rhetoric* is at odds with that of the *Nicomachean Ethics* where it is denied that *arete* is merely a capacity, and its status as a fixed habit is stressed. It is also valued there for itself, and not merely as productive of other goods.[14] But there is probably no real contradiction, only a difference in emphasis. A habit is in one of its aspects a fixed capacity, and though Aristotle is concerned in the *Rhetoric* with the legal and political character of *arete*, the treatment of the praiseworthy given here makes no sense unless he regards the *aretai* as also valuable in themselves, as a modern commentator has ably argued.[15]

It is in this rhetorical context that Aristotle finds justice and courage foremost among the *aretai*: the former because it denotes a kind of fair treatment of other people that is necessary to the functioning of the state in peace and war, the latter because it is essential in war. But self-control (or what might be called prudence) is also necessary to effective citizenship. Magnificence, the public display of wealth and possessions (in its less virtuous manifestations, conspicuous consumption), is less important, as are magnanimity, which is a kind of generosity of spirit, and liberality, which denotes the philanthropic kind of generosity.[16] Finally, and most important among the *aretai*, is common sense, the capacity to make intelligent moral choices in politics and in private affairs. It is to be distinguished from wisdom, the capacity to apprehend the basic principles of the specialized sciences. Common sense and wisdom are not the same; while one should not equate the former with "street smarts," there is unquestionably that aspect to it; possession of the latter does not necessarily imply the former. The *Rhetoric* is especially addressed to persons of common sense, and it is an important constituent of the *ethos* of the speaker. Elsewhere, Aristotle considers common sense less valuable than wisdom; here it is of primary importance. Of course the rhetorical inventory can be used by people of little sense, but using it well requires the kinds of choices only a person of good sense could make.[17]

Missing from the list of *aretai* are gentleness and compassion. Gentleness is given among the *aretai* in the *Nicomachean Ethics*. In the *Rhetoric* both gentleness and compassion are discussed among the *pathe* ($II_3$ and $II_8$); that is, they are considered conditions under which one's choice is altered rather than ends for which one chooses. In spite of the obvious relationship of this list to the early Platonic dialogues, nothing is said here about piety, the subject of Plato's *Euthyphro*. Honesty is not explicitly mentioned, though it may be implied in the kind of fair treatment that is the essence of justice. It is a somewhat different list from a Victorian or even a modern one.

Just as the various goods are the objects of rational choice, so also are what is noble and excellent as ends of human action. Indeed, it is not enough to praise someone for having done good deeds; what he has done must be interpreted as having been done for the sake of moral excellence. Lastly, it should be noted that these epideictic speeches do not contain an elaborate enthymematic proof. They consist mostly of long passages of narrative, the facts of which are taken on trust rather than being subject to proof. These passages are interspersed with shorter ones using the common *topos* of more and less to build up the importance of the subject's deeds and connect them to the *aretai*.

Aristotle opens the section on forensic discourse with a definition of wrongdoing, or, in modern legal terminology, crime: doing voluntary harm contrary to law. Voluntary implies not being done because of chance or some kind of compulsion; harm implies damage to a victim, and contrary to law implies some clear prohibition about which the accused should have been informed. Aristotle comes close to stating that voluntary implies knowledge, a position developed by Plato in the *Apology* and elsewhere. Ignorance is akin to chance; criminal action requires choice. Aristotle's development of the *topoi* of forensic discourse proceeds deductively from the parts of this definition. Like everyone else, a criminal chooses either goods or pleasures; hence one needs an account of the pleasures as motives of crime and the states of mind of those who choose to act criminally and some notions about proving that they have violated the law. Then, since it is victims who are damaged, one must know something about them and the seriousness of the crimes that have damaged them.

This description moves a long way toward a modern conception of crime, implying as it does an established body of law, knowledge, criminal intent, and perceptible damage to a victim.[18] Aristotle also makes the distinction, so important in his time, between public indictments and private indictments. This is not quite the same as our distinction between criminal and civil cases. In the city-states, if someone's house was robbed or he was assaulted, he brought action against the criminal as a private action; if he was murdered, his family brought the action. Only if someone desecrated a temple or refused to serve in the armed forces or consorted with the enemy in time of war was the action public, that is to say it was prosecuted as a public action because it was a crime against the state.

The definition of pleasure (*hedone*) as a certain motion of the *psyche*, a perceptible settling into its accustomed state, has been traced to Plato's *Philebus*.[19] There, pain is characterized as a loss of harmony or a disruption of a natural state of equilibrium; presumably the modern way of putting this is that pain as an antecedent to pleasure grows out of frustration and deprivation. Pleasure in the *Philebus*, and in some modern theories, is by definition, then, a restoration of the natural state.

This definition of pleasure, requiring that there be a perceptible, or as it might be translated, a sensible, movement of the soul, connects pleasure with sensation (*aisthesis*) as opposed to intellection (*noesis*). That is, perhaps, what people intuitively believe; even the pleasure of drawing a simple inference as experienced when reading a story and finding ourselves one step ahead of the detective is accompanied by warmth and excitement. The definition seems at odds with that in the *Nicomachean Ethics*, where Aristotle denies that pleasure is a motion (*kinesis*) and insists that it is an unimpeded activity. This difference may be due to the fact that the passage in the *Rhetoric* pre-dates a more mature doctrine in the *Ethics*, but there is an additional quite probable explanation: pleasure in the *Rhetoric* is viewed primarily as the motive to criminal action, and within that framework what is most important to stress is a fast movement to relieve pain rather than the sustained activity that is more closely connected to happiness.

One might expect Aristotle to give prominence to pleasures arising from gratification of physical appetites, these being the motives to crime most recognized by the layman. Instead, he elaborates on pleasures of skill and victory and games and friendship. The central position in his list, not coincidentally, is occupied by wonder and learning, from which are derived the pleasure one takes in the imitative arts; one reasons from the artistic representation saying to himself, "Ah, that is a such and such"; thus he learns (see *Poetics*, $1448b_{5-6}$). The primacy of more intellectual pleasures can be deduced from Aristotle's twofold division of desire into reasonless appetites as opposed to desires for which there is a reason ($1370a_{5-6}$). The latter kind of desires he gives more space. The former are to be connected with inartistic proofs; food and sex are often a kind of bribe to changing conduct. But the desires with reason are brought about by persuasion. Indeed, people can be persuaded to long for imagined events from the past and anticipated experiences in the future ($1370a_{6-8}$); such imagined pleasures are almost as powerful as those that are being perceived right now. It is, then, the pleasures connected with persuasion that are most appropriate to laying out the inventory of artistic proofs.

The notion that the strict operation of the law should be modified by equity or fairness (*epieikes*) may grow out of the discussion of distributive justice in Plato's *Republic*. Fairness is also a good translation because this notion is somewhat different from the modern legal concept called equity.[20] Aristotle gives the sound reason why such equity is needed: that no deliberative body can foresee every possibility when framing laws, so that a law too rigidly enforced in an individual case is likely to cause injustice. The rules of equity are embodied in one species of unwritten law; they are common rules that everyone agrees should be followed. The example from Empedocles, "nature has made no one a slave," is given by the anonymous medieval scholiast; it seems a little peculiar in the light of Aristotle's spirited defense of slavery elsewhere (*Politics*, $1253b_{15}-1254b_{40}$), but it is probable that though Aristotle defended the institution, he recognized a deep, ingrained prejudice that was held by free Greeks against it. Arnhart aptly points out that Aristotle avoids tracing unwritten law to the gods. The second example he cites of it is from Sophocles' drama; in citing it he trims Antigone's lines to avoid her invocation of divine sanction.[21]

The inartistic or extrinsic proofs (*atechnoi pisteis*) are the final subject covered under the head of forensic speaking. They are handled with a dialectical symmetry unusual even for Aristotle, e.g., if the written law is against the advocate, he should appeal to equity, but if it is in his favor he should state that a law not enforced might just as well not have been passed. The prevailing custom in the city-states was to examine slaves under torture; though symmetry is preserved in Aristotle's treatment of this kind of testimony, he weights the balance somewhat against it; the reasons he gives for disbelieving slaves are more compelling than those for believing them.[22] Aristotle surprises us by stating that testimony of the poets about events in history is perhaps more probable than that of witnesses appearing in court since the poets cannot be bribed. This premise is contrary to our modern empirical bias.

Though the inartistic proofs lie outside the art of rhetoric, the allocation of this much space to them is obviously justified. Directions must be given for handling the artistic aspects of inartistic proofs. Aristotle does not tell how to find a witness or torture a slave; he does set out an inventory of premises for making enthymemes if the advocate has a witness or slave to testify for him. Witnesses and other inartistic proofs are only as good as the arguments interpreting them; it is these arguments, their arrangement and their phrasing in language that make up the study of rhetoric.

The inartistic proofs complete Book I of the *Rhetoric*; Aristotle now proceeds to consideration of *ethos*, the *pathe*, and adaptation of the discourse to the various ages and fortunes of people.

## BOOK II

### B. Topoi *for Establishing the Speaker's* Ethos (II₁)

Since bad advice is given either through lack of sense or lack of integrity or dislike of the auditors, it follows that a speaker will seem trustworthy if he shows common sense, moral excellence, and good will. A speaker must show his common sense and his moral excellence by using the *topoi* set forth in relation to praise and blame ($I_3$); he shows his good will using the *topoi* for friendliness, one of the *pathe* ($II_4$).

## C. Topoi *for Leading the Auditors Into Certain States of the* Pathe *($II_{2-11}$)—Definition of* Pathe

The *pathe* are psychological emotional states through which people when passing alter their decisions: they always occur together with pain and pleasure. To lead someone into such a state, a speaker must consider three factors: the dispositions of people prone to pass into that state of feeling, against whom or for whom it is felt, and under what circumstances people are likely to feel it.

### For a State of Anger ($II_2$)

Let anger be defined as a desire accompanied by pain for a conspicuous revenge; it is caused by a manifest and undeserved slight against a person himself or others for whom he cares. This definition implies that someone who is angry is always angry at an individual and not at mankind in general, and he is angry because that person has acted or intends to act against him or those he cares about. Anger also involves pleasure, since visualizing revenge is pleasurable.

People prone to anger are those who are frustrated in achieving their desires, especially those who live in danger, who are invalids, or deeply in love; and also those who are entitled to better treatment than they get from others. They get angry at those they consider their inferiors, particularly when inferiors get in the way of achievement and they get angry at those from whom they do not expect slights: members of their families, their children, and their close friends. They are angered at those who mock them and scoff at them and do them violence, and particularly at those who show disrespect for what they take pride in (e.g., philosophers get angry with those who do not respect philosophy). And people get angry with those who ignore their suffering or even rejoice in their misfortunes.

Special circumstances conducive to anger are when the slight is public, particularly if it occurs in the presence of our rivals or those we admire or those we would like to have admire us or people before whom we are embarrassed or who are embarrassed on our behalf. We are also especially angered on behalf of our parents and other members of our families.

### For a State of Gentleness ($II_3$)

Gentleness can be defined as a settling down or allaying of anger. It is felt by those who have not been slighted or who have been treated with respect. People toward whom we feel gentle include those who respect us, and those who we respect and fear (for fear inhibits anger). People who, having slighted us, admit their fault and humble themselves often make us feel gentle. And we are less angry with those who themselves have acted against us in anger, since obviously they did not enjoy slighting us. The opposite circumstances from those conducive to anger are those in which people are likely to become gentle.

### For Friendship (II₄)

Friendship is wishing for another person what one thinks good for himself, and wishing it for that person's sake. Friends are those who love and feel loved in return, who share pleasure in the good things of life and pain in the bad ones, who rejoice and are distressed at the same events, and who usually have the same friends and the same enemies. People feel friendly toward those who have conferred benefits on them or those they care for, and those who have common desires and interests with them. Ordinarily we want to be friends with people of moral excellence, especially the just (who we think capable of being good friends). And we want to be friends with those we admire, and those who are pleasant to deal with and ready to joke or take a joke. And we want friends who are neat and orderly. Also, we want to be friends with those before whom we are not easily embarrassed, and those who habitually speak well of other people and even of the dead, and above all, those who are not too intimidating. We feel friendship under certain circumstances, such as when we have received benefits, especially those conferred on us unasked and in the absence of publicity.

### For Hatred (II₄)

Enmity or hating is the opposite of friendship [presumably it is wishing evil on others not because damaging them results in good things for us but because they belong to a detested class]. We feel hatred when we observe classes of people [who are destructive] even though they may not have done us personal harm. It follows that hatred is disinterested and does not involve revenge; therefore, unlike other *pathe*, it is accompanied by neither pain nor pleasure. We naturally feel hatred toward thieves and informers. People who anger us may see that anger turn to hatred; spite and slander also produce hatred. Anger can be cured by time and the coming of pity; hatred is incurable.

### For Fear (II₅)

Fear is pain or distress arising from an image of some impending evil of a destructive or painful sort. Evils that are especially destructive are most fearful, and fear is most felt when the evil is near and by people who consider themselves weak. Persons who are powerful and have acted effectively in the past are the very type of those in the presence of whom we feel fear, especially if they are angry or hate us, or if they have a motive for crime against us and a state of mind conducive to committing it. People in circumstances where they do not expect to suffer do not fear: such are the wealthy, the powerful, and those with many friends. The poor and friendless, rather, are likely to fear. But no one fears who has suffered so much that he has given up altogether; there must be hope if there is to be fear.

### For Confidence (II₅)

Confidence is the opposite of fear; it is the hope of deliverance from danger, together with an image of deliverance being near, while dreadful things do not exist or are far off. It is felt in the absence of those who cause fear: when we have not offended powerful figures or those we have offended are far off. It is also felt by those who have little experience of danger or who believe that they are skillful in handling dangers, and also by persons with superior resources and weak enemies. And those who feel strongly that they have been wronged and think that the gods are with them; such people become angry, and anger makes for confidence.

### For Shame and Shamelessness (II₆)

Shame is pain or distress about those evils past, present, or future, that bring obvious disrepute; shamelessness is a belittling of, or imperviousness to, such pain. Actions considered shameful by us and others are those originating from vices, e.g., throwing away one's armor and deserting in battle, or having sex with inappropriate partners or at inappropriate times and places: the former springs from cowardice, the latter from lust. Plundering someone weaker than ourselves is especially shameful. Boastfulness is shameful and selling one's sexual services also.

### Persons Who Feel Shame—Circumstances Conducive to Shame

Persons who are honorable and of distinguished ancestry are prone to shame, as are those with many or with distinguished admirers. One feels shame most in the presence of his admirers, or those by whom he wants to be admired, and before people who do not act shamefully themselves. In general one is ashamed of acts done publicly and conspicuously and before people who are prone to gossip. One seldom feels shame before those he considers his inferiors or before infants or small animals. The opposite of these *topoi* should be used to bring auditors into shamelessness.

### For Graciousness (II₇)

Graciousness is a state in which one gives a favor to someone in need, not in exchange for anything, but for the recipient's sake alone. The favor is greatest when the need is greatest, or when what is given is hard to get, or when the one who gives it is the first or most able to give it. Needs are desires, and those in pain from a desire for something (e.g., from deprivation of sex) or those in danger are especially grateful recipients of favors. One who stands by a person in poverty or exile is especially gracious, for at a critical time a small favor produces much gratitude. Ungraciousness is produced by showing that a person who did an apparent favor really acted because of a reward or from compulsion, or because the favor was trifling.

### For Pity (II₈)

Pity is the pain felt at a visible destructive or painful evil occurring to someone who does not deserve it, when we expect that evil might occur to ourselves or members of our family. Hence a person feels pity who believes that he can suffer harm, perhaps because he is older and more experienced, or is a person of good sense, or is educated, or, on the other hand, if he is a coward.

### Persons Pitied—Circumstances Conducive to Pity

Pity is felt for people suffering what corrupts and destroys, e.g., torture, disease, or desertion by friends. Also for those who deserved good but got evil and those who never had a good thing happen to them. We feel pity for those who are like us, in particular, friends or acquaintances or members of our own family. And those who suffer the destructive things that come by chance are pitiable; indeed if someone deserves the destruction that comes upon him, we do not pity him. One feels pity in circumstances that are not too fearful; indeed if great danger is upon someone, he thinks only of himself not others. If things are so good that he becomes too confident, however, a person suffers arrogance (*hubris*), which also inhibits pity. Like fear, pity is felt when suffering is near at hand; this seems to be so when the signs of suffering are visible. For this reason speakers often display the nonverbal behavior of sufferers or the clothes of those who have suffered, or they recite their last words.

### For Indignation (II₉)—Persons Who Cause Indignation

The proper opposite to pity is indignation (*nemesis*); it is pain not at undeserved misfortune but at undeserved good fortune; both pity and *nemesis* are felt by morally excellent persons. One's sense of justice is violated when a wrongdoer is rewarded. Because of the connection to justice, *nemesis* has been attributed to the gods. Indignation is not felt at persons whose good fortune results from moral excellences, and it is felt at those who have beauty and good birth only if they lack moral excellence. Someone who has recently come into wealth or power or another such acquired good is especially a target of indignation (the *nouveau riche* rather than those who inherit old money); also a lesser person who has the gall to contest with a greater one.

### People Who Easily Feel Indignant

People are prone to indignation who are worthy of great goods and possess them. Also, persons of moral excellence, especially those who take themselves seriously, are prone to indignation. And above all, those who are ambitious and see others receiving the objects of their ambition. Speakers prevent decision-makers from feeling pity by using these *topoi* that lead them into indignation.

### For Envy (II₁₀)—Persons Who Are Envied

Envy is the pain we feel at manifest prosperity among our equals of the same kind that prompts indignation. Envy comes not because we want what they appear to have, but because they have it. It follows that those who have many equals in birth, age, moral habits, reputation, or possessions are prone to feel it, as are persons of good fortune and fame, and especially those who are ambitious, but also those who lack that generosity of spirit noted among the *aretai* (I 9 1366b₁₇). We tend to envy our competitors (e.g., rivals in love), especially those close to us (e.g., our siblings). We envy those who succeed more easily than we, or whose success is a reproach to us. Decision-makers will not feel pity if the speaker brings them into a state of envy.

### For Emulation (II₁₁)—People Who Feel Emulation—Those Who Are Emulated

Emulation is the pain we feel at the manifest presence among our equals of the good things that are honored and are possible for us to acquire. Emulation comes not because they have these things, but because we want them; thus, it is felt by a noble person, while envy is more felt by a worthless one. People are emulous who think that they deserve goods they do not have; these are often the young and those with generosity of spirit. People who are honored and have goods appropriate to being the objects of honor tend to be emulous, as do those with good families and connections. The *aretai* are objects of emulation since they are by definition good and praiseworthy, and they are sources of goods and benefits for others. Goods that can be shared with friends are even more the objects of emulation than other kinds of goods. Persons who possess such goods and virtues are the ones we emulate, especially those who have power and can benefit many other people and are the objects of praises and *encomia* (speeches of praise). Those without characteristics that may be emulated are usually despised by the emulous, especially those who have had good fortune without it having brought them anything of lasting value.

### Choice of Topoi as Affected by the Ages and Fortunes of Speakers and Auditors (II₁₂₋₁₇)

People's characters are obviously affected by these states of feeling and by their habitual moral choices (see the section on the *aretai*, I₉). The kinds of arguments made to them need to change; arguments should also change according to the age of the speaker, whether young, in the prime of life, or elderly, and also the ages of the auditors. Likewise, arguments need to change according to the status which fortune has conferred on speakers and their auditors—whether they are well born or rich or powerful or the opposite of these states.

### The Young (II₁₂)

The young have stronger desires than those at the other ages; of the desires of the body the most likely to overcome them is the sexual. Their desires are intense, but short-lived. They tend to act from honor rather than calculate expediencies, and though they love honor, they love victory even more because youth desires superiority. They tend more than the other groups to act in anger. Not having been often deceived, they are prone to believe. They live mostly by hope, for hope is of the future, and for them the future is long. They are also courageous from a combination of desire and hope.

### The Old (II₁₃)

The old have, by and large, the opposite character. Weaker in desire, they err on the side of timidity and act more for gain than from lust. They often calculate expediencies rather than act from honor, and they are shameless in these calculations. They tend to be stingy since experience has taught them how hard money is to get, and how easy it is to lose. Having often been deceived, they are suspicious and slow to believe and even think that most human endeavors will turn out badly. They live in memory more than in hope, for their past is longer than their future: this is the reason for their long-windedness.

### Those in the Prime of Life (II₁₄)

The character of those in the prime of life lies midway between that of youth and of age. Neither rash nor timid, neither skeptical nor overtrusting, they usually make choices on a true basis. They are not given to excess in desire, or to lack of feeling or parsimony. They live respecting both honor and expediency. In short, the most useful traits of youth and age are theirs.

### The Well Born (II₁₅)

The well born are ambitious, for anyone who starts with an advantage tries to add to what he started with, and good birth is inherited advantage. They are disdainful, even of contemporaries with achievements equal to those of their ancestors because honor from afar is thought better than that achieved nearby. The term "well born" denotes excellence of family, as distinguished from noble, which means that a descendant has not deteriorated from the excellence of his ancestors. Nobility is not so common among the well born; there seems to be a trend in nature toward deterioration of the line.

### Character as Influenced by Wealth (II₁₆)

Wealth alters character by making persons possessing it insolent and overbearing. The rich value everything by money. They are prone to luxury and conspicuous consumption. Since money is the measure of all things, they consider themselves entitled to everything, especially to rule. They do wrong more from incontinence than from malice. In sum, they become prosperous fools, and the *nouveau riche* have these vices in more excessive forms.

### Character as Influenced by Power (II₁₇)

Power influences character in similar but somewhat better ways than wealth. The powerful are more ambitious and more heroic because they aspire to achieve what power can achieve. They are more energetic and serious than other people because of their need to maintain power. They temper their tendency to be overbearing into a dignified reserve. Rather than petty crimes, they tend to commit crimes of a certain magnitude.

### Character as Influenced by Good Fortune (II₁₇)

The influence of fortune on character is similar to that of good birth, wealth, and having power, since these are the most important results of good fortune. It also provides advantages to a person's body and to his family. Though it makes those who come into it more arrogant and irrational, it also makes them more pious, for the gods seem to have given them much. The characters of the meanly born, the poor, the powerless, and the unfortunate are obviously the opposites of those presented here.

Aristotle has already characterized *ethos* as perhaps the most authoritative of the rhetorical proofs or *pisteis*. He has also stated that it should not be left to prior impressions, but should be enhanced by the speech itself. Prior impressions, based perhaps on reputation, belonging to a certain social class, physical attractiveness, or dressing the part, are stressed by modern social scientists, but they are not considered a relevant part of the art in the *Rhetoric*. This is because of a self-imposed limitation: the art of rhetoric is about those factors which are intrinsic to that art. Social class and age are treated under the heading of the characters often, but only insofar as these influence the choice of enthymemes an advocate makes; the other sociological traits are extrinsic to the art. A speaker develops *ethos* artistically by showing common sense, the virtue by which one makes right judgments about practical affairs, and good moral character, the other virtues such as justice and courage, and also good will, which Aristotle takes as the equivalent of arguing that one is in an emotional state of friendliness toward the auditors.[23] A speaker reminds the audience, for example, that his family has farmed the territory near Athens for generations, his forebears have given services to the state, and he has grown up facing the same problems as his fellow citizens. Making such statements provides materials from which the auditors infer similarity between themselves and the speaker; they have common backgrounds and common interests and goals. These considerations are used to bring others into a state of friendliness.

The *pathe* are defined as those psychological states through which people when passing alter their judgments about subjects under consideration. They are usually accompanied by pleasure or pain; that is they have a physiological dimension. For the purposes of rhetoric, Aristotle is not much interested in this dimension; it is mentioned, and occasionally, as in the case of anger and the pleasure of revenge, it is used to deduce some aspects of the state. It is their basis in perception and judgment, however, that constitutes the larger part of the treatment he gives to each of the *pathe*.

The focus is on what factors are useful to the advocate for leading an auditor into this emotional state. The treatment follows a standard pattern: first a definition of the *pathos*, then an outline of the state of mind of those who feel it, then a list of those people or happenings in the face of which it is felt, then a list of circumstances in which it is apt to be felt. Several of the *pathe* receive full development of this pattern; some are regarded as of lesser importance and receive more cursory treatment. Since Aristotle often treats anger as his paradigm, and he gives it a full treatment, it will be adopted as a basis for the following comments about the perceptual and judgmental bases of the *pathe*.

To feel angry, a person must perceive that someone else has committed an offending action that he feels is an intentional and undeserved slight, a belittling of his personhood. By calling it an "apparent slight," Aristotle leaves open the possibility that the offending action may not have been intended to belittle or may have been in some way deserved; it may even have been done by the other without consciousness of the slighted party's being on the scene. But the angry man could take this lack of consciousness as evidence for a (fallacious?) enthymeme based on the premise that "someone who acts against me and does not even know that I exist is one who has belittled me." It is easy to reason from this premise if the party slighted is already frustrated and looking for someone to blame for his frustrations. It is even easier if the one who has acted against him is a friend or a subordinate, since we all think that friends and subordinates ought to be conscious of what our interests are: that is part of the definition of both friend and subordinate.

In addition, if someone perceives that other people, especially his rivals, think that he has been slighted (someone whispers to him, "Are you going to take that?"), then he is sure to feel angry. At every step, from the initial perception of the action, to the awareness of who did it and that others saw it done, the angry man reasons from his perceptions to the judgment that he is slighted and that he is justified in feeling angry.

It is also possible to refute this reasoning using the *topoi* for leading others into a state of gentleness, the opposite emotion from anger. The advocate points out that the slight was not real; the other party actually had no grounds even to suspect the presence of one who now feels slighted; the real premise should be someone who acts completely in ignorance could not intend to belittle another: "And someone like you who has had so few frustrations would have to be petty and mean to take offense at the mere appearance of a slight. As for those other people who think you were slighted: you are too intelligent to let them decide how you should feel." The advocate argues that if one perceives a deliberate action, he is not seeing things clearly; if he judges the action to be a slight, he is not thinking straight; though temporary frustrations will lead to a state of mind in which it is hard to think straight, an intelligent person does not abide for long in that state. Altogether, there really is no justification for being angry.

That the *pathe* are subject to this kind of argument is one of the features that distinguish them from the appetites or irrational desires. If someone is thirsty, it is not natural to try to argue him out of his desire for a drink: it is hard to say, "You're not the kind of person who ought to suffer thirst, and besides, the drink that you think you see is really a mirage, and you only think it's hot enough to dehydrate anyone." Exactly the same kinds of arguments that might be persuasive for a person who is angry are difficult even to make for someone who is thirsty.

As has been remarked, imagination (*phantasia*) functions as a weak kind of perception. Aristotle takes account both of *pathe* that are founded on accurate perception and those that are founded on images of reality. Anger arises from an apparent slight, e.g., from the image of a slight, and the image of taking revenge is part of the experience of anger; fear is caused by an image of a destructive impending evil; confidence is connected to the hope of safety and the image that the means of deliverance are near; if we imagine that someone belongs to a detested class, we are apt to hate him; pity is pain at the appearance of fearful evil overtaking someone who does not deserve it: in these and other cases the *pathe* are specifically connected to the imagination. To the extent that judgments are made on the basis of accurate perceptions, Aristotle views them as appropriate. But one of the functions of rhetoric is to stimulate the consciousness to produce an image of something that is not immediately perceptible: an image remembered from the past, or one extrapolated from past experience to the future.

Because the *pathe* are dependent on perceiving and judging, it has been said that the *Rhetoric* presents us with a cognitive theory of the emotions.[24] His theory is consistent with modern cognitive theories of emotions. It contrasts with views of the emotions as arising from an uncontrolled, undifferentiated subconscious. It is a limitation of the *Rhetoric* that it does not deal with hysterical emotional states or the verbal triggers thereto. This limitation is inherent in a conception of rhetoric that makes argumentation its primary characteristic. But the great advantage of this cognitive theory is that it makes a virtually complete integration of emotional proofs with the proofs made by the reasoned arguments in the discourse. Auditors are led into the states of feeling by making judgments on the basis of arguments; once in these states they alter their decisions to accept or reject the conclusions of other arguments. Aristotle does not remark on a corollary to this kind of theory: the emotions as distinct from the appetites are more keenly felt by intelligent persons than by the slow-witted, because it is intelligent people who can understand the arguments and make the right judgments.

Cognitive theories have had their defenders among contemporary philosophers. Arnhart points out that the well-known phenomenologist, Martin Heidegger, adopts a format studying the emotions similar to the one given in the *Rhetoric*. Fear is considered from three perspectives: the attitude of fearing, that about which we fear, and that before which we fear. Heidegger, too, understands these perspectives as founded on reasoned judgments about reality, and he claims that "the fundamental ontological interpretation of affectivity in general has been able to take hardly one noteworthy step forward since Aristotle."[25] One of the modern features of Aristotle's treatment is precisely that it depends so little on introspection. Aristotle describes the pattern of stimuli and the inferential basis for judgments made about that pattern; he does not speculate about the internal states of individuals who are experiencing the emotions.

The *Rhetoric* treats the emotions in pairs of opposites: anger and gentleness, friendship and hatred, fear and confidence, shame and shamelessness, graciousness and ungraciousness. Pity is said to have two opposites: indignation and envy. Pity itself requires that we recognize a similarity between ourselves and the persons who are the objects of our pity; indignation that we note the difference between those who do not deserve good fortune and the deserving like ourselves; envy, again, that we observe the similarity between ourselves and the objects of our envy, who have had the good fortune that we have not had. This scheme contrasts with that in the *Nicomachean Ethics* where the division is threefold because *arete* in relation to the *pathe* is a mean between two extremes, that is, gentleness is said to be the mean between irritability and lack of irritability; it is not the absence of anger as in the *Rhetoric* but being angry at the right time with the right people and for the right purpose. This makes gentleness into a virtue rather than an emotional state.[26] The bipolar framework probably works better for rhetoric while the tripartite framework, stressing the mean, works for the study of ethics. Pairing polar opposites and suggesting terms in between lends itself to making arguments.

When considering friendship (*philia*) it is notable that Aristotle does not mention sexual love (*eros*). This seems peculiar, because passing through an erotic state certainly makes people alter their decisions even when faced with logical arguments. Aristotle uses the phrase "rational wish" to describe what a friend wants the other person to have for his own sake, which is the essential feature of that *pathos*.[27] He apparently considers erotic love to be an appetite quite unconnected with such a rational wish; therefore it is not much subject to the rhetorical art. Something of the tradition of romantic love with its elaborate rhetoric of courtship must have been known to him, since it is clearly reflected in the *Phaedrus* and the *Symposium*. One must probably conclude that courtship was uncongenial to his nature.

Only slightly related to his inventory of the *pathe*, Aristotle says that the rhetor should undertake a demographic analysis that divides speakers and auditors into age groups and also groups that have characters influenced by several kinds of fortune: good birth, wealth, accession to positions of power, and unspecified other kinds of good fortune. He only mentions, but does not develop, the opposites to these fortunes, such as mean birth or poverty. This section is an attempt to carry out Plato's prescription (*Phaedrus* 271D–272D) for a classification of kinds of souls in order to construct a matching set of arguments. Aristotle states two related purposes for this classification: first, the speaker should alter his choice of *topoi* and enthymemes derived from them to appeal to the interests of the various groups, and second, he should choose to present his *ethos* differently when speaking to one group as opposed to another. To an audience of the elderly, for example, a young speaker should point out prudent actions in his past and show, if possible, that he is the kind of person who understands the special concerns of people who have lived long. A striking example of a rhetor pursuing this advice is contained in the debate in the *ecclesia* about sending an expeditionary force to Sicily, as reported by Thucydides. The speaker is the young Alkibiades, who states:

> Remember that I brought about a coalition of the greatest powers of the Peloponnese, without putting you to any considerable danger or expense, and made the Spartans risk their all on the issue of one day's fighting at Mantinea, and though they were victorious in the battle, they have not even yet quite recovered their confidence. So, in my youth and with this folly of mine which is supposed to be so prodigious, I found the right arguments for dealing with the power of the Peloponnesians, and the energy which I displayed made them trust me and follow my advice. Do not therefore be afraid of me only because I am young, but while I still have the vigor of my youth and Nikias the reputation for being lucky, make the best use you can of what each of us has to offer.[28]

Obviously other demographic divisions are possible, like those into occupations, or by residence in urban or rural areas, or by ethnic origins, or levels of education. But Aristotle is guilty of the traditional stereotypes. His observations by and large catalog the conventional wisdom: the young are optimistic and competitive and given to rashness, the old are cautious to a fault, and the powerful are proud with a tendency to insolence. The presentation of the prime of life as a mean between youth and age, possessing the virtues of both these extremes without their defects, is one of the few places in the *Rhetoric* where this paradigm is used.

At this point Aristotle has concluded his presentation of the *topoi* for inventing arguments in the specialized areas, including those for building the speaker's *ethos* and those for leading the auditors into the various *pathe*. He now turns to the *topoi* that are common to all subjects and types of discourses.

## III. *Topoi* for Invention of Arguments Common to All Subjects and Kinds of Discourses

### Summary and Transition to the Koina

All discourses are directed toward a decision (*krisis*), even when the decision-maker is only a single individual. Epideictic speeches, too, are composed as if the spectators were decision-makers.

Now that premises for each of the kinds of discourse have been covered and also the choosing of premises adapted to the various ages and fortunes of men, it remains to deal with the *koina*, premises common to all discourse. These are: (1) the possible and impossible, equally important for the three kinds; (2) past fact, which is most important for forensic discourse; (3) future fact, which is important for deliberative, and (4) more or less, the premise most important for epideictic.

### A. Topoi *for Proving Something Is Possible or Impossible (II$_{19}$)*

One proves something is possible using premises such as these: if the opposite of something is possible, the thing itself must be possible (if a person can be healthy, it follows that he can be sick); if a difficult form of something is possible, then an easy form is possible (if there are hard riddles, easy riddles must also exist); if something is the object of desire or of an art or science, it is possible, for nature does not lead us to desire what is impossible (if there are passionate gardeners, there must be gardens). The opposites of such premises can be used to prove the impossible.

### B. For Establishing the Probability That Events Have Occurred in the Past (II$_{19}$)

One proves that something has occurred with premises such as these: if the less probable event has occurred, so has the more probable (if a man has hit his father, he has probably also insulted him at some time); if the antecedent has occurred, so has the expected consequent (if two enemy armies have marched toward each other, there has probably also been a battle); if a person or state has the power to do something and the desire to do it, it will be done (if an armed man has met his enemy alone in the woods he has probably killed him). The opposites of these premises are used to prove that events have not occurred.

### C. For Predicting the Probability That Events Will Occur (II$_{19}$)

By turning the preceding premises to the future tense, arguments for proving predictions can be invented: the premise about having power and desire turns into, if a person or state has the power to do something and the desire to do it, it will probably be done (if a man has built the foundations and had the means to build a house, he has probably gone on to do so).

### D. For Proving What is More or Less (II$_{19}$)

Some species of good is the end for all discourses, the advantageous for deliberative speeches, the honorable for epideictic speeches, and the just for judicial speeches. About largeness and smallness and more and less as it concerns each of these genres enough has been said in a previous chapter (I$_7$).

These *topoi* that are common to all speeches and subjects are, of course, probable premises: it is obviously not always true that when the antecedent has occurred, so has the consequent; oftentimes some force will intervene to prevent the normal consequent from occurring. Such less than scientific arguments are often decisive when making policy even in advanced countries; for example, it is assumed that persons informed of the consequence of committing a violent felony is capital punishment will be deterred from committing violent felonies, but since no one knows how many felonies have actually been deterred, this assumption amounts to nothing more than a special case of Aristotle's probable premise "where the antecedent has occurred, so has the expected consequent." Someone proposing a punishment of death may state this assumption as an axiom or rule, but that does not make the assumption any more or less a probability.

Turning away from the content and onto the structure, Aristotle next outlines the various forms that arguments can take.

## IV. Forms of Enthymemes and Related Proofs ($II_{20-25}$)

### A. The Example (Paradeigma) ($II_{20}$)

Examples are of two kinds: actual events or fictitious events. The fictitious kind can be short parallels like those in Socratic dialogues or stories like Aesop's fables. Fictitious parallels are easier to provide; historical parallels carry more conviction. When examples are the only proof, a speaker needs many, but when they are added to enthymemes, they function as witnesses.

### B. The Maxim (Gnome) ($II_{21}$)

Maxims are general statements [often truisms] about human affairs. They serve either as conclusions or premises of enthymemes and become complete enthymemes if a reason or conclusion is added. Some are obviously true without a reason, e.g., "If you don't know where you're going, any road will get you there." Others require a reason. If the maxim is paradoxical or controversial, the reason may be stated first, e.g., "Since the rich can afford more, tax the rich." Making maxims is more suitable to the elderly and those experienced in a subject; it is inappropriate for those who are younger, and is foolish for the inexperienced. Maxims are effective because they state as a general rule the opinions people hold about particular cases; additionally they are effective because speeches create good *ethos* when they show moral choice; since maxims are public declarations of moral principles, they necessarily show moral choice.

### C. The Enthymeme ($II_{22}$)

The enthymeme has already been characterized as a kind of *syllogismos* ($I_2$). A speaker should not make enthymemes in a long chain or try to include everything, lest his speech not be persuasive to the auditors. He should draw his arguments from opinions held by a particular group of auditors, such as the ones making a decision in this case, or from people they respect. He should also argue more from probable premises than from necessary ones. Connecting his claims to first principles and necessary grounds might be tiresome or unclear, both of which are qualities that a speaker must avoid.

### Enthymemes Based on Specialized Topoi

First and foremost the speaker must know the special subject matter about which he is to speak; otherwise he will have no basis on which to build conclusions, e.g., he can only advise Athenians to go to war by knowing about their army and navy, its kind and quality and size, and also about their other resources and their potential allies and the outcomes of previous wars they have fought. And they can only be adequately praised or blamed on the basis of specifics rather than generalities: the victories at Marathon and Salamis, or the enslavement of the people of Aegina and Potidaea.

### Constructive and Refutative Enthymemes

Just as in dialectic, proofs are divided into syllogism and refutation, enthymemes are divided into those which are constructive and those which are refutative. The former proceed from premises on which advocates agree to the conclusion that something is true or false; the latter use these premises to show that our adversaries are inconsistent for not accepting the obvious conclusions.

As has been noted, Aristotle relates the argument from example (*paradeigma*) to induction. An example (as opposed to an enthymeme by example) does not establish a rule, but reasons directly from singular case to singular case. This can be done either in the form of a historical parallel or of a fable.

At this point Aristotle does not relate the example to stylistic tools like simile and metaphor; he discusses both examples and maxims solely in terms of their logical force. Most later rhetoricians treat them, especially the fictitious kind, as devices of style. Maxims they characterize as being sententious in form—short, pointed, and sloganeering. To be sure, the examples that Aristotle uses are of this sort, but his comments ignore the stylistic form and emphasize their function in making enthymemes and building *ethos*.

Defined technically, an enthymeme is a *syllogismos* from signs and probabilities. We will treat signs first. A sign is an event or characteristic that accompanies another event or almost always accompanies it; in modern parlance: a correlation. Acting dishonestly usually goes with acting secretly, so secrecy can be taken as a sign of the likelihood of dishonesty.

Though Aristotle defines being grounded in probabilities and signs as the essential characteristic of the enthymeme, some of his explanations have given rise to the idea that the absence of one or more parts necessary to form a complete syllogism makes any utterance an enthymeme, e.g., "Why didn't he act in secret if he was being dishonest?" This idea has been corrected in modern interpretations of the *Rhetoric*, which have demonstrated that while enthymemes are often presented in a brief form, their brevity is not a defining characteristic.

If signs are correlations, probabilities are high likelihoods. Distinguishing between enthymemes based on probabilities and those based on signs is difficult because of the apparent ambiguity in the way that Aristotle uses the term "probability." He sets up an opposition between first principles and probable principles. First principles (*archai*) are the foundations of the sciences; in the *Prior Analytics* and *Posterior Analytics* he assumes that they are the basis for reasoning. Probable principles are the foundations of reasoning in the *Topics* and the *Rhetoric*. The first principles express the real causes of things; probabilities (the rhetorical counterpart) are either about hypothesized causes or about empirical determinations of how things will turn out. Aristotle often treats them as if they are an inferior kind of first principles; indeed, this is implied by his word for them, *eikota*, likenesses or resemblances. They are truth-like statements. There is no good English term for *eikos*, as there is in German where the word *Wahrscheinlichkeit* means apparent truth as well as probability. Often though, Aristotle uses *eikos* to mean a little more than apparent truth; in some cases it is a statement not yet fully proved, one that has the potential to become a true first principle.

Now to the ambiguity of the concept. It is used to cover several kinds of phenomena. One might divide probabilities into four classes: (1) value statements held by people of good sense; (2) empirical generalizations rooted in unexamined experience; (3) empirical generalizations supported by systematic induction (or at least partially supported by such induction); (4) propositions that are on the way to becoming *archai* but have not yet been sufficiently tested to be confirmed as first principles.

The first two classes are called *doxa*, or received opinions. The third class comprises a series of events where one has reason to expect that the next member of the series will be like the preceding ones. This third kind somewhat resembles a modern frequency theory of probability. The fourth kind Aristotle calls first principles of a sort. All such statements, of course, are to be distinguished from genuine *archai*, which show the causes of things and their essences.[29] Only these principles, and statements deduced from them, are part of a scientific system—a closed deductive system something like Euclidean geometry. When Aristotle states in Book I that rhetoric does not give instruction, he means that it does not deal with such scientific matter.

The validity of this distinction between scientific principles and probabilities is somewhat problematic. Such a distinction is basic if one believes in Aristotelian science, the science of the closed deductive system. Most modern scientists believe that scientific truth is also probable, and that the most one can know is a statistical prediction of the frequency with which events will occur. If that is so, then in the technical sense all reasoning is enthymematic; the distinction between enthymeme and scientific syllogism loses much of its importance.

Next, Aristotle presents a catalogue of typical forms for enthymemes and typical forms for sham enthymemes, i.e., fallacies. This catalogue constitutes a rhetorical analogue of Aristotle's dialectical treatises, the *Topics* and the *Sophistical Refutations*. For these formal topics a complete statement consists of three parts: (1) the name of the relationship between terms that gives rise to this form of argument (such relationships as contraries, multiple meanings of a word, and comparison of advantages and disadvantages); (2) an abstract pattern for arguments based on this relationship; and (3) one or more concrete examples. These *topoi* are said to form both constructive and refutative enthymemes.[30]

### D. Typical Forms for Enthymemes (II₂₃)

1. From contrary opposites.

    From the correctness of a (positive or negative) predicate of a subject, one can reason to the contrary opposite predicate of the contrary opposite subject. Reasoning from p(A) to -p(-A). Example: "*If the war is the cause of present evils, things should be set right by making peace*"[31] (1397a₁₁).

2. From grammatical inflections.

    From the correctness of a predicate of a concept, one can reason to the correctness of the predicate of the same concept expressed in a different grammatical form.

Reasoning from p(A) to p(A-ness) or to p(being A). Example: *"the just is not entirely good; for then what is done justly would be a good, but as it is, to be put to death justly is not desirable"* (1397a$_{22}$).

3. From reciprocal relations.

From the value of an action, one can reason to the same value of the corresponding reception and vice versa. Reasoning from p(giving A) to p(taking A). Special attention must be paid to the question whether the correct agent does the giving and taking. Example: *"If it is not shameful for you to sell them, neither is it for me to buy"* (1397a$_{27}$).

4. From the more or less (and the analogous).

From the correctness of a less plausible or likely predicate of a subject, one can reason to the correctness of a more plausible or likely predicate of the same (or a similar) subject. Similarly, one can reason with the same predicate about more and less likely subjects. Also, one can reason from the correctness of one predicate of a subject to the correctness of the same predicate of a similar subject. Example: *"[A] person who has beaten his father has also beaten his neighbors"* (1397b$_{15}$)— assuming that beating one's parents is a more heinous crime, and therefore less likely than beating random neighbors.

5. From examining time.

From the correctness of a claim or demand at an earlier period in time, one can reason to its correctness now, especially if events in the meantime are likely to have strengthened the original claim. Reasoning from p$_{prior}$ to p$_{now}$. Example: *"If, before accomplishing anything, I asked to be honored with a statue if I succeeded, you would have granted it. Will you not grant it [now] that I have succeeded?"* (1397b$_{28}$).

6. From using what the opponent has admitted against him.

From the quality that the accuser claims about himself, the defendant can reason to a similar quality about himself (the defendant), especially if the defendant is generally more likely to possess the quality in question. Reasoning from p (person A) to p (person B). Example: *"And [there is] the argument Iphicrates used against Aristophon when he asked [the latter] if he would betray the fleet for money. After [Aristophon] denied it, [Iphicartes] said, 'If you, being Aristophon, would not play the traitor, would I, Iphicrates?'"* (1398a$_{6}$).

7. From definition.

From the correctness of a predicate of a *definiens*, one can reason to the correctness of the same predicate of the *definiendum*, or vice versa. Reasoning from p(A) to p(Def$_A$). Example: *"What is the divine? Is it not either a god or the work of a god? Still, whoever thinks it is the work of god must also think that gods exist"*[32] (1398a$_{16}$).

8. From multiple meanings of a word.

From the correctness of a predicate of a homonym, one can reason to the correctness of the same predicate of at least one of its meanings. Or, from the incorrectness of a predicate of one of the meanings, one can reason to the incorrectness of the predicate of the complete homonym.[33] Reasoning from p(x/y/z) to p(x or y or z), or reasoning from non-p(z) to non-p(x/y/z). Modern example: *"It is not true what you say that all flukes (=fish) make good meals, for who would like to eat a part of an anchor (=fluke)?"*

9. From division.

From the incorrectness of a predicate of any of the alternatives, one can reason by elimination to the incorrectness of the same predicate of the entire concept. Reasoning from non-p(a$_1$) and non-p(a$_2$) and non-p(a$_n$) to non-p(a). Example: "*All people do wrong for one of three reasons: either for this, or this, or this; now two of these are impossible, but even [the accusers] themselves do not assert the third*" (1398a$_{30}$).

10. From induction.

From a number of examples that have a certain quality and a predicate, one can reason to the correctness of the predicate of the present case which has the same quality. Reasoning from p(a$_1$) and p(a$_2$) and p(a$_3$) to p(a$_4$). Example: "*as Alcidamas [argued], that all honor the wise; at least, Parians honored Archilochus despite the nasty things he said [about them]; and Chians Homes, though he was not a citizen; and Mytilenaeans Sappho, although a women*" (1398b$_{10}$).

11. From previous judgment.

From the previous judgment of authorities worthy of admiration on the same or a similar or opposite case, one can reason to the truth of their statement. Reasoning from A claims p to p. Example: "*And as Isocrates wrote about Helen, that she was virtuous, since Theseus so judged*" (1399a$_1$).

12. From subordinate parts.

From the correctness of a predicate about a genus, one can reason to the correctness of the same predicate about at least one of its species. Reasoning from p(A) to p(a$_1$) or p(a$_2$) or p(a$_n$). Example: "*Against what holy place has he profaned? Which gods that the city recognizes has he not believed in?*" (1399a$_9$).

13. From consequences.

From the positive value of a consequence, one can reason to the positive value of its cause. Reasoning from p(consequence) to p(cause). Example: "*being envied is an evil result of being educated, but the wisdom [acquired] is a good thing; therefore, [it may be argued,] one should not be educated, for one ought not to be envied. On the other hand, one should be educated, for one ought to be wise*" (1399a$_{13}$).

14. From contrasting opposites.

From an action with two contrary alternatives, each of which has a positive and a negative consequence, one can reason either do engage in or to stay clear of this action. Example: "*a priestess did not allow her son to engage in public debate: 'For,' she said, 'if you say what is just, the people will hate you, but if what is unjust, the gods will. On the other hand, you should engage in public debate; for if you speak what is just, the gods will love you, if what is unjust, the people will'*" (1399a$_{21}$).

15. From hypocrisy.

In responding to a statement from an opponent whom one suspects of openly stating one thing but secretly supporting another, one might be well advised in using the opponent's professed statement as a starting point for alternative reasoning. A modern example can be found in Abraham Lincoln's letter to Joshua Speed: "*You say that if Kansas fairly votes herself a free state, as a Christian you will rather rejoice at it. All decent slave-holders talk that way, and I do not doubt their candor. But they never vote that way. Although in a private letter or conversation, you will express your preference that Kansas shall be free, you would vote for no man for Congress who would say the same thing publicly.*"

16. From consequences by analogy.

   From the absurd consequences of an analogue case, one can reason to the error in the present case. Reasoning from p' leads to c' and c' is bad, therefore p is bad. Example: *"when they tried to force his son who was underage to perform public services because he was tall, Iphicrates says that if they deem large boys men, they should vote that small men are boys"* (1399a$_{34}$).

17. From identity of results to identity of causes.

   From the identity of the results of two numerically different items, one can reason to the similarity or identity of the items. Reasoning from p leads to c and p' leads to c to p equals p'. Example: *"Xenophanes said that those who say that the gods are born are as impious as those who say that they die; for in both cases, the result is that at some time the gods do not exist"* (1399b$_6$).

18. From the inconsistency between choices at different times.

   From a previous opposing choice, one can reason to the error in the present choice. Reasoning from p(t$_1$) to not non-p(t$_2$). Example: *"[It would be terrible] if when in exile we fought to come home, but having come home we shall go into exile in order not to fight"* (1399b$_{16}$).

19. From identifying possible purpose with real cause.

   From a plausible purpose of a certain action, one could reason to this purpose being the real cause. Reasoning from p leads to c to c being the motivating cause of p. Example: *"God gives great good fortune to many, not out of good will, but so that the disasters people experience may be more obvious"* (1399b$_{22}$).

20. From incentives and deterrents.

   From the presence of incentives and the ability to do an action as well as from the absence of effective deterrents, one can reason to the action having been committed by the respective person. Reasoning from the motivation for p to the commitment of p. *Socrates cites as a deterrent to his having corrupted the youth intentionally that "if a man with whom I have to live is corrupted by me, I am very likely to be harmed by him"* (13).

21. From the implausible.

   From the fact that something is believed even though it is implausible, one can reason that it must then be true, because otherwise people would not believe what is implausible. Reasoning from implausibility of p together with popular belief in p to the truth of p. *See, for instance, the statement erroneously attributed to Hitler's aide, Dr. Goebbels: "Tell such a big lie that no one would believe you would dare to utter it unless it were true."*

22. From inconsistencies.

   From a contradiction between the statement of the opponents and his earlier words or actions, one can reason to the falseness of the statement. Reasoning from prior, stronger non-p to the falseness of the present p. Example: *"And he says I am litigious, but he cannot show that I have brought any case to be judged in court"* (1400a$_{19}$).

23. From explaining the cause of prejudice.

   By explaining the cause of a false impression, one can dissuade the audience from the wrong belief. Example: *"Odysseus tells Ajax why he [Odysseus] does not seem braver than Ajax, although he really is"* (1400a$_{28}$).

24. From cause to effect.

    From the presence or absence of a cause, one can reason to the presence of absence of its effect. Reasoning from p(c) to p(e). Example: *"when Leodamas was defending himself aginst Thrasybulus' charge that his name had been cut out [from the inscription] in the time of the Thirty [Tyrants], he said it was not possible; for the Thirty would have trusted him more if his hatred of democracy had remained inscribed"* ($1400a_{33}$).

25. From a better plan.

    From the existence of a better alternative than the discussed course of action for the person concerned, one can reason that the worse path has not been chosen by that person (unless the better alternatives were not known at the time) because no one willingly choses what is worse. Reasoning that p is worse than q (in the perception of the agent) to non-p. Modern example: *"Why do you believe I would have murdered him with a knife although I knew that he was much stronger than me and I had a gun at my disposal."*

26. From contrasting opposing actions.

    From the inconsistency of the consequences of two actions, one can reason to the inadvisability of at least one of them. Reasoning from p1 leads to c1 and p2 leads to c2 and c1 is inconsistent with c2 to either non-p1 or non-p2. Example: *"when the people of Elea asked Xenophanes if they should sacrifice and sing dirges to Leucothea or not, he advised them not to sing dirges if they regarded her as a god, and if as a human being not to sacrifice"* ($1400b_6$).

27. From past mistakes.

    Based on admittedly having committed (minor) mistakes one can build an accusation, or based on what would have been a mistake, one can build a defense. Example: *"some accuse her [Medea] on the ground that she killed her children. At any rate, they are not to be seen; for Medea made the mistake of sending the children away"* ($1400b_{10}$).

28. From the meaning of a name.

    From the meaning of a name that an agent carries, one can reason to that agent having (some of) the qualities expressed in the name. Reasoning from name (agent) to quality (agent). Example: *"and of Dracon the lawgiver that his laws were not those of a human being but of a drakon ['snake']"* ($1400b_{22}$).[34]

## E. Typical Forms for Fallacious Enthymemes (II₂₄)

These are *topoi* for utterances that appear to be enthymematic but really are not.

1. From deceptive uses of language: (a) stating a conclusion in the absence of sufficient proof [non sequitur] (b) to create a deceptive homonym. [fallacy of equivocation]
2. From attributing the characteristic of a part to the whole. [fallacy of composition]
3. From building up the horror of an action the fact being unproved.
4. From fallible sign. (He must have a fever since he's breathing rapidly.) [But he could have just finished running a race.]
5. From accident. Stressing a quality that is not relevant for the point in question.
6. From making the consequent convertible. If people that have one quality also have a second, one (still) cannot reason from the presence of the latter to the former.

7. From claiming what is not a cause to be the cause, especially when an event happens at the same time as another or follows another, since people often assume "after this, therefore because of this" [post hoc ergo propter hoc.]

8. From omitting the circumstances of time and manner. Generalizing what is true only under certain conditions for cases beyond those conditions.

9. And taking particular probability as universal generates an apparent enthymeme. Since improbable things do happen, what is improbable can be said to be probable. This is the case when the strong man accused of assaulting a weak one pleads that it is improbable he committed this crime since everyone would think it probable that he did it. (But what is universally probable is that strong men attack weaker, not the reverse. See the discussion of Corax and Tisias in Chapter 2.)

## F. Refutation of Enthymemes (II$_{25-26}$)

Refutation can be either by counter-argument or objection. It is by counter-argument when the speaker uses the foregoing *topoi* to draw opposite conclusions from those of his opponents. It is by objection when brought in any of the following ways: from redefining the original enthymeme so that it contradicts the opponent's conclusion, or by redefining a similar or related enthymeme so that the conclusion is contradicted, or from the contrary when it indicates a conclusion incompatible with the opponent's, or from the decision of some well-known person that indicates an opposite conclusion to the opponent's.

Enthymemes from probabilities are fallaciously refuted by bringing an exception to the rule as objection; if there were no exception, the premise would be certain, not probable. But no decision-maker should accept such refutation; the burden is on the refuter to show that the conclusion is not probable rather than that it is not necessary. Fallible signs are easily refuted by objection; infallible signs can only be refuted by denying the facts.

Neither amplification nor making a counter-argument or an objection should be considered a kind of *topos*; all of these processes must be accomplished by using *topoi* from the foregoing inventory.

It is difficult to know why Aristotle thinks that the list of formal *topoi* in II$_{23}$ yield valid enthymemes, while those in II$_{24}$ yield only fallacies. To be sure, some of the classical fallacies are listed in II$_{24}$: e.g., equivocation and *post hoc ergo propter hoc*. But are these any more fallacious than treating a conceivable cause as the actual cause as advised by *topos* 19? Or by punning on a name as in *topos* 28? Perhaps it's basically fallacious nature is the reason that while a pun on the name is common in ancient tragedy, it is, according to an authoritative Chicago researcher, not present at all in ancient Greek oratory.[35] And, is it universally more probable that the strong man will attack the weak one? Perhaps but perhaps not.

Aristotle's list of 28 *topoi* is, however, not just of interest by itself, but also as one of the earliest studies of modes of reasoning. While many of the divisions and hypotheses about fundamental aspects of persuasion in the *Rhetoric* have been largely confirmed by modern rhetorical research, Aristotle's collection of *topoi* has been developed significantly. Modern taxonomies of so called "argument schemes" take the same idea—to collect ways in which humans reason and persuade—but offer a considerably more systematic and complete approach that Aristotle's ad hoc list of *topoi* can.

With the remark that neither amplification nor refutation is a kind of *topos*, Aristotle concludes his treatment of invention, having made an inventory of the *topoi* that are specialized to the kinds of discourses and to the fields of ethics and politics and criminology, as well as those for building *ethos* and for the various *pathe* and for depicting the stock characters of humankind. He has also covered those kinds of *topoi* that provide basic forms for making enthymemes about any of the relevant subjects. A retrospective glance shows that this is his conception of the process of invention: the composer of a discourse invents by checking through an inventory or inventories of the stock lines of argument. They constitute the available means of persuasion that rhetoric examines in relation to the subject of any discourse. The inventory developed in these chapters is itself the proper exegesis of the celebrated definition of rhetoric ($I_2$). Throughout, Aristotle conceives of invention as a conscious choice from among a fixed stock of alternatives. He does not give a role to creative imagination and never mentions insight issuing from the unconscious in a dream or inspiration from on high. His word for invention, *heuresis*, or the English "heuristic," emphasizes examining alternatives rather than creating. This view of getting the right materials for the discourse is compatible with that of other ancient rhetoricians; it is however not fully compatible with the notion of rhetoric as inspired by Plato's *Ion*, or even by that implied by the second speech of Socrates in the *Phaedrus*.

Aristotle now turns to the other divisions of the art of rhetoric. Books I and II did not announce any treatment of delivery, style, and arrangement; they found no place in Aristotle's overview of rhetoric and are not necessarily implied by his definition. It has, therefore, been thought that Book III, in which these are the subjects, was originally a separate treatise that was added to the others by an early editor. The third book begins with some remarks on the delivery of speeches, which Aristotle connects closely with style.

## BOOK III

## V. Language of the Discourse—Style ($III_{1-12}$)

### A. Suggestions for a Treatise on Delivery ($III_1$)

Delivery has not yet been treated systematically. It has to do with the right management of the voice to express each of the *pathe*. The voice varies in volume, pitch, and rhythm. In a strict sense only the proofs constitute the art of rhetoric, but since rhetoric aims at appearances, delivery and style also need to be studied.

### B. Qualities of Style (Lexis) ($III_2$)

The two great virtues (*aretai*) of style are clarity and appropriateness. Clarity comes from choosing words easily defined by current usage. But enough words that are unusual should be chosen to impart a subtle air of strangeness to the discourse; otherwise it will lack dignity. And the discourse will seem inappropriate if young persons or persons speaking about trifling things use elevated language. Besides current terms the speaker should use some terms appropriate to specialized subjects and certainly metaphors as was stated in the *Poetics*.

## Metaphor (Poetics, xxii)

(Metaphor is the application to one thing of the name that belongs to another. It is of four kinds: the name of the genus applied to the species, of the species applied to the genus, of one species applied to another species, or proportionally among four terms where the second and fourth are interchangeable.)

## Simile (Eikon) (III₄)

Simile is a metaphor introduced by specific words of comparison [in English, "like" or "as"]. Since a simile is actually a metaphor differing only by addition of a word or two, what has been said of metaphor applies equally to simile.

## Appropriateness of Metaphor to a Speaker's Intentions (III₁)

Metaphor is even more important to prose than to verse, for prose has fewer resources. Above all, metaphors should correspond exactly to the thing expressed and to the intention of the speaker. If one means to disparage, he draws the metaphor from something worse in its class; to adorn, from something better. [Stealing and liberating are both species of taking. Troops in occupied territory say: "We liberated six bottles of wine."] Epithets [stock adjective formulas] may also be taken from the good or bad side of anything [blue sky or gray sky, depending on the rhetorical purpose of the speaker]. Diminutives can also be used to make a bad thing less bad or a good thing less good.

## Vices of Style (Frigidities) ta psychra (III₃)

Vices of style or frigidities result from the following: (1) over-compounding (e.g., the beggar-poet-toady); (2) use of archaic or dialect words [e.g., the dastardly criminal poltroon]; (3) overwriting with long, untimely, or crowded epithets (e.g., not laws, but laws, sovereigns of states); (4) inappropriate metaphors, either because they are too extravagant (e.g., Alkidamas called philosophy a "fortress against the laws") or too far-fetched [e.g., Emily Dickinson's moving conveyance, that neighing, stopped to feed itself by tanks, presumably the iron horse or train. This metaphor makes for interesting poetry where the reader may take pleasure in re-reading and puzzling it out; such metaphors do not serve the purpose of rhetoric, where persuasion demands language that is almost instantly intelligible].

## Clarity Derived From Correctness (III₅)

Right Hellenic usage is the foundation of good style. It is achieved by: (1) correct choice of conjunctions; (2) use of terms that accurately describe the subject of the discourse; (3) avoidance of ambiguous terms; (4) proper attention to gender and number; and (5) avoidance of solecism [e.g., he saw the birds in the trees singing loudly (trees do not sing)]. One should also avoid unnecessary embedding so that there are natural pauses in the line, and one can always tell what modifiers go with what nouns.

### Clarity Derived From Using Augmentation and Diminution (III₆)

It is often desirable to augment the weight of an utterance [to give it more presence] and sometimes also to diminish it. Describing something instead of naming it adds weight, naming instead of describing makes for conciseness. The right metaphors and epithets add weight, as does using the plural when literally the singular is intended. Also, using the article with each of two paired nouns, though only one use is required is augmentation. If one omits the article altogether it gives conciseness. The same comments apply to conjunctions: *polysyndeton* augments, *asyndeton* diminishes. One may also augment by taking time to describe by negation.

### Appropriateness of Style (III₇)

Style will be appropriate if it conveys the states of feeling (*pathe*), depicts characters (*ethe*), and is proportionate to the subject matter. But if a speaker goes too far, making his discourse similar in all these ways, the audience will distrust him: hence if his words are extremely harsh, either his voice or his features should be only moderately harsh.

Aristotle does not show much interest in delivery, probably because it is not a very philosophical subject. After stating that the art is undeveloped even in relation to poetry, he adds a basic principle that the speaker should manage the volume, rhythm, and pitch of his voice to express each of the *pathe*. Nothing is said about action, which is a little surprising considering its importance in dramatic presentations. Nor does he mention voice or action for the depiction of character. Yet he feels compelled to apologize for the little that is said, explaining that we have to attend to factors outside the art of rhetoric, which, strictly speaking, is restricted to proofs, only because of the depravity of the audience.

Aristotle reduces the *aretai* that serve as general criteria for judging style to two: clarity and appropriateness: language cannot achieve its function if it is not clear, and it will not persuade if it is not appropriate. Aristotle accomplishes this reduction by subsuming correct usage and giving weight to the discourse under clarity, but it is clear that these characteristics could stand independently as qualities of style. And, surprisingly, he does not mention forcefulness (*deinotes*), a quality dear to other rhetoricians.

### C. Composition Rhythm, Periodic Structure, and Figures of Syntax (III₈₋₉)—Rhythm (III₈)

The language of the discourse must be rhythmical but not metrical. Dactylic, spondaic, and trochaic rhythms are too clearly metrical: iambic, the rhythm of conversation, too undistinguished. The foot that one needs is one with an uneven ratio: this is the paeon, consisting of either one long foot and three short ones (/uuu) or three short feet and one long one (uuu/); the latter is particularly useful for making a cadence at the end of a period.

### The Period (III₉)

Style is either strung together like pearls on a necklace or tightly structured like strophe and antistrophe of a song. Structured style comes in periods. It is more satisfying than the strung-together style, because each unit can be counted and implies an answering unit moving toward a definite end. Periods are either divided into *cola* or simple, that is consisting of one *colon*. A divided period with its several *cola* is either coordinate [simple parallelism] or antithetical; periodic structure may be reinforced by *parison* and *paromoiosis*.

### D. Wittiness of Style (III$_{10-11}$)

Some of the elements previously listed when used together make for wittiness (or urbanity) of style (*ta asteia*). The general principle is: those devices that impart new knowledge quickly give the most pleasure.

### E. Metaphor is a Source of Wittiness (III$_{11}$)

Metaphor, especially that involving a little deception, imparts quick knowledge best; simile is only second best; a proverb is another kind of metaphor. Antithesis is also another source of wit. And an important source is vivid representation [*energeia*] or setting a thing before the hearer's eyes. Adlai Stevenson once said of Eleanor Roosevelt that, "she would rather light one candle than to curse the darkness." Puns are also witty. Hyperbole, like simile, is a common kind of metaphor, particularly characteristic of the young.

### F. Kinds of Style for the Three Kinds of Discourses (III$_{12}$)

Style must be appropriate to the discourse. Deliberative and forensic speeches assume an actual contest, so their style is agonistic; epideictic speeches are more literary. The agonistic style is more suited to delivery. The deliberative speaker paints in broad strokes and uses the most obvious rhetorical artifices; the forensic style is more finished, and the speaker makes a greater attempt at clarity of detail. The literary style is the clearest and most finished of all: an epideictic speaker excels at character portrayal; forensic speakers also portray character but excel at bringing the auditors into the proper states of feeling.

Aristotle was writing at a time of great transition from the oral, poetic style to the written, prose style. Aristotle's general statement that rhetorical style should be rhythmical but not metrical is probably a statement that reflects that transition. He is probably reacting to the poetic style of Gorgias and the prose style of Isocrates, and arguing that the speaker's style should approximate the mean between the two. His preference for the *paeon*, however, can only be justified for speeches in a language in which one can distinguish long and short syllables; most modern languages count meter by stressed and unstressed syllables, not by long and short ones. The division of style into loose or strung together versus periodic is historically important, constituting in traditional rhetoric a distinction between random and artistic composition. Artistic composition is done in parallel members (Aristotle's cola): in simple parallelism, e.g., Daniel Webster's "Union and liberty, now and forever, one and inseparable." Here are three members with their coordination reinforced by parallel stress and repetition of the conjunction "and." It is also done in a complex parallel or antithetical structure where the members double back on each other: e.g., John F. Kennedy's, "Ask not what your country can do for you, ask what you can do for your country." Here "your country" as actor in the first colon is in antithesis with "you" as actor in the second, while 'you' as receiver of the action in the first colon is balanced against "you" as actor in the second. This particular construction was known to later rhetoricians as *chiasmus* or *antimetabole*; Aristotle does not use these terms, but he would recognize the construction as one of several kinds of complex period.

Parallelism and antithesis are reinforced by *parison*, or approximate equality of the cola in their number of syllables and *paromoiosis*, or parallel similarity in sound. Consider Bill Clinton's remark that, "There will come a day when America is known for the power of its example rather than the example of its power." In Abraham Lincoln's address at Gettysburg, the initial sound echoes of each colon are reinforced by the end rhymes in the first two phrases of "We cannot dedicate, we cannot consecrate, we cannot hallow this ground." *Paromoiosis* of end rhymes, as in "dedicate" and "consecrate," is also called *homoioteleuton* by Aristotle: literally similar end. One is struck by the simplicity of this classification of devices of composition. Aristotle handles in five or six terms what later rhetoricians deal with in 20 or more.

Since Aristotle often reasons from the principle that humans by nature get pleasure from drawing inferences and acquiring knowledge (see I$_{11}$), it is not surprising that he finds the special effect of a good metaphor to be the joy of quick and easy learning. He especially recommends in the section on wittiness the metaphor that involves a little deception. In this case, the hearer expects something different from what he finally understands, and what he has learned is made plainer by the contrast to his false expectation. An Aristotelian example is: "an arbitrator and an altar are the same—for each is the refuge of injured innocence."

In his remarks on vivid representation of action (*energeia*), Aristotle recognizes that one of the most important functions of metaphor is to give animation to the inanimate. Most of his examples come from the Homeric epics: "Back toward the plain rolled the shameless stone" and "the arrow quivering with eagerness to fly to its mark." Animating metaphors such as these are striking, though sometimes such metaphors become so common that they pass unnoticed, e.g., "the neck of a bottle," "a head of lettuce," "the face of a mountain." But an animating metaphor never heard before has peculiar force and vividness.

Aristotle assumed that a unique style is appropriate to each of the three kinds of discourse. When he says that the deliberative speaker paints with broad strokes (like a scene painter) he has in mind a meeting of a large group, like the assembly at Athens, a large body of citizens; his comment might not apply to meetings of a subcommittee. The characterization of forensic speakers as always aiming at clarity, describes the practice of a court with legal requirements for proof, so that speakers must present coherent structures of facts and arguments. The literary finish that Aristotle claims for epideictic speeches grows out of the notion that auditors come to them as spectators to enjoy and critique.

The last major division of Aristotle's *Rhetoric* is concerned with the arrangement of speech.

## VI. Organization of the Discourse (III$_{13-19}$)

### A. Four Necessary Parts of the Discourse (III$_{13}$)

The necessary parts of the discourse are a simple statement of what is to be proved and the proof: there can be no proof without first making the statement and a statement without proof is obviously inadequate. The four-part division, proem, narrative statement, proof, and epilogue, is basically absurd (although we will use it); a narrative statement is useful only in forensic speeches; indeed, in the running debate of deliberative speaking one can even dispense with a proem and in some other speeches the epilogue. The height of absurdity is to set up such additional parts as a preliminary narrative, refutation, and supplementary refutation. At most one should divide into only the four parts: proem, statement of facts, proof, and epilogue.

## B. The Proem (III₁₄₋₁₅)

The proem of the epideictic speech can be irrelevant and loosely connected to the rest by a transition; it is ordinarily drawn from praise and blame but may be from premises proper to other kinds of speeches. The forensic proem must explain the object of the speech. All other proems have in common that they are drawn from materials related to either to the speaker, hearer, subject, or adversary. When the proems are related to speaker and adversary, they have as their end to rouse and dispel prejudice; when related to the hearer, to bring him into a state of feeling (enmity or friendliness) or to compel his attention; when related to the subject, to stress its importance to the interests of the hearers. In the proem one usually refutes prejudice either by explaining away suspicion about the cause in general, or saying that a deed was a mistake, misfortune or unavoidable, or that the prosecutor has also done misdeeds, or is untrustworthy, or is a habitual litigant, or the like. But the actual issues raised by the case must also be met [see Proofs]. The proem must signal the *telos* or end of speech.

## C. The Statement of Facts (III₁₆)

In epideictic speeches the narrative should be interspersed with the proof rather than continuous. The rule that it should be fast is absurd; it should hit the functional mean in speed as also in length. The narrative should depict one's character favorably; his opponent's unfavorably. It should also give details showing the moral character of the persons acting in it and showing them acting from conscious moral choice, either good or bad; and the people in it should be presented acting in the various states of feeling.

## D. The Proofs (III₁₇₋₁₈)

In a forensic speech the proofs will make a demonstration [i.e., a case] if they support the following four issues: that the accused did or did not commit an act, that the act was or was not harmful, that the harm was or was not substantial, and that the act was or was not criminal. Proofs will make a demonstration in a deliberative speech if they show that the consequences will or will not occur, or, on the negative side, that they will or will not be just if they occur, or will be advantageous or disadvantageous and significant or insignificant. Examples are more suited to deliberative speaking; enthymemes to forensic, since demonstration is more nearly possible for past fact. If at a loss for material to develop a deliberative speech, one borrows additional *topoi* from accusation and defense. If at a loss to develop an epideictic speech, he praises relatives of the subject of the speech or virtues in general.

Refutation is not a separate section from proof, since it is done with the same means as the rest of the proof: an objection is really a kind of example and a counter-argument a kind of enthymeme. Ordinarily constructive arguments come first, then refutation, but if an adversary's proofs have been overwhelming, then the obstacles to the auditors' accepting our proofs must be removed by refuting first. We will often put arguments that build good *ethos* into the mouth of some person other than ourselves.

### Cross-Examination (III₁₈)

Speakers cross-examine their adversaries when it is obvious that an admission has been made such that if another question is asked the absurdity of the adversary's position will seem complete, or when one premise is obvious and we can get the desired conclusion by asking the other as a question, or when there is an inconsistency to expose, or when our opponent must answer us with so many qualifications that he appears evasive. If one cannot accomplish one of these ends, he should not cross-examine. When we reply to cross-examination, we will make our opponent define his terms, and if we expect to contradict ourselves, explain the contradiction away even before he has a chance to make it clear to the decision-makers. If he phrases the conclusion of the argument as a question, we will append an explanation that weakens its force. Jokes may also be used to weaken the force of an opponent's arguments.

### E. The Epilogue (III₁₉)

Four elements comprise the epilogue: reinforcement of a favorable attitude to ourselves and an unfavorable one to our opponents, amplification of the significance of the facts that are favorable to us, reinforcement of the emotional states favorable to acceptance of our arguments and recapitulation of the arguments themselves. The speech can fittingly close with an *asyndeton*: "I have spoken; you have heard; you have the facts; judge."

The sophists usually organized their arts of rhetoric around systems of the parts of the speech: they started out with what to say in the proem, and prescriptions for the narrative statement and the rest, whereas Aristotle starts with putting rhetoric into its proper relation with the other branches of his works about logic (see I₁). Aristotle's critique of the practice of organizing the treatises around what should be done in each of the parts of the discourse echoes that of Plato in *Phaedrus*, 266–267. This critique would lead us to expect something like Plato's doctrine of the speech as an organism (see *Phaedrus*, 264). But no such doctrine is presented in the *Rhetoric*—in the *Poetics,* yes, but not in the *Rhetoric*. Instead we find the traditional system of parts criticized and then used, to be sure without the separate section on refutation, but still pretty much intact. Friedrich Solmsen once remarked that the last seven chapters of the *Rhetoric* constitute a little sophistic art that is superficially complete in itself and organized around a system of parts of the speech.[36] For each of the parts there are *topoi* from which proofs are drawn, e.g., the lines of argument for dispelling prejudice in the proem (III₁₅), the stock issues for forensic speeches (III₁₇). There are also remarks about style, such as that the narrative statement should hit the functional mean in length and speed, and in some section statements about arrangement, like the one that constructive proof precedes refutation except when the opponent's attack has been very strong (III$_{17}$). In this way some precepts not made within the broader framework of Aristotle's treatise are covered in a context familiar to students of rhetoric in his time.

In this section cross-examination is almost treated as a fifth part of the speech, one that would naturally come after constructive proofs and before the epilogue. This treatment reflects the practice of forensic speaking in the ancient courts: witnesses testified by deposition; it was the opponent who stood cross-examination at the end of the proof in an effort to lead him to confirm the speaker's conclusions from his own mouth. By contrast, in modern courts witnesses are the ones cross-examined in order to lay the basis for a closing statement that makes a final summation of proofs.

In the section on proof, Aristotle covers the issues that a speaker must meet to make his case, though it is remarkable that he says nothing about indicting the status quo. The deliberative speaker must meet four issues: that the consequences of the proposal will occur, that they will be substantial, and they will be advantageous, and they will be just. The forensic speaker must prove the act, that harm was done, that it was substantial, and that this harmful act can be defined as a crime. This section is important historically because it foreshadows the Hermagorean status system that dominated Latin rhetorics up to modern times.[37] Aristotle clearly believed that ordinarily a speaker should give an expanded epilogue rather than a brief concluding statement. The proofs should be reinforced and in some cases amplified, and the auditors should be drawn once again into the requisite *pathe*. A certain amplitude in the epilogue is required to do these things.

---

*We have seen that Aristotle's* Rhetoric *demands of the rhetor knowledges and capacities undreamed of by his predecessors like Gorgias and Plato. His so-called "definition" in I.2 proves to be no more than a summary of the demands he places on the rhetor; the Romans, as we are about to see, called this* facilitas, *or the rhetoric-ness of the speaker.*

*Even though the authority of Aristotle's great name gave a certain amount of influence to the* Rhetoric *in the history of this field, subsequent arts of rhetoric tend to carry on parts of his vision without accepting his whole message. For example, many carry on the distinction between inartistic and artistic proofs, that is between data and interpretation, much as Aristotle presented it. Later treatments of* ethos *are by no means as systematic as that of Aristotle, at least not until modern times, but most of them show his influence. His division of speeches into deliberative, forensic, and epideictic genres was universally adopted in later Roman rhetorics. The tradition of the* topoi, *or stock lines of argument, is also carried on, as are the basic forms of enthymemes and of fallacious enthymemes. Some of the fallacies in this latter list appear in logic textbooks even to this day. A large part of the presentation about goods and virtues as ends of deliberative and epideictic speaking reappears in later rhetorics also.*

*In two important aspects Aristotle's* Rhetoric *seems to have had little following among writers in that field. His detailed analysis of the* pathe *is not reproduced or developed by other rhetoricians: they ignore the systematic deductive scheme, starting with a definition of each* pathos *carefully framed, followed by a description of the kinds of persons prone to feel it, those apt to cause it, and the conditions under which it is felt. The overlooking of these chapters, lasting until the late Renaissance, is most surprising because they are among the most subtle and finished in Aristotle's treatise.*

*It is also the case that the connection of the enthymeme to a detailed system of formal logic was not much followed until the late Renaissance: it was remarked by logicians, but writers on rhetoric usually treated the enthymeme as if it were a device of style. Yet most modern students of rhetoric would now rank Aristotle's emphasis on the importance of the enthymeme and its connection to (formal) logic as his greatest single achievement in that study.*

*However, we are most concerned here with the influence of Aristotle and his* Rhetoric *on ancient writers, particularly those in the Hellenistic Period as we shall see in the next chapter, and in the Roman Period starting in the middle of the 2nd century BCE as we shall read about in Chapters 5 and 6. While Aristotle's influence on the Hellenistic Period is quite direct, his influence on the Roman rhetoricians Cicero and Quintilian is more indirect. Cicero studied in Athens and was familiar with some Aristotelian ideas. He may even have read the* Rhetoric. *The Roman educator Quintilian cites Aristotle more than 50 times in his landmark work on rhetorical education,* The Institutes of Oratory. *Both Cicero and Quintilian, however, drew their knowledge of rhetoric primarily from the Hellenistic writers whose system was formally adopted by the Romans in the late 2nd century BCE. It is to that critical period of transition that we now turn.*

# Chapter 4

# From Greek to "Roman" Rhetoric, with Synopses of Three Pragmatic Handbooks

I have omitted to treat those subjects which, for the sake of futile self-assertion, Greek writers have adopted.

Anonymous, *Rhetorica ad Herennium* (circa 86 BCE)

We turn now to the period between the two masterminds of classical rhetoric, Aristotle and Marcus Tullius Cicero. Aristotle died in 322 BCE, and some 220 years elapsed before the appearance of the first recognizably "Roman" treatises, Cicero's youthful *De Inventione* and the anonymous ("pseudo-Ciceronian") *Rhetorica ad Herennium* in the period 90–80 BCE.

What happened to ideas about rhetoric during that long period, and how did its practitioners move from the broad-based metarhetoric of Aristotle to the highly specific, pragmatic system that has come to be called "Roman" rhetoric?

We do know from numerous references that rhetorical textbooks were common from the earliest times. Isocrates is said to have composed a *techne* (handbook) now lost. Plato (*Phaedrus* 226) denigrates "the books that have been written about the art of speech." In fact even Aristotle himself complains (*Rhetoric* I.1354a) that "current treatises on rhetoric have constructed but a small portion of this art."[1]

It is a truism of book history that books used in classrooms are the least likely to survive, both because of heavy use and because of the low esteem accorded to "mere" handbooks.

It should not be surprising then, to find that with three notable exceptions the texts of the rhetorical handbooks of this long period have not survived, and the others are available to us only in fragments or in references made to them in existing texts. The influential ideas of Hermagoras (see below), for example, have had to be reconstructed from others' references because his own text has not survived. Nevertheless, the two and a half centuries between 340 BCE and 90 BCE contain some rhetorical treasures that can teach us important lessons about the art of speaking. Anaximenes of Lampsacus and Hermagoras of Temnos, for example, left a lasting impression on the discipline. This period also sees the downfall of Greek influence after the battle at Chaeronea in 338 BCE and the rise of the Roman republic as the main political power of the Mediterranean region and beyond. Since rhetoric flourishes best under conditions of democratic decision-making paired with civic changes, it comes as no surprise that the epicenter of rhetorical theory also shifts from Athens to Rome during this time.

The three major surviving handbooks of this period are the Greek *Rhetorica ad Alexandrum*, written by a contemporary of Aristotle, and two Latin school-influenced works written centuries later, the *Rhetorica ad Herennium* by an anonymous author, and the ambitious *De Inventione* composed as the first of a projected five books about rhetoric by the young Marcus Tullius Cicero.

What these three works can offer us much better than their more famous counterparts is an insight into the rhetorical practice of their times. They are written for the average student, not for the rhetorical expert. They avoid all unnecessary philosophical, ethical, or psychological reflections that are not immediately useful for the student, and give clear and simple (sometimes too simple) rules about how to structure a speech, how to find an argument, and how to respond to common rhetorical situations. As one modern observer has noted, "A deliberative speaker would find more practically useful advice in the *Rhetorica ad Alexandrum* than in Aristotle's excessively schematized *a priori* construction."[2]

## Rhetorica ad Alexandrum (about 340 BCE)

The *Rhetorica ad Alexandrum* is at least as interesting for what it is as for what it is not: it is not one of the philosophically reflective and masterful works of Aristotle.[3] Instead, what we can find in the *Rhetorica ad Alexandrum* is a clear account of the standard textbook tradition, one that is similar to the rhetorical teachings that were sharply criticized by Plato (in his *Gorgias* and *Phaedrus*), Aristotle, and Isocrates. The *Rhetorica ad Alexandrum*, or "Rhetoric to Alexander," owes its name to a spurious letter that was attached to it in later centuries, dedicating the book to Alexander the Great, son of Philip of Macedon and student of Aristotle. This letter and the false classification of the *Rhetorica ad Alexandrum* as one of Aristotle's works is most likely the only reason why the treatise survived through the Middle Ages.[4] In the time before the invention of the printing press, copying and thereby preserving a book took an enormous effort and hundreds of hours of writing by hand. Accordingly, it led to a careful selection of works that were deemed worthy over others that were abandoned and not copied. This selection often favored the writings of famous individuals and it is also responsible for the fact that the vast majority of Greek speeches that have been preserved were created by only ten men—the ten canonical "Attic" orators. The *Rhetorica ad Alexandrum* is not the only example of an important rhetorical textbook that was preserved by virtue of being attributed to a famous author, one of the others being the *Rhetorica ad Herennium* in the "Ciceronian" corpus, as we shall see below.

Actually, due to references in Quintilian's *Institutio oratoria* (see Chapter 6), we now believe that *Rhetorica ad Alexandrum* was written by Anaxamines of Lampsacus, another teacher of Alexander.

The *Rhetorica ad Alexandrum* was written during Aristotle's lifetime, around 340 BCE.[5] The last event that is mentioned in the book is 341 BCE. At this time, some of the most important elements of the later Roman handbooks had not been fully developed yet or at least not come to prominence in the rhetorical literature. Among them is *stasis* theory, a model of legal defense that fills up a significant part of the *Rhetorica ad Herennium*, Cicero's *De Inventione*, and Quintilian's *Institutio Oratoria*. Even more importantly, the model of the *officia oratoris*, the tasks that an orator has to go through while preparing his speech, plays no significant role yet. Accordingly, while some of the contents concerning speech organization and rhetorical devices overlap, the structure of the entire book differs significantly from later handbooks.[6]

The following synopsis gives an overview over the structure of the *Rhetorica ad Alexandrum* and its main contents.

## Synopsis of the *Rhetorica ad Alexandrum*

Introductory letter
(Spurious) dedication to Alexander. On the importance of reasoning and rhetoric as
    well as miscellaneous advice about life and politics.

### *Part I – The kinds of oratory*

*(1) Speech genres and general arguments*
    There are three speech genres: political, ceremonial, and forensic. They fall into seven species:[7] exhortation and dissuasion, praise and blame, accusation and defense, and investigation. The main aspects of political speeches include justice, legality, expediency, honor, facility, pleasure, practicability, and necessity. Reasoning can be developed by analogy and the use of kinds of opposites.

*(2) Political speeches*
    Political speeches must have as their main topic one of the seven: religious ritual, legislation, the constitution, alliances and treatises, war, peace or finance. Each of the seven can be developed with help of the seven aspects above and general stock arguments. Advice about just laws in different forms of government.

*(3) Ceremonial speeches*
    Speeches of praise or blame must amplify virtues and marginalize vice (or vice versa). Praiseworthy objects are what is just, lawful, expedient, noble, pleasant, or easy. Ways of amplification include presentation based on: the results, authoritative judgment, comparisons, the opposite, and the intentions of the person.

*(4) Forensic speeches*
    In accusing, one must show that the act was breaking a law and caused harm. The former is crucial for laws with fixed punishments, the latter for flexible punishment. A defense of lack of intent can be anticipated. The defendant must show that either he did not commit the act, or that he was justified, or plead forgiveness based on error or misfortune.[8]

*(5) Investigations[9]*
    The aim of the investigation is to find inconsistencies and contradictions within the opponent's speech or between the speech and the orator's actions or intentions, or between any other aspect of the opponent's life and conduct.

### *Part II – General proofs and figures of speech*

*(6) Rhetorical techniques as they apply to speech genres*
    The main aspects (expedience, honor, etc.) are most important in political speeches. Amplification and minimization are especially useful for ceremonial speeches. Proofs (*pisteis*) are central for forensic speeches. Additional techniques apply to all speech genres similarly.

*(7)  Probabilities*

There are two groups of proof, direct and supplementary. Direct proofs include a) probability (*eikos*), b) example (*paradeigma*), c) indication of inconsistency (*tekmerion*), d) enthymeme (*enthymema*), e) maxim (*gnome*), f) sign (*semeion*), and g) irrefutable direct proof (*elenchos*).[10] Supplementary proofs consist of a) opinion of the speaker, b) witness evidence, c) evidence under torture, and d) oath. Arguments based on probabilities can be derived from common emotions, customs, or motivation of profit. They can be employed by the accusing side and must be refuted by the defense. Arguments based on probability are also useful for other speech genres.

*(8)  Examples*

There are two types of examples, those illustrating the common expectations and those running against them. The former strengthen probable argumentation, the latter show that it is not fully reliable. Depending on the speaker's intention either can be a useful way of reminding the audience of the evidence provided by the past.

*(9)  Indications of inconsistency*

Indications of inconsistency are infallible signs that contradict the reasoning of the opponent and thus attack his credibility.

*(10)  Enthymemes*

Enthymemes are concise statements that point out an inconsistency or tension between the speech and actions, or motivations if one attacks the opponent. They can also be employed for one's own speech by showing that the speech is contrary to negative values. Enthymemes can be obtained with the techniques introduced in the chapter on investigations.

*(11)  Maxims*

Maxims are memorable expressions about general matters of conduct. To construct such a point the orator should analyze the particular nature of the case, or use a hyperbole, or consider a parallel.

*(12)  Signs*

A sign is an indication that something will happen, has happened, or is about to happen. Signs can also be used as indicators of varying strengths for the absence of something that would have brought about the sign in question.

*(13)  Irrefutable direct proof*

A irrefutable direct proof is a non-defensible statement that points out an inconsistency in the opponent's claim or else demonstrates a necessary truth that requires no further argument.

*(14)  Differences between various kinds of direct proof/supplementary proofs*

Probabilities are previously familiar to the audience, examples are newly introduced. Enthymemes can be produced from more sources than just word and deed. Signs produce clearer knowledge in the hearers than most other proofs, irrefutable direct proof teaches the judges the truth.

The first form of supplementary proofs is the speaker's opinion. A speaker can use his own authority as a proof in personally supporting a claim and pointing out that he has experience in the topic and an incentive to speak the truth.

*(15)  Voluntary evidence*

Favorable evidence from voluntary testimony can be amplified by pointing out the plausibility of the statement and the credibility of the person. Unfavorable evidence can be attacked based on the content and on the person, by showing that the person might have ulterior motives or is otherwise untrustworthy.

*(16) Evidence under torture*

*Topoi* (i.e., common lines of argument) in favor of the credibility of a statement made under torture include the argument, that people who are tortured tell the truth immediately to stop the pain. *Topoi* against include arguments based on the hostility of tortured slaves towards their masters and their willingness to confess anything to end the torture.

*(17) Evidence under oath*

The fourth kind of supplementary proofs is testimony with an appeal to the gods. A *topos* in favor of the credibility of testimony under oath is the fear of the witness to be punished by the gods for perjury. A *topos* against is the ruthlessness of a criminal mind that will fear neither gods nor men.

*(18) Anticipation (prokatalepsis)*

In political speeches the orator can reduce the resistance of the audience by offering reasons why he has the right and duty to offer counsel on the topic at hand. In speeches of defense the orator can use similar arguments and additionally point to the importance of hearing both sides in a fair trial.

Anticipating the opponent's arguments before his speech takes away their novelty and some of their strengths and allows one to misrepresent them. In defense against anticipations the orator can clarify and must insist of giving an unaltered perspective.

*(19) Postulation (aitema)*

The speaker can demand agreement from the audience on some basic premises if they are in accordance with the law or reasonable procedure. He must be attentive to his opponent if unjust postulates are presented and rebut them.

*(20) Recapitulation*

At the end of both a section of the speech and the entire speech the orator should remind his audience of the main points, by either calculating the results or enumerating his main arguments, or making a proposal, or posing a question.

*(21) Irony*

Irony can be used either in the form of pretending to pass over an aspect while thereby mentioning it[11] or by using one term while actually meaning its opposite.

*(22) Style and length of a speech*

Virtues of style include enthymemes in which the audience fills in part of the thought, maxims, and word variety. Adding divisions and internal summaries can lengthen speeches. They can be shortened with the help of a careful wording and concise grammatical structures.

*(23) Word arrangement*

Words can be simple, compound, or metaphorical. They can be linked in different ways, especially concerning the beginning and ending of words on a vowel or a consonant.

*(24) Twofold statements*

Statements can be brought into juxtapositions with each other to form twofold statements that are set parallel or in opposition to each other. There are six varieties of these combinations.

*(25) Clarity*

Clarity can be achieved by using the proper terms for all entities and by avoiding ambiguities on the word or sentence level. Introducing grammatical markers can help the audience to understand the speech more easily. If homonyms are unavoidable they must be accompanied by other expressions to make the intended meaning clear.

*(26) Antithesis*

Sentences can be antithetical in wording or meaning or both. Antitheses consisting of terminological and content opposites are the strongest, but the single options are also useful.

*(27) Parisosis*

Parisosis is a parallelism in sentence structure where two parts of the sentence are metrically equal to each other and thus produce a figure that is comparable but not as strong as antithesis.

*(28) Paromoeosis*

Paromoeosis is a parallelism in sound produced by choosing similar syllables in different word. By not only providing a harmonic metric, but also elements of rhyme it is a stronger variety of parisosis.

This concludes the explanation of the main aspects of the speech and their sources as well as general proofs and stylistic devices. The next section will be devoted to structure of speeches in the different rhetorical genres, starting with the introduction, which is similar in all genres.

### Part III – Speech structure and special considerations in each genre

*(29) Introduction (Prooimion) in political speeches[12]*

The main purpose of the introduction is to gain attention and good will from the audience. Attention is gained mainly through exposing the main topic in the light of an important aspect. Good will can be taken for granted with a favorable audience. In an indifferent audience it must be amplified by flattery and by reminding them of the importance of hearing advice. A hostile audience must be persuaded that the hostility toward the person or the proposition is unwarranted or has no bearing on the case at hand. Prejudices against the speaker based on his age or the frequency of his speeches can be reduced with reference to the importance of the topic.

*(30) Narrative*

The narrative of past events must be clear, concise, and convincing. This can be achieved by presenting the events in chronological order and by employing precise and adequate wording. Depending on the success or failure of a past activity the orator must emphasize or minimize the part he himself played in the event.

*(31) Arrangement of narrative*

Depending on the size of the exposition and the knowledge of the audience, the narrative can be either included in the introduction or attached to it, or presented as an independent section of the speech.

*(32) Confirmation*

The confirmation section in political speeches uses the kinds of proof already discussed, especially the customary course of events, examples, considerations, and speaker's opinion. If the individual facts do not need to be supported then the orator can directly proceed to showing that the proposal is just, lawful, expedient, honorable, pleasant, easy, practicable, and necessary—in that order.

*(33) Anticipation*

In anticipating his opponent's arguments the orator makes use of amplification and matches one or more of his own arguments with the anticipated points such that they are outweighed.

*(34) Emotional appeal*

If possible the orator should incite the audience to feel gratitude, compassion, friendship, or similar emotions toward the author of a proposal or the opposite to his opponent.

*(35) Structure of ceremonial speeches*

The introduction of speeches of praise or blame is similar to political introductions. The body of a praise contains a narrative of the person praised, outlining his or her external goods and virtues. Goods external to virtue include high birth, strength, beauty, and wealth. Virtues include wisdom, justice, courage, and temperance. Vituperations are constructed along the same topics but with a negative orientation. Ceremonial speeches should be delivered in a dignified style.

*(36) Structure of forensic speeches*

The structure of the introduction in speeches of accusation and defense is similar to political speeches. Beyond gaining the audience's attention a speaker should, depending on his side, arouse or diminish the prejudices against his client by anticipating the opponent and shifting the blame for the case on him. The narrative in an accusation also follows rules similar to political oratory. Next follows the confirmation employing the forms of proof outlined earlier, beginning with testimonies. The final sections are an anticipation of the defender's possible lines and a brief recapitulation including emotional appeals. The structure of speeches of defense is similar to accusations. A defense should end with an appeal to compassion for the accused and incite adverse feelings for the accuser.

*(37) Structure of investigational speeches*

Examinational oratory consists of an introduction, preparing for a benevolent reception by the audience; second, the examination of the words, life, or conduct of a person or administration; finally a brief conclusion. The tone of an examination should be mild for optimal oratorical effect.

*(38) Miscellaneous*

Oratorical success is the consequence not only of adhering to the rhetorical rules, but also the result of proper conduct in one's personal and public life.

The *Rhetorica ad Alexandrum* gives very valuable insight into the practical rhetoric of the 4th century BCE. Its instructions lack the sophistication of Aristotle's rhetoric and are partially tied to the necessities of the time, but they are easily accessible and include many observations that remain useful for the modern speaker.

## Hermagoras of Temnos

Rhetoric is a decidedly practical art. It flourishes when it is needed and it decays in times of great stability, such as lasting monarchies or tyrannies. It comes as little surprise that many of the greatest rhetoricians lived in times and places with heavy political struggles, either within democracies or between democracies and rising dictatorships. This is true of ancient rhetoric for the sophists in 5th century Greece, Aristotle and Anaximenes in 4th century Greece, and Cicero and the Auctor ad Herennium in 1st century Rome, as well as the modern rhetoric of Chaim Perelman and Lucie Obrechts-Tyteca and Kenneth Burke in Europe and North America. During these times, political rhetoric tends to hold the highest esteem within the rhetorical genres because its implications affect the most people.

The time following Alexander's rise and the downfall of the Greek city-states does not present these kinds of opportunities for political rhetoric. Instead, the attention shifts to more detailed questions in poetics and style and most notably to forensic rhetoric. The most influential rhetorician of the 2nd century BCE is Hermagoras of Temnos. His work reflects precisely this shift, and the advances he made to rhetorical theory are mostly situated in the forensic genre of accusation and defense. Other than his birthplace, little is known of the man himself. Unfortunately, his work also did not survive. His main theory—the theory of stasis—has been reconstructed from fragments and testimonies. Due to the diligent work, mainly of two German scholars during the 1950s and 1960s, Dieter Matthes and Karl Barwick,[13] who compared all references to Hermagoras in the works of Cicero, the Auctor ad Herennium, Quintilian and (Pseudo-)Augustine (as well as many others) with surviving fragments, we now have a fairly clear understanding of his stasis model.

Stasis theory is a method of finding the vital issues in a rhetorical disagreement involving a penal norm. The term "stasis" derives from the Greek word for "stand" or "standstill." According to legend, this term was chosen with reference to the stance boxers would assume at the beginning of a competition before engaging with the opponent. There are clear traces of early stasis theory in the oratorical praxis of Antiphon and Gorgias as well as the rhetorical theories of Aristotle and Anaximenes.[14] Accordingly, Hermagoras did not create his model *ex nihilo* (as was long believed by rhetorical scholars), but he did polish it and brought it to a new level of complexity. After him, stasis theory has been one of the backbones of rhetorical invention in nearly all important classical rhetorical textbooks.

Classical stasis theory implicitly rests on the fact that rhetorical disagreements in the *genus iudiciale*, or forensic genre, differ from the other two *genera* (deliberative and epideictic) with respect to the uneven distribution of the burden of proof of the opponent.[15] This distinction manifests itself in the presumption of innocence of the accused. Because the defendant can make use of this presumption, the accuser has to prove a variety of sub-standpoints in order to be successful. These sub-standpoints of issues are expressed in the stasis model. From the point of view of the defendant this means that there is a menu of alternative defense strategies that can be employed. In classical stasis theory there is no clear distinction between vital issues that are sufficient for the complete defense against the accusation and non-vital issues that lead to a mere delay of the case or reduction of the punishment, nevertheless understanding the model can be very useful for the accuser and defender as well as for the judge or critic who needs to make a decision about the merits of the case. Finally although classical stasis theory was developed for courtroom rhetoric,[16] its usefulness expands beyond legal accusations into moral conflicts.

## Hermagoras' Stasis Model

The model Hermagoras developed is a rather complex system of issues with multiple layers of subdivisions. Within the model, Hermagoras shows a clear preference for divisions of four. Accordingly, at the top level of the stasis model proper (not counting the legal questions) there are four main issues: issues of fact (stochasmos), issues of definition (horos), issues of quality (poiotes), and issues of competence or legal process (metalepsis). The third issue, quality, divides into four sections that most likely address the four ends of the speaker: expediency, honor, justice, and practicability. Of these justice (dikaiologike) falls into two kinds of issues: complete justification (antilepsis) and incomplete justification (antithesis). The latter finally contains four more issues that complete the system. By adding the four legal questions that are concerned with the interpretation of norms and norm systems, the model illustrated by Figure 4.1 is reached.

This model thus consists of eight rational staseis and four legal staseis. A stasis, or central issue of the case, is largely determined by the choice of the defender. Hermagoras and later theorists presented a sophisticated method of judging the issue at hand based on the first turns of an accusation and defense. An attentive listener or participant will, however, easily recognize the main issue without such an instrument.

From a defender's point of view there are accordingly eight "stances" that can be taken individually, combined, or consecutively, illustrated for the example of a murder accusation, these are as follows:

1.  Issue of fact (*stochasmos*)—Did the accused commit the act?
    The first issue materializes if the accused denies a direct involvement with the act outright, by stating that the act has not been committed by anyone or at least not by the accused.
    *Example: I did not murder the victim. At the time of her death I wasn't even in the same city.*
2.  Issue of definition (*horos*)—Has the act been defined correctly?
    In this issue the defender attempts to redefine the act so that it is no longer covered by the relevant law. If successful this will lead to an accusation under a lesser law or a complete acquittal (if there is no other law under which the redefined act can be subsumed).
    *Example: I might have killed her, but I certainly did not act with malice or premeditation so it could not have been a murder such as I am accused of.*
3.  Issue of justification (*antilepsis*)—Are there other laws in the same norm system that cancel the broken law?
    This issue contains cases of full justification of the act. The kinds of justification that can be used depends on the norm system in question. The most famous justification is the killing of a tyrant to save the country.
    *Example: Yes, I killed him. I did it to protect the state and to rid the country of a dictator.*
4.  Issue of collision of duties (*antistasis*)—Did the accused have any alternative that would not have led to a similar or even graver transgression?
    A defense in this issue invokes a legal dilemma for the accused. While this does not necessarily justify the act, it usually at least excuses the accused who has no

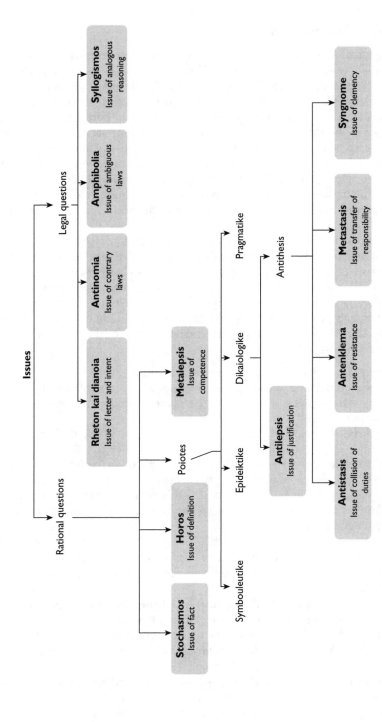

*Figure 4.1* Hermagoras stasis diagram

malignant intent and no better option that would not have broken a law. There is a smooth transition between this and the preceding issue.

*Example: Yes, I killed him by closing the floodgates, but only in order to save many others who would otherwise certainly have died.*

5. Issue of resistance (*antenklema*)—Could the accused be expected to act in accordance with the original law after the victim changed the legal situation?

In this issue the defendant transfers the guilt for the act onto the victim of the transgression. The most typical case of this issue is the claim to self-defense or defense of others against an imminent attack.

*Example: Yes, I killed him. What else was I to do after he drew the knife on me and threatened to stab me?*

6. Issue of transfer of responsibility (*metastasis*)—Could the accused be expected to act in accordance with the original law after a third party changed the legal situation?

This issue differs from the preceding one in that it transfers the responsibility not onto the victim but onto a third party.

*Example: Yes, I killed him. I acted under direct military orders and had no information about the circumstances.*

7. Issue of clemency (*syngnome*)—Are there mitigating circumstances that make the act of the accused a less grave transgression?

This is undoubtedly the weakest defense in the model. If the accused has no other options then the final resort is an apology and a request for leniency.

*Example: I did not mean to kill her. I am terribly sorry, I was in a rage and I did not know what I was doing. I wish I could undo my deeds.*

8. Issue of competence (*metalepsis*)—Are the accuser and judges competent to move the case forward at this time and place?

This issue differs from all preceding staseis by not attempting to show that the accused is not guilty (or at least should not be punished as harshly), but rather by preventing the accusation from even going forward. If successful, a defense in the issue of competence averts the entire process without even engaging in questions of guilt. Contrary to its position in most stasis models this put the stasis of metalepsis logically prior to all other issues.

*Example: Whether or not I killed her, the incident happened in another country so you have no right to judge over me.*

The four legal questions do not supply an independent basis for a defense against an accusation. Their purpose is comparatively more modest and centers on providing different angles to interpret the norm. Even if the defendant is successful in interpreting the norm in a beneficial way for the case at hand, he or she will still need to use one of the rational issues to complete the defense. The four legal questions provide argumentative starting points in cases where the intention of the author of the document clearly differs from the actual wording of the text (*rheton kai dianoia*), in cases of conflicting laws (*antinomia*), in cases of ambiguous phrasing with a law (*amphibolia*), and in cases where there is no law that directly applies, but the possibility of invoking an analogous norm (*syllogismos*) which does. Hermagoras also provides a list of four types of cases that are incapable of a rational solution (*asystaton*), but these seem rather artificial and of little value to the modern user.

One of the great strengths of the stasis model as designed by Hermagoras and revised by later rhetoricians is that it is not systematically limited to courthouse rhetoric but can serve in everyday discourse as well. Whenever there is an accusation of any kind the same system of defense options applies.

Classical stasis theory thus reveals a quality that is representative for classical rhetoric as a whole. Beyond a thin layer of seemingly complicated terminology and instruction it contains concepts that can be very useful for a better understanding of contemporary discourse and effective participation in public or private deliberation.

## Early Roman Rhetoric

Rhetoric in Rome developed under very different conditions compared to Greek rhetoric. Not only did the Romans have access to much of the Greek writings, but they also lived in a very different culture. When trying to grasp something so complex as an entire culture of a large state it is very easy to oversimplify matters. There were of course huge distinctions between various Greek city-states and within the Roman republic. Even acknowledging these internal differences, there are some obvious cultural paradigms that distinguish 5th and 4th century Greece from 2nd and 1st century Rome. The most obvious of these paradigms is the Greek appreciation of the *agon*— the playful or serious competition—in many fields of society ranging from sports (including the Olympic Games) to oratory to politics. It is this appreciation for the *agon* that allows rhetoricians like Gorgias and Isocrates to engage in a playful praise of one of the most despised historical figures: Helen of Troy. It also forms the background of many of Plato's dialogues and the teachings of the sophists, including Protagoras' famous saying that he could make the better case appear to be the worse. A second important aspect of Greek culture that is not shared on a comparable level by the Romans is the value given to the freedom of speech. Athens in particular was known to grant a very large amount of *parrhesia*—freedom to say almost anything— to its citizens. This concept and the related *isegoria*—literally: free access to the podium—were criticized by some of the more conservative Greek intellectuals, including Isocrates, Plato, and Xenophon, for being exaggerated beyond good judgment. At its core, however, it was an integral part of Athenian culture that provided an important foundation for the free development of oratory and rhetoric. While there is some appreciation for freedom of speech in Rome, the dominant paradigm is less open and playful and more influenced by the ethos of male integrity and loyalty that is fitting for a heavily militarized society. One episode in the 2nd century BCE illustrates this difference quite clearly. In 161 and 155 two philosophical envoys traveled from Greece to Rome. The latter included the famous philosophers Carneades, Critolaus, and Diogenes. As part of their presentation the philosophers gave public lectures. Following the agonistic spirit, one of the lectures consisted in praising justice on one day as a virtue and in the following day attacking it. Far from appreciating this pair of lectures as an attempt to expose the full scope of the concept and engage the audience in their own thoughts, it instead led to a movement for the expulsion of the entire envoy.

Very little of the Roman oratory of the early republic is preserved and the earliest complete rhetorical textbooks that survived are the *Rhetorica ad Herennium* and Cicero's *De Inventione* from the early 1st century BCE. Some fragments are still extant and the person who probably best embodies 2nd century Roman oratory and rhetoric is Marcus Porcius Cato.

## Cato the Elder

Marcus Porcius Cato—or Cato the censor, named after one of the high offices he reached in the republic—perfectly embodies the pre-Ciceronian Roman attitude to rhetoric. He was known to be a very skilled orator and some fragments of his speeches still survive. He probably even wrote a small collection of rhetorical rules. Yet he advises his son Marcus firmly against studying too much of the Greek theory. Among the instructions he left for his son are two that are particularly interesting. The first, *"rem tene, verba sequentur"*—"know the material and the words will follow," expresses one of the key reservations that have been leveled against rhetoric: if you are only competent enough in the topic itself, then you do not need the artificial tools that the rhetorical art can teach you. It expresses the sentiment of an arch conservative man in an already conservative society. Cato is well known for many sentiments that would seem strange in a modern culture. Decades of students of Latin have learned his *"ceterum censeo Carthaginem esse delendam"*, the sentence that demands the total destruction of Carthage, the opponent of Rome in the Punic wars, with which he is said to have ended every speech. Other anecdotes about him include an episode where he used his office of censor to expel a Roman senator from the senate for kissing his wife in public in front of his daughter and the publication of a book in which Cato laments the decline of domestic violence because it leads to a lack of authority of the husband. Nevertheless the statement itself—stick to the materials and the words will follow—is as current in modern culture as it is false. Ancient and modern history is full of people who have been experts in their field but were unable to express themselves persuasively and thus failed to gain the assent of the public. It might accordingly even be said, against Cato, that a person who has knowledge and cares about society has the ethical duty to learn to express the knowledge in a persuasive manner to the benefit of others.

The second quotation that won Cato a lasting fame among rhetoricians is his definition of the orator: *"Orator est, Marce fili, vir bonus, dicendi peritus"*—"An orator is, dear son Marcus, a good man speaking well." This definition is noteworthy for the clear expression of a moral category with the description of an orator. In other words, only a *vir bonus*, a good man, can ever be judged to be a worthy speaker. The question about the relationship of rhetoric and ethics is a lot older than Cato. Plato already raises it in his dialogue *Gorgias*, when he lets Socrates ask Gorgias whether he would accept a rhetorical student who was lacking in moral fiber. Gorgias answers that "Yes, he would, but he would also teach him the morals he needed." This answer is revoked later in the dialogue and the underlying question remains. Cicero and Quintilian later pick up the notion of Cato's *vir bonus* and develop it into a central concept of their rhetorical theory. There is a slight historical irony to using Cato's definition as the starting point of this question in rhetorical theory. Elevating the *vir bonus* concept into a rhetorical idea suggests that there is something special about the rhetorical skills that make them so powerful that they must be accompanied by moral instruction or else may only be taught to an upstanding citizen. Yet, this is probably not what Cato had in mind. He seems to rather focus on a general appeal to the Roman citizenry that is not limited to rhetoric, but expands into all crafts as shown in his definition of a farmer as a *"vir bonus [...], colendi peritus, cuius ferramenta splendent"*—"a good man, plowing well, whose tools are shining."

## Marcus Antonius and Lucius Licinius Crassus

The best bridge between the eloquent but professedly anti-rhetorical Cato and the exceedingly eloquent and openly pro-rhetorical Cicero is provided by two of the protagonists of Cicero's *De Oratore*: Marcus Antonius and Lucius Licinius Crassus. While *De Oratore* is one of Cicero's late rhetorical works, its dramatic date is set at 91 BCE, which is at the height of the influence and political activity of the historical Antonius and Crassus.

Marcus Antonius, the grandfather of the triumvir Mark Antony, was consul in 99 BCE, influential statesman and one of the most accomplished orators of his time. Cicero and later authors mention that Antonius had written a short rhetorical treatise, but unfortunately once again this text has not survived and we are limited to very few fragments. One of these fragments mentions a rudimentary tripartite stasis theory that is similar to the one later found in the *Rhetorica ad Herennium*. Perhaps even more interesting than this fragment is a sentiment that Cicero's Antonius expresses in *De Oratore* (II, 153) and which probably coincides with the belief of the historical Antonius: in order to be successful in front of an audience an orator must appear as natural and as ignorant of the rhetorical art as possible. This *dissimulatio artis* (hiding of the art) is one of the single most important precepts of ancient rhetoric and at the same time one of the most tempting to neglect. It puts the highly skilled orator into a paradox: adhere to this rule and hide your art but be unable to shine for your true skills or be more effective but appear merely lucky and in support of an obviously easy case. If the historical Antonius followed this rule as much as Cicero has us believe then he provides a good testimony for the oratorical success that can result. Contrary to many of his contemporary orators Antonius did not publish his speeches because he did not want to open himself up to a charge of inconsistency, but the few fragments that have survived, such as his defense of Norbanus, show him as a supremely effective orator.

The other protagonist of *De Oratore*, Lucius Licinius Crassus, was also hugely successful both as a statesman (consul in 95 BCE and censor in 92 BCE) and as an orator. He was well known as a very thorough and well-educated speaker and maybe best remembered for his role in the *causa Curiana*, an inheritance case. Cicero describes this famous court case as the battle between the lawyer most skilled in rhetoric (Scaevola) against the orator most skilled in law (Crassus)[17] and thereby also provides a landmark in the slow drifting apart of two disciplines that used to be one. In the *causa Curiana* the orator prevailed and with him a very nice example of a plea for the spirit of the law against the literal interpretation.[18]

Perhaps the most interesting aspect of Crassus' influence on the history of rhetoric was not his actual oratory or teaching, but a famous edict that he passed together with his fellow censor Domitius Ahenobarbus in 92 BCE.[19] In this edict the censors denounce the opening of Latin schools of rhetoric (presumably especially that of a certain Plotius Gallus) and condemn it as against the common values and educational traditions of their forefathers:

> A report has been made to us that certain men have begun a new kind of teaching, and that young men are going regularly to their school; that they have taken the name of teachers of Latin rhetoric (*Latini rhetores*): and that our young men are

wasting their whole days with them. Our ancestors ordained what lessons their children were to learn, and what schools they were to frequent. These new schools are contrary to our customs and ancestral traditions, and we consider them undesirable and improper. Wherefore we have decided to publish, both to those who keep these schools and to those who are accustomed to go there, our judgment that we consider them undesirable.[20]

To put this edict in context, it was issued at a time when conservative Romans saw schools, especially Latin-language schools, as a threat to ancient traditions of family education. For centuries it had been the custom that boys destined for public life—and it was a male-centered society—were first tutored by their fathers and then privately by a teacher (usually a Greek slave) before going off to what amounted to a public apprenticeship at the feet of some practicing orator or lawyer.[21]

The edict was not a formal ban of the schools but was intended as a strong discouragement for reputable Roman families. Nevertheless it was not successful in impeding the spread of schools of rhetoric that would give instructions in Latin. But why even try? The categorical resistance against rhetorical theory that was so vividly expressed by Cato the censor was no longer prominent. Antonius, Crassus, and certainly Cicero a few years later would openly excel in rhetorical theory and oratorical praxis alike. The precise motivations for the edict are still debated but it is fair to assume that one of the significant reasons for trying to limit rhetorical studies to the Greek language was the attempt to keep this potentially dangerous weapon in the hands of a select few. Keeping rhetoric Greek meant limiting its reach to the nobility with a classical and expensive education. Once the rules of rhetoric are taught without the detour of Greek literature and philosophy they would be available to a wider public and could no longer be used as an instrument of aristocratic governance.

But note the date of the decree (92 BCE). It was already too late. Within a decade Rome saw the appearance of two school-related Latin-language handbooks which established a set of standardized rhetorical principles known as "Roman rhetoric" for the next 1,500 years. There were the *De Inventione* (*On Invention*) of a young Cicero, and the anonymous *Rhetorica ad Herennium* (which takes its title from its dedication to an unknown Herennius). They appeared within a few years of each other, not long after the edict of Crassus and Ahenobarbus; both were apparently a Latinized set of Greek ideas coalesced in Greek-language rhetoric schools; both set out almost identical plans based on a scheme of five "parts" of rhetoric: Invention, Arrangement, Style, Memory, and Delivery. And both proved to have long-range influence in western culture far beyond what a reader might expect from reading each of them.

## The *De Inventione* of Marcus Tullius Cicero

Precise dating of the *De Inventione* is impossible. On the basis of textual evidence Cicero was approximately 20 years old when he wrote it.[22] There are more important considerations than dating the book, however. Cicero apologizes for the book in his later years,[23] and the rigid, pompous, and didactic manner of presentation more than warrants his apology. Furthermore, if ever a book became famous for the wrong reasons, the *De Inventione* is such a book. Later rhetoricians seized on this manual as their guide and their criterion for excellence. Yet Cicero's treatment of the types of argumentation is, politely phrased, unclear. The key term, argument (*ratiocinatio*), is not defined and it can be interpreted as reasoning, deduction, rhetorical inference, enthymeme, or epicheireme.[24] Moreover, Cicero's pedantic insistence that Hermagoras is wrong in dividing general questions into deliberative, demonstrative, forensic, and interpretive categories becomes tiresome. Cicero was simply not able to synthesize various philosophical systems at this time.[25]

What, then, can be gained by reading the *De Inventione*? First, it allows us to understand the general nature of rhetorical instruction in the 1st century. Also, we can only appreciate the richness of Cicero's mature speculation by comparing and contrasting both the content and form of the *De Inventione* with, for example, the artistry and penetrating insights of the *De Oratore*.

These paraphrased accounts of Cicero's rhetorical treatises maintain the lines of discussion and points of view found in the Latin texts. Approximate section references are placed in parentheses within the text to assist the reader in locating specific passages. To consider these synoptic accounts as precise translations would be a serious mistake. If these synopses encourage the reader to consult the original treatises, their purpose will be accomplished.

## De Inventione

### BOOK I

I believe that oratory has been helpful to mankind, but wisdom must accompany eloquence.

Historically, some unknown man recognized the power of the intellect and of eloquence and by using these he brought about a society devoted to the common good—a society based on justice, not on physical strength.

(5) The best Romans—Cato, Laelius, Africanus, and the Gracchi—possessed wisdom and eloquence. Consequently, I think men ought to study oratory in order that charlatans may not attain political power harmful to good citizens and to the community.

Men excel animals by having the power of speech. And the person who excels other men in the ability of eloquence possesses an exceptional ability. Let me therefore talk about the nature of the art itself, its functions, goals, materials, and components.

Rhetoric is an important part of politics. The function of eloquence is to speak in order to persuade an audience; its goal is persuasion by speech. The function, in other words, is what the speaker ought to do; the end is the purpose for which he ought to do it. The material of the art of rhetoric is those subjects about which oratory is concerned. Gorgias of Leontini assigned all subjects to rhetoric. Aristotle, however, assigned to rhetoric three classes of subjects: the epideictic, the deliberative, and the judicial. The epideictic is concerned with praise and blame of a particular person; the deliberative subjects occur in political debates; the judicial branch concerns accusation and defense. I think the art and ability of an orator must be concerned with these three divisions.

The parts of rhetoric are invention, arrangement, style, memory, and delivery. Invention is the discovery of true or apparently true arguments that make an argumentative case probable; arrangement is the distribution of invented arguments in their proper order. Style is the fitting of the proper language to the invented materials. Memory is the firm mental grasp of arguments and language. Delivery is the control of the voice and body adapted to the importance of the material and language. Since invention is the most important part of rhetoric, I want to consider its divisions.

(10) The question from which the entire case arises is called an issue. An issue can be conjectural when it concerns a question of fact or definitive when a term must be defined. The issue may be qualitative when the nature of the act is disputed or translative when the case involves a possible change of venue.

Hermagoras was in error to divide the qualitative issue into the deliberative, epideictic, judicial, and legal genera. (15) On the contrary, I believe that there are three genera of arguments—the forensic, epideictic, and deliberative. Each genus utilizes all four kinds of issues.

When the issue has been determined one must consider whether the case is simple or complex. A simple case involves a single question; a complex case is made up of several questions.

There are six parts of an oration: the exordium, the narrative, the partition, the confirmation, the refutation, and the peroration.

(20) An exordium is a passage that brings the mind of the auditor into a proper condition to receive the rest of the speech by making him well-disposed, attentive, and receptive. Depending on the type of case being argued, different exordia should be constructed. The exordium is divided into the introduction and the insinuation. An introduction is that which directly and in plain language makes the auditor well-disposed, receptive, and attentive. Insinuation is that which by dissimulation and indirection discreetly lodges in the mind of the auditor.

Good will can be gained by talking about ourselves, our opponents, the members of the jury, or the case itself. Our audience will be attentive if we show that what we are about to discuss is important, new, unbelievable, or if we discuss the scope of the matter. When, however, the audience is hostile, one must begin with an insinuation.

(25) If your opponent has won over the audience, attack the strongest argument which he made. Or express doubt about where to begin so that the jury will think they have evaluated the case too hastily. Or begin with something new and humorous. The narrative is an exposition of events that have occurred or are alleged to have occurred. There are three kinds. One type contains only the case and the rationale for the dispute; a second kind consists of a digression that is made for the purpose of attacking somebody or of amusing the audience or for amplification. The third kind is unconnected with the issue but is given for amusement and, at the same time, for valuable information.

(30) The partition makes the entire speech clear and lucid. It has two general forms: one indicates where we agree with our opponents and what is still left in dispute; the second is a preview of the remainder of our argument. The confirmation is that part of a narration that, by marshaling arguments, lends force, authority, and support to our case. Let me, therefore, set down the raw materials from which all arguments are drawn.

(35) All propositions are supported in argument by attributes of persons or of actions. Attributes of persons are: name, nature, manner of life, fortune, habit, feeling, interests, purposes, achievements, accidents, and speeches that have been made by the person. The attributes of actions are partly connected to the action itself, partly

considered in connection with the performance of it, partly adjunct to it, and partly consequent. All argumentation drawn from the topics that I listed will be either probable or necessary. Necessary arguments are those that cannot be proved otherwise, and they are usually phrased as a dilemma, an enumeration, or a simple inference.

(45) Probability is that which usually happens or which is found in men's ordinary beliefs, or which contains in itself some resemblance to these qualities.

(50) Every kind of argument can be discovered under the headings that have just been given, but style and arrangement make the speech attractive. Previous writers on the art of rhetoric have neglected to show how the rules of argument may be combined with the theory of argumentation. All argumentation is to be carried on either by analogy or by the enthymeme. Analogy is a form of argument that moves from assent on certain undisputed facts through approval of a doubtful proposition due to the resemblance between what is granted and what is doubtful. This style of argument is threefold: the first part consists of one or more similar instances, the second part is the point we wish to have conceded, and the third is the conclusion that reinforces the concession or shows the consequences of the argument.

(55) Enthymematic reasoning is a form of argument that draws a probable conclusion from the facts under consideration. Some say this type of reasoning has five parts, others argue that it cannot have more than three parts.

I believe the five-part division is more acceptable, but let me give my reasons.

(65) Since there are times when the proof of the major premise is optional it seems to be a distinct part. Proof, therefore, is from premise. The same is true for the proof of the minor premise. It is, therefore, untrue that an argument cannot have more than three parts.

The word "argument" has two meanings. First, it can mean a statement on any matter that is either probable or certain.

(75) Second, the term can mean the artistic embellishment of such a statement. I am primarily concerned here with methods of embellishment.

Now that I have discussed in detail the confirmatory part of an oration it is time to consider the remaining parts.

The refutation is that part of an oration in which arguments are used to disprove or weaken the confirmation and proof in our opponent's speech.

(80) Every argument is refuted in one of these ways: either one or more of its assumptions is not granted, or, if the assumptions are granted, it is denied that a conclusion follows from them, or the form of the argument is shown to be fallacious, or a strong argument is met by one equally strong or stronger.

The peroration completes the speech and has three parts: the résumé of what has been discussed throughout the speech, the arousing of animosity against your opponent, and, finally, the arousing of sympathy for your own client.

(100) To add even more variety to your summation you may use personification to present the illusion that either the author of a given law or the law itself is speaking. In that portion of the peroration in which you arouse animosity and hatred against your opponent you can generally use the same topics that were discussed under the precepts of the *confirmatio*.

(105) A third subdivision of the peroration is that place in which we arouse the pity of the jury. To accomplish this end the orator should use commonplaces that treat themes of the power of fortune and the infirmities of men. Once you have succeeded

in arousing the emotions of the jury, however, do not linger long, because nothing dries more quickly than tears.

## BOOK II

(5) I can only hope that my treatise on rhetoric will prove as valuable as the models on which it is based.

(10) In this book I hope to give more specific attention to the arguments suited for the confirmation and refutation. Every speech necessarily turns on one of the stases, but there are specific rules for each kind of speech because speeches that have different purposes cannot have the same rules. In view of this difference I wish to discuss first the rules applying to forensic speeches.

(15) I shall begin with the conjectural stasis. If, in a given case, the allegation is "you have committed murder," the answer in the conjectural issue is "I did not commit murder." The question for judicial decision and the stasis on which the jury's decision must rest is "did he commit murder?" A number of topics are helpful for adducing material in the conjectural stasis. We can consider these topics under the categories of the cause of the action, the person involved, and the nature of the act itself.

Under the cause of an action we must consider the difference between impulse and premeditation. An action done on impulse is characterized by an absence of planning and is committed because of some emotion. Premeditation, on the other hand, is the careful and thorough reasoning about doing or not doing something.

Let us turn now to a consideration of the arguments that can be adduced from the person of the accused. Sometimes a person's name can be used as an indication of his temperament or, if his name is quite common, perhaps you can establish mistaken identity.

(30) An exploration of the person's habits, emotions, interests, purposes, accomplishments, past actions, and speeches may be useful in creating conjectural suspicions.

The prosecutor must show that the character of the defendant is in some way compatible with the crime.

(35) The defense attorney must show that the defendant's life has always been honest and praiseworthy, since a man with a blameless life is not likely to change overnight. Certain tentative conclusions and inferences may be drawn from the act itself. We should examine what occurred before the act, as well as what was actually done during the deed and what followed. We should look to the place, the time, the occasion, and the facilities.

(40) We should examine the adjuncts of the affair. Also, we must look at the consequences of the action and at whether such an action has been approved or disapproved in the past. The most important questions to be asked in the conjectural issue are whether a given act could have been performed by anyone else, or whether the necessary means were available, or whether the action had to be done. Moreover, the motive, either premeditation or passion, must be established.

(50) In the conjectural issue there are numerous common topics; for example, one should and should not trust rumors, witnesses, evidence secured from torture, and so on. Some of these common topics are limited to the prosecution, others to the defense,

but in each case their chief purpose is amplification. The second stasis gives rise to the issue of definition. The prosecutor should first give a precise definition of the word used to designate the criminal act and then point to the relationship and similarity between the action committed by the accused and the definition proposed.

(55) The defense attorney must advance a definition of the word in question, support it with examples, and demonstrate clearly that the act in question does not correspond to the definition. The next stasis generates the translative or procedural issue, which concerns the question of transferring the case to another court.

The qualitative issue and its subdivisions of the legal and the equitable must be considered next.

(65) The legal issue involves a point of civil law, which may be derived from nature or may be part of the codified statute law. In any case, there are common topics available for each.

The equitable subdivision encompasses not only the nature of justice and injustice but also the principles of reward and punishment, and it is to this latter that I now turn. (110) Many speeches request some sort of reward, and there are four topics that can be used when discussing the concept of reward: the services performed, the person himself, the type of reward, and the ability to make the reward.

(115) Now that I have discussed legal cases, which involve general reasoning, I wish to turn to forensic cases, which involve interpretation of a document. Controversy can arise from five sources in the nature of written documents: from ambiguity, from the letter and intent of the document, from a conflict of laws, from analogous reasoning, and from definition.

(120) A legal argument can arise from ambiguity when there is doubt about what the writer meant.

(125) A controversy can arise from a dispute over the letter and intent of a written document when one person follows the precise wording and the other argues from what he believes the writer meant.

(145) When two or more laws seem to disagree, a legal controversy can arise. The orator should compare the laws and consider which law treats the most important subject; that is, the orator should consider which law is most recent, and whether the law commands or merely permits a certain action.

(150) A controversy can also arise from analogous reasoning when one argues that Case A is similar to Case B and Case B is covered by existing statute law.

(155) The controversy can also arise from definition when a word that has a disputed meaning exists in a given law. This type of case can be argued in the same way in which I explained the stasis of definition.

Let us turn now to the precepts for deliberative oratory. The qualities of things to be desired should be the honorable and the advantageous, whereas things to be avoided are characterized by baseness and disadvantage. Things to be sought or avoided are inherently related to necessity and condition.

(160) The honorable is anything that is sought for its own sake either wholly or in part, and the honorable is composed of wisdom, justice, courage, and temperance.

(170) Let me next discuss the qualities of necessity and condition that accompany honor and advantage. Necessity is something that no force can resist; condition is a change of affairs caused by the influence of time, actions, or the interests of men. In epideictic, in speaking, the orator is concerned with praise and blame. Arguments for

praise and blame can be drawn from my earlier discussion of the attributes of persons. I have said enough about invention.

## The Rhetorica ad Herennium of "Pseudo-Cicero"

The anonymous *Rhetorica ad Herennium*,[26] composed about 90 BCE, is the oldest complete Latin textbook on rhetoric. It thus covers invention, arrangement, style, memory, and delivery—the five standard "parts" or "canons" of rhetoric as it was taught by the Romans. It contains the oldest surviving treatment of the art of memory, a section on style featuring a detailed study of 64 figures of speech and thought that add *dignitas* to language, and a complex section on delivery that analyzes gesture, voice, and facial expression. The treatment of invention is reminiscent of Hermagoras, and is very close to the ideas of Cicero in his *De Inventione*. The author proposes two different theories of arrangement for speeches, one of which is a method of invention through arrangement. The *Rhetorica ad Herennium* is, in short, a highly technical document reflecting the crystallized state of Hellenistic rhetorical doctrine at the beginning of the 1st century before Christ.

The author is unknown. A recent edition, however, attributes it to a certain "Cornificius." It is so close in tone to Cicero's *De Inventione* that for 1,500 years it was regarded as a book actually written by Cicero. Hence the unknown author is frequently termed "Pseudo-Cicero." It had virtually no influence in the ancient world, but at the beginning of the Christian intellectual movement of the 4th century, Saint Jerome and others recommended it and it remained popular for more than a thousand years. During the Renaissance, Book IV on Style again influenced rhetoricians interested in tropes and figures.

This book, and all the other major Roman works on rhetoric, accepts the division of rhetoric into five "parts." While we do not know the precise origin of this particular scheme, some modern scholars have argued that each of the five parts can be found in Aristotle's *Rhetoric*, either explicitly or implicitly. This declaration of the five-part division, however, is strictly a Roman one. Its astonishing longevity is probably due to its pragmatic efficiency. It is actually a psychologically valuable sequence. The five parts are not mere philosophical distinctions, but chronological action steps toward the preparation and delivery of an oration to an audience. This plan asks the rhetor to do five things, one after another:

1. **Find** ("invent") ideas
2. **Arrange** them in an order
3. Put **Words** ("style" to the ideas)
4. **Remember** the ideas, their order, and their words
5. **Deliver** (transmit) the ordered and worded ideas to audience through sound, facial express, and gesture.

As a whole, the sequence covers the entirety of the oratorical process.

Once rhetoric is conceived of as a five-part process, moreover, each part can be studied by itself. Studying rhetoric using this five-part division (or the "canons of rhetoric" as they are sometimes called) simplifies the learning process, but then there is a danger that the wholeness may tend to disappear. As we shall see in the next chapter, even Cicero wrote a separate book on Invention (*De Inventione*) and another (*Orator*) on Style.

The importance of Invention can be seen in the fact that the author devotes most of the first three books to it. He is keenly aware of the differing problems of each of the three oratorical genres inherited from Aristotle: deliberative, forensic or judicial, and epideictic. And he lays out a six-part oration pattern—the "parts of an oration" (I.3)—which become a template for specific steps in planning each case.

At the same time, the modern reader should be aware that the amount of space devoted to Style (91 pages in the Caplan translation) does not mean that the author regards it as more important than Invention. Rather, as in the case of all discussions of Style, the necessity of providing numerous detailed language examples makes any such treatment a lengthy one.

## The Figures of Speech and Thought

The *Rhetorica ad Herennium* is the first ancient work to provide a detailed nomenclature of "figures," or devices of language variation. The principle of variation, of course, is much older than this work. Gorgias for example uses them but does not name them. Aristotle discusses the basic concept of variability in *Poetics*, sections 22–23, as well as in *Rhetoric* III.1–2. In the *Poetics* he declares that "Diction becomes distinguished and non-poetic by the use of unfamiliar terms, i.e., strange words, metaphors, lengthened forms, and everything that deviates from the ordinary means of speech" (22:1458a.22). Yet, Aristotle does not attempt to provide a taxonomy of names for such deviations. He is, of course, more interested in the principle itself, using examples only to illuminate the principle.

This attitude was to change with the Romans. The author of the *Rhetorica ad Herennium* is relentlessly taxonomic, intending to classify every aspect of the subject. This is the way he introduces the figures:

> To confer Distinction (*dignitas*) on style is to render it ornate, embellishing it by variety. The divisions under Distinction are Figures of Diction and Figures of Thought. It is a figure of diction if the adornment is comprised in the fine polish of the language itself. A figure of thought derives a certain distinction from the idea, not the words. (IV.xiii.18)

Then, without a transition, he launches into definitions and examples of 64 figures—45 figures of diction (or speech) and 19 figures of thought.

This naming and classifying of variation devices is a Roman pattern that was to influence rhetorical theory for more than 2,000 years. Unfortunately, the ordering of figures in the *Rhetorica ad Herennium* is not as systematic as it looks at first glance. There are several overlaps, omissions, and ambiguities. For example "antithesis" and "hyperbole" occur both as figures of speech and figures of thought, while some figures—e.g. colon, comma, period—could also be seen as matters of grammatical description rather than rhetorical variety. Why should "maxim" (literally, a sententious thought) be named as a figure of speech? The closer the examination, the less systematic the array of figures becomes. Nevertheless, this particular grouping of figures, in this particular order, became a standard for centuries.

One question remains: once the principle of language variation is accepted, why is it necessary to give names to the variations, and to classify them into groups? Perhaps the answer lies in the Roman impulse to lay out explicit rules, with the enumeration of specific parts of each subject. Perhaps it is a schoolmaster's approach to a subject. Whatever the cause, the fact is that the *Rhetorica ad Herennium* presents us with these figures for the first time, just as it spells out as a standard the five parts of rhetoric and the six parts of an oration.

## Topos and Figura: Cause and Effect?

It seems clear that the author of the *Rhetorica ad Herennium* inherited—i.e., did not create—the set of figures detailed in Book IV. (As we shall see later in Chapters 5 and 6, both Cicero and Quintilian are familiar with the same figures.) Did Hellenistic classifiers of the period 300–100 BCE look to logical *topoi*—already a classification system for finding inventional arguments—to set up a parallel system for identifying types of language variation? There are some interesting parallels between the two sets of ideas. For example the "antithesis" which occurs as both a figure of speech and a figure of thought in the *ad Herennium* also occurs in Aristotle's set of 28 sample *topoi* in *Rhetoric* II₂₃ as "opposites." The "synecdoche," which is a figure of speech here dealing with part-and-whole, is in Aristotle the twelfth topic for producing enthymemes. Moreover, the "comparison," which is a figure of thought in *ad Herennium*, covers four of Aristotle's listed topics. The first Aristotelian topic listed in *Rhetoric*, "inflections of words," describes half a dozen of the figures of speech in this book. These are but a few examples. The point is that there are indeed some similarities between the two sets of ideas, similarities which might be worth studying further. While we lack clear historical evidence about how this particular set of figures achieved the form seen in the *ad Herennium*, it is nevertheless interesting to note the parallel to the earlier Greek inventional system of topics (*topoi*). The prevalence of these figures among all the Roman rhetoricians is of course another evidence of the homogeneity of the Roman rhetorical system. Evidently, Cicero and Pseudo-Cicero are so similar because they both share a common school training. This is not to say that they had the same teacher, however. Rather, they were both products of a Roman rhetorical training that by about 90 BCE had been highly systematized and standardized. Furthermore, it remained substantially unchanged for many more centuries, for we note that Quintilian (writing in 95 CE) describes a rhetorical curriculum very much like the one Cicero himself describes in several of his works. Saint Augustine taught a similar program in Carthage and Milan as late as 380 CE, and since Roman cultural systems were introduced all over Europe in the wake of conquests by the Roman army, the Roman rhetorical schools survived the barbarian invasions in some places in Gaul and Germany even after 500 CE. Because of this standardization of rhetorical education, it is possible to identify a "Roman tradition" of rhetoric. It is almost equally appropriate to call it a "Ciceronian tradition" because of the close similarity between the school doctrines and Cicero's seven rhetorical works. This tradition is built around the five "parts" of rhetoric, each of which can be analyzed separately for the sake of study: invention, arrangement, style, memory, and delivery. The anonymous *Rhetorica ad Herennium*, as the first book to present a full-blown discussion of this complete five-part system, ranks as one of the major works in that Roman rhetorical tradition.

## *Rhetorica Ad Herennium*

### BOOK I

1. Prefatory Letter to C. Herennius. This is a practical treatise, and does not include those matters that the Greeks have adopted for the sake of futile self-assertion. Remember that theory without continuous practice in speaking is of no avail, so it is to be understood that the precepts offered here should be applied to practice.

2. The task of the public speaker is to discuss capably those matters that law and custom have fixed for the uses of citizenship and to secure as far as possible the agreement of his hearers. There are three kinds of causes that the speaker must treat: epideictic, deliberative, and judicial. The epideictic kind is devoted to the praise or censure of some particular person. The deliberative kind consists of the discussion of policy, and embraces persuasion and dissuasion. The judicial is based on legal controversy, and comprises criminal prosecution or civil suit, and defense. The speaker should possess the faculties of invention, arrangement, style, memory, and delivery.

   (1) Invention (*inventio*) is the devising of matter, true or plausible, that would make the case convincing.

   (2) Arrangement (*dispositio*) is the ordering and distribution of the matter, making clear the place to which each thing is to be assigned.

   (3) Style (*elocutio*) is the adaptation of suitable words and sentences to the matter invented.

   (4) Memory (*memoria*) is the firm retention in the mind of the matter, words, and arrangement.

   (5) Delivery (*pronuntiatio*) is the graceful (*venustate*) regulation of voice, countenance, and gesture.

   All these things we can acquire by (1) theory, or a set of rules that provide a definite method; (2) imitation, or the stimulation to attain the effectiveness of certain models; and (3) practice, or assiduous exercise and experience in speaking.

3. Invention is used for the six parts of a discourse: introduction, statement of facts, division, proof, refutation, and conclusion. Given the cause, in order to make a more appropriate introduction, we must consider the kind of cause it is. The kinds of causes are four: honorable (*honestum*), discreditable (*turpe*), doubtful (*dubium*), or petty (*humile*).

4. There are two kinds of introductions: direct (*principium*) and subtle (*insinuatio*). Hearers must be made receptive, well-disposed, and attentive. We can make our hearers well-disposed by four methods: (1) by discussing our own person; (2) by discussing the person of our adversary; (3) by discussing that of our hearers; and (4) by discussing the facts themselves. 5–7. Details of these methods.

8–9. Statement of facts includes either narrative based on facts or narrative based on persons. 10. The division of the cause involves first telling the audience where we agree or disagree with our opponent, and then setting forth the points we intend to discuss, which is called distribution.

11–16. Proof and refutation will be possible if we know the type of issue that the cause presents. Though others say four, my teacher said there are three: (1) conjectural, a question of fact; (2) legitimate, based on interpretation of a text; and (3) juridical, when an act is admitted but its right or wrong is in question.

## BOOK II

1. The juridical is the most difficult of these three causes; invention is the most difficult and most important of the speaker's tasks.
2–8. There are six divisions in the conjectural issue: probability, comparison, signs pointing to guilt, presumptive proof, subsequent behavior, and confirmatory proof. 9–12. There are rules for arguing on the issue of legitimacy in the cases of variance between letter and spirit of a document, or when there is ambiguity, or when argument is based on definition, transference, or reasoning from analogy.
13–17. Under the juridical issue we argue from (1) nature, (2) statute, (3) custom, (4) previous judgments, (5) equity, or (6) agreement. 18–29. The most complete and perfect argument in any of these causes is composed of five parts: (1) proposition, (2) reason, (3) proof of the reason, (4) embellishment, and (5) résumé or conclusion. 30–31. Conclusions are tripartite, consisting of (1) summing up, (2) amplification, and (3) appeal to pity (which should be brief).

## BOOK III

1–5. Deliberative speeches present a legislative audience with either two choices or more than two choices. Their aim is advantage for the state, which has the subdivisions of security and honor. While security depends upon military power, honor deals with the right and the praiseworthy. The right has the four topics of wisdom, justice, courage, and temperance; the praiseworthy depends upon the opinion of authorities, allies, other citizens, or our descendants.
6. Since epideictic speeches deal with praise or censure, the topics for praise will serve for both. The following, then, can be subject to praise: (1) external circumstances (descent, education, wealth, kinds of power, titles to fame, citizenship, friendships); (2) physical attributes (agility, strength, beauty, health); and (3) qualities of character (wisdom, justice, courage, temperance). 7–8. The introduction may be drawn from persons or from the subject matter itself, in which case there is no need for a statement of facts. The division should point out what we intend to praise or censure, with the topics of character being used throughout the speech. The conclusion should be a brief summary. This concludes the most difficult part of rhetoric—invention.
9. There are two kinds of arrangement, one from rhetoric (six parts of speech and five parts of an argument) and the other from the particular circumstances of the case. 10. In proof and refutation it is best to put the strongest arguments at the beginning and the end, with the weakest in the middle.
11–15. Many have said that the faculty of greatest use to the speaker is delivery, which includes voice quality (volume, stability, and flexibility of tones) and physical movement (facial expression and body movement). Good delivery ensures that what the orator is saying seems to come from the heart.
16–22. Memory, the treasure house of the ideas supplied by invention, the guardian of all the parts of rhetoric, is of two kinds: (1) natural memory, which is aided by discipline; (2) artificial memory, which depends upon backgrounds and images. Backgrounds are such scenes as are naturally set off on a small scale, complete and conspicuous, so that we can grasp them easily by the natural memory.

An image is a figure, mark, or portrait of the object we wish to remember. To remember an object we must place its image in a background. The backgrounds should be in a series in some desert place, to avoid confusion, with each fifth one marked. Likeness of objects or works is the criterion for choosing images. 23–24. The speaker must learn various methods of searching his memory. Memorizing words is appropriate when done for the sake of training.

## BOOK IV

1–11. I shall divide the teaching of style into two parts: first, the kinds of style, then those qualities that style should always have. There are three kinds or types of style to which discourse, if faultless, confines itself: the grand (high) style, consisting of smooth and ornate arrangements of impressive words; the middle style, consisting of lower yet not of the lowest and most colloquial class of words; and the simple (plain) style, which is brought down even to the most current idiom of standard speech. Variety of styles is useful.

12. Each of these three styles should have the qualities of taste (*elegentia*), artistic composition (*compositio*), and distinction (*dignitas*); the last of these, distinction, is achieved through the judicious use of figures (*exornationes*). Figures are of two kinds: figures of speech (diction) occur if the adornment is comprised in the fine polish of the language itself; figures of thought derive a certain distinction from the idea, not the words.

### Figures of Speech

*Editor's Note: In order to facilitate study of the figures, selected examples from the readings in Part II have been added to some of the definitions below. Not every figure named here occurs in those readings, though of course they are used to good purpose in many other ancient works. Readers are encouraged to find other examples in the readings as they study, discuss, and/or recite them. The number that occurs after the reference indicates the paragraph in which the example appears.*

1. Epanaphora (*repetitio*) occurs when one and the same word forms successive beginnings for phrases expressing like and different ideas. This figure has much charm and also impressiveness and vigor in a high degree; therefore it ought to be used for both embellishment and amplification.

    *Pericles (7): Our love of what is beautiful does not lead to extravagance; our love of the things of the mind does not make us soft. We regard wealth as something to be properly used, rather than as something to boast about.*

2. Antistrophe (*conversio*) occurs when we repeat, not the first word in successive phrases, but the last.

    *Cicero, Catiline (8): But now what is this life of yours? For I shall speak to you, so that men may feel I am swayed, not by hatred, as I ought to be, but by pity, non of which is due you.*

3.  Interlacement (*complexio*) is the union of both figures, the combined use of antistrophe and epanaphora; we repeat both the first word and the last word in a series of phrases.

> *Plato (7): I could not help thinking that he was not really wise, although he thought he was wise by many, and still wiser by himself, and thereupon I tried to explain to him that he thought himself wise, but was not really wise; and the consequence was that he hated me, and his enmity was shared by several who were present and heard me.*

4.  Transplacement (*traductio*) makes it possible for the same word to be frequently reintroduced, not only without offense to good taste, but even so as to render the style more elegant. To this kind of figure also belongs that which occurs when the same word is used first in one function and then in another. (See also "Polyptoton" Chapter 2, *Gorgias*.)

> *Plato (6): If you ask me what kind of wisdom, I reply, wisdom such as may perhaps be attained by man, for to that extent I am inclined to believe I am wise, whereas the persons of whom I was speaking have a kind of superhuman wisdom, which I know not how to describe, because I have it not myself. Cicero, Catiline (16): Thou wilt punish living and dead with eternal punishments.*

5.  Antithesis (*contentio*) occurs when the style is built on contraries.

> *Pericles (8): We make friends by doing to others, not by receiving good from them.*

6.  Apostrophe (*exclamatio*) is the figure which expresses grief or indignation by means of an address to some man or city or place or object. If we use apostrophe in the proper place, sparingly, and when the importance of the subject seems to demand it, we shall instill in our listener as much indignation as we desire. (Caplan: Quintilian, 9.3.97, assigns *exclamatio* to figures of thought.)

> *Cicero, Catiline (1): Is it nothing to you that the Palatine has its garrison by night, nothing to you that the city is full of patrols, nothing that the senate is convened in this stronghold, is it nothing to see the looks on all these faces?*

7.  Interrogation (*interrogatio*) reinforces the argument that has just been delivered, after the case against the opponents has been summed up; but not all interrogation is impressive or elegant.

> *Cicero, Catiline (17): Those things which I have spoken, without regarding the habits of the forum or judicial usage, both concerning the genius of the man and my own zeal on his behalf, I trust have been received by you in good part.*

8.  Reasoning by question and answer (*ratiocinatio*) occurs when we ask ourselves the reason for every statement we make, and seek the meaning of each successive affirmation. This figure is exceedingly well adapted to a conversational style, and

both by its stylistic grace and the anticipation of the reasons, holds the hearer's attention. (Caplan: Quintilian, 9.3.98, assigns it to figures of thought.) This figure is to be distinguished from *ratiocinatio*, the type of issue which employs reasoning from analogy.

> *Plato (7): When I heard the answer, I said to myself, What can the god mean? And what is the interpretation of his riddle? For I know that I have no wisdom, small or great. What then can he mean when he says that I am the wisest of men?*

9. A maxim (*sententia*) is a saying drawn from life, which shows concisely either what happens or ought to happen in life. Maxims may be either simple or double, and be presented either with or without reasons. We should insert maxims only rarely, that we may be looked upon as pleading the case, not preaching morals. When so interspersed, they will add much distinction. Furthermore, the hearer, when he perceives that an indisputable principle drawn from practical life is being applied to a cause, he must give it his tacit approval.

> *Isocrates (10): Those, however, who are rightly governed should not cover the walls of the porticoes with copies of the laws, but preserve justice in their hearts; for it is not by decrees but by manners that cities are well governed, and while those who have been badly brought up will venture to transgress laws drawn up even with the greatest exactitude, those who have been well educated will be ready to abide by laws framed in the simplest terms.*

10. Reasoning by Contraries (*contrarium*) is the figure which, of two opposite statements, uses one so as neatly and directly to prove the other, as follows: "Now how should you expect one who has ever been hostile to his own interests to be friendly to another's?" (Caplan: Quintilian regards this as more a kind of argument than a figure of speech, and notes the similarity to Aristotle's *a fortiori* commonplace.)

> *Lysias (5): For the wealthy purchase with their money escape from the risks that they run, whereas the poor are compelled to moderation by the pressure of their want. The young are held to merit indulgence from their elders; but if the elders are guilty of offence, both ages unite in reproaching them.*

11. Colon or Clause (*membrum*) is the name given to a sentence member, brief and complete, which does not express the entire thought, but is in turn supplemented by another colon. (Caplan: The doctrine of Colon, Comma, Period is Peripatetic in origin; Quintilian excluded Comma and Colon from the list of figures.)

> *Explanation: In modern usage, a "dependent clause."*

12. Comma or Phrase (*articulus*) occurs when single words are set apart by pauses in staccato speech.

> *Explanation: In modern usage, "a phrase."*

13. A Period (*continuatio*) is a close-packed and uninterrupted group of words embracing a complete thought. We shall best use it in three places: (1) Maxim, (2) Contrast, or (3) Conclusion.

> *Helen (1): Fairest ornament to a city is a goodly army and to a body beauty and to a soul wisdom and to an action virtue and to speech truth, but their opposites are unbefitting.*

14. Isocolon (*conpar*) is the figure comprised of cola which consist of a virtually equal number of syllables. (Caplan: Isocolon, Antitheses, and the next three figures—Homoeoptoton, Homoeoteleuton, and Paronomasia—are the so-called "Figures of Gorgias.")

> *Helen (6): Now if for the first reason [fate, the gods, etc.], the responsible one should right be held responsible: it is impossible to prevent a god's predetermination by human premeditation, since by nature the stronger force is not prevented by the weaker, but the weaker is ruled and driven by the stronger; the stronger leads, the weaker follows.*

15. Homoeoptoton (*similiter cadens*) occurs when in the same period two or more words appear in the same case, and with like terminations.

> *Helen (6): For either by fate's will and gods' wishes and necessity's decrees she did what she did or by force reduced or by words seduced or by love induced.*

16. Homoeoteleuton (*similiter desinens*) occurs when the word endings are similar, although the words are indeclinable.

> *Helen (6): If therefore, by fate and god the cause had been decreed, Helen must of all disgrace be freed.*

17. Paronomasia (*adnominatio*) is the figure in which, by means of a modification of sound, or change of letters, a close resemblance to a verb or noun is produced, so that similar words express dissimilar things. This is done in three ways:

  (1) through slight change or lengthening or transposition
    (a) by thinning or contracting the same letter
    (b) by the reverse
    (c) by lengthening the same letter
    (d) by shortening the same letter
    (e) by adding letters
    (f) by omitting letters
    (g) by transposing letters
    (h) by changing letters
  (2) through greater changes
  (3) through a change of case in one of the nouns. (Caplan: The author knows only four parts of speech, so that "noun" would include "adjective.")

> *Helen (1): Man and woman and speech and deed and city and object should be honored with praise if praiseworthy, but on the unworthy blame should be laid; for it is equal error and ignorance to blame the praiseworthy and to praise the blameworthy.*

These last three figures are to be used very sparingly when we speak in an actual cause, because their invention seems impossible without labor and pains.

18. Hypophora (*subiectio*) occurs when we inquire of our adversary or ask ourselves what the adversaries can say in their favor, or what can be said against us. (Caplan: Quintilian, 9.3.98, assigns this to figures of thought.)

> *Plato (6): I dare say, Athenians, that someone among you will reply, "Yes, Socrates, but what is your occupation? What is the origin of these accusations which are brought against you; there must have been something strange which you have been doing? All these rumours and this talk about you would never have arisen if you had been like other men: tell us, then, what is the cause of them, for we should be sorry to judge hastily of you."*

19. Climax (*gradatio*) is the figure in which the speaker passes to the following word only after advancing by steps to the preceding one. (Caplan: This figure joins with Epanaphora, Antistrophe, Interlacement, and Trans-placement or Antanaklasis (*traductio*) to form a complete theory of Repetition.)

> *Cicero, Catiline (1): Do you not see that your conspiracy is bound hand and foot by the knowledge of all these men? Who of us do you think is ignorant of what you did last night, what you did the night before, where you were, whom you called together, what plan you took? What an age! What morals!*

20. Definition (*definitio*) in brief and clear-cut fashion grasps the characteristic qualities of a thing. (*NB: Definitio* is also the subtype of "Legal Issue," I.ii.19 of the *Rhetorica ad Herennium*.)

> *Socrates (10): He O men, is the wisest, who, like Socrates, knows that his wisdom is in truth worth nothing.*

21. Transition (*transitio*) is the name given to the figure which briefly recalls what has been said, and likewise briefly sets forth what is to follow next. (Caplan: This figure combines the functions of *enumeratio* and *propositio* used by the author in the Division and Conclusion.)

> *Cicero, Archias (1): For as far as ever my mind can look back upon the space of time that is past, and recall the memory of its earliest youth, tracing my life from that starting-point, I see that Archias was the principle cause of my undertaking, and the principle means of my mastering, those studies. And if this voice of mine, formed by his encouragement and his precepts, has at times been the instrument of safety to others, undoubtedly we ought, as far as*

*lies in our power, to help and save the very man from whom we have received that gift which has enabled us to bring help to many and salvation to some.*

22. Correction (*correctio*) retracts what has been said and replaces it with what seems more suitable.

> *Cicero, Archias (12): For if any one thinks that there is a smaller gain of glory derived from Greek verses than from Latin ones, he is greatly mistaken, because Greek poetry is read among all nations, Latin is confined to its own natural limits, which are narrow enough.*

23. Paralipsis (*occultatio*) occurs when we say that we are passing by, or do not know, or refuse to say that which precisely now we are saying. (Caplan: Sometimes *praeteritio*. Quintilian, 9.3.98, puts this in figures of thought.)

> *Demosthenes (2): When, then, men of Athens, when I say, will you take the action that is required? What are you waiting for? "We are waiting," you say, "till it is necessary." [but what must we think of all that is happening at this present time? Surely the strongest necessity a free people can experience is the shame which they must feel at their position!]*

24. Disjunction (*disjunctum*) is used when each of two or more clauses ends with a special verb. (Caplan: Quintilian, 9.3.64, says that devices like this and the two following are so common that they cannot lay claim to that art which figures involve.)

> *Cicero, Archias (12): Wherefore, if those achievements which we have performed are limited only by the bounds of the whole world, we ought to desire that, wherever our vigor and our arms have penetrated, our glory and our fame should likewise extend.*

25. Conjunction (*conjunctio*) occurs when both the previous and the succeeding phrases are held together by placing the verb between them.

> *Cicero, Archias (10): They say that the great Themistocles, the greatest man that Athens produced, said, when someone asked him what sound or whose voice he took the greatest delight in hearing, "The voice of that by whom his own exploits were best celebrated."*

26. Adjunction (*adiunctio*) occurs when the verb holding the sentence together is not placed in the middle, but at the beginning or end.

> *Cicero, Archias (9): Who of us was of so ignorant and brutal a disposition as not lately to be grieved at the death of Roscius, who, though he was an old man when he died, yet, on account of the excellence and beauty of his art, appeared to be one who on every account ought not to have died?*

27. Reduplication (*conduplicatio*) is the repetition of one or more words for the purpose of Amplification in Appeal to Pity. The reiteration of the same word makes a deep impression upon the hearer.

   *Cicero, Archias (9): Should not I, then, love this man? Should not I admire him? Should not I think it is my duty to defend him in every possible way?*

28. Synonymy or Interpretation (*interpretatio*) is the figure which does not duplicate the same word by repeating it, but replaces the word that has been used by another with the same meaning. The hearer cannot but be impressed when the force of the first expression is renewed by the explanatory synonym. (Caplan: Quintilian, 9.3.98, denies that this is a figure.)

   *Cicero, Archias (7): But all books are full of such precepts, and all the sayings of philosophers and all antiquity are full of precedents teaching the same lesson.*

29. Reciprocal Change (*commutatio*) occurs when two discrepant thoughts are so expressed by transposition that the latter follows from the former although contradictory to it, as follows: "You must eat to live, not live to eat."

30. Surrender (*permissio*) is used when we indicate in speaking that we yield and submit the whole matter to another's will. It is especially useful for evoking pity.

   *Cicero, Archias (16): And as this is the case, we do entreat you, O judges, if there may be any weight attached, I will not say to human, but even to divine recommendation in such important matters, to receive under your protection that man who has at all times done honor to your generals and to the exploits of the Roman people.*

31. Indecision (*dubitatio*) occurs when the speaker seems to ask which of two or more words he had better use.

   *Cicero, Catiline (266–267): The Senate knows these things, the consul sees them. Yet this man lives. Lives, did I say? Nay, more, he walks into the Senate, he takes part in the public counsel.*

32. Elimination (*expeditio*) occurs when we have enumerated the several ways by which something could have been brought about, and all are then discarded except the one on which we are insisting. (Caplan: Cicero, Quintilian, and Aristotle all regard this as a form of argument, not a figure. It is known in modern argumentation as the Method of Residues.)

   *Demosthenes, Philippic (255): When, then, men of Athens, when, I say, will you take the action that is required? What are you waiting for? "We are waiting," you say, "till it is necessary." But what must we think of all that is happening at this present time? Surely the strongest necessity that a free people can experience is the shame which they must feel at their position! What? Do you want to go round asking one another, "Is there any news?"*

33. Asyndeton (*dissolutum*) is a presentation in separate parts, conjunctions being suppressed.

> *Cicero, Catiline (5): You cannot remain with us longer; I will not bear it, I will not tolerate it, I will not permit it.*

34. Aposiopesis (*praecisio*) occurs when something is said and then the rest of what the speaker had begun to say is left unfinished. (Also: *interruptio*.)
35. Conclusion (*conclusio*) deduces, by means of a brief argument, the necessary consequences of what has been said or done before. (Caplan: Quintilian, 9.3.98, denies that this is a figure.)

> *Demosthenes (12): As it is, I do not know what will happen to me, for what I have said: but I have chosen to speak in the sure conviction that if you carry out my proposals, it will be for your good; and may the victory rest with that policy which will be for the good of all!*

There remain also ten Figures of Diction, which I have intentionally not scattered at random, but have separated from those above, because they all belong to one class. They indeed all have this in common, that the language departs from the ordinary meaning of the words, and is, with a certain grace, applied in another sense. (Caplan: These ten figures of diction are *tropi*, a term which the author here does not employ. Quintilian, 8.6.I, defines a trope as "an artistic change of word or phrase from its proper signification to another." It is to be noted that tropes are not here separated from figures of diction.)

36. Onomatopoeia (*nominatio*) is a figure which suggests to us that we should ourselves designate with a suitable word, whether for the sake of imitation or for expressiveness, a thing which either lacks a name or has an inappropriate name.
37. Antonomasia or Pronominatio (*pronominatio*) designates by a kind of adventitious epithet a thing that cannot be called by its proper name.
38. Metonymy (*denominatio*) is a figure which draws from an object closely akin or associated an expression suggesting this object meant, but not called by its own name:

    (1) by substituting the name of the greater for that of the lesser
    (2) by substituting the name of the thing invented for the inventor
    (3) by substituting the instrument for the possessor
    (4) by substituting the cause for the effect
    (5) by substituting the effect for the cause
    (6) by substituting the container for the content
    (7) by substituting the content for the container.

39. Periphrasis (*circumitio*) is a manner of speech used to express a simple idea by means of a circumlocution.
40. Hyperbaton (*transgressio*) upsets the word order by means of either

    (1) Anastrophe (*perversio*), or reversal of natural order, or
    (2) Transposition (*transiectio*) changes the word order to gain more favorable rhythm.

41. Hyperbole (*superlatio*) is a manner of speech exaggerating the truth, whether for the sake of magnifying or minifying something. This is used either independently or by comparison.
42. Synecdoche (*intellectio*) occurs when the whole is known from a small part or a part from the whole.

    (1) The whole may be understood from the part, or part from the whole.
    (2) Singular may be understood from plural, and plural from singular.

43. Catechresis (*abusio*) is the inexact use of a like and kindred word in place of a more precise and proper one.
44. Metaphor (*translatio*) occurs when a word applying to one thing is transferred to another, because the similarity seems to justify this transference. It is used

    (1) for vividness
    (2) for brevity
    (3) to avoid obscenity
    (4) for magnifying
    (5) for minifying
    (6) for embellishing.

    > *Isocrates (3): A city's soul is nothing else but its political principle, which has as great influence as understanding in a man's body.*

45 Allegory (*permutatio*) is a manner of speech denoting one thing by the letter of the words, but another by their meaning. It assumes three aspects:

    (1) Comparison, when a number of metaphors originating in a similarity in the mode of expression are set together.
    (2) Argument, when a similitude is drawn from a person or place or object in order to magnify or minify.
    (3) Contrast, when one mockingly calls a thing that which is its contrary.

## Figures of Thought

1. Distribution (*distributio*) occurs when certain specified roles are assigned among a number of things or persons.
2. Frankness of Speech (*licentia*) occurs when, talking before those to whom we owe reverence or fear, we yet exercise our right to speak out, because we seem justified in reprehending them, or persons dear to them, for some fault. (Caplan: Quintilian, 9.2.27, denies that this is a figure.)
3. Understatement (*diminutio*) occurs when we say that by nature, fortune, or diligence, we or our clients possess some exceptional advantage, and in order to avoid the impression of arrogant display, we moderate or soften the statement of it.
4. Vivid Description (*descriptio*) is the name for the figure which contains a clear, lucid, and impressive exposition of the consequences of an act.
5. Division (*divisio*) separates the alternatives of a question and resolves each by means of a reason subjoined. There is this difference between the present kind of Division and that other which forms the third part of a discourse (in Book I): the

former division operates through the Enumeration or Exposition of the topics to be discussed throughout the whole discourse, whereas here the division at once unfolds itself, and by briefly adding the reasons for the two or more parts, embellishes the style.

6. Accumulation (*frequentatio*) occurs when the points scattered throughout the whole cause are collected in one place so as to make the speech more impressive or sharp or accusatory.

7. Refining (*expolitio*) consists in dwelling on the same topic and yet seeming to say something ever new. It is accomplished in two ways:
   (1) by repeating the same idea
      (a) in equivalent words
      (b) in different styles of delivery as we change words
      (c) by the treatment
         (I) in dialogue form
         (II) in arousal form
   (2) by descanting upon the theme
      (a) by simple pronouncement
      (b) by reason
      (c) by a second expression in new form
      (d) by comparison
      (e) by contrary
      (f) by example
      (g) by conclusion.

8. Dwelling on the Point (*commoratio*) occurs when one remains rather long upon, and often returns to, the strongest topic on which the whole cause rests. There is no appropriate example of this figure, because this topic is not isolated from the whole cause like some limb, but like blood is spread through the whole body of discourse.

9. Antithesis (*contentio*) occurs when contraries meet. The Antithesis which is a Figure of Diction presents a rapid opposition of words, while in the Figure of Thought the opposing thoughts will meet in a comparison.

10. Comparison (*similitudo*) is a manner of speech that carries over an element of likeness from one thing to a different thing. It has four forms of presentation, each of which has a separate aim:
   (1) Contrast, whose purpose is embellishment
   (2) Negation, whose purpose is proof
   (3) Abridgment, whose purpose is clarity
   (4) Detailed Parallel, whose purpose is vividness.

11. Exemplification (*exemplum*) is the citing of something done or said in the past, along with the definite naming of the doer or author. (Caplan: Examples are drawn from history.)

12. Simile (*imago*) is the comparison of one figure (*forma*) with another, implying a certain resemblance between them. It is used for either praise or censure.

13. Portrayal (*effictio*) consists in representing and depicting in words clearly enough for recognition the bodily form of some person.

14. Character Delineation (*notatio*) consists in describing a person's character by the definite signs which, like distinctive marks, are attributes of the character. (Caplan: Quintilian, 9.3.99, excludes this from the figures.) [Following this brief

definition, the author supplies the longest single example of the book, portraying the character of a bragging beggar, iv.50.63–64.]

15. Dialogue (*sermocinatio*) consists in assigning to some person language which as set forth conforms with his character. (Caplan: Quintilian, 9.2.29, joins this figure and Personification as one.)

16. Personification (*conformatio*) consists in representing an absent person as present, or in making a mute thing or one lacking form articulate, and attributing to it a definite form and a language or a certain behavior appropriate to its character. (Caplan: This figure sometimes became a *progymnasma*, or composition exercise.)

17. Emphasis (*significatio*) is the figure which leaves more to be suspected than has actually been asserted. It is produced through:
    (1) Hyperbole
    (2) Ambiguity
    (3) Logical Consequence
    (4) Aposiopesis
    (5) Analogy.

18. Conciseness (*brevitas*) is the expressing of an idea by the very minimum of essential words. (Caplan: Quintilian does not admit it as a figure, 9.3.99, but does treat it as a form of Asyndeton in 9.3.50.)

19. Ocular Demonstration (*demonstratio*) occurs when an event is so described in words that the business seems to be enacted and the subject to pass vividly before our eyes.

If you exercise yourself in these figures, Herennius, your speaking will possess impressiveness, distinction, and charm. As a result you will speak like a true orator, and the product of your invention will not be bare and inelegant, nor will it be expressed in commonplace language.

Remember always that you must combine both study and exercise to master the art.

If we follow these principles above, our Invention will be keen and prompt, our Arrangement clear and orderly, our Delivery impressive and graceful, our Memory sure and lasting, our Style brilliant and charming. In the art of rhetoric, then, there is no more.

---

*The Rhetorica ad herennium, then, is a workmanlike, pragmatic document. While it lacks the philosophical depth of Aristotle's Rhetoric, it takes an opposite tack by specifying in detail the practical operations of the Roman five "parts" of rhetoric. Note too that the author declares at the outset that "I have omitted to treat those topics which, for the sake of futile self-assertion, Greek writers have adopted" (I.1). If Aristotle's Rhetoric is a masterful discussion of what a rhetor needs to **know**, the Rhetorica ad Herennium is a masterful statement of what the rhetor needs to **do**.*

*The section on style in Book IV is one of the most influential treatments of that subject in the history of rhetoric, just as the section on memory carves out its own long-lasting influence. It is also worth noting that the author concludes his treatise with same advice with which he began—that is, that rhetorical capacity is acquired from the three sources of theory, imitation, and practice. This is Isocrates' trilogy of sources. This is another evidence of the homogeneity of Roman rhetoric, for it is* echoed in the author's contemporary, Cicero, and laid out in full detail later in Quintilian. It is also a proof of the continuity of Roman education. But handbooks like these three just discussed can seem to be simply long lists of things to do. For readers stupefied by the relentless pragmatism of the Rhetorica ad Alexandrum, the almost arrogant self-confidence of De Inventione, and the stultifying detail of the Rhetorica ad Herennium—especially in the seemingly endless march of figures and tropes in Book IV—this type of codified rhetoric can seem to be just the opposite of the ideals sought after by Plato, Isocrates, and Aristotle. It can seem to be mechanical, not human.

Fortunately for us, and for western civilization, Rome also gave rise to one of the most influential orators and rhetoricians in our culture—Marcus Tullius Cicero, the humane student of human behavior whose dialogue De oratore has a rank in rhetorical history on a level with Aristotle's Rhetoric as a statement of the highest ideals of rhetoric. The mature Cicero is the subject of our next chapter.

# Chapter 5

# The Rhetorical Theory of the Mature Cicero, With Synopses of His Major Rhetorical Works[1]

> I do maintain that the complete and perfect orator is he who can speak about all subjects with fullness and variety.
>
> Crassus, in Cicero's *De oratore*

## Introduction

Practically the first thing that Marcus Tullius Cicero did when he took up a serious writing career in 55 BCE was to repudiate a little rhetoric handbook he had produced when, in his words, he was an "adolescent"—"the sketchy and unsophisticated work that found its way out of my notebooks when I was a boy, or rather, a youth" (*De oratore* I.5). He was of course referring to the *De Inventione* we have just discussed in the preceding chapter.

By then after 30 years of successful law practice, as well as service in the highest levels of the government of the republic, it is clear that by then his school notebooks no longer provided enough for him or anyone else.

If indeed handbooks like the anonymous *Rhetorica ad Herennium* and Cicero's youthful *De Inventione* had been the only Roman rhetorical texts to survive from the period of the republic, we would have a rather restricted view of Roman rhetoric as being purely prescriptive, rules-laden, and somewhat mechanical.

Fortunately for western culture, and for us, the mature Cicero set a much higher, more humane standard in both theory and practice. Marcus Tullius Cicero (106–44 BCE)[2] so far eclipsed his contemporaries that even today the term "oratorical style" could be easily be termed "Ciceronian style," and "Roman rhetoric" has become virtually interchangeable with "Ciceronian rhetoric." Cicero was not only a major ancient force, but his theories informed medieval rhetoric as well, and during the European Renaissance his theories dominated rhetorical thought. Moreover, his numerous works on ethics, political science, and philosophy were widely disseminated. His letters reshaped the form of letter-writing in Europe and America. He was admired by Americans like Thomas Jefferson. This towering figure represents the best of Roman humanism.

His rhetorical theories reflect his understanding of the art from the schoolroom enterprise to the platform of an accomplished orator-statesman. As he matured, so too did his insight into the ways of persuasion. Not only a theorist, Cicero practiced his art, pitting his genius and talent against gifted opponents in the Roman Senate and the Roman Courts (see below, Part II). His practice informed his theory, his theory his practice. More was involved, of course, for Cicero was a man of letters, something of a scholar. His writings include 774 surviving letters, 58 speeches, and 25 treatises on ethics, government, philosophy, law, criticism, and a host of other topics. This literary penchant also provides a background for the singular excellence of his conception of rhetorical theory. More than any other theorist, Cicero possessed self-reflexivity, the ability to know what he was doing as he was doing it and he had the literary talent to explain, comment on, and theorize from his oratorical experience and success.

A man of passion, Cicero passionately believed that rhetoric, properly understood, involved more, much more, than the dry formulas of the school courses. For him, the rhetorician-orator-writer needed as wide a range of capacities as Aristotle had demanded: wide and deep reading; mastery of philosophy, law, history; command of humor, amplification, and digression; and psychological control of an audience. For many modern readers Cicero's conception of rhetoric may seem an unattainable ideal. Yet Cicero exemplified and realized that ideal.

Let us turn now to who he was and what he believed the rhetorical art to be.

Marcus Tullius Cicero was born near Arpinum, a small town in central Italy, in 106 BCE.[3] He was a member of the equestrian order, or, to use modern terms, he belonged to the social and economic upper middle class. Following the established custom of members of their order, Cicero and his brother moved to Rome to pursue their education. As we have seen in the preceding chapter, Cicero first took part of his education in Rome and then moved to the Greek island of Rhodes, returning with the new five-part scheme of rhetorical organization that underlay his own handbook and that of the anonymous author of the *Rhetorica ad Herennium*.

In that sense he was a product of two generations, influenced by the older, more conservative, family-centered educational plan harking back to the days of Cato and Crassus, but influenced strongly also by the newer Greek-originated rhetorical schematics imported from Rhodes.

We shall see in the next chapter on Quintilian that Roman society quickly adopted not only the new rhetorical precepts but also the systematized educational program which helped make Roman schools the transmitters of these ideas throughout the known world. The family, the state, and religious institutions had served educational functions in Rome until the middle of the 2nd century BCE. With Rome's military expansion to the east, however, came its discovery of Greek civilization and, more important, of Greek education. As a result, Rome adopted the Hellenistic system of formal education, a system of "schools" that was intellectual in content and conducted by professionals, each an expert in his discipline. Quintilian, living in what we call the first Christian century, explains that system to us in great detail. But this is a subject of another chapter.

Cicero never forgot his republican instincts of public service, the rule of law, and the respect for institutions like the Senate. At the same time he never forgot his rhetorical training. As a mature practitioner of the art which he also explained, he was thus able to provide both his speeches, for example, and his humane concepts of the place of rhetoric in society.

Refining and polishing rhetorical theory occupied a great portion of Cicero's literary life.[4] At the age of 20, as we have seen, he had published the treatise *De Inventione*. In 55 BCE, the first of his three great works on rhetoric, the *De Oratore*, appeared, intended to correct the weaknesses of the youthful work. Nine years later Cicero wrote the *Brutus* (46 BCE) and the *Orator* (46 BCE). As a trilogy these books contain the best of Cicero's theory. In the same year, Cicero also produced the *De Optimo Genere Oratorum*, which was the preface to his lost translation of Demosthenes' and Aeschines' *De Corona*.[5] He subsequently wrote for his son, Cicero, the *De Partitione* (45 BCE), a catechetical discussion of the speaker's resources, the components of a speech, and the nature of both causes and audiences. The *Topica* (44 BCE), an application of Aristotelian dialectic to Roman oratory, was Cicero's last contribution to rhetorical theory.

J. W. H. Atkins appraises these treatises by noting their sources:

> Cicero aimed at acquainting his generation with the best that had been thought and said on the subject of rhetoric; and not content with the scholastic teaching, he returns to the fountain-heads, to Plato and Aristotle, Isocrates and Theophrastus, and with their work as a basis he attempts a new synthesis, selecting, combining and extending, in accordance with his own genius and his experience as an orator.[6]

But learning the rules was considered only part of the Roman orator's education. In 89 BCE Cicero attended the legal consultations of Quintus Scaevola, a prominent attorney. Apprenticeship to a practicing lawyer, common in the early days of our own country, served a dual function: knowledge of the law could be gained in a realistic situation, and knowledge of legal speaking could be learned by imitation, inquiry, and observation.

Cicero, after his legal apprenticeship to Scaevola, had at his disposal numerous sources of law, chief of which were the Twelve Tables. These were statute laws (*leges*) in the fullest sense of the term and dated from the 4th century. Certain forms of actions (*actiones legis*) were framed at about the same time which specified certain legal rights and liabilities. The *Responsa Prudentum*, or answers given by learned lawyers when consulted by clients on points of legal difficulty, formed the body of civil law (*jus civile*). The popular assemblies issued their decrees in the form of a plebiscite; the Senate in the *senatus consultum*. Each of the praetors (originally two, one for the city and one for foreigners, but in the late republic this group of magistrates in charge of legal suits probably numbered 12) issued edicts which were considered legally binding. In addition to all these branches of written law, there existed the large body of accumulated customs (*consuetudines*).

Most civil suits were tried before elective panels of juries chosen from "The Hundred" (*centumviri*) or "The Ten" (*decemviri*). The *centumviri* comprised the official jury members. Numbering 175 (five each from the 35 tribes) this group could serve individually as a single judge if both parties agreed, or panels, as was usually the case, could be employed. The judge sat on a raised dais, the jury, the litigants and their advocates on rows of benches. Although the procedural processes were quite complex, it will suffice to understand that a summons was issued, and a preliminary trial was held to discern whether the suit should go before a jury. In this first stage of a Roman trial, the defense had a negative objective. The right to bring the suit (*actio*) at all could be contested on technical grounds. The praetor heard speeches from both sides and if the praetor decided to grant a jury trial, the suit then moved to the second phase, i.e., that of the trial proper.

The Romans had a number of standing courts (*quaestiones perpetuae*) which dealt with extortion, treason, embezzlement, bribery, assassination, poisoning and arson, breach of trust, forgery, personal injury, personal violence, etc. The praetors were the customary presiding officials. Juries were drawn from a list of qualified senators (later, the Knights and tribunes of the treasury) and their number ranged from ten to 75 depending on the type of suit. The number of advocates on either side varied from two to 12 in a single case. Special laws placed time restrictions on the advocates: the chief prosecutor had four hours, each assistant two. The defendant was allotted twice as much time.[7]

After his study with Scaevola, Cicero reports that he listened eagerly to the speeches of the eloquent tribune Sulpicius Rufus, and in 87 BCE, he returned to his study of oratory under Molo of Rhodes.[8] Cicero was introduced to philosophy by Philo the Academic and Diodotus the Stoic, but there is little reason to believe that his initial exposure to philosophy had any immediate effect.

Cicero began his literary activity in 86 BCE in a traditional way, by publishing translations from Aratus, Homer, Plato, and Xenophon.[9] John Rolfe supplies this overview of the political situation that confronted Cicero:

> In Cicero's Rome the control of the government had fallen into the hands of a body of highly trained men, a ruling class theoretically fitted for duties of the most varied kind. The leading men of the Roman senate, the flower of her aristocracy, had filled the higher Roman magistracies, they were supposed to be able to take the field as commanders of armies equipped with the necessary military knowledge, and to govern provinces in various parts of the Roman world, which presented a great variety of administrative problems. In such a body there was a place for men of prominence, but all were expected to be controlled by patriotism, precedent, and inherited custom.[10]

Cicero was a practicing orator as well as a rhetorician. At the age of 25 he began his public career as a lawyer. After successfully defending several victims of Marius, the Roman dictator, he spent two years traveling throughout Asia Minor. Whether his trip was motivated by political expediency, reasons of poor health,[11] or an interest in advanced education is uncertain. In 81 BCE he returned to his study of rhetoric under Demetrius the Syrian and Molo of Rhodes.

On his Asian trip Cicero continued his study of philosophy, this time under the guidance of Antiochus, the head of the Academy at Athens, gaining a familiarity with Platonic and Aristotelian concepts that is revealed in most of his later writings.

Thirty years of legal and political experience intervene between the publication of the *De Inventione* and the appearance of the *De Oratore*. Cicero undertook dozens of lawsuits, and, early in his career, sided with the popular democratic factions in Rome. Although he did not belong to the patrician class, his eloquence and political sagacity earned for him a favorable reputation and a constituency. State offices were traditionally restricted to patricians, but Cicero managed to gain office largely as a consequence of his oratorical ability. He was elected quaestor, aedile, praetor, and finally consul, positions that correspond in some respects to our offices of governor, state supreme court justice, chief justice of the Supreme Court, and president. Cicero's Rome was convulsed with change. The republic was soon to become the empire, and power shifted from the people to the government and finally to the military. The law courts through which Cicero had attained eminence were in the process of dissolution. As he advanced in political power Cicero became increasingly conservative, and he suffered a corresponding loss of popular support.[12] Disliked by the patricians and distrusted by the people, Cicero turned to writing as an outlet for his many energies.

From a letter written to his friend Atticus in mid-November 55 BCE we know that Cicero finished the *De Oratore* in that year after spending much time and effort on it.[13] In this work, the methods of rhetorical training that were fully detailed in the *De Inventione* are relegated to a lesser position. The great orator-statesman, Cicero seems to say, should be acquainted with the rules and precepts, but he must not depend on oratorical schooling alone.[14] Cicero's ideal orator is a man widely read in philosophy, but he is more than this.

He will need knowledge of civil law and history. He must have a sense of humor, and psychological insight to enable him to anger or to touch the judge. He must be able to pass from the particular to the general, to see in each individual case the application of universal law. He must adapt his speeches to occasions and persons: his openings must be tactful, his statement of facts clear, his proof cogent, his rebuttals trenchant, and his perorations vehement.[15]

Cicero wanted rhetoric, as it was properly understood, to be a system of general culture. This was not an original goal. Isocrates had stated that the study of rhetoric was valuable for refined statesmanship several centuries earlier, and Cicero frequently acknowledges his debt to the Greek theorists.[16]

In marked contrast to his perfunctory discussion of the emotions in the *De Inventione*, Cicero maintains in the *De Oratore* that the orator must actually experience and feel the emotions that he tries to arouse. Wit and humor are added to the requisite weaponry of the advocate, and Cicero's statements on prose rhythm, although they are vague, do allow the reader to appreciate, in part, the careful revisions needed for oratorical success.

Cicero chooses the dialogue format for this treatise. At the Tusculan villa of Lucius Licinius Crassus in 91 BCE, he assembles Rome's preeminent orators to discuss oratory. One of the characters in the *De Oratore*, Crassus, a patrician and ex-consul, had actually tutored Cicero in rhetoric. Cicero uses Crassus as the exponent of his own views on the subject, namely, that rhetoric is a mode of life itself, and that the orator is a cultured mixture of philosopher, lawyer, and politician. To oppose the views of Crassus, Cicero uses Marcus Antonius, grandfather of the triumvir. Historically, it is the position of Antonius that has endured. Publius Sulpicius Rufus and Gaius Aurelius Cotta are introduced as foils for the main characters. Quintus Mucius Scaevola appears in Book I to represent the position of a legal theorist who doubts the need for both rhetoric and broad cultural education in an orator. In the later books of the treatise Cicero presents Quintus Lutatius Catulus, a military official, and Gaius Julius Caesar Strabo Vopiscus, a lawyer who agrees to speak about wit and humor.

In reading the following synopsis of the *De Oratore* one should remember that educated men, before and after Cicero, placed a value on theoretical discussions of style, rhetoric, and grammar that seems odd to us. However, by publishing this treatise Cicero "offered a target to which were drawn the shafts of opposing opinion. From this time on until the *Orator* at the end of the year 46 there are traces of this literary debate."[17]

# De Oratore

## BOOK I

My youth was spent during the civil war; my consulship was an exhausting struggle to save our country; afterward my energies were directed against the political factions intent on overturning the republic. You have asked that I write on the subject of what eloquent men have thought about oratory. Despite my urgent duties I will do as you request.

(10) Few men have attained preeminence in oratory. In other academic disciplines—philosophy, mathematics, poetry, literature—those who are considered great have comprehended the entirety of their subject matter. The art of oratory, concerned as it is with the obvious practices and customs of men, is somehow more difficult than those branches of learning concerned with less obvious subjects. Yet no discipline yields greater rewards or has done more for civilization than oratory.

Oratory demands knowledge of many subjects, mastery of style, understanding of men's emotions, a charming, cultured wit, a memory filled with history, comprehension of civil law. In addition, oratory demands an understanding of delivery and a commanding memory. Since oratory demands so much we can understand why its ranks number so few.

When Philippus was consul and the tribuneship of Drusus was under assault, Lucius Crassus retired to his villa at Tusculum. (25) Quintus Mucius and Marcus Antonius accompanied him. Gaius Cotta and Publius Sulpicius, candidates for the tribunate, also were in the party. After spending the first day in melancholy discussion about politics, Scaevola suggested that the conversations continue under a plane tree as Socrates did in the *Phaedrus*.

(30) Crassus opened the discussion by saying, "Oratory has flourished only in free, peaceful, and tranquil nations. How incredible it is that few men, using the abilities given to most men, have the power to interest, motivate, and persuade their fellow men. No other art could have unified humanity, maintained civilization, or established civic laws and duties. The perfect orator, therefore, maintains not only his own dignity, he maintains the State as well."

(35) Scaevola politely challenged, "I doubt that orators established social communities, and I seriously question whether an orator can converse about all of humanity. Instead of eloquence, wise counsel probably established communities. (40) Tiberius Gracchus won for us our constitution with only a word. His sons, gifted in eloquence, nearly destroyed the State. Are not religion and law more relevant? Moreover, your claim that an orator is supreme in dialectic conversation is groundless. You should be content to say that an orator is able to make his case seem more credible and his policies more astute."

(45) Crassus replied, "Your views are those of the Greek philosophers. I disagree with them as I disagree with Plato who sponsored the notion. (50) The unique trait of good speakers is their embellishment, distinct, and arranged presentation; in other words, their style, yet style without substance is ludicrous. An orator must know how to rouse or quell men's emotions. Words alone are insufficient. (55) He needs a profound understanding of human nature, the province of philosophy.

"A statesman is expected to know political theory; the orator must go further and give spirit to these theories. The perfect orator, again, is one who can speak copiously and with variety on all subjects.

(60) "If an orator's client belongs to the military, the orator must know the facts of military science; if he speaks on governmental policy, he must know political science; if he must rouse emotions, he requires the teachings of natural philosophy.

(65) "The orator must know the facts of his case. If he doesn't then he must learn them from a subject specialist, and then, I maintain, the orator will present this material better than the specialist could.

"Training in the liberal arts is as necessary to the orator as knowledge of color is a prerequisite for a painter."

Scaevola smiled and said, "Crassus, you have apparently overturned my argument. If it were conceivable that any man could possess the abilities demanded by your definition, I would certainly admire him.

(75) "And if any man approached such an ideal it would seem to be you. But you have not yet mastered the wide scope of learning that you require in an orator; consequently, I suspect your standards are idealistic."

Crassus replied, "I have not been describing myself. If, as you say, you admire what limited abilities I possess, imagine how great that orator would be who possessed both my skill and the cognate learning that I believe necessary."

(80) Antonius interjected, "You have argued well, Crassus, but the knowledge of subject matter that you require is impossible to attain in the hectic life we advocates lead.

"I recall a visit to Athens during which many learned men discussed the proper function of an orator. Mnesarchus, a Stoic, held that orators were only glib practitioners, and he believed a man possessing the single virtue of eloquence possessed all virtue.

(85) "Charmadas of the Academy argued that no man could be a skilled speaker unless he studied the precepts of philosophy.

"Later I published a pamphlet in which I defined an orator as a man who can express his ideas clearly to an ordinary audience. I reserved eloquence to one who spoke in an admirable style, capable of amplifying any subject, and knowledgeable of whatever he chose as his topic.

(95) "I confess that my legal practice prevents me from achieving eloquence, but I think Crassus has, in fact, succeeded in this quest."

Sulpicius said, "Cotta and I wanted you and Crassus to discuss this very subject as part of our education about the nature of oratory, but you have avoided the subject in the past."

Crassus then said, "As you wish. I think there is no art of oratory in the strict sense. No precise knowledge of oratory is possible because our language and subject matter are constantly changing.

(110) "However, rules have been abstracted from the practice of oratory and this collection of precepts can be considered an art. In the course of my career, however, I have made several observations about oratory that I will share with you.

"Natural talents must be present in anyone who wishes to be an orator. Art provides an agreeable finish to a speech, but unless a native capacity is present, no amount of instruction and practice will make an appreciable difference. Those with some degree of natural capacity have been recognized in past years as popular orators."

Antonius noted, "Your remarks, Crassus, on the necessity of natural ability are well taken. A quick mind, a fluent tongue, and a restrained bearing are needed in no other profession except oratory. Indeed, nearly all characteristics praised in a man when found singly must be combined in the orator."

(130) Crassus added, "Any blemish or error in an orator is immediately apparent. We demand total perfection in any person whom we designate as eloquent.

"Both of you possess natural ability and each of you gives every promise of becoming an eloquent orator. What remains is the acquisition of judgment and discerning taste, but no art can teach these virtues. Enthusiasm and a determined motivation must also be present. But you wanted to know about my procedure in preparing myself for a career in oratory.

"From my school course in rhetoric I learned that it is proper for an orator to speak in such a way that audiences become convinced.

(140) "I was taught that every case involves either a general or a specific question and that the stasis doctrine must be applied to each question. In addition to these prescriptions, I learned commonplaces for judicial, epideictic, and deliberative speeches. I was taught that an orator must locate and evaluate his proofs, garnish them in stylistic language, commit them to memory, and deliver them effectively. I was told to divide my oration into parts, each part serving a separate yet necessary function. My diction was supposed to be correct, clear, elegant, and appropriately graceful. Many rules for delivery and memory were given as well.

"Such training in rhetoric, in my opinion, was useful. Eloquence does not result from applying these rules, but the art of eloquence does. Knowledge of the rules is the first step towards oratory, practice is the second.

(150) "It is necessary to exercise and test your forensic skills before you enter the law courts. In your private exercises you should prepare carefully and frequently write out and revise your practice speeches. Writing out your speeches is invaluable training for precision in oral discourse. I discovered that my declamations on subjects treated by Latin authors were ineffectual.

"They had already used the best expressions; consequently, I recommend translating Greek speeches and declaiming on them.

"To perfect our delivery we must study the habits of actors. To perfect our memory we can use the mnemonic tricks taught in the schools."

(160) Cotta asked, "Would you, Scaevola, ask Crassus to amplify his discussion?" Crassus, yielding to the unanimous entreaties, continued, "Can you consider a man, ignorant of common law, an orator? Far too many cases are carried on by advocates who are apparently unacquainted with our laws.

(170) "Any man who pretends to give legal protection to his clients and at the same time is ignorant of the law is a scandal to our profession.

"I will presume on your good will to hear me out on the available sources for the study of law. In fact, the whole of common law is set down in only a few books. Anyone studying history or political science will discover that these subjects are closely related to legal theory. Philosophy itself is based on the common law in that both the philosopher and the lawyer discuss obligations, rewards, sanctions, control of the emotions, ownership, and so on. Few books are as useful as the one that contains the Twelve Tables.

(200) "I think an orator must know public law in order to speak effectively in the Senate and assemblies, as well as in the courtroom. Any man who assumes the duties of protecting the innocent and prosecuting the guilty must have more learning than is given in the schools of rhetoric."

Mucius and Sulpicius, after expressing their gratitude, encouraged Crassus to return to his discussion of oratory, but he declined and suggested that Antonius present his theories on the subject.

Antonius replied, "I usually try to avoid speaking after Crassus, but in this instance I request that you expect no lofty diction, since I never attended a school of rhetoric. What I can pass on to you are my observations gained in my actual practice of oratory.

(210) "If we were discussing the nature of military science or politics or philosophy, I would undoubtedly posit a definition of the subject and preview the areas of development which I intended to follow. Accordingly, I will define an orator as one who uses pleasing language and convincing arguments in forensic and deliberative situations. I would also desire that he be instructed in voice, delivery, and a certain charm.

"Crassus seemed to claim political theory as part of the true province for his orator. I disagree. Men like Marcus Scaurus, a politician of the first rank, attained preeminence through their competent grasp of political science, not oratory. In fact, no amount of rhetorical training will ensure that an individual possesses the requisite knowledge or skill to institute national policy.

"You argue, Crassus, that only by studying and knowing natural philosophy can an orator incite or allay the audience's emotions. (220) I suggest that such a goal is impractical and unnecessary. Impractical because we are too busy in the courts to afford this luxury. Unnecessary, because an orator can observe in everyday affairs what is praiseworthy or blamable.

"Your concern for common law is understandable when we consider your respect for Scaevola and your long study of the subject. If you equate lawyers and orators, I approve. But you maintain that many learned men are not orators and, as a result, you defame the legal profession. Sometimes an advocate does not know the proper formulae because the laws are frequently vague or contradictory. In these instances an orator is more successful than a pedantic lawyer.

"Furthermore, many laws are irrevocable and unassailable. With these an orator need not be concerned. You yourself have often won your cases with charming pleasantries instead of carefully wrought legal subtleties. I think you have oversimplified the relative ease with which legal theory can be learned since you also admit that law is not yet considered an art. Moreover, I doubt that pleasure accompanies legal studies.

(250) "Nor do I think an orator needs detailed and painstaking study in the mechanics of delivery. A speaker simply does not have time to do vocal drills for exercise. Although vocal control and correct gesticulation are necessary skills for any orator, proficiency in these skills is a long-term process.

"If the need arises to know more about history or culture I can again consult specialists in these disciplines. The practice sessions involving assignments, drills, written compositions, and criticism that you recommend are probably suitable, but they are time-consuming.

(260) "I define an orator, therefore, as a man who can speak in such a way that he persuades his listeners. To accomplish this end he must immerse himself in public affairs and practice his art continuously."

Crassus replied, "I suspect you have contradicted my statements in the manner of the philosophers for the sake of contradiction itself. I was discussing the role of an orator in society; you restricted the orator to a legal milieu. Let us continue this debate another day."

## BOOK II

(10) Your reluctance to become an orator still puzzles me, but I am grateful that you want me to help you understand the practice of oratory. To do this let me continue my account of the discussion.

On the second day Quintus Catulus and Gauis Julius Caesar arrived at the villa. They reported that Scaevola had informed them of the discussion on oratory, and both asked to stay for the day.

Crassus responded, "You are welcome, but I am afraid I should not have spoken about oratory yesterday, since I do not have the necessary education for such a subject. You are fortunate, though, because Antonius will have more to say about oratory."

Caesar said, "If you do not wish to speak on the subject, I will not urge you to do so. I certainly do not want to be tactless."

Crassus replied, "I think the Greeks demonstrate a gross lack of tact when they plunge into a discussion on any subject regardless of their knowledge on the topic, but that is precisely what I did yesterday."

(20) Catulus urged Crassus to make an exception in view of the pleasant physical circumstances and the long holiday.

Crassus answered, "I think the Greeks would prefer physical exercise to dialectic pursuits. In any event a holiday should be spent in relaxation, not in intellectual discussions. It is quite natural to spend leisure time in idleness. Moreover, I am reluctant to talk about oratory in the presence of so many distinguished orators. Do stay with us today and hear Antonius."

Antonius exclaimed, "By all means listen to a man discuss a topic which he never learned!"

(30) After the laughter subsided, he continued, "Oratory depends more on ability and less on art. The orator deals, for the most part, with opinions, not with known data. I do maintain, however, that nothing more outstanding exists than a complete orator. No music, no poem, no drama is more delightful or gives more pleasure than a brilliant oration. An orator must be dignified when giving counsel, passionate when treating virtue and vice, forceful in prosecution, powerful in defense. He makes history immortal by his diction, his embellishments, his proofs, and even by his organization."

(40) Crassus added, "You have certainly changed your conception of an orator since our conversation yesterday."

Antonius answered, "My purpose yesterday was to refute you. Now, however, I wish to explicate my own views. It seems that the next question to pose is what the function of an orator should be. In my opinion oratory is properly restricted to panegyrics. No knowledge of rules and formalized precepts is necessary to praise a person.

"I do not wish to claim that the proper scope of rhetoric is every conceivable subject. Just because a person must sometimes give testimony in a trial is no reason to draw up lists of rules on presenting evidence.

(50) "The same is true for delivering official messages, which have no rightful place in rhetorical classifications yet require eloquent diction.

(65) "Frequently orators must encourage, console, advise, and warn their listeners. Rhetoric offers no rules for these functions. Furthermore, although many claim

argumentation on general questions as a legitimate province of oratory, no precepts are taught for such topics as the good, the useful, duty, loyalty, and so on. The orator must learn to speak skillfully on subjects involving society, politics, psychology, and morals, but when he can change men's minds, he has mastered the core of this subject."

(75) Catulus interjected, "I would like to know how this great power of oratory can be acquired. Certainly no Greek rhetorician can teach this type of eloquence." Antonius replied, "I have encountered many teachers of rhetoric, and I find their theories foolish."

(85) "My ideal orator, therefore, must have some learning and physical ability. If he is morally sound and receptive to constructive criticism I will teach him what practice has taught me in the same way that I helped Sulpicius by suggesting that he study under Crassus. My first principle of rhetoric, therefore, is imitation of an excellent model. Only the best qualities of the model, not the irrelevant characteristics, should be chosen for emulation.

"My second rhetorical principle is that an orator should have thorough and exhaustive preparation for each legal case he undertakes.

(105) "When I have full knowledge of all the circumstances, I know instinctively whether to argue from disputed facts, the nature of the action, or from definition.

"After I have classified the case I search for ways to prove my assertions, to convince my listeners that my client and I are trustworthy, and to arouse their emotions. In order to establish my allegations I can use evidence and reasoning. The rhetoricians provide abundant commonplaces for managing evidence, and little talent is required to deploy them effectively.

(120) "Reasoning, however, is part of the orator's art, but the greater part is skillful delivery. Instead of giving you a detailed account of how the orator should invent, embellish, and deliver his oration, I prefer to yield to Crassus, since of all the Greek and Roman orators he is without doubt the best."

Crassus responded, "It is not fitting that I should elaborate on your concept of the orator. In fact, I have witnessed your soaring eloquence on many occasions, and I would prefer that you tell us more about your methods of speaking."

(130) Antonius continued, "Three principles comprise my method, namely, to conciliate, to teach, and to excite my listeners.

"Each specific case relates to one of several types of cases. To assume, as the rhetoricians do, that each case is unique is to become lost in the complexity of individual cases. Just as a law encompasses many specific actions, and one studies laws, not each court case, to learn the subject, so too with the orator.

(145) "He must know how to manage general questions and how to relate specific cases to them. Whoever wishes to be eloquent will know these general types of arguments.

"In order to invent arguments, intelligence, art, and diligence are required. Diligence enables us to locate and study every facet of the case, of our client, and of our opponent."

Catulus replied, "I know that Aristotle prescribed topics for both dialectic and rhetoric."

Antonius continued, "Although I have always maintained that the best orator conceals his art and resists any Greek philosophy, I do admit that sometimes we can profit from their teaching.

(155) "Romans have seldom trusted philosophers, and if an orator displays his philosophic learning, his credibility and influence are diminished.

"If I should ever encounter a student with an aptitude for oratory, I would encourage him to study with the Academic philosophers. There he would learn that proofs are either extrinsic or intrinsic—extrinsic if they are derived from external authorities, intrinsic if they are fashioned by the orator.

(165) "Intrinsic topics are definition, division, etymology, conjugates, genus and species, similarity and dissimilarity, contraries, consequences, antecedents, contradictories, causes, effects, and comparative size."

My brief sketch of these topics will be sufficient for the talented orator who will apply his abilities to the task at hand. Once the material is located it must be structured in various ways to avoid monotony. Sometimes you should make explicit conclusions, sometimes let them be implicit, sometimes argue from analogy. In every proof, however, care should be taken to relate it to some emotion, since most decisions are made on the basis of an emotion. In a similar way the orator must carefully analyze the initial attitudes and sentiments of the jury. If they are favorably disposed, I proceed with my arguments. If they are open-minded my task is more difficult, since the verdict rests on the power of my presentation.

Antonius continued, "Let me add several principles that I have found useful. Not every case calls for intense emotional outpourings. Sometimes you must appear to be defending good men, sometimes you should show how a future benefit will occur if you are given a favorable verdict. Hatred, fear, and jealousy must be excited with great caution, since they are difficult to repress.

(210) "Pity can be evoked by relating the action to some part of the jury's own experience.

"In both the mild and the emotional types of speaking the introduction and conclusion should be paced and leisurely delivered. Emotions are slow to awaken, and to open with your full force would jar your listeners. You must overthrow the proofs of your opponent and evoke emotions opposite to those aroused by your adversary. Humor and wit are often effective, but these are products of natural talent. Since you, Caesar, excel in the use of wit, perhaps you will explain its nature to us."

Caesar answered, "As you suggest, wit is, in my opinion, a native ability and talent which cannot be taught by any system of rules. There are two kinds of wit: irony, which flows throughout the entire speech, and raillery, which is intermittently located in the oration.

(220) "At best I can only recite many examples of wit in legal cases, but no art can teach a person how to cultivate a sense of humor. No witticism should detract from a person's dignity, but you have asked for my concept of what is laughable, and I shall mention its nature, source, propriety, restrictions, and its types.

"I must confess ignorance about the nature of humor, but there are certain philosophers who claim to know its essence. Humor draws upon the incongruous for its object.

(240) "Wit can take the form of impersonation or anecdote. Laughter will result when some aspect of a person's character is displayed as ludicrous. We should not resort to puns every time the opportunity arises, because they are the stock-in-trade of professional comedians. Restraint, therefore, differentiates the witty orator from the jester.

"Witticisms can be drawn, as I said, from facts or from words. The subjects of humor are, generally speaking, the same as those subjects that can be treated seriously.

(250) "Puns, when used with restraint, produce laughter because they usually contain equivocal words.

"Humor that is derived from the nature of the subject matter tends to produce greater pleasure than that gained from word play. Also, humorous stories drawing on the absurd or what is confusing or suggestive or unexpected should be used by the orator. A delightful form of humor occurs when we are able to seize on the words of our opponent and use them as a retort.

(290) "To summarize my statements on the laughable, let me repeat that humor derives from unfilled anticipations, ridicule, restrained imitation of another's faults, and by juxtaposing materials that are at variance with each other. For example, a stern, severe person can usually evoke more humor that a gay individual because the contrast is greater."

Antonius resumed, "Your account of humor was indeed entertaining and you have explained the point quite well. After I have thoroughly studied all the relevant data in a given case, located and evaluated by arguments in terms of the desired emotional response I wish to achieve, I customarily divide the good and bad points. I amplify and embellish the strong aspects of the case and minimize the others. At all times I concentrate on what will best convince my listeners. When I encounter a vexing argument I tend to bypass it, and I try not to advance my case; rather, I bend every effort to avoid damaging it."

(295) Caesar asked, "Why do you value this principle of avoiding whatever could damage your case?"

Antonius responded, "Remember that I am not discussing an ideal orator. I am describing my own meager achievements. In a lawsuit, however, the sheer number of variables make my principle necessary. Sometimes witnesses should not be cross-examined if they are angry or if they have great influence with the jury. Sometimes a client is unpopular, or you unwittingly attack a reputable person. Far too many cases are lost because advocates fail to avoid whatever can damage their position.

"The arrangement of a speech can arise from the nature of the case or from the instinct of the speaker. The overall structure of a speech is easily learned, but the placement of proofs within the speech requires great skill. I tend to discard weak proofs as a matter of policy.

(320) "Every introduction should contain a statement of the case or some part of it. Moreover, you can profitably adduce statements suitable for the introduction from your clients, your opponents, from the legal charge, or from members of the court.

"Because each audience is most receptive at the beginning of a speech, the statements made at that time probably carry more probative weight than later proofs. A suggestion of what will follow may help involve the jury with our position.

"The narrative should be brief, and by this I mean the absence of superfluities, not length. Let the narrative be as clear as your painstaking ability permits.

(330) "The statement of the case with relevant proofs follows the narrative. Care must be exercised not only to establish your position, but also to refute your opponent's proofs. Little need be said about the conclusion of a speech except that it should be designed to sway the audience.

"Dignity is essential in deliberative speeches. To argue mere expediency seldom meets with success in our country. Whether you argue from moral worth or from expediency, you must consider the possible and the impossible. Above all else, the deliberative orator must know how the state operates.

(340) "Panegyric oratory, in my opinion, is a lesser form of oratory. Still, since we must praise individuals at various times, I will discuss the subject. You can find much to say about a person by considering how he managed his natural endowments of family connections, health, wealth, and so on. Look also to a person's use or abuse of virtue for panegyric materials. We tend to praise most those deeds that were done without profit or reward as well as those that involve great effort and personal danger. We also esteem those who have suffered setbacks without losing their dignity. In short, if the orator knows all the virtues, he can quickly compose a panegyric.

(350) "Founding the art of memory is credited to Simonides of Ceos, who reconstructed the seating arrangement of those who had been crushed to death while attending a banquet. Orderly arrangement, therefore, associated with familiar visual images, can assist an orator in retaining his material and proofs. In my opinion, a strong memory is a gift of nature and not something gained from rule books.

"Now I see that the hour is late, and I fear that I have bored you with my narration. You shall hear about style from Crassus."

## BOOK III

I appreciate your concern for my safety, and your requests that I relinquish my career are probably wise. But part of my consolation will be the continuance of the discussion which took place at Crassus' home. According to Cotta who reported the conversation to me, everyone rested until mid-afternoon. After exchanging some initial pleasantries Crassus began.

(20) "Because of your friendship I dare not refuse to discuss my theories on the embellishment of oratory. Every speech consists of substantive matter and words. Each depends on the other in much the same way that nothing in the universe is self-sufficient. No matter the subject or goal of any oration, it must consist of matter and form, and although neither can be separated except in the abstract, I will give my views on style, the form which language should take.

"Each of our senses can yield pleasurable sensations that are agreeable in differing degrees. In the arts, too, the diversity within each genre of art gives rise to various intensities of praise or blame. In oratory, however, different styles abound. There are probably as many styles of speaking as there are practicing orators.

"With such diversity, how, then, can there be rules for style? Some students are allowed to develop their distinctive styles in various schools of rhetoric, but it is a rare and gifted instructor who can bring this about. In any event I shall discuss the style of that orator whom I most approve.

"The best speaking style is one which is correct, clear, ornate, and appropriate. Little need be said on the value and necessity of speaking proper and pure Latin, nor do I need to dwell on the virtue of being understood. But let us agree to leave the matter of correct Latinity to the schools, to reading, and to learned conversation.

"Clarity is achieved by speaking correct Latin, by avoiding ambiguity, by grammatical precision, and by uncluttered sentence structure. In fact, these subjects of correctness and clarity are such simple matters that no orator is ever praised for them. He is held accountable, however, for their absence.

(55) "The perfect orator must have learned everything that pertains to the life of man because this is his province. Eloquence, the greatest of all virtues, gives expression to the substantive matter with which an orator deals.

"Socrates, himself a master rhetorician, separated philosophy and rhetoric, and, as an unfortunate consequence, we must now learn to think with the guidance of the philosophers and to speak with the rhetoricians. Numerous schools were developed by Socrates' pupils: for example, Aristotle founded the Peripatetic School; Plato, the Academy; Antisthenes, the Cynic and Stoic Schools; Aristippus, the Epicurean branch of philosophy.

"In my opinion the perfect orator will have little use for the Epicurean teachings. And, although the Stoics equate eloquence with virtue, their logic is self-defeating, and their sparse, nerveless style of speaking is not suitable for our orator. There remains the philosophy of the New Academy. Carneades and his followers tend to avoid stating any opinion but prefer to dispute the assertations made by others.

(70) "I think it is a mistake for an orator to study only the Asiatic rules and regulations of speaking since this restricts him to a narrow scope of operation. Much more preferable is the Attic concept that true eloquence depends on a wide knowledge of philosophy, psychology, sociology, and politics. I suggest, therefore, that our orator study well the teachings of both the old and new Academies.

"Those who declaim against rhetoric do not realize that eloquence, properly understood, encompasses nearly all knowledge, especially knowledge of human behavior. Since philosophy is, in the last analysis, based on experience, even a second-rate orator drawing on the same human experience can defeat a philosopher in a debate.

(80) "An orator, therefore, must have a wide educational background drawn either from philosophy or from experience, and the energetic enthusiasm needed to convey this message."

Catulus said, "Never before have I understood the necessary relationship between philosophy and rhetoric. How did you find time to learn philosophy?"

Crassus replied, "In the first place you should understand that we are discussing the ideal and supreme sort of orator. Even though you think such a designation fits me, I assure you I have not attained preeminence of that kind. However, your question is well taken. I have not had sufficient time to read and study philosophy as I should have done. Nonetheless, I believe that an intelligent person who has had considerable experience in the courts and the Senate probably requires less time to learn philosophy than those who make a career in the pursuit of wisdom.

(90) "Two characteristics of style remain, namely, ornateness and appropriateness. These traits should be understood to mean the style is pleasing, interesting, filled with substance.

"Ornateness is best defined as that element in a speech that is restrained, pleasing, learned, wonderful, polished, and sensitive. Embellishment should not be spread evenly throughout the speech; rather it should be clustered at various points. No one knows what things are most or least pleasing to the senses, but objects that provoke extreme sensory responses tend to become unpleasant.

(100) "Disgust and revulsion are located quite close to great pleasure.

"Any subject capable of discussion, whether general or specific questions, has as its goal either acquiring knowledge or performing an action. To acquire knowledge we may use conjecture, definition, and implication. By using conjecture we seek to determine the essence of something. Definition explains the power possessed by something, and implication is a method for exploring consequences. Conjecture involves four questions: What exists? What is its origin? What is its cause? What can change?

"Definition involves the questions: What is something generally believed to be? What is its essential property? What are its parts? What is its defining characteristic?

"Those subjects that have as their object the performance of an action deal with obligations or with inciting and quelling emotions.

(120) "Embellished speeches always move the consideration of the subject from specific questions to the more general issue. Accomplishing this task cannot be achieved by studying the school books on rhetoric; instead, the orator must have wide learning and command of much factual information. Therefore, I think the orator not only can but must seize as his rightful province the discussion of general questions and the methodology that assists such discussions."

Catulus added, "I agree that the orator should be allowed to address himself to abstract discussions, especially since the early Greek sophists, Hippias, Prodicus, Protagoras, Gorgias, claimed all areas of discourse for their own.

(130) "Why do the Greeks no longer advance the discipline of oratory?"

Crassus replied, "Each of the arts has undergone an unfortunate specialization and fragmentation. Many years ago the Greek statesmen—Thales, Pisastratus, Pericles, and others—were distinguished by their wisdom, their cultural background, and their eloquence. They had an educational system that encompassed all the learning necessary for the career of a statesman. Isocrates, focusing his instruction on the nobility of style, graduated many excellent orators and politicians. His success caused Aristotle to revise the style of his philosophical writings.

"In short, I do not care whether we use the label philosopher or orator so long as the individual in question presents substantive matter in an eloquent manner. Each discipline is necessary for the success of the other."

Crassus continued, "You all know about ornateness, but I will discuss the subject for you. An orator's words are either the usual designations of things or unusual significations, or new expressions. Words may derive their force and impact because they are antiquated, newly invented, or metaphorical. Of these divisions I have learned that audiences derive more pleasure from metaphorical expressions than any other. I suspect listeners enjoy the discovery of new relationships between commonly used terms. Consequently, the relationship between words expressed in a metaphor should have some resemblance to each other and not be too extreme. Some metaphors should be softened, and, if there is any suspicion that the metaphor will prove obscure, wisdom would dictate not using the expression.

"A natural standard for the period is the number of words that a person can produce with one breath. An artistic standard, however, differs in the cadences chosen for eliciting maximum pleasure. Some authorities recommend the iambus or trochee, but these are stultifying if used excessively."

(185) Aristotle considers the paean more suitable.

"Rhythm results from subdividing a continuous flow of words. Each part of the period must be manipulated in such a way that clauses that follow each other are equal or longer in quantity than those that precede.

(195) "Most of an oration's power comes from its style. Instinctively, it seems, men can discriminate and evaluate whatever is applied to their senses. Few men understand the nature of a balanced, rhythmic speech, but nearly all men can detect a blemish.

(205) "Our orator will find great value in amplifying his statements, since audiences perceive this technique as an effort to clarify confusing matters. Moreover, there are dozens of figures of thought that can be deployed throughout the oration, for example, exaggeration, impersonation, and so on. Figures of language will be second nature to our orator, and his artistry in the use of climax or alliteration or inversion or any such figures will add great power to his presentation.

(213) "I claim that delivery is the supreme factor in successful oratory. The best of the Greek orators know that without a suitable delivery eloquence was impossible to attain. The emotions that an orator wishes to evoke from his audience dare not be artificial. Nature has assigned special looks and tones to each emotion, and any artifice is quickly discovered. And of all gesticulation, our eyes are the most crucial.

(225) "Any orator who wishes to be eloquent must learn to control his gaze. Variety in tone and intensity can add heightened distinction to the oration. Each voice is unique and must be manipulated in such a way that the highest and lowest notes are avoided, but the entire register of tones ought to be used effectively.

"Now the hour is again late, and I have finished my assigned task."

---

In 46 BCE Cicero published an introduction to a volume of translations entitled *De Optimo Genere Oratorum* (*On the Ideal Classification of Orators*). In the nine years that intervened between the *De Oratore* and the *De Optimo*, Cicero's political fortunes had become increasingly bleak. Caesar had conquered Britain and Gaul; civil rioting in Rome became commonplace in the absence of restraining authorities; Pompey and Caesar used both their political henchmen and their armies as they dueled for supreme command of Rome and the empire.[18] A look back at an older masterpiece may have given Cicero some relief from the increasingly tense political situation.

The *De Optimo* is brief. Cicero presents Demosthenes as the greatest orator of all time, able to speak eloquently in all three styles, and an Attic orator worthy of emulation. Historically, Demosthenes and Aeschines had met in legal combat on the legality of Athens' awarding Demosthenes a crown.[19] Cicero recognized that the forensic speeches that occurred in the course of the trial were masterpieces of eloquence, and translated them. The *De Optimo* was the preface to these translations. No record of the translations themselves remains.

## De Optimo Genere Oratorum

The ideal orator should instruct, delight, and move his audience. His diction should be pure and flawless, his words decorous and appropriate. (5) His language should be adapted to the three ends of oratory. He will arrange his ideas in the best way, and he will know the principles of memory and delivery. In short, the perfect orator is supreme in managing the five canons of oratory.

There is only one kind of oratory, namely, the Attic, whose purity is unmarred by meanness.

(10) We would do well to imitate the simplicity of Lysias, a splendid model of Atticism. Speaking in the Attic mode, therefore, means speaking well. In my translations of Aeschines and Demosthenes, I tried to maintain their general style and language.

(15) I made these translations in order that Romans may realize what Attic oratory can be. I do not consider either Thucydides or Isocrates as the ideal orator; instead, the honor must go to Demosthenes.

(20) To reconstruct the setting of this debate you will recall that Ctesiphon proposed to award a crown to Demosthenes for his service to the city during the war. Ctesiphon made this proposal before Demosthenes' accounts had been audited and, as a result, Aeschines indicted Ctesiphon. Conflicting laws are examined in their speeches, and a comparison of the public lives of both statesmen can be gained by studying their orations. Both men had prepared for this encounter, and both were filled with personal antagonism.

---

Although the evidence is incomplete, it seems that a sizable group of Roman philosophers, orators, and writers had settled on the characteristic of "Attic simplicity" as the critical ideal in their system of discourse. Caesar followed this Attic style as seen in his *Commentaries*, which are straightforward and devoid of stylistic embellishment. The self-proclaimed "Atticists" took as their models Thucydides, Xenophon, and Lysias, all of whom had paid little attention to ornate or rhythmical language. These Romans attempted to emulate the "pure" vocabulary and grammar used by the 5th-century Greeks.[20] They believed that faultless Latinity, when joined to propriety in word choice, could not be reconciled with the redundant, copious, and emotional language of oratory.

At the other extreme was the group known as the Asiatics. The foremost practitioner of this style was Hortensius, Cicero's great forensic rival. The aim of the Asiatic style of speaking was "to impress and secure the attention of an audience either by fluency, by florid and copious diction and imagery, or by epigrammatic conciseness."[21] In a literary debate of the middle 40s, Cicero was not only charged with speaking in the Asiatic manner, but also accused of non-Atticism. The need to answer these charges placed Cicero in his traditional role as defense attorney for his rhetorical theory, and early in 46 BC he wrote the *Brutus*, a subjective history of Roman oratory in dialogue form.

In this treatise Cicero assumes the primary role as the main speaker and his foils are Titus Pomponius Atticus, a trusted friend, and Marcus Junius Brutus, who was later immortalized by Shakespeare in Julius Caesar.

To vindicate his position as an Attic orator Cicero marshals an account of over 200 Roman orators, evaluating them variously on the basis of the five canons of oratory, the three functions of the orator, and the three classifications of style. Within this sterile format Cicero displays his ability as a rhetorical critic.

## Brutus

(15) Brutus then asked, "When are you going to take up your pen again? You have not written anything since your books on the state. But let us discuss the matter that we came for originally.

(20) "Namely, let us talk about orators and when they first appeared and who they were and what sort of orators they were."

"I will try to do as you ask," I said.

Whereupon Atticus interjected, "I recall that our former conversation on this subject began when you were deploring the lack of eloquent orators in our courts and forum."

"Indeed, it is as you say," I said, "and I still worry about what career lies open for Brutus now that eloquence has become silent." Brutus replied, "You are correct in your observation; however, much pleasure remains in the study and training which oratory involves. No one can be a good speaker who is not a sound thinker."

"True," I said, "the rewards of oratory are the fairest and most noble in all of public life.

"Greece, for example, and especially Athens, can be called the birthplace of the orator.

(30) "Then arose the teachers of rhetoric, Gorgias, Thrasymachus, Protagoras, Prodicus, and Hippias, who taught their students how to make the weaker case seem the stronger.

"In response to these teachers, Socrates developed his ethical theory and Isocrates opened his school of eloquence.

(35) "Lysias, a writer of extraordinary attainments, is rivaled only by Demosthenes for the title of the perfect orator. Demosthenes' eloquence is characterized by a simple diction, compression, and a direct style. His sentences possessed power, dignity, and beauty.

"I realize that there are conflicting accounts about the deaths of Themistocles and Coriolanus, both of whom were famous orators of their era. Pericles, you must remember, was the first orator trained in the principles of philosophy.

(45) "The age of Pericles, marked as it was by peace and tranquility, was also characterized by a magnificence of oratory.

"Aristotle, for example, points out that Corax and Tisias were the first to assemble theoretical principles of rhetoric and prescribe a definite method for speaking. The point I am trying to make here is that oratory flourished only recently in Greece, although from our historical vantage point it appears quite ancient.

"But let us discuss the early Roman orators despite the paucity of historical records about them.

"Marcus Cornelius Cethegus is the first Roman of whose oratorical skills we have an extant record. Ennius called him a sweet-speaking tongue and the marrow of persuasion.

(60) "The styles of Cato and Lysias are both pointed, elegant, and brief.

(65) "Even though Lysias is studied today and Cato is overlooked, his orations are marked with every oratorical excellence. Cato's language is considered archaic, but if one revises his orations, no one can be found to excel Cato. Although his language is rich in tropes and schemes, I readily admit that his orations lack a certain completeness.

(80) "At the time of Cato's death many young orators were flourishing in our state, and, of these, Galba was preeminent. He could digress as a means of embellishment; he could delight and move his audience; he could amplify and use motivational proofs as well as commonplaces.

(85) "The speeches of Laelius, in my opinion, are pleasing but archaic. His contemporaries agreed that Laelius was highly regarded in the art of oratory; you will recall, however, the incident in which Laelius twice defended a group of men and then told the defendants that Galba would be a better advocate in the case in question because Galba possessed a more somber and forceful method of speaking. Galba was successful."

(90) Brutus asked, "If Galba was as skillful as you claim, why does this not appear in his orations?"

To which I replied, "Some orators do not write out their orations after they are delivered; others simply do not realize that writing can improve one's style in speaking. Some men realize that they speak better than they write, and such was the case with Galba.

"Tiberius Graccus and Gaius Carbo were orators of the first magnitude. Their orations are pointed as well as substantive and literary. (105) Carbo is famous for his vigorous delivery and his engaging wit. We know that he devoted much attention to declamations and written exercises, and that he was considered the best lawyer of his era.

"Rutilius, on the other hand, spoke in an arid style because he was educated in the doctrines of Stoicism. Stoic oratory is extremely systematic and not suited to convincing a popular audience.

(115) "Rutilius, following the Stoic doctrine of self-sufficiency, defended himself rather than enlist the greatest orators of the time, Crassus and Antonius. He lost his case. Rutilius represents the Stoic schools of oratory; Scaurus, the Roman school."

Brutus then said, "The orators who profess the Stoic doctrines are most competent in the careful form of disputatious argument; however, when they are placed in an oratorical situation they are usually found lacking."

I replied, "The reason is that Stoics pay little attention to style. Cato, as you know, did study philosophy under the Stoics, but he learned to speak from rhetoricians. I would suggest that a student learn the precepts of the Peripatetic School, since they not only teach the dialectical method but also present the virtues of good style."

(120) Whereupon Atticus said, "Let us go on to the orators and historical periods that remain."

(125) I agreed to do so and said, "Gaius Graccus possessed many natural and acquired oratorical abilities, and if he had lived longer, his many talents would have equaled or excelled those of his ancestors. His word choice was lofty, the concepts about which he spoke were characterized by wisdom, and his style was at all times dignified.

"Publius Scipio was the equal of any man in the purity of his Latinity, and in witty rejoinders none was his equal. Fimbria should be recognized for his thorough preparation as well as for his energetic intellect, although, if I may say so, his style was harsh and abusive.

(130) "His contemporary, Calvinius, although plagued by ill health, was a man of discerning intellect and precise speech. As a prosecuting attorney, Marcus Brutus, one of your ancestors, was inordinately vehement and distasteful in his speaking style.

"But it is only with Antonius and Crassus that we finally come to the best orators, those who attained a degree of eloquence rivaling that of the Greeks.

(140) "Antonius was attentive to the smallest detail, placed his arguments in the most appropriate places, possessed a perfect memory, and always appeared to speak

as if he had not prepared at all. The words that he used in his orations, however, were not chosen with painstaking care, and this was a blemish on his oratorical ability. He was most artistic in connecting his words into precise sentences. His embellishment served to enhance the thoughts that he expressed by providing more ornate settings for his ideas. The gestures that Antonius used were always in harmony with the thought he was expressing. Crassus must be considered on the same elevated plane as Antonius. Personally he possessed great dignity and wit. His Latinity was without blemish, the arguments and analogies that he used were clear and praiseworthy, but his most amazing skill consisted in diminishing or amplifying a presumption of guilt. Few men have been more resourceful than Crassus.

(145) "So competent was he in cases involving the interpretation of codified laws that he was considered the most competent lawyer among the orators. His most noteworthy opponent, Scaevola, deserves our respect and admiration for the clarity with which he could present legal issues, but I must also point out that Scaevola was unable to amplify, embellish, and refute the arguments of his opponent."

Brutus interjected, "I did not realize that Scaevola was considered a speaker of such ability." "Indeed he was," I replied. "Both men possessed a certain elegance and a certain terseness, but each in differing degrees."

(150) Brutus then remarked, "From your discussion of Crassus and Scaevola, I can see certain similarities between you and Servius Sulpicius."

I replied, "You are quite right about Servius. Few men have studied the precepts of rhetoric with the zeal and attention that he has. And he has done so to maintain his preeminence as a master of civil law."

Brutus asked, "Is Servius better than Scaevola?"

"Yes," I responded, "Servius made an art of civil law. He could only have done this as a result of his many years of training in dialectic. To this knowledge of dialectic and civil law he applied the fruits of his study in grammar and rhetoric. (155) In my opinion he surpassed his teachers in diligence, subtlety, and efficiency.

"Do allow me to continue my discussion of Crassus. In my opinion this orator was always prepared and was heard eagerly and attentively. (160) Although his language was extremely forceful and, at times, filled with anger, the gestures that he used were in good taste and always reserved. Of all the legal cases in which Crassus was involved, his most famous was the speech of advocacy that he made on the Servilian law.

"The speeches of Crassus have been a textbook for me. His speech on the Servilian law was given to a hostile audience, yet he spoke with such sincerity and charm that he won even his enemies over to his side.

(165) "There is another classification of orators who were either Latins or allies of Rome. Men such as Vettianus, Valerius, and Barrus were able to plead their cases eloquently."

(170) Brutus asked, "How are these orators different from our own?"

I replied, "These non-Roman orators differ in no respect except their lack of an urban tone. I am not able to define precisely what I mean by an urban tone except that it is a certain quality of intonation and pronunciation that somehow seems to characterize our city orators.

"Let me return again to the contemporaries of Crassus and Antonius.

(175) "Philippus, for example, was not only inventive but gifted in the use of language and humor. He made good use of his wit when he engaged in legal debates.

Gaius Julius Caesar Strabo is unsurpassed in all of the history of Roman oratory for his clever wit."

Atticus asked, "Is it necessary to win the approbation of the multitude, or is it sufficient to be acclaimed by the critics who appreciate and understand eloquence?"

(185) I replied, "An orator who is approved by the public must eventually be approved by the critics. A master of the art of oratory will be able to evaluate how well a given speaker instructs, gives pleasure, and arouses emotions. The ultimate test of a speaker's success, however, is the approval of the people. I should suspect that the common people would have agreed with me in my ranking of the most famous Roman orators, since it is their approval that has formed a major part of my criterion. The common people, when hearing a real orator, will be affected and not know why. The critic, on the other hand, understands the principles involved in affecting an audience. It should be apparent that what the people approve must be approved by the critics.

"An orator must have an audience if his speech is to be successful. Frequently the common people mistakingly give their approval to a mediocre orator because they are unable to compare him to someone better.

(195) "By way of illustration, let me remind you of the case in which Scaevola defended Caponius. The common man who heard this speech was undoubtedly impressed with Scaevola's knowledge of testamentary law and his ability to determine the precise meaning of written documents. Crassus, however, arguing against Scaevola, captured the attention of his listeners with his pleasant presentation. Crassus advanced a series of arguments that won belief from his audience, and, finally, with an abundance of admirable examples and illustrations, he convinced the jury.

"The important distinctions between the trained critic and the untrained multitude are these: first, the trained critic knows the principles of eloquence that ought to affect the audience;

(200) second, he is able to distinguish and judge which is best of two orators considered equally successful by the multitude; third, he is able to recognize the degree of an orator's skill by the effects that are produced in the audience.

"Returning to my discussion of Cotta and Sulpicius, I contend that two types of good oratory exist. One is simple and brief, the other elevated and full.

(205) "Sulpicius published none of his speeches; Cotta engaged Lucius Aelius, a learned Stoic and sometime speech writer, to write several of his orations. These six advocates, then, were in demand by the multitude: Antonius and Crassus, Philippus and Caesar, Cotta and Sulpicius.

(215) "Everyone knows that competence in the art of speaking depends on mastery of the five arts. Antonius excelled in delivery, Crassus in style. Curio, however, was distinguished only for his diction. His invention, arrangement, delivery, and memory were, at best, ridiculous and confused. So weak was his memory that he forgot what he wrote as soon as it was written. Nonetheless, as a consequence of his magnificent diction, Curio was ranked next to the best orators of the day.

"Quintus Hortensius won the approval of critics and populace alike when he was only nineteen years old. Like all other artists he is inevitably compared to older and younger practitioners. As a youth he excelled the elder Philippus; among his contemporaries he was always ranked first.

(230) "I was eight years younger than he, and we were rivals for many years.

"Others will talk about me, but do allow me to discuss Marcus Crassus, a contemporary of Hortensius. Few have excelled this orator in sheer zeal and industry. His material, however, lacked stylistic flourish, and his delivery was lifeless."

"I do wish," said Brutus, "that you would critique Julius Caesar and Marcellus even though we have both heard them. The orations that Marcellus gives please me greatly.

(250) "I know that he studied and practiced the art of eloquence with painstaking care. I doubt if he lacks anything essential in a statesman; in fact, he seems to resemble you in his accomplishments. In any event, I do wish you would address yourself to the speaking of Caesar."

Atticus responded, "I have heard Cicero state on many occasions that he considers Caesar's diction to be without blemish. His industrious scholarship on the subject of Latinity was, in fact, dedicated to Cicero."

Brutus interjected, "Then we do have an orator on a par with the eloquence of Greece."

(225) "Possibly," I said, "if Caesar was not merely being friendly. I do agree that eloquence has done more for civilization than the military; however, utility is not a criterion for oratory; rather, we should consider the value of the art itself. But do continue your discussion of Caesar."

Atticus continued, "Pure diction is the basis for eloquence. Formerly, all Romans learned correct Latin at home; later, impurities were introduced. Cotta, for instance, used broad vowels; Catulus spoke with rural accents.

(260) "Caesar tries to restore correct usage in his orations and writings. In my opinion he is an orator of the highest rank and noble in every utterance."

"I disagree," I said, "since the language of his *Commentaries* is clear and correct, but no ornamentation can be found in them. Let me return, if you wish, to orators no longer living.

"Sicinius, a student of the Hermagorean school, excelled in invention, not in embellishment. Varro, who displeased the public with his oratory, should be famous for his superior diction and terse expression. (265) Torquatus, widely read and gifted with the ability to explain technical subjects, and Triarus, a man of measured words, should be given the recognition they so richly deserve."

Atticus asked at this point, "You seem to be including everyone who ever addressed an audience."

(270) I replied, "My purpose is to show how few orators Rome has produced, and of these, how few have earned distinction. For example, my son-in-law, Gaius Piso, was unsurpassed in industry or in talent. He could marshal all five of the arts of oratory.

(280) "Curio and Calvus died before they could excel as orators. Curio sought political power instead of honor. Calvus, on the other hand, was well-trained and frequently original in his treatment of subject matter. He thought he was an Atticist, and spoke with an abbreviated, lifeless style. Avoiding bombast should be sought as much as avoiding aridity.

(285) "There are numerous Attic models, and to imitate only one is to deny that the others were Atticists. Moderation is the best rule to follow. If you wish to imitate an Attic orator, let that one be Demosthenes. I would hope that when the perfect orator speaks, the audience is engulfed by the power of his words. (290) Not all who speak in an Attic style speak well, but all who speak well should be called Attic."

Atticus said, "There is much virtue in irony when talking about something to deny it in oneself yet attribute it to those who pretend to possess it. (295) Your praise of many Roman speakers seems to lack scruples. Cato and Galba were not orators in any sense of the word. You seem to confuse and intermingle great men and great oratory. In brief, you have been overly generous in your unstinting praise."

I answered, "You are suggesting a topic for another discussion, Atticus. My model in my youth was, indeed, Crassus, and there has been no irony in my account of Rome's orators. Do let me continue my discussion of Hortensius.

(300) "His memory was more accurate than any I have known. If he was not speaking in the forum, he declaimed at home. His use of previews and internal summaries were unique to his method of speaking. Hortensius deployed words in a telling manner; his voice and delivery were without flaw.

"You can see how parallel my career was with that of Hortensius. While Hortensius held the first place among the practicing advocates, I studied Stoicism with Diodotus and received a thorough training in dialectic from him.

(310) "When a stable government was again restored, I undertook my first criminal case, a defense of Sextus Roscius. Without doubt my frail physique and overworked lungs caused my friends to worry about my health. I went to Asia Minor in order to modulate my intemperate speaking practices.

(315) "At Athens I studied philosophy with Antiochus and rhetoric under Demetrius. My traveling companions were the finest orators in Asia Minor, but I went to Rhodes to study with Molo. He repressed my excesses so that upon my return to Rome I appeared a different orator.

"Cotta and Hortensius were still the leading orators, and after my return from Sicily, Hortensius and I met in court.

(320) "In my opinion Hortensius relaxed his pursuit of eloquence after his consulship and decided to enjoy his reputation. I did not cease in my efforts. Few spoke more, wrote more, studied more, or exercised the arts of eloquence more than I. After my consulship Hortensius and I were frequently heard on the same side of many cases. Posterity will judge our success."

---

Cicero continued his polemic with the so-called Atticists by releasing the *Orator* late in 46 BCE. Written in the form of a letter to Brutus, the treatise presents Cicero's view of the perfect orator. The dominant theme of the book is the general notion that two kinds of orators exist: those who speak in plain terms for useful, instructive purposes and those who rely on their exuberance, verbosity, and rhythmic cadences to sway their auditors. Cicero prefers the latter. Again assuming a defensive point of view as he did in the *Brutus*, Cicero discusses his theory of prose rhythm. He draws upon Plato's concept of "ideas" to illustrate his conception of the ideal orator, but the discussion of style belongs to Cicero alone.

By arguing for the interrelationships between the three functions of the orator—to teach, to please, to move—and the three levels of styles—plain, middle, and grand—Cicero offers an approach to oratory that is unified and coherent. If one places undue stress on the parts of orations or the number of premises in a proof—in short, if one takes the curricular approach to rhetoric—he will eventually lose sight of the entity, the wholeness, that is an oration. Cicero claims that style is the unifying principle of oral discourse; moreover, style adds an aesthetic dimension to oratory. The *Orator* clarifies Cicero's theory of style.

## Orator

(15) Philosophy is an essential component in the education of the ideal orator. Pericles and Demosthenes studied philosophy, and their success was due, in part, to their training in philosophy. On the other hand, rhetoric is needed to embellish the materials gleaned from philosophy. This schism between the disciplines accounts for the paucity of truly eloquent orators.

(20) There are only three styles; few men have mastered all of them. Those who spoke in the grand style were forceful, skilled in the nuances of diction, and able to evoke emotional responses. Orators who used the plain style were gifted with the qualities of clear exposition devoid of embellishment. Some modeled their style upon the traits of an unskilled speaker. Between these extremes is the middle style, which lacks both impact and intellectual appeal, but is gentle and occasionally uses a figure of speech.

Rome has produced no orator capable of sustaining the grand style. Indeed, those who wish to be Atticists can do no better than imitate the master of the Attic orators, Demosthenes.

Few realize that many kinds of Attic style exist. Some presently believe that to be an Atticist all they need do is speak in an unaffected and plain manner, but they are in error. Lysias was a master of the plain style, but his eloquence was never inept. Widespread difference of opinion exists on the nature of the ideal. Nonetheless, there is something of the ideal in all things, but only an expert can recognize it.

An orator must know what to say, in what order, and in which manner. Do not expect me to present rules for these divisions, since I am only concerned with the superior form of eloquence. Locating and deciding what to say is, after all, a matter of ordinary intelligence.

(45) The perfect orator, nonetheless, must know the topics of argumentation and the topics of reasoning. He must know that evidence is needed to argue whether an action took place, that definitions answer the stasis of what was done, and that ethical principles are needed to discuss the qualitative stasis. The perfect orator always moves the discussion from the particular instance to a more general principle.

(50) Our ideal speaker will arrange his material into an introduction, a confirmation, a refutation, and a conclusion. How the orator presents his material is most crucial, and describing the best style is, indeed, difficult. Some prefer smooth fluency; others, a severe, broken style. Since Memory is common to many arts, I will not discuss it here.

(55) The manner of presentation is twofold: delivery and use of language. The perfect orator will know that delivery—the tone of his voice, his gestures, his countenance—is essential to persuasion. Eloquence is impossible without a total mastery of delivery.

(60) The perfect orator is eloquent in that he excels in the use of language.

(65) Delighting audiences by their stylistic flourish is the goal of the sophists. Historians use decorous language to embellish their narratives, and poets use measured cadences to garnish their language. The perfect orator, however, will prove his case, charm his listeners, and sway them to his position.

(70) While proving his case he will use the plain style, reserving the middle style for pleasing, and the grand style for compelling his audience. Accomplishing this task requires a man of discerning judgment, skilled in knowing what is appropriate.

(75) We must, therefore, explicate the essence of the true Attic orator. He is characterized by restraint and simplicity, uses ordinary language, avoids rhythmical cadences and hiatus, excludes obvious figures of speech, speaks pure Latin, chooses pleasing words and phrases. Metaphors are used in the plain style to make the meaning clear, not for entertainment. He will avoid elaborate, contrived symmetry and repetition as well as the more powerful figures of speech.

(85) Moderate vocal variety and slight gesticulation are typical of an orator speaking in the plain style. He will use humor and wit to charm and ridicule his opponents.

The middle style is more robust than the first type. Ornamentation is appropriate. Metaphor, metonymy, catachresis, allegory may all be used effectively. The orator using this style will present his arguments in detail and in depth.

The third style is described by the words full, ample, stately, and ornate. An orator using the grand style undoubtedly has the greatest force. Eloquence of this sort sways and moves an audience. Anyone who speaks only in this mode should be despised, since the clarity and precision of the plain style and the charm of the middle style must be used to prepare an audience.

(100) We have, then, the form of the ideal orator in our minds. Remember that I am discussing the concept of the perfect orator, not his existence in the real world. That man is eloquent who can speak about ordinary subjects in a simple way, great subjects grandly, and topics between these extremes moderately.

This perfect embodiment of eloquence will know the science of logic in addition to the art of oratory.

(115) Zeno and Aristotle spoke frequently of the relationship between logic and rhetoric, and, in my opinion, our orator should be versed in logic as taught by Aristotle or Chrysippus. He should know the nature of words, singly and in predication, the methods of determining truth and falsity, ways of resolving ambiguity, the manner of defining what a thing is, and the relationships that adhere between genus and species.

In addition to logic our ideal orator will know how to discuss the philosophic concepts of religion, duty, good, pleasure, and so on, because the eloquent speaker encounters situations when these subjects must be developed.

(120) A ready command of civil law is also needed, as is a knowledge of history. To remain ignorant of what happened before you were born is to remain forever a child.

The facts of a case are easily gathered, but the manner in which the orator manipulates his subject matter is the essence of eloquence. He will win benevolence in his introduction, his narrative will be brief, his refutation and confirmation will be conclusive, and his peroration will arouse the emotions of his listeners.

A man's character (ethos) often wins agreement from a jury, but oratory is better served by appeals to the emotions (pathos).

(130) Appeals to pity need not be mentioned. Genuine sympathy must be present if one expects the jury to respond to piteous appeals. You can find copious examples of many kinds of appeals to pity in my speeches or those of Hortensius and certainly the speech of Demosthenes for Ctesiphon.

(135) Additional refinements of style can be achieved by using figures of language, for example, assonance, consonance, alliteration, repetition, antithesis, climax, and so on. Figures of thought are more important, since these devices contribute greatly to eloquence, and embellishment is the essence of oratory. Our perfect orator will deploy such figures as extenuation, digression, interrogation, dissimulation, division, and so on.

He will deprecate and interpolate. He will warn and suppress and protest and conciliate and use every resource of ornate language at his command.

(140) All of these figures, however, must be packaged in words, and I fear that critics will be displeased with what I have to say on the subject. When I consider, however, the role eloquence has played in maintaining the Republic, I need not apologize for my attempts to teach eloquence to younger men. A student of law need only listen to an advocate advise his clients to learn civil law, but with eloquence it is necessary to train and to teach.

I wish to discuss next the very roots of eloquence, specifically, combinations of words and the quantity of their syllables. Words must be arranged to avoid hiatus, be arranged in agreeable periods, and be arranged rhythmically.

(150) An orator must train his mind to preview his intended utterances in order that clashing consonants and vowels do not occur. Precise usage of our language demands that we avoid the unpleasant sounds created by hiatus, despite the contrary precedent established by the Greeks. Not even poetic license can forgive the illiterate use of hiatus.

(155) For the sake of creating a pleasing sound some consonants are omitted, some words shortened, others combined. Many poets use variations of common usage, but I prefer the correct forms of words. In nearly each case where words have blended together you will find the resulting word agreeable to the ear. Many times the common people are the first to alter accepted pronunciation for euphony. Always let your ear be the judge of sounds and cadences.

The orator should use ordinary language, avoiding rough, harsh, and foreign terms.

(165) Sentences, too, must appeal to the ear, and this is accomplished by casting our ideas into periods. When the clauses are either balanced or antithetical, the sentence has a natural harmony.

Prose rhythm, the planned cadence of a periodic sentence, is also adjudicated by the ear. Granted, our ancestors were unaware of the impact that a rhythmic period can have, but their custom should not be imitated by our ideal orator.

(170) When the material of a speech is worthwhile, it is proper to have a suitable and appropriate cadence that congeals the sentence.

I know that you, Brutus, want me to discuss the origin, cause, nature, and use of prose rhythm; consequently, I will do so.

(175) Thrasymachus discovered prose rhythm, but Isocrates perfected it. Gorgias was intemperate with this device, but Isocrates applied and taught restraint in its use. I can only speculate on the reasons why the Greeks failed to recognize the phenomenon of cadenced prose. Evidently they did not recognize the natural charm produced by the periodic style.

(180) To discuss the nature of prose rhythm would require a longer treatise than I intend to write. I suggest, however, that different types of prose rhythm exist for exposition, narration, and persuasion. Furthermore, this prose rhythm differs from that used in poetry, and derives its pleasurable impact from the arrangement of agreeable sounds. Poetry has obvious melodies, in fact. Greek lyrics depend almost entirely upon their musical accompaniment.

(185) In prose, however, words are the material made pleasant by measure.

The ancients recognized diction, but left us no guidelines for creating prose rhythm. Yet, if our periods are to move with vitality, the cadenced arrangement of our words is necessary. Although we agree that versification should not occur in prose, we must ask if the rhythms of prose are those of poetry.

(190) Both prose and poetry use the foot, either the dactyl of the iambus or the paean, as the basic ingredient for rhythm. Concerning these three much dispute and controversy has arisen about which best serves the needs of an orator. Some favor the iambus, others the paean, still others the dactyl. Aristotle agreed, and I concur in his judgment, that the paean, three short intervals followed by a long interval or one long and three short, is at the same time the most pleasant and most elegant cadence.

(200) The question is frequently raised whether rhythm should permeate the entire period or occur only in the initial and terminal positions. The conclusion of every period must be rhythmical, but some degree of appropriate cadence must also be incorporated throughout the period. Sometimes, of course, prose rhythm emerges from the concinnity and form of words.

Several questions remain. Where should rhythm be used within the period? (205) What is the difference between rhythm and rhythmical quality? What is the best way to divide the period?

Everyone agrees that the periodic style is essential in historiography and in epideictic orations. Such consensus does not exist with regard to judicial and deliberative orations. Even the most illiterate audiences recognize the artificiality of excessive periods in a trial or a senate speech. The resolution of this difficulty, I think, lies in a moderate use of periodic style.

(210) Rhythmical qualities are suited to passages of praise, and you may examine my speeches against Verres for suitable examples. In amplification, in the peroration, and in those cases when the audience has been won over, periodic style is desirable. Throughout the rest of the speech, however, we must accomplish our ends by restricting rhythmical characteristics to the cola, the structural parts of a period.

(215) An orator may use a ditrochee, a series of intervals that follow the pattern: long, short, long, short, to conclude his sentence as Gaius Carbo did when addressing the assembly. Or the cretic, a series of long, short, long intervals, and the paean can be used to secure a rhythmical structure. Although the spondee moves sluggishly with its two long intervals, it does lend a certain dignity to the shorter cola.

(220) A natural rhythm is sometimes generated by the structure of words, by balanced and antithetical clauses, but in other cases an orator must arrange his words rhythmically. Since each period dare not be rhythmic, the pleasurable cadence sometimes must be transferred to its components. A full period has four *membra* and contains from twelve to seventeen syllables; however, we must vary not only the number of membra but the syllables within the membra as well, ending sometimes with a ditrochee, sometimes with a spondee.

(225) What, then, is the reason for speaking in a rhythmic, periodic style? Utility. An orator's thought and diction must be flexibly arranged to elicit pleasure from the listener. Much learning and training and practice are needed to avoid the errors of obvious rhythm and jejune style.

I can only hope that my discussion has clarified for you, Brutus, my notions of ideal eloquence.

---

Near the end of 46 BCE Cicero published the *De Partitione Oratoria* (*On the Divisions of Rhetoric*). Cicero's son, Marcus, is presented as an interested student of oratory who poses questions to his father. In this treatise the tenets and divisions of rhetorical theory as taught by the Academicians are presented in a terse, crisp fashion. Amplifications and digressions appear infrequently, and the tone of the essay is somewhat impatient. As a capsule summation of Ciceronian rhetoric, however, the *De Partitione Oratoria* is unexcelled. Three main subjects are discussed: the five arts of the orator, the parts of the oration, and the divisions of discourse—that is, limited and unlimited questions.

In some respects this dialogue resembles the *De Inventione*. Both prescribe rules for effective speaking, and both possess an assertive finality as though little else can be said on the subject. The *De Partitione Oratoria* is distinguished, however, by greater clarity, by a wider conception of discourse, and by Cicero's plea for philosophical as well as rhetorical training for an orator.

## De Partitione Oratoria

I agree to answer questions put to me by you, my son. The theory of discourse can be divided into three parts: the speaker's personal resources, the speech itself, and the question.

The first of these, the speaker's personal resources, are divided into matter and language, and these may be considered under the headings of invention, arrangement, style, delivery, and memory. The oration itself falls into four parts: the exordium, the statement of facts, the proof, and the peroration. The question, however, is divided into general inquiry and a cause.

(5) Let me now discuss invention. Since an orator is concerned with convincing his auditors he should seek out arguments derived from topics.

(10) Once they are located, arguments must be arranged. Since the case varies according to the type of audience you are addressing, it is necessary to know whether audiences are concerned with judgment or with deliberation or with embellished speeches.

In a speech designed to give pleasure, a speech of embellishment, the arrangement might be chronological, or in terms of size, or in terms of complexity. In a deliberative speech the organization is: an introduction that is brief or absent, a narration that is brief or absent, depending on the situation, and an argument that is convincing and affective.

(15) In a judicial case the prosecutor relies primarily on evidence, whereas the defendant must concern himself with securing good will, locating evidence, and using appropriate digressions. The peroration must, above all else, arouse compassion.

With regard to style, single words must be chosen carefully, and when combining words we must strive for rhythm and correct grammar.

(20) The criteria to apply to word choice are clarity, brevity, credibility, brilliance, and charm. Another type of style, as you know, consists in the modification of words. Delivery enhances one's style, and memory employs a system of mental images.

(60) Let me now turn to a discussion of the question which is the basis for a given inquiry. There are two kinds of questions. One refers to specific occasions and particular persons, and this type is called a cause. The second is unlimited and called a thesis. A thesis is either concerned with knowledge or with action, and the stasis doctrine enables us to analyze the first type. Action involves approach or avoidance, advantage or utility.

(65) The same topics for securing credibility in a speech may be used in discussing a thesis, and the arrangement is likewise similar. Causes are subdivided into two categories, one that aims at giving pleasure and a second that has as its goal the demonstration of a case.

(70) An example of the first type of cause is the panegyric, which is concerned with praise and blame. A panegyric does not establish doubtful propositions; rather it amplifies what is already known. Words should be chosen for their brilliance in a panegyric.

(75) In a deliberative speech one must consider the possible and the necessary in terms of the proposed action. The proponent of a measure must show that the course of action is useful and possible.

(85) The useful is concerned with distinguishing between good and bad, some elements of which are necessary, others not, some desirable in themselves, others as means to other goods. When addressing audiences who are unlearned and lacking in cultural refinement it is best to argue utility. When speaking to an educated, sophisticated audience it is best to argue true worth. Since men are more prone to avoid what is evil than to search out what is good, it is usually best to motivate your audiences in terms of how to avoid the evil.

(95) When you must argue that your proposal is easily implemented, you will find comparison to be the most useful method of argumentation to establish practicality.

Finally, let me discuss legal speaking for you. This genre has equity as its goal. It is extremely necessary to know civil law if one is to be successful in judicial speaking. Here again the stasis doctrine must be employed, and the topics of invention will provide the arguments for each of the three stasis positions.

(115) Frequently, circumstantial evidence can serve to corroborate your position. Extrinsic proofs, evidence from witnesses, evidence secured under torture, and so on, must be made credible, and you must establish confidence in these.

The stasis of definition, now that we have finished considering the conjectural stasis, must be considered.

(125) The prosecution generally should argue from the common meaning of a given term, whereas the defense may find contraries more suitable.

In the third stasis, that of quality, we must consider what is equitable. Equity is further divided into nature and law. Each of these is further divided into divine rights and human rights.

(130) Within these divisions it is possible to argue from written rules of conduct as well as the unwritten customs of a nation. Occasionally it will happen that a case rests on an interpretation of a written document. In such an instance it is necessary to make your interpretation seem intelligent, and that of your opponent absurd. One may also argue the distinction between what the writer meant and what he wrote.

(135) When it happens that the case turns on the meaning and intention of a given law, you may argue from the intent of the lawmaker or an interpretation of the meaning of the law. Or you may argue from conflicting laws. This ends my discussion of the theory or discourse.

---

Cicero wrote the *Topica*, his final essay on a rhetorical subject, in 44 BCE. During the two years that passed between the publication of the *De Partitione Oratoria* and the publication of the *Topica* Cicero's daughter, Tullia, had died. Torn with personal grief, he turned again to writing philosophical essays. In March, 44 BCE, Caesar was assassinated, and Cicero withdrew from public life for nearly six months, devoting his energies to the composition of the *De Divinatione*, *De Fato*, *De Gloria*, *De Senectute*, *De Amicitia*, and the *Topica*.

Trebatius, a close friend, had read Cicero's copy of Aristotle's *Topica* and, expressing confusion, requested that Cicero explain the subject of rhetorical topics. In response, Cicero wrote his *Topica*. Aristotle's treatise was intended to provide guidelines and rules for conducting a dialectic argument. Cicero, however, does not produce a similar manual on philosophical discussion. On the contrary, he borrows heavily from Aristotle's list of enthymematic topics found in Book II of the *Rhetoric*. The same Ciceronian topics that are presented in the *Topica* also appear in *De Oratore* (II, 162–173), which would suggest that Cicero is using a source other than Aristotle. The importance of the *Topica* rests in the attempted fusion of philosophic and rhetorical invention. Throughout his career Cicero repeatedly tried to show the relationship between the two disciplines, and in the *Topica* he is suggesting that philosophy and rhetoric have a common inventional methodology.

## Topica

(5) I wrote this essay while on a cruise without my personal library, and therefore, I am relying on my memory.

Every argumentative discourse must be concerned with the invention of arguments and with the judgment of their validity. In our own time the Stoics have pursued the methods of judging in the science called dialectic. Therefore, I will deal with the invention of arguments by discussing topics.

I define a topic as a residing place of arguments, and I define an argument as that which makes a doubtful matter credible. Some topics are inherent in the nature of the subject, others are extrinsic to the subject. The inherent topics are derived from the whole, from the part, from its meaning, and from connection.

(10) Definition is also a topic as is enumeration of parts. Arguments drawn from circumstances are inherent topics. Arguments based on words from the same family are called conjugates. Genus and species also provide useful ways of locating argumentative materials.

(15) Similarity, difference, contraries, adjuncts, antecedents, consequents, and contradictions, efficient causes, and effects can provide frameworks for inventing arguments.

Extrinsic arguments are generally adduced from authority. They are called extrinsic because they are not invented by the art of the orator.

(25) The brief résumé that I have just given is probably sufficient, but allow me to amplify each of them and speak more about their subdivisions.

A definition is a statement that explicates whatever is defined. There are two classes of definition, those that explain in terms of sensible phenomena and those that explain in terms of mental concepts. Definitions can be made by enumeration of parts and numbers, or by division into the species that come under the genus being defined.

(30) As I said earlier, enumeration is concerned with listing the parts, whereas division is concerned with genus and species relationships. A genus is a concept that encompasses many different species. A species is a concept whose defining characteristic

can be referred to as a single genus. A concept, moreover, is that which is innate. Sometimes an orator can define his subject by using comparison, but I think this is a sufficient discussion of definition.

Division is useful in argumentation only if the orator enumerates all of the parts. (35) An argument may also be developed from the meaning of a word, and this is called arguing from etymology.

The next topic of circumstances gives rise to several subdivisions. The first is the topic from conjugates, which concerns words that are etymologically related. Similarity can yield a desired argument by means of several comparisons, either by using parallel cases or by comparing two nearly identical cases or by citing examples.

(45) Difference, the opposite of similarity, is the next topic. We should also consider the topic of contraries. There are many sorts of contraries, for example, words that are opposites, privatives, and those that express degrees of difference as well as negatives.

(50) The argument from adjuncts helps one inquire what took place before, during, and after an event.

We should also inquire into the topics that have found special favor with the logicians, namely, consequents, antecedents, and contradictories. Consequents are what necessarily follow from something, whereas antecedents necessarily precede something, and contradictories can never be associated with something.

Another topic is that of causes and effects. There are really two kinds of causes. The first is the efficient cause, which does or produces something. The second is a material cause insofar as something cannot happen unless this material cause is present.

(60) In argumentation, however, it is best to argue from efficient causes whenever possible, since the results from efficient causes are inevitable.

An orator can derive arguments from a careful study of the effects of causes as well.

Finally, I wish to discuss the topic of comparison made between things that are greater or less or equal. Remember that considerations of quantity, quality, value, and relationship are useful when deriving arguments from this inferential mode. For example, more good things are preferred to fewer good things, and those things that are sought for their own sake are preferable to those that serve as means for something else.

(70) An example of an evaluative comparison would be the premise that an efficient cause is more important than one that is not. And, finally, with respect to relation, the desires and interests of the majority of leading citizens are more important than the minority.

Let us next turn to the extrinsic topics, specifically, those external or derived from sources outside the subject matter that I have been discussing. I define testimony as everything that is brought in and secured from some external circumstance for the purpose of gaining a conviction. The best witness, therefore, is one who has, or is perceived by the jury to have, authority. Physical or mental necessity also can assist an advocate in securing credibility.

(75) For example, evidence that has been derived as a result of torture frequently has the appearance of truth. The concurrence of random events and public opinion may also be considered as types of testimony. Sometimes one may incorporate the pronouncements of the oracles or interpret heavenly signs and portents to win credibility.

Or, the sayings and writings of men who are popularly regarded as virtuous can serve to secure plausibility. This concludes my discussion of the topics of argumentation.

I wish to point out that there are two kinds of inquiry or questions. The particular question is called a hypothesis or a cause or a case, whereas the general question is called a thesis or proposition.

(80) A case involves definite persons, places, times, action, or affairs, but a proposition is only part of a case and entails only one or several of these factors.

Since some topics of argumentation are better suited to one question or another, I shall now make suggestions about which topics to use for the cognitive or pragmatic questions. Causes, effects, and conjuncts are best suited to conjecture. A knowledge of definition is necessary if one is to argue about what a thing is. Similarity and dissimilarity as well as antecedents, consequents, and contradiction, cause and effect, are also useful for locating and arguing a question involving definition. When the question involves the nature of thing, the topic of comparison is extremely useful. (90) Enough has been said about the two kinds of general inquiry or proposition.

I wish to consider the hypothesis or the particular case. There are three kinds of particular case: the judicial, the deliberative, and the encomiastic. Each has as its end justice, equity, and honor respectively. The stases can be applied to judicial cases, and they are effective in deliberative and encomiastic orations.

Even the parts of an oration can be assisted by using the topics of argumentation. The introduction should render the audience well-disposed, docile, and attentive. The narrative should be plain, brief, clear, credible, restrained, and worthwhile. After the narrative it is necessary to establish belief, and this, indeed, has been my purpose in discussing the topics of argumentation. The peroration incorporates amplification in order to move the emotions of the audience in a direction that is advantageous to your case. I have given in other books the rules for the parts of speech; consequently, I think what I have said should be sufficient for you. Even though I have included more than you requested, I think you will appreciate what you have received.

---

*What were Cicero's contributions to the theory of oral discourse? He believed that the orator must have a firm foundation of general knowledge. He condemned the shallowness of orators who depended exclusively on perfect diction and elegant words that lacked substance. He felt that the perfect orator should be able to speak wisely and eloquently on any subject with dignified, restrained delivery. Cicero's ideal was the philosopher–statesman–learned orator who used rhetoric to mold public opinion.*

*For Cicero, oratory was more than legal pleading or a school subject. He considered oratory "the highest form of intellectual activity, an instrument indispensable for the welfare of the state."[22]*

*He joined the three functions of the orator to the three levels of style. He gave his contemporaries a broad interpretation of Atticism, and he revitalized the best of the Greek theoreticians and practitioners of oratory. J.W. H. Atkins has summarized his contributions:*

> *In an age of disintegration, artistic confusion, and unrest, he first held up the mirror to antiquity; and by means of a sustained constructive effort he recalled to his contemporaries the same ideals and standards of the past. What he aimed at*

*primarily was an adaptation of Hellenic doctrine to the needs of Rome; and with a wise eclecticism he drew freely on all the great teachers, selecting and interpreting, and in the end producing a new body of doctrine. Thus does he warm into new life many of the earlier commonplaces; and in making Greek thought dynamic in the Roman world he corrects abuses and enlarges the vision of his contemporaries.*[23]

*In 43 BCE, Cicero was murdered in a proscription*[24] *ordered by Marcus Antonius. The emperor Augustus pronounced a fitting encomium years later in a remark to his grandson, "He was a great orator, my child, a great orator, and one who loved his country well."*

*According to the historian Plutarch, Cicero faced his assassins with the cry, "With me dies the republic." In a sense he was right, in that the highest forms of free speech and rule of law he had known as a youth were being supplanted by civil war, violence, and disregard of law. The ultimate winner of the civil wars, Octavian—who came to call himself Augustus ("blessed")—ruled as the first Roman Emperor for 41 years, from 27 BCE to 14 CE, firmly establishing one-man rule. He named his own successor, Tiberius (emperor 14–37 CE).*

*During the latter years of Tiberius' reign a boy was born in the Spanish provincial town of Callagurris (modern Calahorra) who was to come to Rome and become its most famous teacher, and a famous rhetorician second only to Cicero in his impact on western culture.*

*His name was Marcus Fabius Quintilianus, and he is the subject of the following chapter.*

# Chapter 6

# Quintilian's Place in Roman Rhetorical and Educational Theory, with a Synopsis of His *Institutio oratoria*

> I am proposing to educate the perfect orator, who cannot exist except in the person of a good man.
>
> Quintilian, *Institutio oratoria*, 1. Preface 9

If you could find a single book that not only laid out all the principles of rhetoric but also showed how to teach these principles, would that make it easier for you to understand the subject? One modern scholar has an answer: "Since we are fortunate enough to have a comprehensive treatment by a successful orator and teacher, who includes surveys of other theorists' opinion and his own reflections on rhetoric and its pedagogy, the obvious place to start is Quintilian."[1]

The preceding chapters have laid out a bewildering sequence of ideas from Corax and Tisias through Plato, Gorgias, Isocrates, Aristotle, Hermagoras, Cicero, and a host of other writers. A student once remarked that trying to handle it all was like trying to drink a tidal wave through a straw.

To complicate matters we have seen as well that social and political backgrounds played a significant role in the development of rhetorical consciousness, with a constant close relationship between rhetoric and oratory and the societies in which they were embedded. For example there could have been no role in a place like monarchical Persia for a Demosthenes or a Cicero, or for the kind of Greek analytic spirit that originally tried to understand why some speakers succeed and others fail. That is why we have no ancient Babylonian or Hittite or Sumerian rhetoric. This factor demands that we know enough about Greek and Roman society to understand why matters rhetorical worked out the way they did. Cicero's life is a case in point—he flourished both as theorist and practitioner in a period which enabled creativity.

But Cicero, as we have seen, died at the hands of assassins sent by a leader of a faction in a civil war that was soon to destroy the self-governing republic and set up a dictatorial system which dominated Rome for half a millennium. Emperors, like other tyrants, cannot afford to tolerate free speech. On the face of it, then, it would be natural to expect that rhetoric would die away with the free speech it was designed to encourage.

However, this is not what happened. Rhetoric was too important, too ingrained in Roman education. It was the power tool of the elite classes, and an avenue of upward social mobility for the middle and lower classes. Coupled with grammar, it was also the base for what we would now call "literary" expression. For conquered people

*Figure 6.1* Statue of Quintilian in the town square of his birthplace, Calahorra, Spain (the Roman Caligurris)

throughout the empire it was to become the route to social acceptance in the new Latin order. As a matter of public policy, schoolmasters followed soldiers into newly-conquered territories as part of a grand scheme to Latinize the world. A standardized curriculum enabled schools to flourish everywhere, almost regardless of the skills of teachers. Rhetoric, the theory of human discourse, seems to have survived beyond its original close tie to free public oratory.

Fortunately, we do have from the end of the 1st Christian century, a century and a half after Cicero's murder, a single book which does sum up Greco-Roman rhetorical concepts and describes what was by then the accepted methods of teaching those ideas. If one were to choose only one ancient book of rhetoric to take to the proverbial desert island, this would be it.

The book is *The Education of the Orator* (*Institutio oratoria*) of Marcus Fabius Quintilianus (30?–96? CE).[2]

This account confirms that basic Roman teaching methods and rhetorical theory were in place even in Cicero's lifetime, and we know from other evidence that these remained virtually unchanged until the 5th or 6th Christian century; they influenced the middle ages, and had a great resurgence in Europe and America in the 15th through 19th centuries. A force as potent as this surely deserves our careful study.

Moreover, since Quintilian constantly discusses other writers' viewpoints, he offers what is in essence a comparative study of Greek and Roman rhetoric and education.

Quintilian was the preeminent teacher in Rome of the 1st Christian century, and second only to Cicero in his later influence on European rhetorical education. He began as a lawyer but turned to teaching, and in his retirement wrote a book— the *Institutio oratoria*—that not only presented a complete survey of rhetorical theory but also described in full detail the Roman school system which dominated European education for nearly 2,000 years. Rhetoric was at the heart of it. By coordinating speaking, writing, reading, and critical listening, the Roman school system combined theory and practice to produce orators capable of speaking effectively on any subject.

## The *Institutio oratoria* in Context

Quintilian emphasizes the value of rhetoric as a moral force in the community. "My aim," he says, "is the education of the perfect orator" (I. Pref. 8). Since the function of the orator is to advance the cause of truth and good government, Quintilian says he must by definition be a good man morally and not just an effective speaker.

This was a revolutionary doctrine in the development of rhetoric: Aristotle after all sees rhetoric as morally neutral, a human tool whose moral character resides in the speaker not the art, and Plato's grand ideal of the truth-speaking orator, so nobly laid out in his *Phaedrus*, had no impact at all in antiquity. Cicero, despite his call for humane studies in his *De oratore*, remains a political pragmatist with winning in mind. But Quintilian even goes a step beyond Isocrates' concerns for virtue and justice—as means for a better self-governing society—to make moral goodness integral to oratory.

Quintilian wrote at a time (95 CE) when this idea was especially critical. The republic which Cicero knew had encouraged the free expression of ideas. The whole elaborate apparatus of checks and balances had been designed to support government by laws rather than men. (The framers of the American Constitution looked to that republican structure for many of their ideas.) But by Quintilian's time much had changed.

According to Plutarch, Cicero faced his assassins with the cry, "With me dies the republic." Even allowing for the great self-pride of Cicero, there is some justice in the remark. He was the last great free orator of the republic.

The threats to Roman oratory in the 1st century CE included the loss of political liberty, degraded morality, and the complexity of the empire. It was ironic that the political threat to Roman oratory in the 1st century occurred at a time when rhetoric was the foremost discipline in Roman education. The ultimate winner of the civil wars of Cicero's time, Octavian, ruled from 27 BCE to 14 CE—41 years. Octavian and his successors were clever enough to retain the official institutions of the republic, like the Senate and the law courts, while retaining firm control. The years from the beginning of Tiberius' reign (14 CE) to the end of Hadrian's (138 CE) marked the even firmer consolidation of the apparatus of the Roman empire.

This period coincides with the reigns of all but the first two of Suetonius' 12 Caesars together with the reigns of Nerva, Trajan, and Hadrian. If the empire under Octavian era was relatively personalized, the empire from 14 to 138 CE became organized, perfected, institutionalized, and efficient.

Quintilian himself had to be keenly aware of this situation. After all, the year of his return to Rome from Spain (69 CE) is known as the "year of four emperors"—namely, Galba, Otho, Vitellius, and Vespasian. Quintilian composed his *Institutio* during the reign of Vespasian's successor, Domitian, whom the historian Tacitus called "a monster." During Domitian's reign an active secret police preyed on the population. The slightest suspicion of disloyalty could lead to execution. In a supreme act of irony, Domitian proclaimed himself *censor perpetuus*—protector of public morals. Domitian's manner of death symbolized the level of morality he sustained during his tenure: he was murdered by his wife and guards.

There is a modern debate among scholars as to whether Roman oratory actually declined under these conditions of the empire. For example the *Dialogue on Orators* (*Dialogus de oratoribus*) of Tacitus,[3] written about 103 CE, is often cited as evidence of the decay of oratory, but others point out that the dialogue is a dramatic fiction which cannot be trusted as historical evidence, and cite other evidence for a vigorous public oratory even under the emperors.

Nevertheless conditions in the new empire were in fact inimical to creative oratory: the length of speeches, number of advocates, and duration of court trials were reduced; orators ran the risk of offending the emperor in every speech they gave; the dynamic issues of the past were, for the most part, absent; the power of the autocracy steadily encroached on self-governing bodies like the Senate. The problem of reconciling the organizational requirements of empire and self-government based on a free interchange of ideas proved too difficult for Rome. The result was a general loss of those habits of self-government that had been nurtured in the earlier republic. In short, the social and political conditions productive of creative oratory no longer marked the Roman world.

In this context Quintilian's *Institutio oratoria* was a radical document. His argument was a potentially dangerous one—that people of his time were not doing what they should be doing. It is noteworthy that he seldom uses any contemporary examples—that would have been dangerous in the political climate of his times—but instead points his readers to good and great men of earlier times. For example in Book Ten he analyzes a large number of speakers of the past, virtually ignoring his contemporaries. The implications must have been clear to his readers.

What Quintilian describes for us, then, is the rhetorical-educational environment of a society which dominated the world for five centuries and influenced western culture in so many ways thereafter, right up to the present time. His *Institutio oratoria* is important therefore both for its rhetorical theory and for its account of how Roman rhetoric was taught. No other author in the ancient world has given us such an encyclopedic account of these matters.

## Life of Quintilian

Marcus Fabius Quintilianus held the preeminent place among the *rhetores* of Rome during the 1st century. Martial, in an epigram usually dated 84 CE, proclaimed him as such:

> Quintiliane, vagae moderator summe iuventae, Gloria Romanae, Quintilane, togae Quintilian, premier guide of wayward youth, Quintilian, glory of the Roman toga.
>
> (Martial II.90.1–2)

Quintilian was born between 30 and 40 CE in the province of Calagurris (modern Calahorra) in Spain. Roman civilization seems to have spread into Spain early and more forcibly than into other provinces. For instance, sometime before Quintilian would have attended a *schola grammatica*, Horace recognized the existence of Roman schools in Spain *(Odes*, II. 20. 19). Since Calagurris was a center of Roman culture, Quintilian probably received some of his early training there. However, about 50 CE, his father took him to Rome for further education.

In Rome, several teachers and orators seem to have influenced the young man from Spain. According to the scholiast Juvenal, the prominent grammarian Palaemon taught Quintilian *(Satires*, VI. 452–453). It is certain that Quintilian studied under the orator Domitus Afer, a politician of high rank (consul). Quintilian held him in deep respect and recalled that Afer's treatise *On Witness* was circulated during his boyhood. Quintilian's attachment to Afer continued until Afer's death c.59 CE. Quintilian also ranked Africanus, Servilius Nonianas, Galerius Trachalus, Vibius Crispus, and Julius Secundus high among his early examples.

After Afer's death, Quintilian returned to Spain and it is believed that for the next eight years he practiced law and taught rhetoric. Although there is no extant evidence regarding his career in Calagurris, he must have become connected with Galba, who was governor of Spain at the time, for in the year 68 when Galba went to Rome as emperor, he took Quintilian with him.

Shortly after his return to Rome, Quintilian resumed his career as a lawyer and teacher. Although there are only two known cases in which Quintilian pleaded in the courts, there may have been more. In Quintilian's defense of Naevius Arpinianus, the sole question in the case was whether the defendant threw his wife out of the window or she threw herself. The question was unsettled! He also pleaded in behalf of Queen Berenice, before whom Paul appeared in Caesaria before going to Rome (Acts 25:13ff.). Quintilian defended the Queen as she sat as judge of her own case.

As a teacher of rhetoric, Quintilian enjoyed an eminent public position. Emperor Vespasian subsidized his school in 72 CE. In 87 CE the emperor appointed him head of the state school of oratory in Rome. His teaching covered a span of 20 years from 72 to 92 CE. Counted among his students were Pliny the Younger, Juvenal, Suetonius, and Tacitus, as well as children from the imperial household. According to Juvenal, Quintilian received many honors and great wealth by virtue of his reputation as a teacher *(Satires*, VII. 188ff.).

Quintilian retired from teaching about 92 CE, to secure "rest from my labors, which for twenty years I had devoted to the instruction of youth" *(Institutio oratoria*

I. Preface 1). It is probable that he completed his major treatise, *Institutio oratoria*, about 95 CE. Also during his retirement, Quintilian received from the Emperor Domitian a singular honor—the Consular insignia. Although we know nothing of his subsequent life, it is believed that he died shortly after the reign of Domitian ended in 96 CE.

## The Structure of the *Institutio oratoria*

None of Quintilian's earlier works has survived. The first known published work of Quintilian was his "Defense of Naevius Arpinianus." (He later acknowledged with a degree of embarrassment that he had published this work in order to acquire fame.) No longer extant, this work is apparently the record of Quintilian's successful efforts for his client. A treatise titled *De Causis Corruptae Eloquentiae* (*On the Causes of the Decay of Eloquence*) is known only through Quintilian's references to it in the *Institutio oratoria* (vi. Preface 3; viii. 6. 76). This *alius liber* (other treatise) on educational matters apparently traced the decline of eloquent use of the Latin language. (Because it is similar in subject matter to the *Dialogus de oratoribus* of Tacitus, many Renaissance editors believed that Quintilian was the real author of Tacitus' work.) A work published by his students without his consent, the *Ars Rhetorica*, is no longer extant. Two other sets of sample speeches were published under his name but are believed spurious: *Declamationes maiores* and *Declamationes minores*.

Quintilian's major work, his *Institutio oratoria*, blends the theoretical and educational aspects of rhetoric. Even though he spent only two years in composing his treatise, Quintilian gathers up an educational experience of 20 years. Quintilian clearly states his intention: "I am proposing to educate the perfect orator, who cannot exist except in the person of a good man." Thus Quintilian demands not merely the possession of exceptional gifts of speech, but of all the excellences of character as well (I. Preface 9).

The emphasis on moral purpose as well as rhetorical skill distinguishes *Institutio oratoria*. The fundamental idea of this work is Quintilian's definition of oratory as *vir bonus dicendi peritus*—"the good man speaking well." In its various Latin forms, the phrase "good man" appears in 23 passages throughout the work. The concept of a "good man" is not what one might expect. The definition of the orator as a "good man" goes back to the Elder Cato (234–149 BCE), whom Quintilian quotes. (Cato is discussed in Chapter 4 above.)

What Quintilian means is that the "good man" is one who is publicly active, possessed of both integrity and eloquence, constantly learning, and courageous in pursuing his ideals. His concept of goodness is close to the Stoic ideal of "public duty." No reclusive philosopher can be good in this sense, since active public life is required. As Quintilian points out, "a wise man in the Roman sense is one who reveals himself as a true statesman, not in the discussions in the study, but in the actual practice and experience of public life" (XII.2,7).

It is important therefore to realize that Quintilian intends the entirety of the *Institutio* to be seen as working toward the "perfect orator." From cradle to retirement (and beyond) everything has the same end—the creation of the Roman citizen-orator. While the book may seem overly long to some modern readers looking for quick answers, Quintilian would probably reply that there are no unnecessary parts in it. His own description of the book shows its intended unity:

> My first book will be concerned with the education preliminary to the duties of the teacher of rhetoric. My second will deal with the rudiments of the schools of rhetoric and with problems connected with the essence of rhetoric itself. The next five will be concerned with Invention (in which I include Arrangement). The four following will be assigned to Elocution, under which head I include Memory and Delivery. Finally there will be one book in which our complete orator will be delineated; as far as my feeble powers permit, I shall discuss his character, the rules which should guide him in undertaking, studying and pleading cases, the style of his eloquence, the time at which he should cease to plead cases and the studies to which he should devote himself after such cessation.
>
> (I. Preface 21–22)

In fact the *Institutio* carries out this promised plan quite closely. A brief outline shows how Quintilian adheres to his own projected order:

Book One: Earliest Education of the Young
    Home influences
    Advantages of schools
    Elementary exercises under the Grammaticus
Book Two: Boy sent to *rhetor* when ready
    Advanced *progymnasmata* (exercises)
    Beginning practice in *declamatio*
    Learning nature of rhetoric
Book Three: Rhetoric defined as "the science of speaking well"
    Five divisions of rhetoric: Invention, Arrange, Expression, Memory,
    Delivery, Three kinds of oratory: Epideictic, Deliberative, Forensic
Book 3.6 to Six: Invention
Book Seven: Arrangement
Books Eight to Ten: Elocution/Expression, with tropes and figures
Book Eleven: Memory, Delivery
Book Twelve: The Perfect Orator: character, career, and retirement.

We hope that this simple outline will be of assistance to readers looking over the synopses of the 12 books below.

## Rhetoric in the Roman School System

It is important to note at once that the teaching program described in Quintilian's *Institutio* is not merely his own personal proposal—rather it is a description of actual Roman school practice. This system was apparently already in place by the time of Cicero nearly 200 years earlier; the system itself lasted virtually intact into the 5th Christian century, and its basic teaching methods were transmitted into the middle ages and later the Renaissance—when English colonists brought them to America in the 17th century.

It is not generally recognized today that the Romans were, in effect, the inventors of the concept of "school"—that is, a center for education through standardized teaching methods on standardized subjects using graded steps or stages to reach a desired end product in the student. The Roman school was replicable, exportable, portable. In fact, Roman schools were so successful that they became instruments of imperial power as the schools followed the soldiers, Latinizing the conquered peoples of Europe and Asia. (Nor was this a one-way process, because the conquered peoples also saw the schools as a means of upward mobility for themselves and their sons.)[4]

The "schools" of ancient Greece depended heavily on the personality and philosophy of their founders. While a few Greek centers—such as Plato's Academy—long outlasted their founders, most Greek teaching was highly personalized. (The careers of the sophists discussed in Chapter 2 demonstrate this fact.) The Roman school, on the other hand, was an institution that did not depend on the individual teacher. Naturally some teachers were better than others, but it was the system not the person that prevailed for so long a time. Virtually every element of the Roman educational system was inherited from the Greeks, but it was the Roman genius to coordinate all those individual elements into a system.

Rhetoric and its practice formed the core of the Roman school system. Young men entered school at the age of six or seven, and for the next 11 or 12 years were put through a rigorous training in language use—both written and spoken. The rhetorical theory was that of the five "parts" of Invention, Arrangement, Style, Memory, and Delivery familiar since the days of Cicero and the Pseudo-Ciceronian *Rhetorica ad Herennium*.

Quintilian says that the aim of the training program is *facilitas*, or the ability to improvise effective language—whether oral or written—for any situation. Since the methods are often described very briefly, perhaps because he realized that his readers

*Figure 6.2* Roman school

would already be familiar with them from their own schooling, it may be useful here to present in outline form the overall structure of the Roman teaching system.

## Overview of Roman Teaching Methods Described in the *Institutio oratoria*

Quintilian's primary descriptions of the teaching methods occur in Books One and Two, reinforced in Book Ten with his program for the continuing self-education of the adult orator.

The methods fall into five categories: (1) Precept; (2) Imitation; (3) Composition exercises (*progymnasmata*); (4) Declamation; and (5) Sequencing.

1. Precept: "a set of rules that provide a definite method and system of speaking." Grammar as precept deals with "the art of speaking correctly, and the interpretation of the poets." Rhetoric as precept occupies eight of the 12 books of the *Institutio oratoria*:

   a. Invention
   b. Arrangement
   c. Style
   d. Memory
   e. Delivery

2. Imitation: the use of models to learn how others have used language. Specific exercises include:

   a. Reading aloud (*lectio*)
   b. Master's detailed analysis of a text (*praelectio*)
   c. Memorization of models
   d. Paraphrase of models
   e. Transliteration (prose/verse and/or Latin/Greek)
   f. Recitation of paraphrase or transliteration
   g. Correction of paraphrase or transliteration

3. Composition exercises (*progymnasmata or praeexercitamenta*): a graded series of exercises in writing and speaking themes. Each succeeding exercise is more difficult and incorporates what has been learned in preceding ones. The following 12 were common by Cicero's time:

   a. Retelling a fable
   b. Retelling an episode from a poet or historian
   c. *Chreia*, or amplification of a moral theme
   d. Amplification of an aphorism (*sententia*) or proverb
   e. Refutation or confirmation of an allegation
   f. Commonplace, or confirmation of a thing admitted
   g. Encomium, or eulogy (or dispraise) of a person or thing
   h. Comparison of things or persons
   i. Impersonation (*prosopopeia*), or speaking or writing in the character of a given person
   j. Description (ecphrasis), or vivid presentation of details

    k.  Thesis, or argument for/against an answer to a general question (*quaestio infinita*) not involving individuals

    l.  Laws, or arguments for or against a law

4.  Declamation (*declamatio*), or fictitious speeches, in two types:

    a.  *Sausoria*, or deliberative (political) speech arguing that an action be taken or not taken

    b.  *Controversia*, or forensic (legal) speech prosecuting or defending a fictitious or historical person in a law case

5.  Sequencing, or the systematic ordering of classroom activities to accomplish two goals:

    a.  Movement, from the simple to the more complex

    b.  Reinforcement, by reiterating each element of preceding exercises as each new one appears

Perhaps the most important aspect of these methods is their coordination into a single instructional program. Each is important for itself, but takes greater importance from its place within the whole.[5]

The influence of Isocrates is clear. The Romans, like Isocrates, believe everyone has talent, which can be developed by education and practice. Subjects like ethics, rhetoric, and political science are not lectured about, but are transmitted to students through imitation of good models and through constant exercises which provide them with an increasingly wide range of ways to think, speak, and write. (Quintilian's description of the Roman school system may be compared with the account of Isocrates' school in Chapter 2.)

The following is a book-by-book summary of Quintilian's treatise. The numbers of the paragraphs refer to the chapter divisions of each book as designated in the Loeb Classical Library text. It must be noted at once that Quintilian is extremely difficult to summarize. No quick synopsis like this can transmit the flavor of his humane, sensible approach to his subject. He always cites differing viewpoints, he interposes personal remarks or advice from his teaching experience, and he uses numerous detailed examples. The reader is encouraged to look to the actual text to appreciate all that he has to say.

## Quintilian's *Institutio oratoria*

### BOOK ONE

PREFACE. I have written this book because my friends have asked me to clarify the ideas of previous writers on the art of speaking, and to reconcile their contradictory opinions. I hold that the art of oratory includes all that is essential for the training of an orator and that it is impossible to reach the summit of any art unless we have first passed through the elemental stages. Therefore my book will not be a dry textbook like the others but will lead the reader through every stage from childhood to perfection in the art. My aim is the education of the perfect orator. The first essential for such a person is that he be a good man. Our ideal orator, then, will be a true "philosopher" because he will not only have virtue but be able to practice it.

1. Conceive the highest hopes for your children, for most are quick to reason and ready to learn. There are degrees of talent, but all have some. Be particular concerning your child's earliest training. His nurses must be of good character and speak correctly. Both parents should be as highly educated as possible, and the child's companions ought to be carefully chosen. He should be taught Greek first, because he will learn Latin naturally at home.

2. Group instruction as opposed to private tutoring, for boys must learn quickly to live in society. Group instruction is accused of corrupting morals, but morals may be corrupted anywhere, even at home. Moreover he will learn from the praise and correction given to others and will profit from imitating the achievements of his classmates.

3. Concerning teaching methods, ascertain first the student's ability and character. The surest indication is his power of memory, which should be quick and retentive. The next indication is his power of imitation. I am opposed to corporal punishment, since it is not necessary with the good and hardens those who are not good. Finally, he who is really gifted will above all else be good.

4. The teacher of literature and language (*grammaticus*) should begin as soon as the student has learned to read and write without difficulty. His art consists of two parts: the art of speaking correctly and the interpretation of the poets. Yet all kinds of writers should be studied, not just poets. Grammar is the foundation of oratory, for the art of writing is combined with the art of speaking. Therefore the details of grammar, including pronunciation and spelling, are important to the future orator.

5. Style has three positive attributes: correctness, clarity, and elegance. A student should be taught to select the right word and the one that sounds best for his desired effect. Proper style results when one chooses the more euphonious word when confronted with exact synonyms, when barbarisms (offenses of single words) are eliminated, when solecisms (errors of more than one word) are eliminated, and when current words are chosen. Note though that some phrases, called *schemata*, seem to be solecisms but are not; these will be discussed later [i.e., in Book Nine].

6. Proper spoken language is based upon reason, antiquity, authority, and usage. Reason provides proper language through analogy and etymology. As for antiquity, attractive archaic words should be used sparingly. Language from orators and historians is applicable if not out of date. I define usage as the agreed practice of educated men.

7. Orthography, or the set of rules for writing, is the servant of usage and changes constantly. It demands detailed knowledge of the alphabet, accents, spelling, and the like. Actually, most words should be spelled as they are pronounced. For those who argue that these details are mere quibbles, I reply that it is only the excess of grammar that is a problem: Cicero insisted that his own son be careful in these matters.

8. Reading aloud must be taught mainly by practice. The student must understand what he reads. Oral reading should be manly and dignified, differing from acting in that characterizations are not created. The teacher should accustom students to analysis by lecturing on the details of first Homer and Virgil and then other poets; but to repeat everything that has ever been said on the subject is a sign of pedantry and ostentation. All the tropes and figures should be taught, because they are used by orators as well as poets.

9. Next the student should engage in composition exercises preliminary to rhetorical study. These include written paraphrases of Aesop's fables, the writing of aphorisms (*sententiae*), character sketches (*ethologiae*), and moral essays (*chreia*). In all these exercises the general idea is the same, though the form differs.

10. These remarks about the role of the *grammaticus* have been very brief, not trying to say everything about so vast a subject. There are some other studies the boys should have before being turned over the teacher of rhetoric (*rhetor*); these are for his general education, which the Greeks call *Paideia*. These include the study of music, which aids voice and body control, and the study of geometry, which is allied to logic. After all, both oratory and geometry require proof.

11. The final preliminary is the study of acting, which aids gesture, movement, and expression. Even the study of gymnastics would be helpful in learning body control.

12. On the capacity of students, early age is the best time for such a curriculum of preliminaries. Variety serves to refresh and restore the mind; therefore the student's day should contain a mixture of studies to avoid monotony. For it is easier to do many things continuously than to do one thing continuously. Next we will take up the duties of the teacher of rhetoric.

## BOOK TWO

1. A student should be sent to the rhetorician (*rhetor*) not just at a certain age, but when he is ready. Grammarians sometimes want to take on the role of the rhetorician and keep students with them longer, but each art should have its own sphere. In any case the student will continue some studies with the grammarian even after he starts the study of rhetoric.

2. The rhetorician must be of good character for he leads the student both by example and by strict discipline. His instruction must be free from affectation, his industry great, his demands on his class continual, but not extravagant. He should declaim every day as a model for his students.

3. The student should be taught by the best teachers available, for inferior teachers will provide poor models and will not know how to correct faults or praise good work. Indeed the task of unteaching is harder than that of teaching.

4. The rhetorician should begin with something like the subjects already studied, such as narration. There are three forms of narratives: the fictitious narratives of tragedies and poems; the realistic narratives of comedies; and lastly, the historical narratives, which are expositions of actual fact. Since poetic literature is the province of the teacher of literature, the rhetorician should begin with historical narrative, which has force in proportion to its truth. Exuberance in boys should be encouraged, for its excesses can be corrected, while barrenness is incurable. Among the exercises that follow narration are proof or refutation of the narrative, praise or blame of famous men, comparison of two characters, commonplaces (*communes loci*), questions of comparison (*theses*), and—most difficult of all—the praise or denunciation of laws.

5. The teacher of rhetoric should point to the strengths and weaknesses of the orations that are serving as examples. At times, it will even be useful to read and evaluate speeches that are corrupt and faulty in style. The teacher should test the critical abilities of his students through questions. "For what else is our object in teaching, save that our pupils should not always require to be taught?"

6. In assigning declamation subjects, young students should be given complete directions about what to say; older students need only a hint or two.

7. There is one practice at present in vogue that should be changed. Boys should not be forced to commit their own compositions to memory. If one is to memorize,

*Figure 6.3* Roman tutor

he should memorize the readily-imitated work of a skilled orator and not that of a faltering novice.

8. The good teacher should be able to differentiate between the abilities of his pupils. While the student should be strong in all phases of oratory, style should be especially encouraged.

9. The student should love his master not less than his studies and should regard his master as he does his parents. Just as it is the responsibility of the teacher to instruct, it is the responsibility of the student to learn.

10. Declamations on deliberative topics (*suasoriae*) and forensic topics (*controversiae*) are valuable because they include virtually every one of the other exercises, and because they are close to reality. The subjects chosen should be as true to life as possible. Unrealistic themes will seem foolish to the intelligent observer, for it is ludicrous to work oneself into a passion for the unrealistic.

11. The sound rhetorical student cannot discard all rules. Eloquent speeches are not the result of momentary inspirations but the products of research, analysis, practice, and application.

12. Untrained speakers may seem to be more vigorous, but they cannot match an artistic orator.

13. It is not possible for me to lay down a code of rigid rules on rhetoric. In practice most rules of rhetoric are altered by the nature of the case, circumstances of time and place, and by hard necessity itself. Therefore the greatest talent of an orator is a wise adaptability. But rules are useful, like a paved road we can turn off if we wish. Hence I will now set down the traditional rules.

14. "Rhetoric" is a Greek term for which there is no direct Latin equivalent. Rhetoric is best treated under these heads: the art, the artist, and the work. The art is

that which we should acquire by study, and is the art of speaking well. The artist is the orator whose task it is to speak well. The work is the achievement of the artist, namely, good speaking.

15. What is rhetoric? There are many definitions. Like Plato, I restrict the term orator to those who are good. The end of rhetoric cannot adequately be stated as persuasion as the ancients have so stated, because other things like money, authority, or pity also persuade. Some theorists make rhetoric a part of the science of politics or philosophy, but the definition that best suits its real character is the science of speaking well.

16. Is rhetoric useful? Some have concluded that since rhetoric may be used for social evil, it is not useful. On this basis, other disciplines would also be useless. It is true that rhetoric has also benefited society. If we define rhetoric so as to allow the evil man to be included as an orator, we admit this criticism of its usefulness.

17. Is rhetoric an art? It is sufficient to call attention to the fact that everything that art has brought to perfection originated in nature. Every art has a definite goal, and rhetoric's end is to speak well. If as Cleanthes says, art is a power reaching its end by a definite path, that is, by ordered methods, then no one can doubt that there is such method and order in good speaking.

18. Arts may be categorized as theoretical (i.e. for understanding), practical (for action), and productive (as in painting or sculpture). Although rhetoric draws heavily from the other two categories of arts, it is practical. Rhetoric is concerned with action, since through action it accomplishes that which it is its duty to do.

19. I quite realize that there is a further question as to whether eloquence derives most from nature or from education. The ideal orator must be a blend of both nature and education. To conclude, nature is the raw material for education: the one forms, the other is formed.

20. There is a more important question: is rhetoric a virtue, or is it an amoral and indifferent art? The rhetoric that I am endeavoring to establish befits a good man and will be a virtue. For how can an orator deliver an epideictic speech if he does not know good from bad, or a forensic one unless he knows what justice is? Man excels above all other living things in the power to reason and speak, so it is quite right that Cicero has Crassus say (*De oratore III*) that "eloquence is one of the highest virtues."

21. What is the material of rhetoric? Some have answered: speech, persuasive arguments, or political questions. I hold, like Plato and Cicero, that the material of rhetoric is composed of everything that may be placed before it as a subject for speech. That is why Cicero insists that the orator be widely educated. And Aristotle virtually brought everything into the orator's domain when he divided oratory into the three kinds of speeches: deliberative, forensic, and epideictic—there being nothing that will not fit under one of these three.

## BOOK THREE

1. There is an infinite diversity of opinions among the writers on rhetoric. The history of rhetoric began with Empedocles although Corax and Tisias also wrote early texts. Contemporaries of Socrates developed various aspects of rhetoric. With Isocrates' and Aristotle's schools, rhetoric began to divide. Stoic and Peripatetic philosophers began to study it. The first Roman theorist was Cato the censor, while Cicero was the first Roman to combine eloquence with teaching the art. My own position does not hold to any particular school but is the collection of many opinions.

2. Speech was born with mankind, and not developed later as Cicero says. Usefulness brought study and exercise gave perfection. Observation of effective speech gave rise to its art.

3. Concerning the divisions of rhetoric, most authorities teach that there are five: invention, arrangement, expression, memory, and delivery. Some see these as duties of the oratory or as elements of rhetoric. But they are neither, for they are parts of the art and not of the material. Some wish to add a sixth division, judgment, but that cannot be separate since it belongs naturally to arrangement, expression and memory.

4. As to the kinds of oratory, most ancients accept three: epideictic, deliberative, and forensic. Some base the classification on audiences seeking pleasure, advice, or judgment on causes. However I think we should classify speeches as either judicial or relating to matters outside the courtroom. In the former we require a decision of fact by others, while in the latter we either praise or blame with regard to the certain past or else deliberate the future where there is still doubt. The three-type division is more neat than true. Nevertheless it seems best to follow the majority view.

5. A speech consists of matter and words. Speaking skill is perfected by nature, art, and practice. The orator aims to instruct, move, and charm. The subject may or may not require proof. Questions are either of law or of fact. Questions are either general (indefinite respecting person, time, or place) or specific (special information on person, time, or place). Cicero calls general questions "theses" and specific ones "causes."

6. Every cause rests on a "status" or basis that brings the opposing sides into conflict and from which comes the question of "issue." There is always one point on which a case rests and on which the orator fixes his attention. Some claim there are only two types of status: conjectural and definitive. Others, including Cicero, think that there are three essential bases: conjectural (fact: is it?), definitive (name: what is it?), qualitative (kind: what kind is it?), and perhaps a fourth called legal (action: competence, intent, letter of law). Now we will take up the three types of speeches.

7. I will begin with causes which are concerned with praise and blame. Aristotle and Theophrastus after him divided these from the practical side of oratory; even its name (epideictic) indicates that it was for display. But we Romans include it as practical. Even speeches of display require proof as when we praise the gods for their services to men. Likewise in praising a man, we take account of when and where he lived, his ancestry, achievements, character, physical excellence, fortune, honorable employment of accidental attributes, unique deeds, and memorials he has left. Denunciation will use the same method for opposite effects.

8. Deliberative oratory deals mainly with the future and its function is to persuade in matters where there is doubt. It should deal with the honorable rather than the expedient as many say. The introduction ought to seek the good will of the audience, though a formal *exordium* may not be necessary because the speaker is already well known to those he advises. The narration should set forth the order of facts to be discussed. Regarding proofs, pathetic appeals are necessary as well as ethical proof. The argument will often turn on practicality (an aspect of conjecture).

9. Forensic oratory aims to bring and rebut charges. Its usual parts include:

1. Exordium:
    a. nature of the case
    b. question at issue
    c. points for and against

2.  Statement of facts: prepares for proof
3.  Proof
4.  Refutation
5.  Peroration

To these five some add a Partition of Parts under Proof, and a Digression. (I do not agree with those who think that the Exordium should be written last; speeches should be composed in the order in which they are to be delivered.)

10. In forensic speeches a cause may turn on one or many issues. Comparative (such as questions of inheritance rights) or mutual accusation controversies belong to the two general types of cause. Once we determine the kind of cause we can determine the status point for the speech.

11. When we are clear on the kind of cause, we must then determine the basis. We must consider the main cause on which the case turns and from which the status arises. The view that *status* (basis), *continens* (central argument), and *indicatio* (point of decision of the judge) are identical is valid and concise. But we should not quibble about technical terms: the main point is to know how to argue the case.

## BOOK FOUR

1. My next task is to explain the order to be followed in forensic causes, which present the utmost complication and variety. I must set forth the function of the exordium, the method of the statement of facts and the cogency of proofs. The Latin *exordium* is the Greek *proem*. It is an introduction to the subject. It is a time to win the favor of the judges or the audience. The sole purpose of the exordium is to prepare our audience for the rest of the speech. It may be divided into two parts: the introduction, which is a direct appeal for good will and attention, and the insinuation, by which the speaker insinuates himself into the minds of the judges.

2. The statement of facts, usually brief, indicates the nature of the subject on which the judge will have to give judgment. There are two forms of statement: one that expounds the facts of the case itself and the other that sets forth facts that have a bearing on the case.

3. In the order of things, the confirmation follows the statement; however, a remark on digressions should be made—that is, digress only when the subject permits it.

4. The beginning of every proof is a proposition that is useful when the fact cannot be denied and the question is about the definition, and also in causes that are obscure and complex. There may be several propositions, depending on the nature of the argument.

5. The partition is the enumeration of our own propositions or those of our adversary, depending on the situation. The partition is useful for clarity. Distinguish what is admitted and what is disputed. Then specify the admissions and the propositions that lead from those factors.

## BOOK FIVE

Preface. Proof is the most important element in any case.

1. Aristotle has rightly stated that there are some proofs adopted by the speaker that lie outside the art of speaking, and others that he himself creates out of his case. The former have been called inartistic proofs, the latter artistic proofs.

2. The first kind of inartistic proof is the previous court decision, and contains three species: the decision in a similar case, the decision in one aspect of the present case, and the decision in this issue itself.

3. Second, there is rumor, which will be interpreted as either public opinion or gossip, depending upon its relation to our side of the case.

4. The same may be said of confession under torture: one side will claim infallibility, the other unreliability.

5. Written testimony is vulnerable to the claim of forgery, ignorance, or inconsistency, either internal inconsistency or inconsistency with other facts.

6. Swearing to the truth of one's statements is not without its problems, since offering to swear, refusing to swear, asking for an oath, and refusing to accept one all may prejudice one's case.

7. Handling evidence is a difficult task. Written evidence is easier to handle than examining a witness orally. One may use commonplaces on the value of witnesses in general or of types of witnesses, or even attacks upon individual witnesses.

8. The second kind of proof is the product of art. Proofs of whatever sort have all these characteristics: they must deal with facts or with persons; deal in either past or present time; lead from one thing to another; be cogent in the abstract, apart from particular facts or persons; and be either necessary, likely, or plausible.

9. Artistic proofs are of three sorts—signs, arguments, and examples. Signs from one point of view are inartistic proofs, for they exist beforehand. They may point to a conclusion necessarily or only probably and that conclusion may point to the time past, present, or future. A necessary sign would be that if a woman is pregnant, she must have had intercourse. A probable sign would be, as Hermagoras says, "That Atlanta is no virgin, for she roamed through the woods with young men."

10. Arguments comprise the second type of artistic proof. They are variously called enthymemes, epicheiremes, and examples by the Greeks. The topics (*loci*) for arguments are those areas of the mind to which one may go for specific sources of proof.

11. The third kind of proof is the example. The chief type of example is the historical similarity, though one may argue from other sources such as analogy or simile.

12. We must remark on the uses to be made of proof. First, though proof is said to proceed from something certain, the most effective argument is one in which we must prove in the face of denial that which we adduce is proof. Second, handle strong proofs individually, like thunderbolts; combine weaker proofs, like hail. Third, arguments that deal with motives are best amplified by commonplaces on the emotions; they should not be merely asserted. Some say that the strongest proofs should be first and last, with the weakest in the middle; but this will depend on each case, except that one should never descend from the strongest arguments to the weakest.

13. Refutation is the duty of both sides in a dispute, which is why it is always named as a regular part of the order of a speech. At the same time it follows the same principles as those used in proof. The nature of the opposing argument determines the method of refutation. Sometimes it helps to treat a mass of arguments one by one, sometimes a general denial works.

14. The enthymeme is an incomplete syllogism, a proof-plus-argument, the proof being either a denial of consequences or a set of contradictions. The epicheireme has as many as five parts: major premise, reason, minor premise, proofs, conclusion; I prefer only three parts, that is, major, minor and conclusion. The syllogism

differs from these, not so much in form, but because it deals with truth rather than probabilities.

## BOOK SIX

PREFACE. I can hardly bear to carry on this work now. First my young wife died, then my youngest son. Now my son Quintilian has died, leaving me alone and without the will to live.

1. There are two types of peroration—an appeal to facts and an appeal to the emotions. Repetition and grouping of the facts serve to refresh the memory of the judge and place the whole case before him. The second type is necessary when there are no other ways for securing the victory of truth, justice, and the public interest. Appeals to pity should be short, since tears dry quickly. Displays such as blood-stained garments or weeping children may affect the judge as much as words do.

2. I must now review the peroration in a more exhaustive fashion. The task of the orator arises when the minds of the judges require force to move them, and their thoughts have actually to be led away from the contemplation of the truth. Emotions are divided into ethos and pathos. Pathos is thought to describe more violent emotions such as anger, fear, hatred, and pity. Ethos, connected with a person, describes emotions that are calmer and gentler. It requires the speaker to be a man of good character and courtesy.

3. I must now turn to humor, which dispels the graver emotions of the judge by exciting his laughter. Laughter depends largely upon the nature of the person and upon the opportunity. The application of humor to oratory may be divided into three heads: (1) we either reprove or refute to make light of, or retort or deride the argument of others; (2) we say things that have a suggestion of absurdity; or (3) we may take words in a different sense than usually expected.

4. It is not out of place to mention the principles of debate, in which forensic success depends upon the accomplishment of attack and defense. There are several important requisites for debate: (1) the debater must have a quick mind; (2) he must control his passion; (3) he should be able to lure the opponent into error.

5. While arrangement is of utmost importance, judgment must occupy some of our time. Judgment deals with evident facts while sagacity deals with hidden facts or with facts which have not been discovered.

## BOOK SEVEN

PREFACE. Enough has been said about invention. Next comes arrangement, without which invention is useless. Every case is different but nevertheless there are some principles of arrangement which can be identified.

1. Arrangement of things and parts is the distribution of sections to the places that it is expedient that they should occupy. There are some general principles to consider: the accuser should mass his proofs, the defendant should separate them into parts; the two sides may discuss the same points in different orders; the defense should proceed in climax order, with the strongest argument last; arguments should descend from the general to the particular, to show how this case relates to what is common. Next we discuss the role of the questions of *status* in deciding on arrangement.

2. The *status* of conjecture is concerned either with facts or intention. Each of these may occur in the past, present, or future. Questions concerning facts are either general or definite: some do not concern persons and some do. I agree with Cicero that it is best to discuss the person first before trying to prove his intention for an act. Proof may also be derived from motives such as anger, hatred, fear, greed, or hope.

3. The *status* of definition is the statement of the fact called in question, expressed in appropriate, clear, and concise language. We must establish our definition and destroy that of the opponent. There are three types (species) of definitions: (a) inquiry, whether one particular term is applicable to a given thing; (b) occasions when the question is which of two terms is to be applied to a thing; and (c) times when the question concerns things that are different in species, and we ask whether two different things are to be called by the same name. The basic process of definition is to ask what a thing is (e.g. the nature of sacrilege), and then ask whether the item under discussion fits that description.

4. Sometimes the *status* of quality is used in a sense to cover a number of questions: nature and form, size and number. The strongest defense is to assert that the act that is charged is actually honorable; in other words, an act can be defended by appealing to its motive. The next best course is to shift the charge to another. If none of these work, we must take refuge in ignorance. In the last resort, plead for mercy.

5. He who neither defends nor denies his act must stand on some portion of the law that is in his favor. There are two classes of argument from points of law: those from arguments advanced by the prosecution and those from some prescription put forth by the defense.

6. Questions arise from the law when it presents some obscurity. A second form of question arises when the meaning is in doubt concerning the "obvious expression of the law and its intention." The third method of questioning the law becomes operative when something is found in the actual words of the law that enables the use of the proof that the intention of the legislator was different from that which the prosecutor claims.

7. The next subject is contrary laws. Authorities agree that in such cases there is a separate *status* for the letter of the law and for the intention of the law. This view is justified by the fact that, when one law contradicts another, both parties attack the letter and raise the question of intention, and the point in dispute, as regards each law, is whether we should be guided by it at all.

8. The syllogistic *status* resembles the one concerned with the letter and intention of the law, since whenever it comes into play, one party rests his case on the letter. The syllogistic *status* deduces the uncertain from the letter of the law.

9. Next is the problem of ambiguity. Single words give rise to error when the same noun applies to a number of persons or things. This is primarily a language difficulty and is best solved by changing grammatical case, altering the position of words, or by adding additional words to make the meaning clear.

10. There is an affinity among all these types of *status*. In definition we inquire into the meaning of a term, and in the syllogism we consider the meaning of the writer, while it is obvious that in the case of contrary laws there are two bases, one concerned with the letter, and the other with the intention. Nevertheless, success in oratory depends on the art and energy of the speaker rather than mechanical use of techniques like these. For example, the gift of arrangement is to oratory what generalship is to war.

## BOOK EIGHT

PREFACE. We have now covered invention and arrangement, so critical to the orator, but it must be remembered that young students should not be overwhelmed with every detail; let them learn an easy road from which they can diverge later if they need to do so. We now turn to style, the most difficult subject. Cicero says that anyone can use invention and arrangement, but it takes a true orator to be eloquent. Yet remember that overemphasis on words alone will actually destroy eloquence.

1. Style (*elocutio*) is revealed both in individual words and in groups of words. As regards the former, we must see to it that they are good Latin, clear, elegant, and well-adapted to produce the desired effect. As regards the latter, they must be correct, aptly placed, and adorned with suitable figures.

2. Clearness is the first essential of a good style. It results above all from propriety in the use of words. It is proper, first of all, to call things by their right names, unless doing so makes the language obscene or in any way undesirable. The propriety of a term, in this case, depends not upon the word itself, but upon the meaning of the word, and must be tested by the touchstone of the understanding, not of the ear.

3. The subject of ornament is very important to the orator. For a speaker wins but trifling praise if he does no more than speak with correctness and lucidity; in fact, his speech seems rather to be free from blemish than to have any positive merit. Ornament is an effective weapon because it appeals not just to the learned, but to everyone. It adds not only pleasure but effectiveness to our case. Like clearness, ornament resides in single words or in groups of words. Three things are needed for eloquence: a clear conception, adequate expression of it, and then an added brilliance or polish which may be called "embellishment." Word-pictures, similes, and emphasis are some ways to achieve this.

4. The real power of language lies in enhancing or amplifying the force of words. Chiefly, this is effected through the words chosen to describe objects, but there are four principal methods of amplification: argumentation, comparison, reasoning, and accumulation of words. Hyperbole, however, is a trope rather than a means of amplification.

5. Rhetoricians are divided in their opinions on the use of striking expressions (*sententiae*). The aphorism is the oldest type, though there are many other types like the epigram; even an enthymeme (a reflexion drawn from contraries) can be used for ornament rather than proof. Some think that they are almost the sole form of adornment, while others think they should never be used. Neither view is satisfactory. For my own part, I regard these particular ornaments of oratory to be, as it were, the eyes of eloquence. On the other hand, I should not like to see the whole body full of eyes. The next subject is that of "tropes" or "modes"; grammarians teach their rules as we have seen [i.e., above, Book One], but it is best to discuss them in detail here, in respect to ornament.

6. By a trope is meant the artistic alteration of a word or phrase from its proper meaning to another. Grammarians and philosophers argue about their genus and species, but I am interested here not in those quibbles but in those most useful to the orator. Tropes can be employed in two ways, to enhance our meaning or to enhance our style. The following kinds of tropes are primarily used to aid our meaning. The metaphor is a trope that is so attractive in itself that "it shines forth with a light that

is all its own." The metaphor can be used to decorate as well as to help with the sense; if it does neither, it is out of place. The metaphor is a very effective way of adorning our style, but overuse tends to produce obscurity. The synecdoche has the power to give variety to our language by making us distinguish many things from one, the whole from a part, the genus from a species, things that follow from things that have preceded; or, on the other hand, the whole procedure may be reversed. Very close to synecdoche is metonymy, in which one name is substituted for another. Another kind of trope found only rarely in oratory is antonomasia, in which something is substituted for a proper name. Onomatopoeia, or the creation of a word where the sound suggests the sense, is barely acceptable to a Roman. Two other tropes involving change of meaning are catechresis and metalepsis. The remaining tropes are those used solely to enhance the style, not the meaning: epithet, allegory, periphrasis, hyperbaton, and hyperbole.

## BOOK NINE

1. Figures and tropes are closely related to each other, but there is a distinct difference. The term "trope" is applied to the transference of expressions from their natural and principal signification to another with a view to the embellishment of style, or, as the majority of grammarians define it, to the transference of words and phrases from the place that is strictly theirs to another to which they do not properly belong. Therefore, the substitution of one word for another is placed among tropes. "Figure" is the term employed when we give our language a conformation other than the obvious and the ordinary. However, what counts is not the names we give to things but their stylistic effect. Most authorities agree that there are two kinds of figures: figures of thought and figures of speech. Their number is not as great as some claim. Cicero in both his *De oratore* [III.52] and his *Orator* [39], which I now quote verbatim, includes as figures all expressions which are striking and which affect the emotions.

2. I wish here to speak only of figures of thought which depart from the direct method of statement. A question involves a figure whenever the question is employed not to get information, but to emphasize our point. Anticipation is used to meet objections before they arise. Hesitation lends an impression of truth to our statements. Concerning various figures of communication, we actually take our opponents or judges into consideration. We take account of what they know and/or leave some questions to the judgment of the jury. Exclamations are useful when they are simulated and artfully designed. There are numerous other figures which can be used: suspense, impersonation, apostrophe, ocular demonstration, ironic negation, aposiopesis, emphasis, hidden meaning, comparison, and antithesis. Some other suggested, like concentration and inference, are not figures but merely ordinary speech.

3. Figures of speech are always changing. There are three main classes of figures of speech: figures of form, which have to do with grammar; figures of rhetoric, which come from the arrangement of words; and figures that attract attention by some resemblance, equality, or contrast in words. Each one must be studied in detail and confirmed with examples, though we will discuss only some of them here. Some figures of speech resemble figures of thought, for example hesitation, correction, or personification. Cicero himself has omitted in his *Orator* some expressions which he earlier termed figures in his *De oratore*. In any case it must be noted that figures well

used will enhance an orator's style, while overuse or inappropriate use will earn him a reputation as one seeking only applause rather than the truth.

4. I must insist again that artistry is essential to the orator, despite the fact that some continue to argue to the contrary. The effect of artistic language can be demonstrated easily by rearranging the order or vocabulary of fine passages to see what results. There are two kinds of style, one closely woven and another loose as in dialogues and letters. Artistic patterns require three things: order of words, connection between them, and rhythm. Prose rhythm, which is both like and unlike meter, can be analyzed by its use of feet. Rhythm must accord with our delivery. My purpose here is not to make the orator a pedantic counter of feet, but rather to make him aware of the powers which rhythm can achieve. Therefore constant practice in careful writing will prepare him to master rhythmical prose when he speaks extempore.

## BOOK TEN NOTE

1. These rules of style are not enough to achieve eloquence. The practicing orator must acquire facility (*facilitas*), which the Greeks call habit (*hexis*). This ease of eloquence is best attained by careful attention to writing, reading, listening, and speaking— but all are so important that no one can be called more important than the others. Here I speak of the discipline an athlete, who has already learned all the exercises, uses to prepare for real contests. Once the student has acquired the elementary skills he must turn to acquiring a copious store of words and matters through deep reading of good writers and speakers. Thus, the choice of models for reading and imitation is critical. Both ancient and modern poets, historians, philosophers and orators are useful for this purpose. [Quintilian then provides a lengthy array (1.37–138) of orators and writers worth studying.]

2. Although invention came first and is all-important, it is expedient to imitate whatever has been invented with success. Simple imitation is not enough, though, for the student should call on his own powers to build on the model to make something new of it. Numerous models help to acquire numerous ways to say things: for example it would be foolish always to speak as Demosthenes or Cicero did.

3. Among the things that the orator cannot obtain from external sources, the pen is the one that brings at once the most labor and the most profit. As Cicero says, writing is the root of eloquence. It is important that writing be careful rather than quick; if you write well you will soon write quickly. A hasty draft, even though corrected later, will always show signs of its haste.

4. Self-correction—addition, erasure, or alteration—is quite as important as the actual writing. If possible, put your writing aside for a time, so that when you return you will see it as new.

5. The point that concerns me now is to show from what sources copiousness and facility may most easily be derived. Translations from Greek to Latin are helpful, for there is much matter and art in the Greek writings worthy of imitation. The paraphrase of Latin authors is helpful for it is one of the best ways of learning the ideas of the best authors. Theses and commonplaces are valuable, since one who has mastered these simple forms will be more fluent in more complex subjects and will be able to cope with any case, for all cases are built upon these kinds of general questions. Writing out declamations of the type used in the schools will be valuable, as will the

writing of histories and poetry. And at a certain point young men who have mastered the rudiments of the art should begin to attend actual trials, and then write out their own speeches on the cases as if they had been participants.

6. Thinking-out (*cogitatio*) a plan for a case derives force from the practice of writing and forms an intermediate stage between the labors of the pen and the more precarious fortunes of improvisation; indeed I am not sure that it is not more frequently of use than either. With a carefully thought-out plan in mind the orator can more readily improvise additional ideas during the course of his speaking.

7. The power of improvisation (*dicendi facultas*) is the highest achievement of the orator. The man who fails to acquire this had better, in my opinion, abandon the task of advocacy and devote his powers of writing to other branches of literature. The orator need not plan to speak extempore, but he should be able to do so if the changing circumstances of the situation require it. This facility (*facilitas*) must be maintained by constant practice, so daily speaking is valuable—to oneself if one cannot find an audience; or if this is not possible it is useful to prepare whole cases in our mind silently. We must study always and everywhere, and think about cases even while doing other things.

## BOOK ELEVEN

1. As Cicero says, one single kind of oratory is not applicable to every situation, or audience, or speaker. To speak appropriately one has to consider both what is expedient and what is becoming to say. Socrates in his *Apology*, for instance, chose personal dignity rather than persuasion as his end. A great variety of factors needs to be considered in each case, since a remark which will be persuasive in one circumstance may be damaging in another. Hence the orator must avoid boasting or anger, must consider the character and rank of opponents and judges, and above all must avoid extravagance of any kind. For mastery of adaptation to audience and occasion, look to Cicero.

2. Some regard memory as being no more than one of nature's gifts; but, like everything else, memory may be improved by cultivation. Memory is the treasure house of eloquence, for it brings to the speaker all his resources of fact and wording. The system of regions and images may be useful for remembering houses or other physical things, but is of little use to the orator in recalling connected speech; in fact using that system would impose a double task on the speaker, to recall both his speech and all those symbols too. My ideas are simpler. Memorize a speech in small parts, preferably in silence, and from the pages we ourselves have written; a well-organized speech will be easier to memorize, since the parts will flow together naturally. Should every word be memorized? Only if the speaker's memory is so strong that he can rely on delivery to make the speech seem natural rather than over-prepared; also, the loss of a single word might doom the whole effort. Above all, constant practice is the key to developing the memory.

3. Delivery is often called action, but the first name is derived from the voice, the second from the gesture. Regardless of its name, it has an extraordinarily powerful effect in oratory. The nature of the speech that we have composed within our minds is not so important as the manner in which we produce it, since the emotion of each member of our audience will depend on the impression made when he hears it.

Delivery has the same four principles as style—that is, that it should be correct, clear, ornate, and appropriate. All of these relate to adaptation to audience, case, and occasion. Daily practice with memorized speeches is best, since the effort of speaking extempore distracts the mind's attention from concentrating on delivery. The orator should study in minute detail the use of hands, fingers, eyes, arms, and the whole body, so that he will be prepared to match gestures to his words.

## BOOK TWELVE

PREFACE. I come now to the most difficult task, describing the character of the perfect orator. Others have written about the rules of speaking, as I have just done, but even Cicero went no further than that. Thus I have no predecessor to guide me.

1. No man can be an orator unless he is a good man. For it is impossible to regard as intelligent those who, when they are offered the choice between the two paths of virtue and vice, choose vice. Unless it first is free from vice, the mind will not find leisure even for the study of the noblest tasks. A bad man says things differently than he thinks, while a good man's words are as sincere as his thoughts. The object of all oratory is to state that which is just and honorable. How can a bad man speak on such matters? And there will always be some who would rather be eloquent than good. The standard to be met is so high that even Cicero does not quite meet it. Yet in the search for the greater good the perfect orator may in some circumstances perform acts which may to some seem not to be good, like defending the guilty or lying in a just cause.

2. Therefore, the orator must devote his attention to the formation of moral character, and must acquire a complete knowledge of all that is just and honorable. The knowledge of these subjects must be sought from the philosophers, who deal in physics, ethics, and dialectic. However the orator should not become a philosopher, who thinks but does not act, but should devote himself to using his knowledge in practical life. He can also learn much from the virtuous deeds of our own Roman citizens.

3. The orator will also require knowledge of civil law and of the custom and religion of the state in which he will practice.

4. Above all, the orator should be equipped with a rich store of examples both old and new; and he ought not merely to know those that are recorded in history or are transmitted by oral tradition or occur from day to day, but also fictitious examples invented by great poets.

5. Loftiness of soul is the most important of all qualities in an orator. Confidence rests on presence of mind coupled with natural advantages of voice and body; all of these can be developed further by art and practice.

6. The age at which the orator should begin to plead depends on his age and his level of preparation. He should begin young, to overcome the fear of public oratory, but only when ready to speak well; if he waits too long, he may never outgrow the habits of the schools.

7. Once the orator has attained some experience he should follow some definite principles in the choice of his cases. A good man will undoubtedly prefer defense to prosecution, but when needed will serve as prosecutor for the good of the society. He must not choose cases simply because the clients are powerful men, nor support inferiors simply to attack those of higher degree. He will not seek to make more money than is sufficient for his needs.

*Figure 6.4*  Roman orator

8. Next is the question of how a case should be prepared. Personal interviews with the client are preferable to relying on written statements, since the orator can question him on all the stock issues (*loci*) we have written about earlier. It is wise to have at least two interviews to check for discrepancies; moreover, clients often lie just as patients often deceive their own physicians. The orator should then act as the opposing lawyer or the judge to test what he has heard.

9. The orator's duty to his client is his primary concern, unless the client wishes him to do something dishonorable like making a personal attack on his opponent. He owes him diligence, so that he pleads as well as he can. Nor should he seek applause merely for the sake of applause; it is the outcome of the case that matters, not his personal gratification.

10. There is as much diversity in different styles of oratory as there is in painting and sculpture. The crisp "Attic" style is superior to the more florid "Asian" style, but because of the difference in languages Greek eloquence is superior to the Latin. Since there is no difference between speaking well and writing well, should the orator speak as he writes? Yes, if at all possible— though he must always be ready to adapt to what occurs in a debate. The orator must not only use all three levels of style—plain, middle, and grand, and their variations—but must do so with ease, as master of eloquence.

11. The orator should retire before his eloquence fades, so that he will not carry on feebly and thus deprive his clients of their due. Yet he can continue his efforts by writing or by teaching, and in any case should continue to learn new things. Now I realize that some may think that I have set too high a standard for the perfect orator, but I ask them to consider what great things men have already done, and how little time men today spend in working to achieve that ideal; if all the energy spent on the theater, feasting, social calls and the like were devoted instead to constant practice, then perhaps we might yet see the perfect orator.

---

*No doubt some modern readers looking at Quintilian's* Institutio *will be tempted to focus on the central books devoted to traditional rhetoric, and to skip over the other sections as being irrelevant or at least old-fashioned. This would be a mistake. Quintilian intends the whole work as one coordinated effort at producing the perfect orator. No one part of it is to be stressed over the others, and each has its own contribution to make. For example, the modern reader should look carefully at Book Ten, which lays out a careful program of self-education for adults. There are some ideas there that are still useful today.*

*If nothing else, Quintilian shows us that, for the Romans, rhetoric was not an isolated skill divorced from society. It was instead the very warp and woof of educated Romanness. The emperors could stifle free speech, but they could not dampen the urge to use language well. Roman schools taught grammar and rhetoric to thousands of Europeans and Africans for hundreds and hundreds of years. The graduates of these schools at least knew Latin well, and even if there were now some limits on free debate in public forums there were other avenues of expression which developed over time The Roman "system" described by Quintilian outlasted the empire and helped shape western culture for almost 2,000 years.*

# Epilogue

## What Happened Next?

Ideal voices, the beloved voices
Of those who have died, or of those
Who are lost to us as if they were dead.

C. P. Cavafy

After the death of Quintilian shortly before the end of the 1st Christian century, it was to be more than a thousand years before the next major development in the arts of discourse in the western world. And this was not to be a rhetorical development but a systematic oral refinement of dialectical process based on Aristotle's system of logic—the *disputatio* of the medieval university.[1]

But over this vast ocean of time the Roman educational and rhetorical system did continue to flourish in various forms through barbarian invasions and enormous social changes. Roman rhetoric with its educational underpinnings outlived its own culture. The world changed, but the "system" did not.[2] Teachers taught in ways Quintilian would have recognized, though after a century or two no one would have recognized the sources of the process. When Christianity emerged as a major force it looked to Ciceronian principles to support its need for preaching.[3] When Charlemagne's advisor, Alcuin, tried to convince his 8th century master of the need for deliberative rhetoric, he wrote a treatise based on Cicero's *De Inventione*.[4]

The old world of the Roman republic with its free Senate and effective orators had by Quintilian's time long been submerged by autocratic emperors who kept all the trappings of the republic but swamped their societies with secret police and draconian laws to suppress free speech.[5] As we have seen, it had long been a truism of the history of rhetoric that rhetoric originated in, and flourished in, free societies. But by Quintilian's time rhetoric had become so much a part of the warp and woof of Roman culture that even dictators could not destroy it and the educational system which supported it. Rhetoric was by then the standard opening to public success, and when the emperors began to use public money for schools, and sent the teachers along with the soldiers to Latinize the conquered lands from Britain to Persia, rhetoric then became the tool for upward mobility in the entire known world.

The practice of rhetoric in the ancient world after Quintilian is more properly a part of social history than of rhetorical history. Basically there were no new major ideas in the field. But boys continued to go to schools, and then later as well-trained orators continued to speak in the Senate and law courts. Ultimately epideictic oratory, a rhetoric of display, came to be increasingly important as deliberative oratory became more dangerous under the emperors, and forensic oratory began to suffer under the strictures of the growing technicality of the law courts. One unusual result of this situation was that a common school exercise, the *declamatio*, originally designed as a test of student ability, became instead a form of public entertainment in which an orator could show off his virtuosity under any situation. Popular declaimers could draw crowds like those to which rock stars are accustomed today, and their published speeches were often best-sellers. An extreme form of this tendency, labeled "The Second Sophistic," lasted into the 4th century of the Christian era.[6]

Under these circumstances it is interesting to see what ultimately became of the major works we have outlined in the preceding chapters.

Paradoxically, it was two 1st century handbooks that came to represent Roman rhetoric—the adolescent *De Inventione* of Cicero and the anonymous *Rhetorica ad Herennium*, which was so close in subject-matter and tone to Cicero's work that it came to be treated as a work of Cicero.

During the middle ages, for example, the *De Inventione* was treated as Cicero's Old Rhetoric (*rhetorica vetus*) and the *ad Herennium* as his New Rhetoric (*rhetorica nova*). They were copied together in manuscripts and printed editions, with appearances of the *ad Herennium* outnumbering those of the *De Inventione*.[7]

On the other hand Cicero's masterful reflection on rhetoric in society, his *De oratore*, essentially disappeared from view until the discovery of a manuscript at Lodi in Italy in 1421 CE revealed to Italian humanists that there was more to Cicero's rhetoric than these two pragmatic handbooks.[8]

Quintilian's *Institutio oratoria*, like the *De oratore* of Cicero, also had little influence in late antiquity. Only a fragment (*textus mutilatus*) circulated in late antiquity and the middle ages. Eventually the Italian book-hunter Poggio Bracciolini found a complete manuscript at a Benedictine monastery in St. Gall, Switzerland, in 1416, leading to a surge of interest among Italian humanists and a new influence on education.[9]

Perhaps Aristotle's *Rhetoric* suffered the same fate as Cicero's *De oratore* because it also was too reflective, too demanding of analytic thought, too abstract, for classroom use. The exigencies of life demanded the readily teachable. No doubt it was easier to drill a young boy on five "parts" of rhetoric than to confound him with concepts of the enthymeme and the psychological implications of *ethos* and *pathos*. The *Rhetoric* was, after all, a Greek text in an increasingly mono-lingual Latin culture. It took Arabic scholars to bring the text to medieval Europe and encourage the first Latin translations in the 12th century as part of an overall Aristotelian revival.[10]

Whatever the fate of individual works, though, the dominant fact is that these classical texts have been re-studied over the past 500 years and have affected Euro-American culture in ways we are just beginning to understand.

The earliest English settlers of North America imported schools with them—schools had become so much a part of life, so fundamental, that even Massachusetts farmers could not do without them on the frontier—and brought Cambridge University scholars from England in 1636 with the curriculum traceable through the European Renaissance back to Cicero and Quintilian.

It is possible that there would have been no American Declaration of Independence and no Constitution without this solid base of classical learning.

John Quincy Adams, the first Boylston Professor of Rhetoric at Harvard University from 1806 to 1809, synthesized the works of Aristotle, Cicero, and Quintilian into 36 popular lectures that every student took. It was this tradition that took root in America and led to the Golden Age of Oratory in the 19th and early 20th centuries. Meanwhile in England the classics-based lectures of George Campbell, Richard Whately, and Hugh Blair helped form the theoretical basis for the rhetorical tradition which affects the teaching of rhetoric even today. Similar classical influences appeared in France, Germany, and Italy. In various forms, then, the classical heritage cited in the Introduction to this book continues to have influence even among many writers who do not realize their own antecedents. The reader of this book, then, may be well equipped to recognize the ultimate sources of many "modern" ideas about speaking and writing.

---

*As we have continually cautioned the modern reader, no synopsis can be a substitute for examining the texts themselves. We shall be grateful if our efforts in this volume will lead readers to look directly at what these writers have tried to tell us about rhetoric as a guide to future language use.*

*Remember that anyone who has ever lived was living in what for him or her was "modern times." Plato and Aristotle and Cicero and all the others urge us to look beyond their "now" to see what can be better in our times ahead. That is the legacy of the "voices" from ancient times that still speak to us today even in the midst of technological revolution.*

*Rhetoric, after all, is about future language. We study now so that we can speak/ write effectively tomorrow. That is what these "voices" have been telling us.*

# Part Two

# Orations For Pleasure and Practice

# Six Classical Texts for Reading, Study, and Discussion

> I do maintain, however, that nothing more outstanding exists than a complete orator. No music, no poem, no drama is more delightful or gives more pleasure than a brilliant oration.
>
> Cicero, *De Oratore, Book II*

While there are innumerable speeches available to us from the classical period, those that follow have been chosen because they exemplify what Cicero says in the epigram above. They are examples of oratory presented by complete orators. They should bring you as much pleasure as your favorite music, poetry, or drama. The speeches chosen should give you a certain "cultural literacy" of the classical period.

There are speeches from all three of the classical genres: forensic, deliberative, and epideictic. One is by Cicero, his Catilinian oration, that exemplifies the use of argument by enthymeme. It also contains a panoply of rhetorical figures. A deliberative speech by Lysias shows the skill of this most famous speechwriter, the *ethopoeia* for which he was most famous. There is an epideictic speech by Gorgias, "The Encomium to Helen," that is written in the poetical style for which he was famous, and which demonstrates the excesses talked about in Chapter Two. And finally, perhaps the two most famous speeches of the period are presented: Pericles, *The Funeral Oration* and Socrates, *The Apology*. Read these two speeches for the sheer pleasure of hearing two of the most famous wordsmiths of the ancient world. We hope that you will enjoy reading these speeches for pleasure but also for the rhetorical brilliance they display.

## Pericles, *The Funeral Oration*

Pericles' *Funeral Oration* stands as the grand exemplar of epideictic oratory, specifically the form of epideictic known to the Greeks as *epitaphios logos*, and to us as a *eulogy*. Delivered in 430 BCE, near the end of Pericles' life and following the first year of the Peloponnesian War, the speech was mandated by the laws of the democracy. Pericles is speaking to the Athenian people who have assembled outside the walls of the city near a large funeral pyre where the bodies have been burned. The purpose of the speech is to honor those who have died in the war.

Pericles saw this occasion as an opportunity to advance themes broader than commemorations, although certainly lament, consolation, and commemoration of the dead are central to the speech. Pericles understood that he must fulfill his responsibility to honor the fallen soldiers, but then to justify their sacrifice by praising the society for which they died. With so many sons, brothers, fathers, and loved ones having perished, and after only one year of what Pericles knew would be a long struggle for Athens against the Spartan alliance, he knew that he would have to raise the spirits of the people and persuade them to continue the struggle by reviewing for them what they have and what they might lose. *The Funeral Oration*, then, is an oration as much about the living as about the dead.

To carry out his purpose, Pericles divided *The Funeral Oration* into four parts: the introduction, praise of the Athenian democracy, praise for the fallen heroes, and advice for the living. He followed the traditional rhetorical practices of the time in each section: humbling himself in the proem as a way of establishing credibility, focusing on the *topoi* for epideictic oratory in the body of the speech, i.e., the *arête* or virtues of moral excellence, and concluding with an emotional appeal to patriotism among those in attendance. As a result, the speech is a classic example of the use of Aristotle's three modes of proof: *ethos*, *logos*, and *pathos*.

*The Funeral Oration* is not preserved exactly as it was written or delivered. The historian Thucydides captured the essence of Pericles' remarks in his notes and transcribed them in his chronicle *The Peloponnesian War*. Following is a translation of Thucydides' account of *The Funeral Oration*.

(1) Many of those who have spoken here in the past have praised the institution of this speech at the close of our ceremony. It seemed to them a mark of honour to our soldiers who have fallen in war that a speech should be made over them. I do not agree. These men have shown themselves valiant in action, and it would be enough, I think, for their glories to be proclaimed in action, as you have just seen it done at this funeral organized by the state. Our belief in the courage and manliness of so many should not be hazarded on the goodness or badness of one man's speech. Then it is not easy to speak with a proper sense of balance, when a man's listeners find it difficult to believe in the truth of what one is saying. The man who knows the facts and loves the dead may well think that an oration tells less than what he knows and what he would like to hear: others who do not know so much may feel envy for the dead, and think the orator overpraises them, when he speaks of exploits that are beyond their own capacities. Praise of other people is tolerable only up to a certain point, the point where one still believes that one could do oneself some of the things one is hearing about. Once you get beyond this point, you will find people becoming jealous and incredulous. However, the fact is that this institution was set up and approved by our

forefathers, and it is my duty to follow the tradition and do my best to meet the wishes and the expectations of every one of you.

(2) I shall begin by speaking about our ancestors, since it is only right and proper on such an occasion to pay them the honour of recalling what they did. In this land of ours there have always been the same people living from generation to generation up till now, and they, by their courage and their virtues, have handed it on to us, a free country. They certainly deserve our praise. Even more so do our fathers deserve it. For to the inheritance they had received they added all the empire we have now, and it was not without blood and toil that they handed it down to us of the present generation. And then we ourselves, assembled here to-day, who are mostly in the prime of life, have, in most directions, added to the power of our empire and have organized our State in such a way that it is perfectly well able to look after itself both in peace and in war.

(3) I have no wish to make a long speech on subjects familiar to you all: so I shall say nothing about the warlike deeds by which we acquired our power or the battles in which we or our fathers gallantly resisted our enemies, Greek or foreign. What I want to do is, in the first place, to discuss the spirit in which we faced our trials and also our constitution and the way of life which has made us great. After that I shall speak in praise of the dead, believing that this kind of speech is not inappropriate to the present occasion, and that this whole assembly, of citizens and foreigners, may listen to it with advantage.

(4) Let me say that our system of government does not copy the institutions of our neighbours. It is more the case of our being a model to others, than of our imitating anyone else. Our constitution is called a democracy because power is in the hands not of a minority but of the whole people. When it is a question of settling private disputes, everyone is equal before the law; when it is a question of putting one person before another in positions of public responsibility, what counts is not membership of a particular class, but the actual ability which the man possesses. No one, so long as he has it in him to be of service to the state, is kept in political obscurity because of poverty. And, just as our political life is free and open, so is our day-to-day life in our relations with each other. We do not get into a state with our next-door neighbour if he enjoys himself in his own way, nor do we give him the kind of black looks which, though they do no real harm, still do hurt people's feeling. We are free and tolerant in our private lives; but in public affairs we keep to the law. This is because it commands our deepest respect.

(5) We give our obedience to those whom we put in positions of authority, and we obey the laws themselves, especially those which are for the protection of the oppressed, and those unwritten laws which it is an acknowledged shame to break.

(6) And here is another point. When our work is over, we are in a position to enjoy all kinds of recreation for our spirits. There are various kinds of contests and sacrifices regularly throughout the year; in our own homes we find a beauty and good taste which delight us every day and which drive away our cares. Then the greatness of our city brings it about that all the good things from all over the world flow in to us, so that to us it seems just as natural to enjoy foreign goods as our own local products.

(7) Then there is a great difference between us and our opponents, in our attitude towards military security. Here are some examples: Our city is open to the world, and we have no periodical deportations in order to prevent people observing or finding

out secrets which might be of military advantage to the enemy. This is because we rely, not on secret weapons, but on our own real courage and loyalty. There is a difference, too, in our educational systems. The Spartans, from their earliest boyhood, are submitted to the most laborious training in courage; we pass our lives without all these restrictions, and yet are just as ready to face the same dangers as they are. Here is a proof of this: when the Spartans invade our land, they do not come by themselves, but bring all their allies with them; whereas we, when we launch an attack abroad, do the job by ourselves, and, though fighting on foreign soil, do not often fail to defeat opponents who are fighting for their own hearths and homes. As a matter of fact none of our enemies has ever yet been confronted with our total strength, because we have to divide our attention between our navy and the many missions on which our troops are sent on land. Yet, if our enemies engage a detachment of our forces and defeat it, they give themselves credit for having thrown back our entire army; or, if they lose, they claim that they were beaten by us in full strength. There are certain advantages, I think, in our way of meeting danger voluntarily, with an easy mind, instead of with a laborious training, with natural rather than with state-induced courage. We do not have to spend our time practising to meet sufferings which are still in the future; and when they are actually upon us we show ourselves just as brave as these others who are always in strict training. This is one point in which, I think, our city deserves to be admired. There are also others:

(8) Our love of what is beautiful does not lead to extravagance; our love of the things of the mind does not make us soft. We regard wealth as something to be properly used, rather than as something to boast about. As for poverty, no one need be ashamed to admit it: the real shame is in not taking practical measures to escape from it. Here each individual is interested not only in his own affairs but in the affairs of the state as well; even those who are mostly occupied with their own business are extremely well-informed on general politics—this is a peculiarity of ours: we do not say that a man who takes no interest in politics is a man who minds his own business; we say that he has no business here at all. We Athenians, in our own persons, take our decisions on policy or submit them to proper discussions: for we do not think that there is an incompatibility between words and deeds; the worst thing is to rush into action before the consequences have been properly debated. And this is another point where we differ from other people: We are capable at the same time of taking risks and of estimating them beforehand. Others are brave out of ignorance; and, when they stop to think, they begin to fear. But the man who can most truly be accounted brave is he who best knows the meaning of what is sweet in life and of what is terrible, and then goes out undeterred to meet what is to come.

(9) Again, in questions of general good feeling there is a great contrast between us and most other people. We make friends by doing good to others, not by receiving good from them. This makes our friendship all the more reliable, since we want to keep alive the gratitude of those who are in our debt by showing continued goodwill to them: whereas the feelings of one who owes us something lack the same enthusiasm, since he knows that, when he repays our kindness, it will be more like paying back a debt than giving something spontaneously. We are unique in this. When we do kindnesses to others, we do not do them out of any calculations of profit or loss: we do them without afterthought, relying on our free liberality. Taking everything together then, I declare that our city is an education to Greece, and I declare that in

my opinion each single one of our citizens, in all the manifold aspects of life, is able to show himself the rightful lord and owner of his own person, and do this, moreover, with exceptional grace and exceptional versatility. And to show that this is no empty boasting for the present occasion, but real tangible fact, you have only to consider the power which our city possesses and which has been won by those very qualities which I have mentioned. Athens, alone of the states we know, comes to her testing time in a greatness that surpasses what was imagined of her. In her case, and in her case alone, no invading enemy is ashamed at being defeated, and no subject can complain of being governed by people unfit for their responsibilities. Mighty indeed are the marks and monuments of our empire which we have left. Future ages will wonder at us, as the present age wonders at us now. We do not need the praises of a Homer or of anyone else whose words may delight us for the moment, but whose estimation of facts will fall short of what is really true. For our adventurous spirit has forced an entry into every sea and into every land; and everywhere we have left behind us everlasting memorials of good done to our friends or suffering inflicted on our enemies.

(10) This, then, is the kind of city for which these men, who could not bear the thought of losing her, nobly fought and nobly died. It is only natural that every one of us who survive them should be willing to undergo hardships in her service. And it was for this reason that I have spoken at such length about our city, because I wanted to make it clear that for us there is more at stake than there is for others who lack our advantages; also I wanted my words of praise for the dead to be set in the bright light of evidence. And now the most important of these words has been spoken. I have sung the praises of our city; but it was the courage and gallantry of these men, and of people like them, which made her splendid. Nor would you find it true in the case of many of the Greeks, as it is true of them, that no words can do more than justice to their deeds.

(11) To me it seems that the consummation which has overtaken these men shows us the meaning of manliness in its first revelation and in its final proof. Some of them, no doubt, had their faults; but what we ought to remember first is their gallant conduct against the enemy in defence of their native land. They have blotted out evil with good, and done more service to the commonwealth than they ever did harm in their private lives. No one of these men weakened because he wanted to go on enjoying his wealth: no one put off the awful day in the hope that he might live to escape his poverty and grow rich. More to be desired than such things, they chose to check the enemy's pride. This, to them, was a risk most glorious, and they accepted it, willing to strike down the enemy and relinquish everything else. As for success or failure, they left that in the doubtful hands of Hope, and when the reality of battle was before their faces, they put their trust in their own selves. In the fighting, they thought it more honourable to stand their ground and suffer death than to give in and save their lives. So they fled from the reproaches of men, abiding with life and limb the brunt of battle; and, in a small moment of time, the climax of their lives, a culmination of glory, not of fear, were swept away from us.

(12) So and such they were, these men—worthy of their city. We who remain behind may hope to be spared their fate, but must resolve to keep the same daring spirit against the foe. It is not simply a question of estimating the advantages in theory. I could tell you a long story (and you know it as well as I do) about what is to be gained by beating the enemy back. What I would prefer is that you should fix your

eyes every day on the greatness of Athens as she really is, and should fall in love with her. When you realize her greatness, then reflect that what made her great was men with a spirit of adventure, men who knew their duty, men who were ashamed to fall below a certain standard. If they even failed in an enterprise, they made up their minds that at any rate the city should not find their courage lacking to her, and they gave to her the best contribution that they could. They gave her their lives, to her and to all of us, and for their own selves they won praises that never grow old, the most splendid of sepulchres—not the sepulchre in which their bodies are laid, but where their glory remains eternal in men's minds, always there on the right occasion to stir others to speech or to action. For famous men have the whole earth as their memorial: it is not only the inscriptions on their graves in their own country that mark them out; no, in foreign lands also, not in any visible form but in people's hearts their memory abides and grows. It is for you to try to be like them. Make up your minds that happiness depends on being free, and freedom depends on being courageous. Let there be no relaxation in face of the perils of the war. The people who have most excuse for despising death are not the wretched and unfortunate, who have no hope of doing well for themselves, but those who run the risk of a complete reversal in their lives, and who would feel the difference most intensely, if things went wrong for them. Any intelligent man would find a humiliation caused by his own slackness more painful to bear than death, when death comes to him unperceived, in battle, and in the confidence of his patriotism.

(13) For these reasons I shall not commiserate with those parents of the dead, who are present here. Instead I shall try to comfort them. They are well aware that they have grown up in a world where there are many changes and chances. But this is good fortune—for men to end their lives with honour, as these have done, and for you honourably to lament them: their life was set to a measure where death and happiness went hand in hand. I know that it is difficult to convince you of this. When you see other people happy you will often be reminded of what used to make you happy too. One does not feel sad at not having some good thing which is outside one's experience: real grief is felt at the loss of something which one is used to. All the same, those of you who are of the right age must bear up and take comfort in the thought of having more children. In your own homes these new children will prevent you from brooding over those who are no more, and they will be a help to the city, too, both in filling the empty places, and in assuring her security. For it is impossible for a man to put forward fair and honest views about our affairs if he has not, like everyone else, children whose lives may be at stake. As for those of you who are now too old to have children, I would ask you to count as gain the greater part of your life, in which you have been happy, and remember that what remains is not long, and let your hearts be lifted up at the thought of the fair fame of the dead. One's sense of honour is the only thing that does not grow old, and the last pleasure, when one is worn out with age, is not, as the poet said, making money, but having the respect of one's fellow men.

(14) As for those of you here who are sons or brothers of the dead, I can see a hard struggle in front of you. Everyone always speaks well of the dead, and, even if you rise to the greatest heights of heroism, it will be a hard thing for you to get the reputation of having come near, let alone equalled, their standard. When one is alive, one is always liable to the jealousy of one's competitors, but when one is out of the way, the honour one receives is sincere and unchallenged.

(15) Perhaps I should say a word or two on the duties of women to those among you who are now widowed. I can say all I have to say in a short word of advice. Your great glory is not to be inferior to what God has made you, and the greatest glory of a woman is to be least talked about by men, whether they are praising you or criticizing you. I have now, as the law demanded, said what I had to say. For the time being our offerings to the dead have been made, and for the future their children will be supported at the public expense by the city, until they come of age. This is the crown and prize which she offers, both to the dead and to their children, for the ordeals which they must face. Where the rewards of valour are the greatest, there you will find also the best and bravest spirits among the people. And now, when you have mourned for your dear ones, you must depart.

## Lysias, *On the Refusal of a Pension to the Invalid*

Lysias began his career as a speech writer (*logographer*), in 411 BCE. Twenty-three of his speeches survive, providing modern readers with an intimate glimpse in the daily lives of Athenians. We meet the outraged husband, Euphiletus, who has murdered his wife's seducer, as he claims, in accordance with Athenian law. We meet a soldier falsely accused of desertion on the battlefield, and another soldier, Mantitheos, accused of having served in the cavalry during the murderous reign of the Thirty Tyrants. Anyone caught in the litigious web that was Athenian democracy might turn to Lysias for a winning oration.

Lysias wrote speeches, as noted in Chapter 2, in the voice of his client, a rhetorical technique known as "*ethopoeia.*" The speeches evoke the personality and the energy of the average citizen seeking redress of his grievances or defending himself as eloquently as his native ability and Lysias' genius allow him.

One of the more typical of the speeches Lysias wrote for his clients is the defense of a cripple. In this speech, presented shortly after the restoration of the democracy, an invalid, i.e., a man who walked with the aid of crutches, is faced with losing his pension. Athens had established a welfare system for those citizens who were incapable of supporting themselves, and each year a list of those pensioners was placed in the Agora for review. Any citizen could challenge any name on the list. In this year, the Assembly had passed legislation raising the pension from one obol per day to two (the difference between a subsistence living and a moderate living); thus, there was more scrutiny than usual among the parsimonious taxpayers. The law specified that the person must be "incapacitated," while in the case of the cripple, he was able to get around on his "sticks," and he actually ran a business, perhaps a shoemaker's shop.

The cripple's pension may have come under even closer scrutiny because his shop was a place where idlers spent their day. The cripple himself is described as a "lusty rascal, a character about the Agora, and delight of young men of the sporting set, who had his shop their resort."[1] The plaintiff may have been a butt of the cripple's jokes, since the cripple was prone to making fun of others. Revenge may have been the ulterior motive of the suit.

The cripple's young friends came to his defense and they raised enough money to hire Lysias to write the speech. Lysias' challenge is to provide a defense that shows the cripple to be in need of a pension even while he is able to work.[2] More than any other speechwriter of his time, Lysias was able to enter into the spirit of the moment as well as into the character of the cripple.

(1) I can almost find it in me to be grateful to my accuser, gentlemen of the Council, for having involved me in these proceedings. For previously I had no excuse for rendering an account of my life; but now, owing to this man, I have got one. So I will try to show you in my speech that this man is lying, and that my own life until this day has been deserving of praise rather than envy; for it is merely from envy, in my opinion, that he has involved me in this ordeal. But I ask you, if a man envies those whom other people pity, from what villainy do you think such a person would refrain? Is it possible that he hopes to get money by slandering me?[3] And if he makes me out an enemy on whom he seeks to be avenged, he lies; for his villainy has always kept me from having any dealings with him either as a friend or as an enemy. So now, gentlemen, it is clear that he envies me because, although I have to bear this sore misfortune,

I am a better citizen than he is. For indeed I consider, gentlemen, that one ought to remedy the afflictions of the body with the activities of the spirit; for if I am to keep my thoughts and the general tenor of my life on the level of my misfortune, how shall I be distinguished from this man?

(2) Well, in regard to those matters, let these few words of mine suffice: I will now speak as briefly as I can on the points with which I am here concerned. My accuser says that I have no right to receive my civil pension, because I am able-bodied and not classed as disabled, and because I am skilled in a trade which would enable me to live without this grant. In proof of my bodily strength, he instances that I mount on horseback; of the affluence arising from my trade that I am able to associate with people who have means to spend. Now, as to the affluence from my trade and the nature of my livelihood in general, I think you are all acquainted with these: I will, however, make some brief remarks of my own. My father left me nothing, and I have only ceased supporting my mother on her decease two years ago; while as yet I have no children to take care of me. I possess a trade that can give me but slight assistance: I already find difficulty in carrying it on myself, and as yet I am unable to procure someone to relieve me of the work.[4] I have no other income besides this dole, and if you deprive me of it I might be in danger of finding myself in the most grievous plight. Do not, therefore, gentlemen, when you can save me justly, ruin me unjustly; what you granted me when I was younger and stronger, do not take from me when I am growing older and weaker; nor, with your previous reputation for showing the utmost compassion even towards those who are in no trouble, be moved now by this man to deal harshly with those who are objects of pity even to their enemies; nor, by having the heart to wrong me, cause everyone else in my situation to despond. And indeed, how extraordinary the case would be, gentlemen! When my misfortune was but simple, I am found to have been receiving this pension; but now, when old age, diseases, and the ills that attend on them are added to my trouble, I am to be deprived of it! The depth of my poverty, I believe, can be revealed more clearly by my accuser than by anyone else on earth. For if I were charged with the duty of producing tragic drama, and should challenge him to an exchange of property, he would prefer being the producer ten times over to making the exchange once. Surely it is monstrous that he should now accuse me of having such great affluence that I can consort on equal terms with the wealthiest people, while, in the event of such a thing as I have suggested, he should behave as he does. Why, what could be more villainous?

(3) As to my horsemanship, which he has dared to mention to you, feeling neither awe of fortune nor shame before you, there is not much to tell. For I, gentlemen, am of opinion that all who suffer from some affliction make it their single aim and constant study to manage the condition that has befallen them with the least amount of discomfort. I am such an one, and in the misfortune that has stricken me I have devised this facility for myself on the longer journeys that I find necessary. But the strongest proof, gentlemen, of the fact that I mount horses because of my misfortune, and not from insolence, as this man alleges, is this: if I were a man of means, I should ride on a saddled mule, and would not mount other men's horses. But in fact, as I am unable to acquire anything of the sort, I am compelled, now and again, to use other men's horses. Well, I ask you, gentlemen, is it not extraordinary that, if he saw me riding on a saddled mule, he would hold his peace—for what could he say?[5]—and then, because I mount borrowed horses, he should try to persuade you that I am

able-bodied; and that my using two sticks, while others use one, should not be argued by him against me as a sign of being able-bodied, but my mounting horses should be advanced by him as a proof to you that I am able-bodied? For I use both aids for the same reason.

(4) So utterly has he surpassed the whole human race in impudence that he tries with his single voice to persuade you all that I am not classed as disabled. Yet if he should persuade any of you on this point, gentlemen, what hinders me from drawing a lot for election as one of the nine archon,[6] and you from depriving me of my obol as having sound health, and voting it unanimously to this man as being a cripple? For surely, after you have deprived a man of the grant as being able-bodied, the law-officers are not going to debar this same person, as being disabled, from drawing a lot! Nay, indeed, you are not of the same opinion as he is, nor is he either, and rightly so. For he has come here to dispute over my misfortune as if over an heiress, and he tries to persuade you that I am not the sort of man that you all see me to be; but you—as is incumbent on men of good sense—have rather to believe your own eyes than this person's words.

(5) He says that I am insolent, savage, and utterly abandoned in my behavior, as though he needed the use of terrifying terms to speak the truth, and could not do it in quite gentle language. But I expect you, gentlemen, to distinguish clearly between those people who are at liberty to be insolent and those who are debarred from it. For insolence is not likely to be shown by poor men labouring in the utmost indigence, but by those who possess far more than the necessaries of life; not by men disabled in body, but by those who have most reason to rely on their own strength; nor by those already advanced in years, but by those who are still young and have a youthful turn of mind. For the wealthy purchase with their money escape from the risks that they run, whereas the poor are compelled to moderation by the pressure of their want. The young are held to merit indulgence from their elders; but if their elders are guilty of offence, both ages unite in reproaching them. The strong are at liberty to insult whom-ever they will with impunity, but the weak are unable either to beat off their aggres-sors when insulted, or to get the better of their victims if they choose to insult. Hence it seems to me that my accuser was not serious in speaking of my insolence, but was only jesting: his purpose was, not to persuade you that such is my nature, but to set me in a comic light, as a fine stroke of fancy.

(6) He further asserts that my shop is the meeting-place of a number of rogues who have spent their own money and hatch plots against those who wish to preserve theirs. But you must all take note that these statements of his are no more accusations against me than against anyone else who has a trade, nor against those who visit my shop any more than those who frequent other men of business. For each of you is in the habit of paying a call at either a perfumer's or a barber's or a shoemaker's shop, or wherever he may chance to go—in most cases, it is to the tradesmen who have set up nearest the marketplace, and in fewest, to those who are farthest from it. So if any of you should brand with roguery the men who visit my shop, clearly you must do the same to those who pass their time in the shops of others; and if to them, to all the Athenians: for you are all in the habit of paying a call and passing your time at some shop or other.

(7) But really I see no need for me to be so very particular in rebutting each one of the statements that he has made, and to weary you any longer. For if I have argued the

principal points, what need is there to dwell seriously on trifles in the same way as he does? But I beg you all, gentlemen of the Council, to hold the same views concerning me as you have held till now. Do not be led by this man to deprive me of the sole benefit in my country of which fortune has granted me a share, nor let this one person prevail on you to withdraw now what you all agreed to grant me in the past. For, gentlemen, since Heaven had deprived us[7] of the chiefest things, the city voted us this pension, regarding the chances of evil and of good as the same for all alike. Surely I should be the most miserable of creatures if, after being deprived by my misfortune of the fairest and greatest things, the accuser should cause me the loss of that which the city bestowed in her thoughtful care for men in my situation. No, no, gentlemen; you must not vote that way. And why should I find you thus inclined? Because anyone has ever been brought to trial at my instance and lost his fortune? There is nobody who can prove it. Well, is it that I am a busybody, a hot-head, a seeker of quarrels? That is not the sort of use I happen to make of such means of subsistence as I have. That I am grossly insolent and savage? Even he would not allege this himself, except he should wish to add one more to the series of his lies. Or that I was in power at the time of the Thirty, and oppressed a great number of the citizens? But I went into exile with your people to Chalcis, and when I was free to live secure as a citizen with those persons I chose to depart and share your perils. I therefore ask you, gentlemen of the Council, not to treat me, a man who has committed no offence, in the same way as those who are guilty of numerous wrongs, but to give the same vote as the other Councils did on my case, remembering that I am neither rendering an account of State moneys placed in my charge, nor undergoing now an inquiry into my past proceedings in any office, but that the subject of this speech of mine is merely an obol. In this way you will all give the decision that is just, while I, in return for that, will feel duly grateful to you; and this man will learn in the future not to scheme against those who are weaker than himself, but only to overreach his equals.

### Plato, *The Apology of Socrates*

Socrates lived between 469 BCE and 399 BCE. His life parallels the years of the Athens Golden Age and its defeat by the Spartans in the Peloponnesian War. He was one of the leading thinkers of his age, perhaps *the* leading thinker. His teachings have influenced western civilization to the present day, forming a body of philosophy that has charged intellectual debate throughout the centuries.

Socrates' life and his teaching are chronicled by two men, Plato and Xenophon, the former Socrates' prized pupil at his school, the Academy. Socrates' ideas are contained principally in Plato's *Dialogues*. The dialogues are written in the form of questions and answers, i.e., the "Socratic method." In most of the dialogues, Socrates introduces a topic of interest to his students, and through the dialogical method he teaches them to find the flaws in the ideas of the other characters. The other characters are leading citizens, including politicians, artists, and sophists. The topics themselves are philosophical or rhetorical in nature, thus lending themselves to endless verbal jousting and debate. Socrates pursues a line of questioning that often leads to a dilemma. In the process, however, he is usually able to show the weakness of his opponent's position, and, at the very best, to illuminate his philosophy through his own rhetoric. His dialogues often led to embarrassment for his opponents, the result being that throughout his lifetime Socrates incurred the wrath of many leading citizens.

Socrates was an antidemocrat, and in his later years, during the Peloponnesian Wars, many Athenians were angered by his political views and his endless questioning of the "justice" of the war, or whether war itself is a "good." At a time when Athens was fighting for its very survival against the Spartan alliance, Socrates seemed to be undermining Athenian resolve. In 404 BCE, when Sparta gained control of Athens, many saw Socrates as a principal cause of the fall of the city.

As discussed in Chapter 2, Socrates was also the leading critic of the sophistic movement. He charged in his *Gorgias* that rhetoric was little more than the art of flattery, that eloquence was often used to deceive and to make the worse argument appear the better. The sophists, whose schools often competed with Socrates' Academy for students, were themselves a powerful political force in Athens, training, as they often did, the political leaders of the city and earning great sums of money for their speeches. Even the more moderate view of rhetoric in the *Phaedrus* failed to allay the anger the sophists felt toward this rival.

The general citizenry also had a dim view of Socrates. In 423 BCE, the playwright Aristophanes produced *The Clouds* for one of the Athenian festivals. In this play, an average citizen, Strepsiades, loses everything through a series of events starting with his decision to send his son, Phidippides, to Socrates' Academy, where the young man learns the art of persuasion, and then turns on his father, beating him and taking his money. While the play was meant to lampoon Socrates, its message was not lost on the citizenry.

By the time he was 70 years of age, Socrates had become disliked by the military, the politicians, the sophists, and the general citizenry. Having temporarily restored the democracy in 399 BCE, leading citizens sought their revenge on those they thought had undermined it. They quickly indicted Socrates and brought him to trial on two charges: that he was corrupting the youth of Athens with his teaching, and, that he was advocating the worship of false gods. The latter charge of atheism was a capital offense.

The indictment was a pretense to stop Socrates and to rid Athens of a man feared by many and loathed by most. Socrates' *Apology* is his speech of self-defense, given at the conclusion of his trial and just prior to the vote of guilt or innocence by the jury. The speech is preserved only in the works of Plato; there exists no actual transcript of Socrates' words on that fateful day. Thus, it must be remembered that the *Apology* is a recounting of Socrates' speech by his most devoted disciple. It is a memorable moment in the history of western civilization, containing as it does one of the most famous definitions of wisdom. I. F. Stone remarks that, "No other trial, except that of Jesus, has left so vivid an impression on the imagination of western man as that of Socrates'." Following is a translation by Benjamin Jowett of this notable oration.

(1) How you, O Athenians, have been affected by my accusers, I cannot tell; but I know that they almost made me forget who I was—so persuasively did they speak; and yet they have hardly uttered a word of truth. But of the many falsehoods told by them, there was one which quite amazed me;—I mean when they said that you should be upon your guard and not allow yourselves to be deceived by the force of my eloquence. To say this, when they were certain to be detected as soon as I opened by lips and proved myself to be anything but a great speaker, did indeed appear to me most shameless—unless by the force of eloquence they mean the force of truth; for if such is their meaning, I admit that I am eloquent. But in how different a way from theirs! Well, as I was saying, they have scarcely spoken the truth at all; from me you shall hear the whole truth, but not delivered after their manner in a set oration duly ornamented with fine words and phrases. No, by heaven! I shall use the words and arguments which occur to me at the moment, for I am confident in the justice of my cause;[8] at my time of life I ought not to be appearing before you, O men of Athens, in the character of a boy inventing falsehoods—let no one expect it of me. And I must particularly beg of you to grant me this favour—If I defend myself in my accustomed manner, and you hear me using the words which many of you have heard me using habitually in the agora, at the tables of the money-changers, and elsewhere, I would ask you not to be surprised, and not to interrupt me on this account. For I am more than seventy years of age, and appearing now for the first time before a court of law, I am quite a stranger to the court of law, I am quite a stranger to the language of the place; and therefore I would have you regard me as if I were really a stranger, whom you would excuse if he spoke in his native tongue, and after the fashion of his country:—Am I making an unfair request of you? Never mind the manner, which may or may not be good; but think only of the truth of my words, and give heed to that: let the speaker speak truly and the judge decide justly.

(2) And first, I have to reply to the older charges and to my first accusers, and then I will go on to the later ones. For of old I have had many accusers, who have accused me falsely to you during many years; and I am more afraid of them than of Anytus and his associates, who are dangerous, too, in their own way. But far more dangerous are the others, who began when most of you were children, and took possession of your minds with their falsehoods, telling of one Socrates, a wise man, who speculated about the heaven above, and searched into the earth beneath, and made the worse appear the better cause. The men who have besmeared me with this tale are the accusers whom I dread; for their hearers are apt to fancy that such inquirers do not believe in the existence of the gods. And they are many, and their charges against me are of ancient date, and they were made by them in the days when some of you were more

impressible than you are now—in childhood, or it may have been in youth—and the cause went by default, for there was none to answer. And hardest of all, I do not know and cannot tell the names of my accusers; unless in the chance case of a comic poet. All who from envy and malice have persuaded you—some of them having first convinced themselves—all this class of men are most difficult to deal with; for I cannot have them up here, and cross-examine them, and therefore I must simply fight with shadows in my own defence, and argue when there is no one who answers. I will ask you then to take it from me that my opponents are of two kinds; one recent, the other ancient: and I hope that you will see the propriety of my answering the latter first, for these accusations you heard long before the others, much oftener.

(3) Well, then, I must make my defence, and endeavour to remove from your minds in a short time, slander which you have had a long time to take in. May I succeed, if to succeed be for my good and yours, or likely to avail me in my cause! The task is not an easy one; I quite understand the nature of it. And so leaving the event with God, in obedience to the law I will now make my defence.

(4) I will begin at the beginning, and ask what is the accusation which has given rise to the slander of me, and in fact has encouraged Meletus to prefer this charge against me. Well, what do the slanderers say? They shall be my prosecutors, and this is the information they swear against me: "Socrates is an evil-doer; a meddler who searches into things under the earth and in heaven, and makes the worse appear the better cause, and teaches the aforesaid practices to others." Such is the nature of the accusation: it is just what you have yourselves seen in the comedy of Aristophanes,[9] who has introduced a man whom he calls Socrates, swinging about and saying that he walks on air, and talking a deal of nonsense concerning matters of which I do not pretend to know either much or little—not that I mean to speak disparagingly of anyone who is a student of natural philosophy. May Meletus never bring so many charges against me as to make me do that! But the simple truth is, O Athenians, that I have nothing to do with physical speculations. Most of those here present are witnesses to the truth of this, and to them I appeal. Speak then, you who have heard me, and tell your neighbours whether any of you have ever known me hold forth in few words or in many upon such matters ... You hear their answer. And from what they say of this part of the charge you will be able to judge of the truth of the rest.

(5) As little foundation is there for the report that I am a teacher, and take money; this accusation has no more truth in it than the other. Although, if a man were really able to instruct mankind, this too would, in my opinion, be an honour to him. There is Gorgias of Leontium, and Prodicus of Ceos, and Hippias of Elis, who go the round of the cities, and are able to persuade the young men to leave their own citizens by whom they might be taught for nothing, and come to them whom they not only pay, but are thankful if they may be allowed to pay them. There is at this time a Parian philosopher residing in Athens, of whom I have heard; and I came to hear of him in this way:—I came across a man who has spent more money on the sophists than the rest of the world put together, Callias, the son of Hipponicus, and knowing that he had sons, I asked him: "Callias," I said, "if your two sons were foals or calves, there would be no difficulty in finding someone to put over them; we should hire a trainer of horses, or a farmer probably, who would improve and perfect them in the appropriate virtue and excellence; but as they are human beings, whom are you thinking of placing over them? Is there anyone who understands human and civic virtue? You must have

thought about the matter, for you have sons; is there anyone?" "There is," he said. "Who is he?" said I; "and of what country? and what does he charge?" "Evenus the Parian," he replied; "he is the man, and his charge is five minas." Happy is Evenus, I said to myself, if he really has this wisdom, and teaches at such a moderate charge. Had I the same, I should have been very proud and conceited; but the truth is that I have no knowledge of the kind.

(6) I dare say, Athenians, that someone among you will reply, "Yes, Socrates, but what *is* your occupation? What is the origin of these accusations which are brought against you; there must have been something strange which you have been doing? All these rumors and this talk about you would never have arisen if you had been like other men; tell us, then, what is the cause of them, for we should be sorry to judge hastily of you." Now I regard this as a fair challenge, and I will endeavour to explain to you the reason why I am called wise and have such an evil fame. Please to attend then. And although some of you may think I am joking, I declare that I will tell you the entire truth. Men of Athens, this reputation of mine has come of a certain sort of wisdom which I possess. If you ask me what kind of wisdom, I reply, wisdom such as may perhaps be attained by man, for to that extent I am inclined to believe that I am wise; whereas the persons of whom I was speaking have a kind of superhuman wisdom, which I know not how to describe, because I have it not myself; and he who says that I have, speaks falsely, and is taking away my character. And here, O men of Athens, I must beg you not to interrupt me, even if I seem to say something extravagant. For the word which I will speak is not mine. I will refer you to a witness who is worthy of credit; that witness shall be the god of Delphi—He will tell you about my wisdom, if I have any, and of what sort it is. You must have known Chaerephon; he was early a friend of mine, and also a friend of yours, for he shared in the recent exile of the people, and returned with you. Well, Chaerephon, as you know, was very impetuous in all his doings, and he went to Delphi and boldly asked the oracle to tell him whether—as I was saying, I must beg you not to interrupt—he actually asked the oracle to tell him whether anyone was wiser than I was, and the Pythian prophetess answered that there was no man wiser. Chaerephon is dead himself; but his brother, who is in court, will confirm the truth of what I am saying.

(7) Why do I mention this? Because I am going to explain to you why I have such an evil name. When I heard the answer, I said to myself, What can the god mean? and what is the interpretation of his riddle? for I know that I have no wisdom, small or great. What then can he mean when he says that I am the wisest of men? And yet he is a god, and cannot lie; that would be against his nature. After long perplexity, I thought of a method of trying the question. I reflected that if I could only find a man wiser than myself, then I might go to the god with a refutation in my hand. I should say to him, "Here is a man who is wiser than I am; but you said that I was the wisest." Accordingly I went to one who had the reputation of wisdom, and observed him—his name I need not mention, he was a politician; and in the process of examining him and talking with him, this, men of Athens, was what I found. I could not help thinking that he was not really wise, although he was thought wise by many, and still wiser by himself; and thereupon I tried to explain to him that he thought himself wise, but was not really wise; and the consequence was that he hated me, and his enmity was shared by several who were present and heard me. So I left him, saying to myself as I went away: Well, although I do not suppose that either of us knows anything really worth

knowing, I am at least wiser than this fellow—for he knows nothing, and thinks that he knows; I neither know nor think that I know. In this one little point, then, I seem to have the advantage of him. Then I went to another who had still higher pretensions to wisdom, and my conclusion was exactly the same. Whereupon I made another enemy of him, and of many others besides him.

(8) Then I went to one man after another, being not unconscious of the enmity which I provoked, and I lamented and feared this: but necessity was laid upon me—the word of God, I thought, ought to be considered first. And I said to myself, Go I must to all who appear to know, and find out the meaning of the oracle. And I swear to you, Athenians—for I must tell you the truth—the result of my mission was just this: I found that the men most in repute were nearly the most foolish; and that others less esteemed were really closer to wisdom. I will tell you the tale of my wanderings and of the "Herculean" labours, as I may call them, which I endured only to find at the last the oracle irrefutable. After the politicians, I went to the poets; tragic, dithyrambic, and all sorts. And there, I said to myself, you will be instantly detected; now you will find out that you are more ignorant than they are. Accordingly, I took them some of the most elaborate passages in their own writings, and asked what was the meaning of them—thinking that they would teach me something. Will you believe me? I am ashamed to confess the truth, but I must say that there is hardly a person present who would not have talked better about their poetry than they did themselves. So I learnt that not by wisdom do poets write poetry, but by a sort of genius and inspiration; they are like diviners or soothsayers who also say many fine things, but do not understand the meaning of them. The poets appeared to me to be much in the same case; and I further observed that upon the strength of their poetry they believed themselves to be the wisest of men in other things in which they were not wise. So I departed, conceiving myself to be superior to them for the same reason that I was superior to the politicians.

(9) At last I went to the artisans, for I was conscious that I knew nothing at all, as I may say, and I was sure that they knew many fine things; and here I was not mistaken, for they did know many things of which I was ignorant, and in this they certainly were wiser than I was. But I observed that even the good artisans fell into the same error as the poets;—because they were good workmen they thought that they also know all sorts of high matters, and this defect in them overshadowed their wisdom; and therefore I asked myself on behalf of the oracle, whether I would like to be as I was, neither having their knowledge nor their ignorance, or like them in both; and I made answer to myself and to the oracle that I was better off as I was.

(10) This inquisition has led to my having many enemies of the worst and most dangerous kind, and has given rise also to many imputations, including the name of "wise"; for my hearers always imagine that I myself possess the wisdom which I find wanting in others. But the truth is, O men of Athens, that God only is wise; and by his answer he intends to show that the wisdom of men is worth little or nothing; although speaking of Socrates, he is only using my name by way of illustration, as if he said, He, O men, is the wisest, who, like Socrates, knows that his wisdom is in truth worth nothing. And so I go about the world, obedient to the god, and search and make inquiry into the wisdom of anyone, whether citizen or stranger, who appears to be wise; and if he is not wise, then in vindication of the oracle I show him that he is not wise; and my occupation quite absorbs me, and I have had no time to do anything

useful either in public affairs or in any concern of my own, but I am in utter poverty by reason of my devotion to the god.

(11) There is another thing:—young men of the richer classes, who have not much to do, come about me of their own accord; they like to hear people examined, and they often imitate me, and proceed to do some examining themselves; there are plenty of persons, as they quickly discover, who think that they know something, but really know little or nothing; and then those who are examined by them instead of being angry with themselves are angry with me: This confounded Socrates, they say, this villainous misleader of youth!—and then if somebody asks them, Why, what evil does he practise or teach? they do not know and cannot tell; but in order that they may not appear to be at a loss, they repeat the ready-made charges which are used against all philosophers about teaching things up in the clouds and under the earth, and having no gods, and making the worse appear the better cause; for they do not like to confess that their pretence of knowledge has been detected—which is the truth; and as they are numerous and ambitious and energetic, and speak vehemently with persuasive tongues, they have filled your ears with their loud and inveterate calumnies. And this is the reason why my three accusers, Meletus and Anytus and Lycon, have set upon me; Meletus, who has a quarrel with me on behalf of the poets; Anytus, on behalf of the craftsmen and politicians; Lycon, on behalf of the rhetoricians: and as I said at the beginning, I cannot expect to get rid of such a mass of calumny all in a moment. And this, O men of Athens, is the truth and the whole truth; I have concealed nothing, I have dissembled nothing. And yet, I feel sure that my plainness of speech is fanning their hatred of me, and what is their hatred but a proof that I am speaking the truth?—Hence has arisen the prejudice against me; and this is the reason of it, as you will find out either in this or in any future inquiry.

(12) I have said enough in my defence against the first class of my accusers; I turn to the second class. They are headed by Meletus, that good man and true lover of his country, as he calls himself. Against these, too, I must try to make a defence:—Let their affidavit be read; it contains something of this kind: It says that Socrates is a doer of evil, inasmuch as he corrupts the youth, and does not receive the gods whom the state receives, but has a new religion of his own. Such is the charge; and now let us examine the particular counts. He says that I am a doer of evil, and corrupt the youth; but I say, O men of Athens, that Meletus is a doer of evil, in that he is playing a solemn farce, recklessly bringing men to trial from a pretended zeal and interest about matters in which he really never had the smallest interest. And the truth of this I will endeavour to prove to you.

(13) Come hither, Meletus, and let me ask a question of you. You attach great importance to the improvement of youth?

Yes, I do.

Tell the judges, then, who is their improver; for you must know, as you take such interest in the subject, and have discovered their corrupter, and are citing and accusing me in this court. Speak, then, and tell the judges who is the improver of youth:—Observe, Meletus, that you are silent, and have nothing to say. But is this not rather disgraceful, and a very considerable proof of what I was saying, that you have no interest in the matter? Speak up, friend, and tell us who their improver is.

The laws.

But that, my good sir, is not my question: Can you not name some person—whose first qualification will be that he knows the laws?

The judges, Socrates, who are present in court.

What, do you mean to say, Meletus, that they are able to instruct and improve youth?

Certainly they are.

What, all of them, or some only and not others?

All of them.

Truly, that is good news! There are plenty of improvers, then. And what do you say of the audience—do they improve them?

Yes, they do.

And the senators?

Yes, the senators improve them.

But perhaps the members of the assembly corrupt them?—or do they too improve them?

They improve them.

Then every Athenian improves and elevates them; all with the exception of myself; and I alone am their corrupter? Is that what you affirm?

That is what I stoutly affirm.

I am very unfortunate if you are right. But suppose I ask you a question: Is it the same with horses? Does one man do them harm and all the world good? Is not the exact opposite the truth? One man is able to do them good, or at least very few;— the trainer of horses, that is to say, does them good, but the ordinary man does them harm if he has to do with them? Is not that true, Meletus, of horses, or of any other animals? Most assuredly it is; whether you and Anytus say yes or no. Happy indeed would be the condition of youth if they had one corrupter only, and all the rest of the world were their benefactors. But you, Meletus, have sufficiently shown that you never had a thought about the young: your carelessness is plainly seen in your not caring about the very things which you bring against me.

And now, Meletus, I adjure you to answer me another question: Which is better, to live among bad citizens, or among good ones? Answer, friend, I say; the question is one which may be easily answered. Do not the good do their neighbours good, and the bad do them evil?

Certainly.

And is there anyone who would rather be injured than benefited by those who live with him? Answer, my good friend, the law requires you to answer—does anyone like to be injured?

Certainly not.

And when you accuse me of corrupting and deteriorating the youth, do you allege that I corrupt them intentionally or unintentionally?

Intentionally, I say.

But you have just admitted that the good do their neighbours good, and the evil do them evil. Now, is that a truth which your superior wisdom has recognized thus early in life, and am I, at my age, in such darkness and ignorance as not to know that if a man with whom I have to live is corrupted by me, I am very likely to be harmed by him; and yet I corrupt him, and intentionally, too—so you say, although neither I nor any other human being is ever likely to be convinced by you. But either I do not corrupt them, or I corrupt them unintentionally; and on either view of the case you lie. If my offence is unintentional, the law has no cognizance of unintentional offences: you ought to have taken me privately, and warned and admonished me; for if I had had instruction, I should have left off doing what I only did unintentionally—beyond doubt I should; but you would have nothing to say to me and refused to teach me. And now you bring me up in this court, which is a place not of instruction, but of punishment.

(14) It will be very clear to you, Athenians, as I was saying, that Meletus has never had any care, great or small, about the matter. But still I should like to know, Meletus, in what I am affirmed to corrupt the young. I suppose you mean, as I infer from your indictment, that I teach them not to acknowledge the gods which the state acknowledges, but some other new divinities or spiritual agencies in their stead. These are the lessons by which I corrupt the youth, as you say.

Yes, that I say emphatically.

Then, by the gods, Meletus, of whom we are speaking, tell me and the court, in somewhat plainer terms, what you mean! For I do not as yet understand whether you affirm that I teach other men to acknowledge some gods, and therefore that I do believe in gods, and am not an entire atheist—this you do not lay to my charge—but only you say that they are different gods. Or, do your mean that I am an atheist simply, and a teacher of atheism?

I mean the latter—that you are a complete atheist.

What an extraordinary statement! Why do you think so, Meletus? Do you mean that I do not believe in the god-head of the sun or moon, like the rest of mankind?

I assure you, judges, that he does: for he says that the sun is stone, and the moon earth.

Friend Meletus, do you think that you are accusing Anaxagoras? Have you such a low opinion of the judges, that you fancy them so illiterate as not to know these doctrines are found in the books of Anaxagoras the Clazomenian, which are full of them? And so, forsooth, the youth are said to be taught them by Socrates, when they can be bought in the book market for one drachma at most; and they might pay their money, and laugh at Socrates if he pretends to father these extraordinary views. And so, Meletus, you really think that I do not believe in any god?

I swear by Zeus that you verily believe in none at all.

(15) Nobody will believe you, Meletus, and I am pretty sure that you do not believe yourself. I cannot help thinking, men of Athens, that Meletus is reckless and impudent, and that he has brought this indictment in a spirit of mere wantonness and youthful bravado. Has he not compounded a riddle, thinking to try me? He said to himself:—I shall see whether the wise Socrates will discover my facetious self-contradiction, or whether I shall be able to deceive him and the rest of them. For he certainly does appear to me to contradict himself in the indictment as much as if he said that Socrates is guilty of not believing in the gods, and yet of believing in them—but this is not like a person who is in earnest.

(16) I should like you, O men of Athens, to join me in examining what I conceive to be his inconsistency; and do you, Meletus, answer. And I must remind the audience of my request that they would not make a disturbance if I speak in my accustomed manner:

(17) Did ever man, Meletus, believe in the existence of human things, and not of human beings? ... I wish, men of Athens, that he would answer, and not be always

trying to get up an interruption. Did ever any man believe in horsemanship, and not in horses? Or in flute-playing, and not in flute-players? My friend, no man ever did; I answer to you and to the court, as you refuse to answer for yourself. But now please to answer the next question: Can a man believe in the existence of things spiritual and divine, and not in spirits or demigods? He cannot.

(18) How lucky I am to have extracted that answer, by the assistance of the court! But then you swear in the indictment that I teach and believe in divine or spiritual things (new or old, no matter for that); at any rate, I believe in spiritual things—so you say and swear in the affidavit, and yet if I believe in them, how can I help believing in spirits or demigods;—must I not? To be sure I must; your silence gives consent. Now what are spirits or demigods? are they not either gods or the sons of gods? Certainly they are.

(19) But this is what I call the facetious riddle invented by you: the demigods or spirits are gods, and you say first that I do not believe in gods, and then again that I do believe in gods; that is, if I believe in demigods. For if the demigods are the illegitimate sons of gods, whether by nymphs, or by other mothers, as some are said to be—what human being will ever believe that there are no gods when there are sons of gods? You might as well affirm the existence of mules, and deny that of horses and asses. Such nonsense, Meletus, could only have been intended by you to make trial of me. You have put this into the indictment because you could think of nothing real of which to accuse me. But no one who has a particle of understanding will ever be convinced by you that a man can believe in the existence of things divine and superhuman, and the same man refuse to believe in gods and demigods and heroes.

(20) I have said enough in answer to the charge of Meletus: any elaborate defence is unnecessary. You know well the truth of my statement that I have incurred many violent enmities; and this is what will be my destruction if I am destroyed;—not Meletus, nor yet Anytus, but the envy and detraction of the world, which has been the death of many good men, and will probably be the death of many more; there is no danger of my being the last of them.

## Gorgias, *Encomium to Helen*

Gorgias' "Encomium to Helen," stands as a prototypical example of his oratorical style, the style Athenians loved and philosophers such as Plato scorned. The date of the Encomium is unknown. It was delivered, according to Kennedy, at various places a number of times.[10] The speech was also available as a pamphlet for sale to the general public. The "Encomium to Helen" is part poetry, part literature, part oratory, and part sheer entertainment. Above all, it is quintessential Gorgian rhetoric.

The subject of the Encomium is Helen. She, of course, is the beautiful Helen of Sparta, the woman so much beloved in Greek literature, and the cause of the ten-year Trojan War chronicled first by Homer in the *The Iliad* and then by playwrights, poets, and storytellers throughout the classical age. In Homer's original story, Helen, wife of the aging but powerful leader of Sparta Menelaus, is raped by Paris and then kidnapped and taken away to his kingdom, Troy. Claiming the blessing of Aphrodite, Paris takes Helen as his wife. Outraged, the Spartans set out in ships to rescue her. The result is the Trojan War.

The story of Helen evolved in the works of later bards, mostly in the explanation of her behavior. The playwright Euripedes raises a question about Helen's motivation by asking whether she went willingly with Paris, and was thus herself responsible for the Trojan War. Did Helen fall in love with Paris and desert her husband? In his drama *Agamemnon*, Aeschylus suggests that Helen was an instrument of fate, a victim of the gods. By the time of Gorgias, Helen had become a central agent in the emerging Greek sense of morality. The explanation one accepted would affect one's view of women, religion, love, and war. For sophists such as Gorgias and Isocrates, the ambiguities surrounding Helen's behavior were perfect grist for their rhetorical mills.

Gorgias did not pass up this opportunity, especially since it allowed him to make good on his boast that he could speak on any subject. The speech is a review of the four reasons that had evolved for Helen's behavior. Gorgias concludes that regardless of Helen's motivation, she is not to blame for her behavior. It is his reasoning that makes the speech interesting and persuasive.

The oration is compelling today for two reasons. First, the four arguments Gorgias reviews in Helen's defense still invite discussion, even about current events of a similar kind. Second, Gorgias' rhetorical style is on full display here: its excesses, its poetic charm, its experimentation in the sound and rhythm of speech. As we read it today, we should read it for both of these reasons. Gorgias' "Encomium to Helen" should be read aloud to experience the art of this virtuoso orator as those in his audience that day must surely have enjoyed. Following is a translation by George Kennedy.

(1) Fairest ornament to a city is a goodly army and to a body beauty and to a soul wisdom and to an action virtue and to speech truth, but their opposites are unbefitting. Man and woman and speech and deed and city and object should be honored with praise if praiseworthy, but on the unworthy blame should be laid; for it is equal error and ignorance to blame the praiseworthy and to praise the blameworthy.

(2) It is the function of a single speaker both to prove the needful rightly and to disprove the wrongly spoken. Thus, I shall refute those who rebuke Helen, a woman about whom there is univocal and unanimous testimony among those who have believed the poets and whose ill-omened name has become a memorial of disasters.[11]

I wish, by giving some logic to language, to free the accused of blame and to show that her critics are lying and to demonstrate the truth and to put an end to ignorance.

(3) Now that by nature and birth the woman who is the subject of this speech was preeminent among preeminent men and women, this is not unclear, not even to a few; for it is clear that Leda was her mother, while as a father she had in fact a god though allegedly a mortal, the latter Tyndareus, the former Zeus;[12] and of these the one seemed her father because he was, and the other was disproved because he was only said to be; and one was the greatest of men, the other lord of all.

(4) Born from such parents, she possessed godlike beauty, which getting and not forgetting she preserved. On many did she work the greatest passions of love, and by her one body she brought together many bodies of men greatly minded for great deeds.[13] Some had the greatness of wealth, some the glory of ancient noblesse, some the vigor of personal prowess, some the power of acquired knowledge. And all came because of a passion that loved conquest and a love of honor that was unconquered.

(5) Who he was and why and how he sailed away taking Helen as his love. I shall not say—for to tell the knowing what they know is believable but not enjoyable.[14] Having now exceeded the time alloted for my introduction,[15] I shall proceed to my intended speech and shall propose the causes for which Helen's voyage to Troy is likely to have taken place.

(6) For [either] by fate's will and gods' wishes and necessity's decrees she did what she did or by force reduced or by words seduced or by love induced.

(7) Now if for the first reason [fate, the gods, etc.], the responsible one should rightly be held responsible: it is impossible to prevent a god's predetermination by human premeditation, since by nature the stronger force is not prevented by the weaker, but the weaker is ruled and driven by the stronger: the stronger leads, the weaker follows. But god is stronger than man in force and in wisdom and in other ways. If, therefore, by fate and god the cause had been decreed, Helen must of all disgrace be freed.[16]

(8) But if she was seized by force and illegally assaulted and unjustly insulted, it is clear that the assailant as insulter did the wrong and the assailed as insulted suffered wrongly. It is right for the barbarian who laid barbarous hands on her by word and law and deed to meet with blame in word, disenfranchisement in law, and punishment in deed, while she who was seized and deprived of her country and bereft of her friends, how should she not be pitied rather than pilloried? He did dread deeds; she suffered them. Her it is just to pity, him to hate.

(9) But if speech persuaded her and deceived her soul, not even to this is it difficult to make answer and to banish blame, as follows. Speech is a powerful lord that with the smallest and most invisible body accomplished most godlike works. It can banish fear and remove grief and instill pleasure and enhance pity. I shall show how this is so.

(10) It is necessary for it to seem so as well in the opinion of my hearers. All poetry I regard and name as speech having meter.[17] On those who hear it come fearful shuddering and tearful pity and grievous longing, as the soul, through words, experiences some experience of its own at others' good fortune and ill fortune. But listen as I turn from one argument to another.

(11) Divine sweetness transmitted through words is inductive of pleasure, reductive of pain. Thus, by entering into the opinion of the soul the force of incantation is wont

to beguile and persuade and alter it by witchcraft, and the two arts of witchcraft and magic are errors of the soul and deceivers of opinion.

(12) How many speakers on how many subjects have persuaded others and continue to persuade by molding false speech? If everyone, on every subject, had memory of the past and knowledge of the present and foresight of the future, speech would not do what it does; but as things are, it is easy neither to remember the past nor to consider the present nor to predict the future; so that on most subjects most people take opinion as counselor to the soul. But opinion, being slippery and insecure, casts those relying on it into slippery and insecure fortune.

(13) What is there to prevent the conclusion that Helen, too, when still young, was carried off by speech just as if constrained by force? Her mind was swept away by persuasion, and persuasion has the same power as necessity, although it may bring shame; for speech, by persuading the soul that it persuaded, constrained her both to obey what was said and to approve what was done. The persuader, as user of force, did wrong; the persuaded, forced by speech, is unreasonably blamed.

(14) To understand that persuasion, joining with speech, is wont to stamp the soul as it wishes, one must study, first, the words of astronomers who, substituting opinion for opinion, removing one and instilling another, make incredible and unclear things appear true to the eyes of opinion;[18] second, forceful speeches in public debate, where one side of the argument pleases a large crowd and persuades by being written with art even though not spoken with truth; third, the verbal wrangling of philosophers in which, too, a swiftness of thought is exhibited, making confidence in opinion easily changed.

(15) The power of speech has the same effect on the condition of the soul as the application of drugs to the state of bodies; for just as different drugs dispel different fluids from the body, and some bring an end to disease but others end life, so also some speeches cause pain, some pleasure, some fear; some instill courage, some drug and bewitch the soul with a kind of evil persuasion.

(16) Thus, it has been explained that if she was persuaded by speech she did no wrong but was unfortunate. I shall now go on to the fourth cause in a fourth argument. If it was love that did these things it will not be difficult to escape the charge of error that is alleged: for [first reason] we see not what we wish but what each of us has experienced: through sight the soul is stamped in diverse ways.

(17) Whenever men at war, enemy against enemy, buckle up in the armaments of bronze and iron, whether in defense or offense, when their sight beholds the scene, it is alarmed and causes alarm in the soul, so that often they flee in terror from future danger as though it were present. Obedience to law is strongly brought home by fear derived from sight which, coming upon people, has made them desire both what is judged seemly by law and thought good by the mind.

(18) But as soon as they have seen terrible sights they have abandoned the thought of the moment. Thus, discipline is extinguished and fear drives out the concept. And many fall victim to imaginary diseases and dreadful pains and hard-to-cure mental aberrations; thus does sight engrave on the mind images of things seen. And many terrors are left unmentioned [in my speech], but those that are omitted are very like things that have been said.

(19) Moreover, whenever pictures of many colors and figures create a perfect image of a single figure and form, they delight the sight. How much does the production

of statues and the workmanship of artifacts furnish pleasurable sight to the eyes! Thus is it natural for the sight sometimes to grieve, sometimes to delight. Much love and desire for many objects is created in many minds.

(20) If, then, the eye of Helen, pleased by the body of Alexander, gave to her soul an eagerness and response in love, what wonder? If love, a god, prevails over the divine power of the gods, how could a lesser one be able to reject and refuse it? But if love is a human disease and an ignorance of the soul, it should not be blamed as a mistake but regarded as a misfortune. For she [Helen] went [with Paris] caught by the nets around her soul, not by the wishes of her mind, and by the necessity of love, not by the devices of art.

(21) How, then, can blame be thought just? Whether she did what she did by falling in love or persuaded by speech or seized by violence or forced by divine necessity, she is completely acquitted. By speech I have removed disgrace from a woman. I have abided by the principle I posed at the start of my speech: I have tried to refute the injustice of defamation and the ignorance of allegation. I wished to write a speech that would be Helen's celebration and my own recreation.

## Demosthenes, *The First Philippic*

Demosthenes was born in 384 BCE, the son of a wealthy sword manufacturer. Upon reaching the age of 18, he attempted to wrest control of his late father's estate from two cousins whose mismanagement of the business had led it to ruin. The arbitration took three years and the case dragged on for two more before Demosthenes finally won, although by this time his father's estate was close to bankruptcy.[19] During this period Demosthenes began his study of rhetoric as a means of helping him win his arbitration. He studied under the notable sophist Isaeus whose influence can be seen in Demosthenes' speeches. Having lost his arms manufacturing business, Demosthenes turned to logography as a profession, writing speeches for others for approximately the next 20 years and doing so successfully. From 351 BCE, until his self-induced death by poison in 323 BCE (to avoid death at the hands of Philip of Macedon's soldiers), Demosthenes turned his talents to public affairs, particularly to rallying the Athenian people against the imminent threat of invasion by Philip.

Demosthenes is considered by many to be the greatest orator of his age. Cicero said of him that he was the complete orator, and that,

> nothing could have been expressed with greater nicety, or more clearly and poignantly, that it has been already expressed by him; and nothing greater, nothing more rapid and forcible, nothing adorned with a nobler elevation, either of language or sentiment, can be conceived, than what is to found in his orations.[20]

And yet Demosthenes did not have the natural abilities which Cicero himself declared were essential to the orator. Indeed, Demosthenes had a weak voice and imperfect delivery, defects which he struggled mightily to overcome. Dobson tells us that, "We are familiar with the legends of his declaiming with pebbles in his mouth and reciting speeches when running up hill, of his studies in a cave by the seashore, where he tried to make his voice heard above the thunder of the waves."[21] Whether fact or legend, Demosthenes did become master of his own style in composition and delivery. He was destined to become the most renowned orator of his time, a man immersed in the struggles of his people, often without success but always passionate in his beliefs.

The Philippics are speeches delivered by Demosthenes between the years 351 BCE and 340 BCE. There are four Philippics orations although Dobson doubts that the fourth is legitimate. The first two Philippics are calls to the Athenian people to resist Philip before Athens itself is threatened with domination by the barbarian from the north. The *Third Philippic* occurs after Philip has gained control of many parts of the Athenian empire and is about to march on the city of Olynthus. Demosthenes pleads urgently and desperately for a military mission to help the Olynthians and prepare for war. Despite his failure in rousing the Athenian people to arm themselves against Philip, Demosthenes' Philippic orations are considered masterpieces of rhetorical invention and technique.

A brief background is necessary to understanding Demosthenes' situation at the time of the *First Philippic*. During the decade of the 360s, the city-states had engaged in constant warring. The Arcadian league, founded in 370 BCE, had been an attempt to secure peace among the states, but the aggressive nature of Sparta and the tribes from Lacedaemon had led to continued bloody conflict followed by peace negotiations followed by more conflict. In 362 BCE, at the Battle of Mantinea, all the city-states met to seek supremacy once and for all. The battle was a disaster for all of Greece, with thousands dead and an enduring enmity among the city-states of Hellas. Isocrates' vision of a unified Greece was forever dimmed. Despite her weakened condition as an empire, Athens continued to hold territories (colonies) far from her own shore. The Athenian empire included all of Attica, Euboea, Syracuse, and, most consequentially, Thessaly and Chalcidice to the north. In the year 383 BCE, during the time when King Amyntas of Macedon was uniting his country, his third son was born, Philip of Macedon. Philip of Macedon had been raised in Thebes and given an Athenian education. From his youth, Philip determined that his people, who were known as barbarians by the Athenians, would be of Hellenic type. When he ascended to power in 359 BCE, he set out immediately to unite the tribes in his country and to build an army of unparalleled size and strength. He seized the gold mines of Mount Pangaeus just beyond the Thracian border and with this newfound source of wealth, Philip was able to expand his sights across his borders, to the east and south—to Hellas. Macedon was landlocked due to the Athenian colonies of Thessaly and Chalcidice which controlled the Macedonian shoreline. In 353 BCE, Philip began his interference in the affairs of Thessaly, which brought him to the attention of Athens. In 352 BCE, he attempted to cross through the pass at Thermopylae and take part in the Sacred War against Phocis; at this time, Athens intervened to stop him. But through intrigue and warfare, Philip soon became master of Thessaly and the greater part of Thrace. He now controlled port towns and he increased his treasury through taxes and customs exacted on the ships that traded there. Athens, still weakened by the wars of the previous decade and focused on internal affairs, was unable or unwilling to mount a campaign against Philip. But in 351 BCE, Philip made a bold move eastward through Thrace toward the Hellespont and the Athenian grain supply route. Now, with control of Athenian shipping and with a stranglehold on their supply routes, the Athenians were alarmed. Most alarmed among them was Demosthenes, the brilliant young speech writer and orator. Once aware of this imminent danger from the north, Demosthenes rose to address his fellow citizens, seeking to rally them to finance an army and prepare themselves for their defense against Philip. The *First Philippic* was delivered in 351 BCE.

(1) If some new subject were being brought before us, men of Athens, I would have waited until most of your ordinary advisers had declared their opinion; and if anything that they said were satisfactory to me, I would have remained silent, and only if it were not so, would I have attempted to express my own view. But since we find ourselves once more considering a question upon which they have often spoken, I think I may reasonably be pardoned for rising first of all. For if their advice to you in the past had been what it ought to have been, you would have had no occasion for the present debate.

(2) In the first place, then, men of Athens, we must not be downhearted at our present situation, however wretched it may seem to be. For in the worst feature of the past lies our best hope for the future—in the fact, that is, that we are in our present plight because you are not doing your duty in any respect; for if you were doing all that you should do, and we were still in this evil case, we could not then even hope for any improvement. In the second place, you must bear in mind (what some of you have

heard from others, and those who know can recollect for themselves), how powerful the Spartans were, not long ago, and yet how noble and patriotic your own conduct was, when instead of doing anything unworthy of your country you faced the war with Sparta in defence of the right. Now why do I remind you of these things? It is because, men of Athens, I wish you to see and to realize, that so long as you are on your guard you have nothing to fear; but that if you are indifferent, nothing can be as you would wish: for this is exemplified for you both by the power of Sparta in those days, to which you rose superior because you gave your minds to your affairs; and by the insolence of Philip today, which troubles us because we care nothing for the things which should concern us. If, however, any of you, men of Athens, when he considers the immense force now at Philip's command, and the city's loss of all her strongholds, thinks that Philip is a foe hard to conquer, I ask him (right though he is in his belief) to reflect also that there was a time when we possessed Pydna and Poteidaea and Methone; when all the surrounding country was our own, and many of the tribes which are now on his side were free and independent, and more inclined to be friendly to us than to him. Now if in those days Philip had made up his mind that it was a hard thing to fight against the Athenians, with all their fortified outposts on his own frontiers, while he was destitute of allies, he would have achieved none of his recent successes, nor acquired this great power. But Philip saw quite clearly, men of Athens, that all these strongholds were prizes of war, displayed for competition. He saw that in the nature of things the property of the absent belongs to those who are on the spot, and that of the negligent to those who are ready for toil and danger. It is, as you know, by acting upon this belief, that he has brought all those places under his power, and now holds them—some of them by right of capture in war, others in virtue of alliances and friendly understandings; for everyone is willing to grant alliance and to give attention to those whom they see to be prepared and ready to take action as is necessary. If then, men of Athens, you also will resolve to adopt this principle to-day—the principle which you have never observed before—if each of you can henceforward be relied upon to throw aside all this pretence of incapacity, and act where his duty bids him, and where his services can be of use to his country; if he who has money will contribute, and he who is of military age will join the campaign; if, in one plain word, you will resolve henceforth to depend absolutely on yourselves, each man no longer hoping that he will need to do nothing himself, and that his neighbour will do everything for him; then, God willing, you will recover your own; you will take back all that your indolence has lost, and you will have your revenge upon Philip. Do not imagine that his fortune is built to last forever, as if he were a God. He also has those who hate him and fear him, men of Athens, and envy him too, even among those who now seem to be his closest friends. All the feelings that exist in any other body of men must be supposed to exist in Philip's supporters. Now, however, all such feelings are cowed before him: your slothful apathy has taken away their only rallying point; and it is this apathy that I bid you put off to-day. Mark the situation, men of Athens: mark the pitch which the man's outrageous insolence has reached, when he does not even give you a choice between action and inaction, but threatens you, and utters (as we are told) haughty language: for he is not the man to rest content in possession of his conquests: he is always casting his net wider; and while we procrastinate and sit idle, he is setting his toils around us on every side. When, then, men of Athens, when, I say, will you take the action that is required? What are you waiting for? "We are waiting," you say, "till it is necessary." But what must we think of all that is happening at this present time? Surely the strongest necessity that a free people can experience is the shame which they must feel at their position! What? Do you want to go round asking one another, "Is there any news?" Could there be any stranger news than that a man of Macedonia is defeating Athenians in war, and ordering the affairs of the Hellenes? "Is Philip dead?" "No, but he is sick." And what difference does it make to you? For if anything should happen to him, you will soon raise up for yourselves a second Philip, if it is thus that you attend to your interests. Indeed, Philip himself has not risen to this excessive height through his own strength, so much as through our neglect. I go even further. If anything happened to Philip—if the operation of Fortune, who always cares for us better than we care for ourselves, were to effect this too for us—you know that if you were at hand, you could descend upon the general confusion and order everything as you wished; but in your present condition, even if circumstances offered you Amphipolis, you could not take it; for your forces and your minds alike are far away.

(3) Well, I say no more of the obligation which rests upon you all to be willing and ready to do your duty; I will assume that you are resolved and convinced. But the nature of the armament which, I believe, will set you free from such troubles as these, the numbers of the force, the source from which we must obtain funds, and the best and quickest way, as it seems to me, of making all further preparations—all this, men of Athens, I will at once endeavour to explain when I have made one request of you. Give your verdict on my proposal when you have heard the whole of it; do not prejudge it before I have done; and if at first the force which I propose appears unprecedented, do not think that I am merely creating delays. It is not those whose cry is "At once," "Today," whose proposals will meet our need; for what has already happened cannot be prevented by any expedition now. It is rather he who can show the nature, the magnitude, and the financial possibility of a force which when provided will be able to continue in existence either until we are persuaded to break off the war, or until we have overcome the enemy; for thus only can we escape further calamity for the future. These things I believe I can show, though I would not stand in the way of any other speaker's professions. It is no less a promise than this that I make; the event will soon test its fulfillment, and you will be the judges of it.

(4) First then, men of Athens, I say that fifty warships must at once be got in readiness: and next, that you must be in such a frame of mind that, if any need arises, you will embark in person and sail. In addition, you must prepare transports for half our cavalry, and a sufficient number of boats. These, I think, should be in readiness to meet those sudden sallies of his from his own country against Thermopylae, the Chersonese, Olynthus, and any other place which he may select. For we must make him realize that there is a possibility of your rousing yourselves out of your excessive indifference, just as when once you went to Euboea, and before that (as we are told) to Haliartus, and finally, only the other day, to Thermopylae. Such a possibility, even if you are unlikely to make it a reality, as I think you ought to do, is not one which he can treat lightly; and you may thus secure one of two objects. On the one hand, he may know that you are on the alert— he will in fact know it well enough: there are only too many persons, I assure you, in Athens itself, who report to him all that happens here: and in that case his apprehensions will ensure his inactivity. But if, on the other hand, he neglects the warning, he may be taken off his guard; for there will be

nothing to hinder you from sailing to his country, if he gives you the opportunity. These are the measures upon which I say you should all be resolved, and your preparations for them made. But before this, men of Athens, you must make ready a force which will fight without intermission, and do him damage. Do not speak to me of ten thousand or twenty thousand mercenaries. I will have none of your paper-armies. Give me an army which will be the army of Athens, and will obey and follow the general whom you elect, be there one general or more, be he one particular individual, or be he who he may. You must also provide maintenance for this force. Now what is this force to be? How large is it to be? How is it to be maintained? How will it consent to act in this manner? I will answer these questions point by point. The number of mercenaries—but you must not repeat the mistake which has so often injured you, the mistake of, first, thinking any measures inadequate, and so voting for the largest proposal, and then, when the time for action comes, not even executing the small one; you must rather carry out and make provision for the smaller measure, and add to it, if it proves too small—the total number of soldiers, I say, must be two thousand, and of these five hundred must be Athenians, beginning from whatever age you think good: they must serve for a definite period—not a long one, but one to be fixed at your discretion—and in relays. The rest must be mercenaries. With these must be cavalry, two hundred in number, of whom at least fifty must be Athenians, as with the infantry; and the conditions of service must be the same. You must also find transports for these. And what next? Ten swift ships of war. For as he has a fleet, we need swift-sailing warships too, to secure the safe passage of the army. And how is maintenance to be provided for these? This also I will state and demonstrate, as soon as I have given you my reasons for thinking that a force of this size is sufficient, and for insisting that those who serve in it shall be citizens.

(5) The size of the force, men of Athens, is determined by the fact that we cannot at present provide an army capable of meeting Philip in the open field; we must make plundering forays, and our warfare must at first be of a predatory nature. Consequently the force must not be over-big—we could then neither pay nor feed it—any more than it must be wholly insignificant. The presence of citizens in the force that sails I require for the following reasons. I am told that Athens once maintained a mercenary force in Corinth, under the command of Polystratus, Iphicrates, Chabrias and others, and that you yourselves joined in the campaign with them; and I remember hearing that these mercenaries, when they took the field with you, and you with them, were victorious over the Spartans. But even since your mercenary forces have gone to war alone, it is your friends and allies that they conquer, while your enemies have grown more powerful than they should be. After a casual glance at the war to which Athens has sent them, they sail off to Artabazus, or anywhere rather than to the war; and the general follows them naturally enough, for his power over them is gone when he can give them no pay. You ask what I bid you do. I bid you take away their excuses both from the general and the soldiers, by supplying pay and placing citizen-soldiers at their side as spectators of these mysteries of generalship; for our present methods are a mere mockery. Imagine the question to be put to you, men of Athens, whether you are at peace or no. "At peace?" you would say; "Of course not! We are at war with Philip." Now have you not all along been electing from among your own countrymen ten captains and generals, and cavalry-officers, and two masters-of-the-horse? And what are they doing? Except the one single individual whom you happen to send to the seat

of war, they are all marshalling your processions for you with the commissioners of festivals. You are no better than men modelling puppets of clay. Your captains and your cavalry-officers are elected to be displayed in the streets, not to be sent to the war. Surely, men of Athens, your captains should be elected from among yourselves, and your master-of-the-horse from among yourselves; your officers should be your own countrymen, if the force is to be really the army of Athens. As it is, the master-of-the-horse who is one of yourselves has to sail to Lemnos; while the master-of-the-horse with the army that is fighting to defend the possessions of Athens is Menelaus. I do not wish to disparage that gentleman; but whoever holds that office ought to have been elected by you.

(6) Perhaps, however, while agreeing with all that I have said, you are mainly anxious to hear my financial proposals, which will tell you the amount and the sources of the funds required. I proceed, therefore, with these at once. First for the sum. The cost of the bare rations for the crews, with such a force, will be 90 talents and a little over—40 talents for ten swift ships, and 20 minae a month for each ship; and for the soldiers as much again, each soldier to receive rations to the value of 10 drachmae a month; and for the cavalry (two hundred in number, each to receive 30 drachmae a month) twelve talents. It may be said that the supply of bare rations to the members of the force is an insufficient initial provision; but this is a mistake. I am quite certain that, given so much, the army will provide everything else for itself from the proceeds of war, without injury to a single Hellene or ally of ours, and that the full pay will be made up by these means. I am ready to sail as a volunteer and to suffer the worst, if my words are untrue. The next question then is of ways and means, in so far as the funds are to come from yourselves. I will explain this at once.

*[A schedule of ways and means is read.]*

(7) This, men of Athens, is what we have been able to devise; and when you put our proposals to the vote, you will pass them, if you approve of them; that so your war with Philip may be a war, not of resolutions and dispatches, but of actions.

(8) I believe that the value of your deliberations about the war and the armament as a whole would be greatly enhanced, if you were to bear in mind the situation of the country against which you are fighting, remembering that most of Philip's plans are successfully carried out because he takes advantage of winds and seasons; for he waits for the Etesian winds or the winter-season, and only attacks when it would be impossible for us to effect a passage to the scene of action. Bearing this in mind, we must not carry on the war by means of isolated expeditions; we shall always be too late. We must have a permanent force and armament. As our winter-stations for the army we have Lemnos, Thasos, Sciathos, and the islands in that region, which have harbours and corn, and are well supplied with all that an army needs. And as to the time of year, whenever it is easy to approach the shore and the winds are not dangerous, our force can without difficulty lie close to the Macedonian coast itself, and block the mouths of the ports.

(9) How and when he will employ the force is a matter to be determined, when the time comes, by the commander whom you put in control of it. What must be provided from Athens is described in the scheme which I have drafted. If, men of Athens, you first supply the sum I have mentioned, and then, after making ready the rest of the armament—soldiers, ships, cavalry—bind the whole force in its entirety, by law, to remain at the seat of war; if you become your own paymasters, your own commissioners

of supply, but require your general to account for the actual operations; then there will be an end of these perpetual discussions of one and the same theme, which end in nothing but discussion: and in addition to this, men of Athens, you will, in the first place, deprive him of his chief source of supply. For what is this? Why, he carries on the war at the cost of your own allies, harrying and plundering those who sail the seas! And what will you gain besides this? You will place yourselves out of reach of disaster. It will not be as it was in the past, when he descended upon Lemnos and Imbros, and went off, with your fellow-citizens as his prisoners of war, or when he seized the vessels off Geraestus, and levied an enormous sum from them; or when (last of all) he landed at Marathon, seized the sacred trireme, and carried it off from the country; while all the time you can neither prevent these aggressions, nor yet send an expedition which will arrive when you intend it to arrive. But for what reason do you think, men of Athens, do the festival of the Panathenaea and the festival of the Dionysia always take place at the proper time, whether those to whom the charge of either festival is allotted are specially qualified persons or not—festivals upon which you spend larger sums of money than upon any armament whatsoever, and which involve an amount of trouble and preparation, which are unique, so far as I know, in the whole world; and yet your armaments are always behind the time—at Methone, at Pagasae, at Potidaea? It is because for the festivals all is arranged by law. Each of you knows long beforehand who is to supply the chorus, and who is to be steward of the games, for his tribe: he knows what he is to receive, and when, and from whom, and what he is to do with it. No detail is here neglected, nothing is left indefinite. But in all that concerns war and our preparation for it, there is no organization, no revision, no definiteness. Consequently it is not until the news comes that we appoint our trierarchs and institute exchanges of property for them, and inquire into ways and means. When that is done we first resolve that the resident aliens and the independent freedmen shall go on board; then we change our minds and say that citizens shall embark; then that we will send substitutes; and while all these delays are occurring, the object of the expedition is already lost. For we spend on preparation the time when we should be acting, and the opportunities which events afford will not wait for our slothful evasions; while as for the forces on which we think we can rely in the meantime, when the critical moment comes, they are tried and found wanting. And Philip's insolence has reached such a pitch, that he has sent such a letter as the following to the Euboeans.

*[The letter is read.]*

(10) The greater part of the statements that have been read are true, men of Athens; and they ought not to be true! but I admit that they may possibly be unpleasant to hear; and if the course of future events would pass over all that a speaker passes over in his speech, to avoid giving pain, we should be right in speaking with a view to your pleasure. But if attractive words, spoken out of season, bring their punishment in actual reality, then it is disgraceful to blind our eyes to the truth, to put off everything that is unpleasant, to refuse to understand even so much as this, that those who conduct war rightly must not follow in the wake of events, but must be beforehand with them: for just as a general may be expected to lead his army, so those who debate must lead the course of affairs, in order that what they resolve upon may be done, and that they may not be forced to follow at the heels of events. You, men of Athens, have the greatest power in the world—warships, infantry, cavalry, revenue. But none

of these elements of power have you used as you ought, down to this very day. The method of your warfare with Philip is just that of barbarians in a boxing-match. Hit one of them, and he hugs the place; hit him on the other side, and there go his hands; but as for guarding, or looking his opponent in the face, he neither can nor will do it. It is the same with you. If you hear that Philip is in the Chersonese, you resolve to make an expedition there; if he is at Thermopylae, you send one there; and wherever else he may be, you run up and down in his steps. It is he that leads your forces. You have never of yourselves come to any salutary decision in regard to the war. No single event do you ever discern before it occurs—before you have heard that something has happened or is happening. Perhaps there was room for this backwardness until now; but now we are at the very crisis, and such an attitude is possible no longer. Surely, men of Athens, it is one of the gods—one who blushes for Athens, as he sees the course which events are taking—that has inspired Philip with this restless activity. If he were content to remain at peace, in possession of all that he has won by conquest or by forestalling us—if he had no further plans—even then, the record against us as a people, a record of shame and cowardice and all that is most dishonourable, would, I think, seem complete enough to some of you. But now he is always making some new attempt, always grasping after something more; and unless your spirit has utterly departed, his conduct will perhaps bring you out into the field. It amazes me, men of Athens, that not one of you remembers with any indignation, that this war had its origin in our intention to punish Philip; and that now, at the end of it, the question is, how we are to escape disaster at his hands. But that he will not stay his progress until someone arrests it is plain enough. Are we then to wait for that? Do you think that all is right, when you dispatch nothing but empty ships and somebody's hopes? Shall we not embark? Shall we not now, if never before, go forth ourselves, and provide at least some small proportion of Athenian soldiers? Shall we not sail to the enemy's country? But I heard the question, "At what point on his coast are we to anchor?" The war itself, men of Athens, if you take it in hand, will discover his weak points: but if we sit at home listening to the mutual abuse and recriminations of our orators, you can never realize any of the results that you ought to realize. I believe that whenever any portion of Athens is sent with the forces, even if the whole city does not go, the favour of Heaven and of Fortune fights on our side. But whenever you dispatch anywhere a general with an empty resolution and some platform-hopes to support him, then you achieve nothing that you ought to achieve, your enemies laugh at you, and your allies are in deadly fear of all such armaments. It is impossible, utterly impossible, that any one man should be able to effect all that you wish for you. He can give undertakings and promises; he can accuse this man and that; and the result is that your fortunes are ruined. For when the general is at the head of wretched, unpaid mercenaries, and when there are those in Athens who lie to you light-heartedly about all that he does, and, on the strength of the tales that you hear, you pass decrees at random, what *must* you expect?

(11) How then can this state of things be terminated? Only, men of Athens, when you expressly make the same men soldiers, witnesses of their general's actions, and judges at his examination when they return home; for then the issue of your fortunes will not be a tale which you hear, but a thing which you will be on the spot to see. So shameful is the pass which matters have now reached, that each of your generals is tried for his life before you two or three times, but does not dare to fight in mortal

combat with the enemy even once. They prefer the death of kidnappers and brigands to that of a general. For it is a felon's death, to die by sentence of the court: the death of a general is to fall in battle with the enemy. Some of us go about saying that Philip is negotiating with Sparta for the overthrow of the Thebans and the breaking up of the free states; others, that he has sent ambassadors to the king; others, that he is fortifying cities in Illyria. We all go about inventing each his own tale. I quite believe, men of Athens, that he is intoxicated with the greatness of his successes, and entertains many such visions in his mind; for he sees that there are none to hinder him, and he is elated at his achievements. But I do not believe that he has chosen to act in such a way that the most foolish persons in Athens can know what he intends to do; for no persons are so foolish as newsmongers. But if we dismiss all such tales, and attend only to the certainty—that the man is our enemy, that he is robbing us of our own, that he has insulted us for a long time, that all we ever expected any one to do for us has proved to be against us, that the future is in our own hands, that if we will not fight him now in his own country we shall perhaps be obliged to do so in ours—if, I say, we are assured of this, then we shall have made up our minds aright, and shall be quit of idle words. For you have not to speculate what the future may be: you have only to be assured that the future must be evil, unless you give heed and are ready to do your duty.

(12) Well, I have never yet chosen to gratify you by saying anything which I have not felt certain would be for your good; and to-day I have spoken freely and without concealment, just what I believe. I could wish to be as sure of the good that a speaker will gain by giving you the best advice as of that which you will gain by listening to him. I should then have been far happier than I am. As it is, I do not know what will happen to me, for what I have said: but I have chosen to speak in the sure conviction that if you carry out my proposals, it will be for your good; and may the victory rest with that policy which will be for the good of all![22]

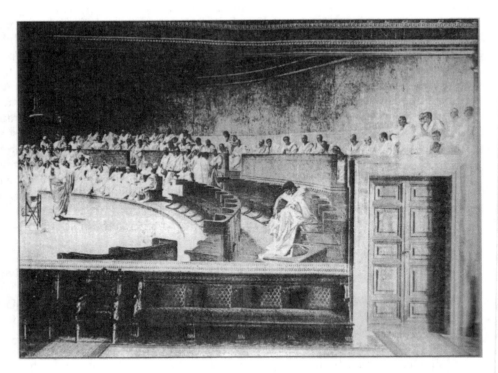

*Figure 8.1* Modern painting of Cicero's oration against Catiline, with the accused sitting isolated on one side of the Senate Chambers

### Cicero, *The First Speech Against Lucius Sergius Catiline*

The Catilinian Orations, which number four, were delivered in November, 63 BCE. Cicero delivered the *First Catilinian* in the Roman Senate on November 8. The prosecution of Catiline was one of Cicero's greatest political triumphs; ironically, his actions in the Catilinian conspiracy would presage his downfall.

Catiline was a member of an ancient but decadent patrician family. He was known in Rome for his debauchery, depravity, and criminal behavior (he had committed many public murders for the Roman emperor Sulla and had even been suspected of murdering his own brother). At the same time, he was known as a brave soldier and the acknowledged leader of many dissolute Roman nobles who peopled the streets of Rome. Delayen captures the essence of Catiline's character most essentially in the following description:

> He had, indeed, gifts equal to his vices: he was fearless, audacious but subject to violent passions, and lacking in prudence; false and crafty, he was capable of counterfeiting everything, dissembling everything. Coveting the property of others, he was at the same time prodigal of his own; he was capable of eloquence and above all he possessed an imperturbable presence of mind: but he was a monster of cynicism, corruption, and perversity.

In 66 BCE, Catiline had returned to Rome from foreign service in the Army of Sulla, during which time he had amassed a large fortune. He began immediately to associate with the most depraved Roman citizens, gambling, drinking, and carousing. During this time, he attempted to seduce one of the vestal virgins, a woman named Fabia, who was the sister of Cicero's wife. Seduction of a vestal virgin was a heinous crime for both parties involved. Charged with the crime by Cicero and with much testimony on the record against him, Catiline set out to bribe the judges and use his family name to get himself acquitted. Cicero took on the prosecution. Despite Cicero's oratory and clear evidence against Catiline, the vote was for acquittal. Cicero and Catiline were to be enemies forever.

Catiline now sought to be elected to the Roman Senate as Consul. He was disqualified as a candidate, however, because of charges of extortion brought against him by his former subjects.[23] The next year, he sought to murder the two Consuls, Cotta and Torquatus, but his conspiracy failed. In 64 BCE, Catiline, having since been cleared of charges against him, sought the Consulship of the Roman Senate along with six others, one of them being Marcus Tullius Cicero. Catiline was easily defeated and Cicero and Antonius were elected.

Catiline now decided to gain the Consulship a third time by conspiracy to destroy Rome. Specifically, his plan was to set Rome on fire and, while the citizenry was diverted, assassinate the Consul Cicero and other Senators. He organized a group of conspirators (most of them former deputies of the murderous Sulla) whose motivation to burn Rome was to destroy the records of their debts. One of Catiline's followers' lovers, Fulvia, was aware of the plans from the start. She and her lover, Quintus Curius, had begun to quarrel and he had recently threatened to kill her. In revenge, she went to Cicero and told him of Catiline's conspiracy.

Cicero took immediate action. On November 8, 63 BCE, Cicero called an emergency session of the Roman Senate. Unaware that he had been betrayed by Fulvia, Catiline was in attendance. Cicero proceeded to his *First Catilinian Oration* detailing the plot by Catiline and, as you will read, repudiating Catiline for his actions. Catiline replied but was shouted down by other Senators. Realizing that sentiment had turned against him, Catiline withdrew from Rome following the oration. Catiline's voluntary withdrawal was a fortunate stroke for Cicero since no actual charges had been brought against Catiline so that he could not have been held involuntarily or tried for any actual crimes. The Senate proceeded to pass an unusual measure to "Let the Consuls see that the State suffers no harm."[24] Cicero realized that such a measure, the equivalent of martial law, was unconstitutional because it allowed the Senate unbridled power to protect Rome. He also realized that he was on dangerous ground in the entire affair since all of his actions were the result of what might have been viewed as the simple vengeful gossip of Catiline's (and his friend's) courtesan, Fulvia. Nevertheless, on the next day, November 9, Cicero ordered armed troops to protect the city and he went himself before the citizens of Rome to justify his conduct in his stirring *Second Catilinian Oration*.

While Catiline was outside the city recruiting troops for his assault, it happened that there was present in Rome a delegation from Gaul, the Allobroges, who had come to petition the Roman Senate for return of some of their possessions that the Roman army had carted off during its conquest of Gaul. They were approached by some of Catiline's conspirators to join the ranks as a way of getting revenge against the republic. They agreed to do so, but soon became concerned for their situation and went to their lawyer, Fabius Sanga, who relayed the news to Cicero. Cicero called the Allobroges delegation to his home and told them to join the conspiracy but to get their instructions in writing on the pretense that they wanted to show the plans to their townsfolk upon returning home. They followed Cicero's orders and upon returning to the home of the conspirators were given the complete plans signed by three of them. With this evidence, Cicero moved swiftly to crush the conspiracy. He arrested the conspirators, tried them before the Senate, rallied public support with his *Third Catilinian Oration*, and sent soldiers to raid the homes of the conspirators and to protect the borders of Rome. Catiline's conspiracy had come to an end and he wandered off to die in anonymity.

The trial of the revolutionaries was held soon thereafter. Cicero had to determine whether to seek the death penalty for them and risk the ire of many citizens who were either relatives or sympathizers. It was unconstitutional at this time for the Senate to pass the death penalty (only a citizen's court could do so), and Julius Caesar rose to eloquently defend that principle. Following Caesar's address, sentiment ran high for life imprisonment. Cicero, while seeming to vacillate between life imprisonment and death, finally decided that it was in the best interests of the republic that the conspirators be strangled by the public executioner. He made his stand in his *Fourth Catilinian Oration*, and by the power of his office in addition to a fiery oration by the venerable Senator, Cato, Cicero's decision was upheld. The conspirators were put to death.

Cicero realized the high point of his political career for his actions in the conspiracy of Catiline. He was recognized by the Senate with the ultimate tribute, "Father of his Country," the first man ever to be so honored for civil service. And yet, this was to be his final moment of glory. He was never forgiven by some for usurping the power of the people in applying the death sentence through the Senate. In addition, he became somewhat arrogant in his triumph and was given to mentioning his bravery and courage too often in public, a trait that led some others to grow weary of his presence. Soon thereafter, he would find himself on the wrong side of the dispute between Pompeius and Julius Caesar for command of Rome (he favored Pompeius), and for this decision he would be banished, later to return but never to his lofty position in Roman political life. He would be put to death in 43 CE by Marcus Antonius. This translation is by Louis E. Lord.

(1) In heaven's name, Catiline, how long will you abuse our patience? How long will that madness of yours mock us? To what limit will your unbridled audacity vaunt itself? Is it nothing to you that the Palatine has its garrison by night, nothing to you that the city is full of patrols, nothing that the populace is in a panic, nothing that all honest men have joined forces, nothing that the senate is convened in this stronghold,[25] is it nothing to see the looks on all these faces? Do you not know that your plans are disclosed? Do you not see that your conspiracy is bound hand and foot by the knowledge of all these men? Who of us do you think is ignorant of what you did last night, what you did the night before, where you were, whom you called together, what plan you took? What an age! What morals! The senate knows these things, the consul sees them. Yet this man lives. Lives, did I say? Nay, more, he walks into the senate, he takes part in the public counsel. He singles out and marks with his glance each one of us for murder. But we, brave men indeed, seem to be doing our duty by the state if we avoid his fury and his shafts. You ought to have been led to death long

ago by the consul's order, Catiline. That destruction which for a long time you have been planning for all of us ought to be visited on you yourself. Shall that distinguished man, Publius Scipio, the pontifex maximus, though he was a private citizen,[26] have killed Tiberius Gracchus, who was only slightly undermining the foundations of the state, and shall we, who are consuls, put up with Catiline, who is anxious to destroy the whole world with murder and fire? For I pass over these precedents as too old, that Gaius Servilius Ahala[27] with his own hand killed Spurius Maelius, who was getting up a revolution. There was once, there was indeed in this state such courage that brave men suppressed a traitorous citizen with more severity than the most hated enemy. We have, Catiline, a decree of the senate against you, potent and stern.[28] The state does not lack the approval nor the support of this body. It is we, I say it openly, we, the consuls, who are lacking.

(2) The senate once decreed[29] that Lucius Opimius, the consul, should "take measures that the state might suffer no harm." Not a single night intervened. There was killed because of a vague suspicion of treason Gaius Gracchus, whose father, grandfather, and ancestors were most distinguished men. There was killed with his children Marcus Fulvius, an ex-consul. A similar decree of the senate[30] entrusted the state to Gaius Marius and Lucius Valerius, the consuls. Did death and the vengeance of the state have to wait a day for the punishment of Lucius Saturninus, the tribune of the people, and Gaius Servilius, the praetor? But we have now for twenty days been allowing the edge of our authority to grow dull. For we have a senate's decree of this kind. But it is merely inserted in the records like a sword buried in its sheath. According to this decree of the senate, Catiline, you should have been instantly executed. You are living—and you are living not to repent, but to augment, your effrontery. I wish, Conscript Fathers, to be merciful. I wish not to seem lax when the perils of the state are so great, but now I condemn myself for inaction and remissness. There is in Italy a camp of enemies of the Roman people, situated in the passes of Etruria, their number is increasing daily; but you behold the commander of that camp and the leader of the enemy inside the walls and even in the senate plotting daily from within the city the destruction of the state. But if, Catiline, I shall order you to be seized, to be executed, I shall have to fear, I suppose, not that all respectable people may say I acted too tardily, but that someone may say that I acted too cruelly! But for a special reason I cannot yet bring myself to do what I should have done long ago. Then at last you shall be executed when no one so depraved, so abandoned, so like yourself, can be found who does not admit that this was done justly. As long as anyone exists who will dare defend you, you will live, and live as you live now, surrounded by many competent guards whom I have set so that you may not be able to move against the state. The eyes and the ears of many shall watch you, although you may not know it, as they have done heretofore.

(3) For what is there, Catiline, for you to wait for longer, if neither night with its darkness can hide your criminal assemblies nor a private house with its walls confine the voices of your conspiracy, if they are patent, if all burst into view? Abandon now that foul plan of yours, be persuaded by me, forget your murder and arson. You are encompassed on all sides; all your plans are clearer to us than the light of day. You may now recall them with me. Do you remember that I said in the senate on the twenty-first of October that Gaius Manlius, a tool and a slave of your bold scheme, would be in arms on a particular day and that that day would be the twenty-seventh

of October? Was I wrong, Catiline, in asserting a thing so crucial, so criminal, so unbelievable, but, what was much more surprising, was I mistaken in that day? I also said in the senate that you had postponed till the twenty-eighth of October the slaughter of the influential citizens though by that time many of the chief men of the state had fled from Rome, not so much to save themselves, as to thwart your plans. Can you deny that, on that very day, shut in by my guards, and by my foresight, you could not move against the state, when you said that, in spite of the departure of the others, you would still be content with killing us who had remained? When you thought that by a night attack you would seize Praeneste actually on the first of November, did you know that that colony was fortified at my command by my guards, my forces, and my troops? You do nothing, you attempt nothing, you think of nothing which I do not hear and see and understand plainly.

(4) Review with me now the events of the night before last.[31] Now you will know that I watch much more vigilantly for the safety of the state than you do for its destruction. I say that the night before last you came into the Street of the Scythe-makers (I will not deal in general terms), you came to the house of Marcus Laeca; to the same place came many of your allies animated by the same madness and wickedness. You do not dare to deny it, do you? Why are you silent? I will convict you if you do deny. For I see here in the senate some who were there with you. O ye immortal gods! Where in the world are we? What sort of a commonwealth do we possess? In what city are we living? Here, here in our very midst, Conscript Fathers, in this most sacred and dignified council of the whole world, are men who plan for the destruction of all of us, who plan for the destruction of this city and even the destruction of the whole world! I, the consul, see them and I consult them on affairs of state, and those who ought to have been slain by the sword I do not yet wound even with my voice! You were, then, at the house of Laeca on that night, Catiline, you apportioned the parts of Italy, you determined where you wished each man to go, you selected those whom you would leave at Rome, those whom you would take with you, you parcelled out the parts of the city to be burned, you averred that you yourself would go presently, you said that you would be delayed a little while because I still lived. Two Roman knights were found who would relieve you of that anxiety and they promised that they would kill me on my couch that very night a little before dawn. I learned all these things almost before your council was dismissed; I fortified and strengthened my home with more numerous guards, I refused admittance to those whom you had sent to salute me in the morning, for those very men did come whose coming at that hour I had already foretold to many eminent gentlemen.

(5) Since this is the situation, Catiline, go whither you had intended, depart at last from the city; the gates are open; get on your way! That camp you share with Manlius has awaited you, its commander, for all too long a time. Take with you all these friends of yours, if not all, then as many as you can; purge the city. I shall be free from my great fear only if there is a wall between us. You cannot now remain with us longer; I will not bear it, I will not tolerate it, I will not permit it.

(6) Great thanks are due to the immortal gods and especially to Jupiter Stator here, the most ancient custodian of this city, because we have already so often escaped this curse of the state, so foul, so horrible, so deadly. The safety of the state ought not to be imperilled too often by one man. While I was consul-elect, Catiline, and you lay in wait for me, I defended myself, not by a public guard, but by my own caution.

When, at the last consular elections, you wished to kill me and your competitors in the Campus Martius, I foiled your wicked attempt by the resources and protection of my friends without arousing any public disturbance; in a word, as often as you threatened me I thwarted you by my own efforts, although I say that my death would bring a great calamity upon the state. Now you are attacking openly the whole state, you call for the destruction and devastation of the temples of the immortal gods, the dwellings of the city, the lives of all the citizens, and all Italy. Therefore, since I do not as yet dare to do that which is most important and which most befits this government and our traditions, I will do this which is more lenient in point of severity and more useful as regards the common safety. For if I shall have ordered you to be killed, there will remain in the state the rest of your conspirators; but if you leave the city, as I have long been urging, the city will be drained of the abundant and pestilent bilge-water of the state—your accomplices. What is wrong, Catiline? You do not hesitate, do you, to do at my command what you were already about to do of your own accord? The consul bids a public enemy leave the city. You ask me, "Is it to be exile?" I do not order that but if you ask my opinion, I advise it. (7) For what, Catiline, can please you now in this city where there is no one, except your fellow-conspirators—ruined men— who does not fear you, no one who does not hate you? What stigma of disgrace is not branded on your private life? What dishonour in personal relations does not cling to your ill fame? What lust has not stained your eyes, what crime has not stained your hands, what corruption has not stained your whole body? To what youth whom you had ensnared by the allurements of your seduction have you not furnished a weapon for his crimes or a torch to kindle his lust? What then? When lately you had made room in your home for a new marriage by murdering your former wife, did you not add to this crime another incredible crime? I do not describe this and I am glad to let it be passed in silence, lest it be thought that the enormity of so great a crime has either existed in this state or has escaped punishment. I pass over in silence the complete ruin of your fortune which you will feel threatening you upon the thirteenth of this month; I come to those things which have to do, not with your private scandals and shame, not with the sordid tangle of your personal affairs but with the highest interests of the state and with the life and safety of us all. Can this light, Catiline, or the breath of this air be pleasing to you when you are aware that all these men know that you, on the last day of December in the consulship of Lepidus and Tullus,[32] took your place in the assembly armed,[33] that you had prepared a band to kill the consuls and the chief citizens of the state, and that no pity nor fear on your part checked your crime and your madness, but the good fortune of the Roman people? But those crimes I do not mention, for they are not unknown and many have been committed since that time:—how often did you attempt to kill me when I was consul-elect and how often after I was consul! How many of your thrusts, so aimed that they seemed unavoidable, I escaped by a slight movement and a dodge, as they call it! You gain nothing, you accomplish nothing, and still you do not cease trying and hoping. How often already has that dagger been struck from your hands, how often has it fallen by some chance and slipped! Still you cannot bear to be deprived of it for a single day. I do not know what sacrifices you made to hallow and consecrate it because you thought that you must plunge it into the body of a consul!

(8) But now what is this life of yours? For I shall speak to you, so that men may feel I am swayed, not by hatred, as I ought to be, but by pity, none of which is due you. You came a little while ago into the senate. Who among all your many friends and

relatives saluted you? If such treatment has been accorded to no one within the memory of man, do you await the condemnation of the spoken word when you have been crushed by this most significant verdict of silence? What of the fact that at your coming all those near-by seats were deserted, that all the ex-consuls whom you have often marked out for murder left all that area of seats vacant and unoccupied as soon as you took your place—with what feelings do you think you ought to bear this? By Hercules, if my slaves feared me as your fellow-citizens, I should prefer not to be seen by my fellow-citizens rather than to encounter the hostile eyes of all; *you* know because you are conscious of your crimes that the hatred of all toward you is just and long due. Do you hesitate to avoid the eyes and the presence of those whose minds and sensibilities you are torturing? If your parents hated and feared you and you could not be reconciled to them in any way, you would, I think, withdraw somewhere from their gaze. Now your native country, the mother of us all, hates you and fears you and decides that you have had no single thought for a long time save for her destruction. Will you neither revere her authority, nor obey her judgements, nor fear her power? She, Catiline, thus confers with you and, as it were, though silent, speaks: "No crime for some years now has come into existence except through you, no outrage without you; you alone have killed many citizens, harried and despoiled the allies unpunished and free; you have been able not only to neglect the laws and the courts but even to thwart and destroy them. I endured as I could those earlier deeds, although they ought not to have been borne, but now that I should be wholly in fear on account of you alone, that, at the slightest sound, Catiline should be feared, that no plan, it seems, can be undertaken against me uninspired by your villainy, that is not to be borne. Therefore depart and free me from this terror; if it is well founded, that I may not be overwhelmed; if it is false, that now at last I may cease to fear."

(9) If our country speaks to you thus, as I have said, ought she not to obtain her request, even though she cannot use force? What of the fact that you gave yourself into voluntary custody, that you said that you wished to live at the home of Manius Lepidus, to avoid suspicion? When he would not receive you, you dared to come even to me and ask me to protect you in my home. From me also you got the answer that I could in no way be safe within the same house-walls with you, since I was in great peril because we were encompassed by the same city walls, you came to the home of Quintus Metellus, the praetor.[34] When he repulsed you, you moved on to that boon companion of yours, that noble gentleman, Marcus Metellus; because of course you thought that he would be most careful to guard you, most shrewd to suspect others, and most brave to defend you. But how far do you think a man should be away from prison and chains who already judges himself worthy of custody?

(10) Since these things are so, Catiline, do you hesitate, if you cannot die with a mind at ease, to go to some other land and devote that life of yours, rescued from many just and long deserved penalties, to exile and solitude? Refer the matter, you say, to the senate; for you demand this and if this body votes that you should go into exile you say that you will obey. I will not refer it; that does not accord with my practice, and still I will so act that you may know what these men think of you. Leave the city, Catiline, free the state from fear; into exile, if you are waiting for this word, go. What is it, Catiline? What are you waiting for? Do you notice at all the silence of these men? They approve it; they are silent. Why do you await the spoken word when you see their wish silently expressed? But if I had said this same thing to that excellent

youth, Publius Sestius, if I had said it to that bravest of men, Marcus Marcellus, upon me, the consul, the senate with most just cause would have laid violent hands in this very temple. In your case, however, Catiline, when they say nothing they express their approval; their acquiescence is a decree. By their silence they cry aloud. And this is true not only of these men whose authority is, forsooth, dear to you, whose lives are most cheap, but also those most honourable and noble Roman knights, and the other brave citizens who are standing around the senate. You could see the crowd of them, their zeal you could perceive, and their voices you could hear a little while ago. For a long time with difficulty I have kept their hands and their weapons from you; I will easily persuade them to accompany you as far as the city gates when you leave all that you so long have desired to destroy.

(11) And yet why do I talk? As if anything could move you, as if you could ever pull yourself together, as if you had contemplated flight, as if you had any thought of exile! Would that the immortal gods might incline you to that purpose! And yet I see, if, terrified by my threats, you were to be persuaded to go into exile, what a tempest of ill feeling would await me, if not now while the memory of your crimes is still fresh, certainly in after times. But it is worth all that, provided your ruin remains a private affair and is divorced from the dangers to the state. But that you should be dissuaded from your vices, that you should fear the punishment of the laws, that you should yield to the needs of the state, that is a thing not to be asked. For you are not the man, Catiline, ever to be recalled from disgrace by shame, or from danger by fear, or from madness by reason. Wherefore, as I have now often said, go, and if you wish to stir up hatred against me, your enemy, as you call me, go straight into exile; with difficulty shall I bear the criticisms of mankind if you do this; with difficulty shall I sustain the load of that hatred if you shall go into exile at the consul's orders. But if you prefer to minister to my praise and glory, take with you that rascally gang of criminals, take yourself to Manlius, arouse the debauched, separate yourself from the upright, bring war upon your country, exult in impious robbery; then it will appear that you have gone not expelled by me to join aliens but invited to join your friends. And yet why should I urge you, for I know that you have already sent men ahead to await you under arms at Forum Aurelium.[35] I know that you have arranged and appointed a day with Manlius and that you have also sent forward that silver eagle,[36] which I trust will be a cause of ruin and a curse for all your band. For this eagle a shrine of iniquities has been set up in your own home. Is it possible that you could longer be separated from this to which you were wont to pay homage as you set forth to murder, from whose altars you often have lifted that impious right hand of yours for the slaughter of the citizens?

(12) You will go, then, at last where that unbridled and furious greed of yours has long been hurrying you; indeed this does not bring sorrow to you but a certain incredible delight. For this madness nature bore you, your own wish has trained you, fortune has preserved you. You never desired peace, nor war even unless it were a wicked war. You have a band of criminals swept up from those whom all fortune and even all hope have deserted and abandoned. In their company what joy will be yours, what delights, what exultation, how you will revel in debauchery, when among so many of your friends you will neither hear nor see a single upright man! For pursuing a life like that those "labours" of yours, of which men speak, have been good practice: to lie on the bare ground not only to lay siege to the object of your lust, but also to perpetrate

crime; to lose sleep not only plotting against the repose of husbands, but plotting also to steal the goods of peaceable citizens. You have an opportunity to show that famous ability you have to endure hunger, cold, a lack of everything; soon you will know that these practices have ruined you. This much I accomplished when I kept you from the consulship: that you might be able to attack the state as an exile rather than to vex it as a consul, and that this undertaking which has been foully conceived by you may be called brigandage rather than war.

(13) And now, that I may prevent our country by entreaty and prayer, Conscript Fathers, from making a complaint that would be almost justified, listen carefully, I pray you, to what I shall say and store it deep in your hearts and minds. For if our country, which is much dearer to me than my life, if all Italy, if all the state should speak to me thus: "Marcus Tullius, what are you doing? This man is a public enemy as you have discovered; he will be the leader of the war, as you see; men are waiting for him to take command in the enemies' camp, as you know: author of a crime, head of a conspiracy, recruiter of slaves and criminals—and you will let him go, in such a way that he will seem to be not cast out of the city by you but let loose against the city! Will you not command him to be cast into chains, to be haled to death, to be punished with the greatest severity? What, pray, hinders you? The custom of our ancestors? But often even private citizens in this state have punished with death dangerous men. Is it the laws which have been enacted regarding the punishment of Roman citizens? But never in this city have those who revolted against the state enjoyed the rights of citizens. Or do you fear the odium of posterity? A fine return you are making to the Roman people who have raised you, a man distinguished only by your own deeds, and by no achievements of your ancestors,[37] so early to the highest office through every grade of honour, if because of the fear of unpopularity or any danger whatever you neglect the safety of your fellow-citizens! But if there is any fear of unpopularity, the unpopularity that comes from sternness and severity is no more greatly to be dreaded than that which comes form laxness and cowardice. Or when Italy shall be devastated by war, when the cities shall be harried, when houses shall be burned, do you not think that then you will be consumed by the fire of unpopularity?"

(14) To this most solemn utterance of the state and of those men who think these same thoughts I will answer briefly. "If I judged that it were best, Conscript Fathers, that Catiline should be put to death, *I* should not give to that gladiator the enjoyment of a single further hour of life." For if our most noble men and most famous citizens were not stained but even honoured by shedding the blood of Saturninus, and the Gracchi, and Flaccus,[38] and many men of ancient time, certainly I should not have feared that when this murderer of citizens has been slain any unpopularity would attach to me in after time. But if that did seriously threaten me, still I have always believed that unpopularity won by uprightness was glory and not unpopularity. And yet there are some in this body who either do not see the disasters which threaten us or pretend that they do not see them; these have fostered the hopes of Catiline by mild measures and they have strengthened the growing conspiracy by not believing in its existence; under their influence many ignorant men as well as villains would be saying that I acted cruelly and tyrannically if I had punished Catiline. Now I know that if he arrives at Manlius's camp whither he is now making his way, no one will be so stupid as not to see that a conspiracy has been formed, no one will be so depraved as to deny it. But if this man alone is executed, I know that this disease in the state can be

checked for a little time, but it cannot be completely crushed. But if he shall take himself off, if he shall lead out his friends with him and gather together to the same place other derelicts now collected from all sources, not only this plague rampant in the state but even the roots and seeds of all evil will be obliterated and destroyed.

(15) For many a long day, Conscript Fathers, we have lived and moved amid these dangers and snares of conspiracy; but in some strange way all these crimes and this long-standing madness and audacity have come to a head in the time of my consulship. If out of this great crowd of robbers this one man shall be removed, we shall seem perhaps for a brief time to be relieved of care and fear. But the danger will remain, and it will be hidden deep in the veins and vitals of the state. Just as often men sick with a grievous disease and tossed about in a burning fever drink cold water and at first seem to be relieved, but later are much more grievously and violently afflicted, so this disease in the state, though relieved by the punishment of this man, will grow much worse so long as the rest remain alive. Therefore let the wicked depart; let them separate themselves from the good, let them assemble in one place. And finally, as I have often said, let them be separated from us by a wall; let them cease to lie in wait for the consul in his own home, to stand around the tribunal of the city praetor, to besiege the senate-house with swords, to prepare fire-spears and fire-brands with which to burn the city; finally, let every man's thoughts of the state be written on his forehead. I promise you this, Conscript Fathers, that there will be such energy in us, the consuls, such authority in you, such courage in the Roman knights, such cordial agreement among all patriotic men, that after the departure of Catiline you will see all things made clear, brought to light, suppressed and punished.

(16) With omens like these, Catiline, go forth to your impious and wicked war, bringing to the state the greatest of benefits, to yourself destruction and annihilation, and to those who have allied themselves with you for all crime and parricide, utter ruin. O Jupiter, thou who wast established by Romulus under the same auspices under which this city was established, rightly called by us the Stayer[39] of this city and empire, thou wilt repel him and his allies from thy temples and from the other temples, from the dwellings of this city and its walls, from the lives and fortunes of all the citizens, and these men, enemies of the upright, foes of the state, plunderers of Italy, who are united by a compact of crime in an abominable association, thou wilt punish living and dead with eternal punishments.

# Notes

## 1 The Origins of Rhetoric in the Democracy of Ancient Greece

1  All dates mentioned in this chapter are from before the Common Era, usually referred to as BCE.
2  Emma J. Stafford, *Life, Myth, and Art in Ancient Greece* (Los Angeles: J. Paul Getty Museum, 2004), 46.
3  Robin Waterfield, *The First Philosophers: The Presocratics and the Sophists* (Oxford: Oxford University Press, 2000), xxii.
4  George W. Botsford, *Hellenic History* (New York: Macmillan, 1924), 45.
5  Douglas M. MacDowell, *The Law in Classical Athens* (New York: Cornell University Press, 1978), 12–15.
6  MacDowell, 18.
7  Stafford, 28–29.
8  Morton Smith, *The Ancient Greeks* (Ithaca, NY: Cornell University Press, 1960), 34.
9  Kathleen Freeman, *The Murder of Herodes: And Other Trials from the Athenian Law Courts* (London: MacDonald & Co., 1946), 14–15.
10  MacDowell, 29.
11  Freeman, 18.
12  Waterfield, 6.
13  Richard Leo Enos, "Ancient Greek Writing Instruction and Its Oral Antecedents," in *A Short History of Writing Instruction from Ancient Greece to Modern America*, ed. James J. Murphy, 3rd edn (New York: Routledge, 2012), 23.
14  Theodore Gomperz, *Greek Thinkers: A History of Ancient Philosophy* (London: J. Murray, 1905), 13.
15  G. Lowes Dickinson, *The Greek View of Life* (Ann Arbor: University of Michigan Press, 1958), 143.
16  Stafford, 32–34.
17  George A. Kennedy, *Aristotle on Rhetoric: A Theory of Civic Discourse* (New York: Oxford University Press, 1991), xii, 81–82, 196, 197.
18  Plato, *Menexenus* (235e, 236b).
19  Christopher Lyle Johnstone, *Listening to the Logos: Speech and the Coming of Wisdom in Ancient Greece* (Columbia, SC: University of South Carolina Press, 2009), 179.
20  Andrea Lunsford, ed., *Reclaiming Rhetorica: Women in the Rhetorical Tradition* (Pittsburgh, PA: University of Pittsburgh, 1995), 23.
21  Dickinson, 173–175.
22  Stafford, 35.
23  Botsford, 264–265.
24  Johnstone, 1.
25  Donald Kagan, *The Peloponnesian War* (New York: Viking, 2003), 12–13.
26  Smith, 64.
27  Dickinson, 71.
28  Dickinson, 73.

29 Botsford, 373.
30 William R. Connor, *Greek Orations, 4th Century B.C.* (Ann Arbor, MI: University of Michigan Press, 1966), 5.

## 2 Rhetorical Consciousness and the Rise of the Sophists

1 John F. Dobson, *The Greek Orators* (New York: Books for Libraries Press, 1919), 1.
2 G. Lowes Dickinson, *The Greek View of Life* (Ann Arbor, MI: University of Michigan Press, 1958), 18.
3 George Kennedy, *The Art of Persuasion in Greece* (Princeton, NJ: Princeton University Press, 1963), 33.
4 Kennedy, 13.
5 George B. Kerford, *The Sophistic Movement* (Cambridge: Cambridge University Press, 1981), 28–29.
6 Richard Leo Enos, "Ancient Greek Writing Instruction," in *A Short History of Writing Instruction*, ed. James J. Murphy, 2nd edn (Mahwah, NJ: Lawrence Erlbaum Publishers, 2001).
7 Kerford, 28.
8 Kennedy, 7.
9 Kennedy, 59.
10 Kerford, 13.
11 Morton Smith, *The Ancient Greeks* (New York: Cornell University Press, 1960), 72.
12 I. F. Stone, *The Trial of Socrates* (Boston: Little, Brown, 1988), 17.
13 Rosamond Kent Sprague, *The Older Sophists* (Cambridge, MA: Hackett, 1972), 2.
14 Lane Cooper, *Plato On the Trial and Death of Socrates: Euthyphro, Apology, Crito, Phaedo* (Ithaca, NY: Cornell University Press, 1941), 5.
15 T. Irwin, *Plato's, Gorgias* (Oxford: Oxford University Press, 1979), 8.
16 Kennedy, 15.
17 Stone, 40.
18 Everett Lee Hunt, *Plato and Aristotle on Rhetoric and the Rhetoricians* (New York: The Century Co., 1926), 3–61.
19 E. Schiappa, *Protagoras and Logos* (Columbia: University of South Carolina Press, 1991), 12.
20 B. A. G. Fuller, *A History of Greek Philosophy* (Cambridge: Cambridge University Press, 1981), 12.
21 Richard Leo Enos, *Roman Rhetoric: Revolution and the Greek Influence* (Prospect Heights: Waveland Press, 1995), 10.
22 Enos 1995, 12.
23 Dobson, 313.
24 Antiphon, Andocides, Lysias, Isocrates, Isaeus, Demosthenes, Lycurgus, Aeschines, Hypereides, Dinarchus.
25 Mario Untersteiner, *The Sophists* (New York: Philosophical Library, 1954), 5.
26 Kerford, 86–87.
27 Sprague, 19.
28 Schiappa, 89.
29 Kerford, 78.
30 Untersteiner, 15.
31 Schiappa, 109.
32 G. W. Botsford, *Hellenic History* (New York: Macmillan, 1924), 280.
33 Schiappa, 141.
34 Kennedy, 34.
35 T. Gomperz, *Greek Thinkers* (London: John Murray, 1905), 441.
36 Kennedy, 52–53.
37 Untersteiner, 92.
38 Kerford, 78.
39 Richard Leo Enos, *Greek Rhetoric Before Aristotle* (South Carolina: Parlor Press, 1993), 57.
40 Untersteiner, 94.

41  Untersteiner, 101.
42  Untersteiner, 101.
43  Untersteiner, 115.
44  Untersteiner, 114.
45  Kennedy, 63.
46  Kerford, 80.
47  Susan Jarratt, *Rereading the Sophists* (Carbondale, IL: Southern Illinois University Press, 1991), 54.
48  Kerford, 78.
49  Enos 1993, 62–63.
50  Kennedy, 64.
51  Dobson, 15.
52  Moses Hadas, *History of Greek Literature* (New York: Columbia University Press, 1950), 160.
53  Kennedy, 15.
54  Gomperz, 477.
55  Untersteiner, 229.
56  Kerford, 50–51.
57  Dobson, 19.
58  Dobson, 19.
59  Kerford, 51.
60  Untersteiner, 254.
61  Gomperz, 437.
62  Dobson, 36.
63  Kennedy, 331.
64  Dobson, 38.
65  Dobson, 32–33.
66  Kennedy, 132.
67  Dobson, 37.
68  Kathleen Freeman, *The Murder of Herodes and Other Trials from the Athenian Law Courts* (London: MacDonald & Co., 1946), 34.
69  William Arnold Stevens, ed., *Select Orations of Lysias*, 8th edn (Chicago: S.C. Griggs and Co., 1891), xiv.
70  W. R. M. Lamb, tr., *Lysias* (London: William Heinemann, Ltd., 1957), v.
71  Richard C. Jebb, *The Attic Orators From Antiphon to Isaeus* (Vol. 1. New York: Russell and Russell, Inc., 1962), 179.
72  Kennedy, 135.
73  J. S. Watson, tr., *Cicero On Oratory and Orators* (Carbondale, IL: University of Southern Illinois Press, 1970), 108.
74  Jebb, 156.
75  Watson, 108.
76  Untersteiner, 289.
77  Botsford, 386–388; Kennedy, 195–196.
78  Kennedy, 181–182.
79  Kennedy, 290.
80  Dobson, 140.
81  Harry M. Hubbell, *The Influence of Isocrates on Cicero, Dionysius, and Aristides* (New Haven: Yale University Press, 1913), 3.
82  Kennedy, 174.
83  George Norlin, tr., *Isocrates* (3 Vols. Cambridge, MA: Loeb Classical Library, 1954–1956), 173.
84  Dobson, 141.
85  Dobson, 137; Norlin, 163–164.
86  Kathleen Welch, *The Contemporary Reception of Classical Rhetoric: Appropriations of Ancient Discourse* (New Jersey: Lawrence Erlbaum Publishers, 1990), 118–120.

87 Dobson, 137; Norlin, 163–164.
88 Kennedy, 174.
89 Dobson, 130.
90 Douglas MacDowell, *Demosthenes: Speeches 27-38* (Austin, TX: University of Texas Press, 2004), 151.
91 MacDowell, 4.
92 Plutarch, *Lives of the Ten Orators*. Tr. Charles W. Barcroft. http://www.attalus.org/old/orators2.html, 844.
93 Kennedy, 224.
94 Jon M. Ericson, "Rhetorical Criticism: How To Evaluate a Speech," in *On the Crown*, ed. James J. Murphy (New York: Random House, 1957), 132.
95 MacDowell, 5.

## 3 Aristotle's Rhetorical Theory

1 This chapter has been revised principally by Michael Hoppmann from the original chapter authored by Forbes Hill. Dr. Hill, sadly, died shortly after the third edition was published. We dedicate this chapter to his memory.
2 Ancient sources suggest that Aristotle wrote four other books on rhetoric, but none have survived. For a review of these sources see: Keith V. Erickson, "The Lost Rhetorics of Aristotle," *Speech Monographs* (now *Communication Monographs*) 43 (1976): 229–237; reprinted in *Landmark Essays on Aristotelian Rhetoric*, ed. Richard L. Enos and Lois P. Agnew (New York: Lawrence Erlbaum Associates, 1998), 3–14.
3 As far as we know, this term is used for the first time in James J. Murphy, "The Metarhetorics of Plato, Augustine, and McLuhan," *Philosophy and Rhetoric* 4 (1970): 201–214. Other studies by the same author are "La Metaretórica de Aristóteles," *Anuario filósofico* 38 (1988): 473–486; "The Metarhetoric of Aristotle, with Some Examples from His *On Memory and Recollection*," *Rhetoric Review* 21 (2002): 213–228.
4 A recent review of the extensive discussion on the origins and dating of the *Rhetoric* can be found in Christof Rapp, *Aristoteles: Rhetorik* (Berlin: Akademieverlag, 2002), Vol. I, 169–193. There are a number of good editions and translations of the *Rhetoric* to date, including George A. Kennedy's very accessible English translation: *Aristotle: On Rhetoric. A Theory of Civic Discourse*, 2nd edn (New York and Oxford: Oxford University Press, 2007). For detailed questions there are three main commentaries: Cope and Sandy's slightly dated but still worthwhile English commentary of 1877, Grimaldi's English commentary of the first two books of the *Rhetoric* (1980 and 1988) and Rapp's masterful German commentary above.
5 The Greek term for common *topoi* is *koina* or, less frequently, *koinoi topoi*. *Koina* literally means commons, probably best translated as common assumptions; Lane Cooper once avoided other translating problems by calling them "universal appliances." In any event, the designation *koina* refers to the lines of argument for showing that some event is possible or impossible, that it has occurred, or that it might occur (past fact or predicted fact), or that it is more important or less. The Greek for special *topos* is *eide* or *idea protases* or just *idea*. The first is the word ordinarily used for species, the latter means specific premises, or just specifics. They could also be called material proofs, because they are based in a subject matter. Aristotle recognizes a third kind of enthymeme-generating element, the *topoi ton enthymematon* of Book II, chaps. 23 and 24. The best translation for *topoi ton enthymematon* is probably basic forms of enthymemes because most descriptions of them given by Aristotle contain not only an assumption, e.g., similar causes will have similar effects, but also an abstract form for the argument drawn from this assumption., e.g. if D causes G, then $\Delta$? Causes. See p. 94.
6 The opposite position: that Aristotle's *Rhetoric* contains in itself a commitment to his ethical theory, has been maintained by Lois S. Self, "Rhetoric and *Phronesis*: The Aristotelian Ideal," *Philosophy and Rhetoric* 12 (1979): 130–145. That some parts of the *Rhetoric* "form a substantive Aristotelian treatise on value" has been argued by Eugene E. Ryan, in "Aristotle's *Rhetoric* and *Ethics* and the *Ethos* of Society," *Greek, Roman and Byzantine*

*Studies* 13 (1972): 291–308. Forbes Hill exhaustively refutes both these positions, maintaining that no moral commitment at all is implicated by the statements used as illustrations in the *Rhetoric*: see Forbes Hill, "The Amorality of Aristotle's *Rhetoric*," *GRBS* 22 (1981): 133–147. It is obvious that Aristotle quite clearly avoids endorsing any particular moral or ethical position, but Whitney J. Oates, in his book *Aristotle and the Problem of Value* (Princeton: Princeton University Press, 1963), 335, states that "Ambivalence" about questions of value is the most striking characteristic of the *Rhetoric*.

7   John Herman Randall, *Aristotle* (New York: Columbia University Press, 1960), 79.

8   Edwin B. Black, *Rhetorical Criticism: A Study in Method* (New York and London: Macmillan Co., 1965), 92.

9   Ernest Havet, *Etude sur la Rhétorique d'Aristote* (Paris: Jules DelaLain, 1846), 5.

10  Compare Michael De Brauw, "The Parts of the Speech," in *A Companion to Greek Rhetoric*, ed. Ian Worthington (Chichester: Blackwell, 2010), 195f.

11  Compare Rapp, Vol. I, 323ff.; M. Hoppmann, "Rhetorik des Verstandes," in *Rhetorik und Stilistik: An International Handbook of Historical and Systematic Research*, ed. U. Fix, A. Gardt, and J. Knape (Berlin: Mouton de Gruyter, 2008), Vol. I, 629–645.

12  This interpretation of the development of Aristotle's deductive schema follows the general outline developed by D. A. G. Hinks, "Tria Genera Causarum," *Classical Quarterly* 30 (1936): 170–182. For a modern comparison of the conflicting definitions of the genres comp. also M. Hoppmann, "Genera Causarum and the Burden of Proof," *Cogency, Journal of Reasoning and Argumentation* 3, 1 (2011): 33–50. The Greek terms for the ends of the three kinds of discourses are: for forensic discourse *to dikaion*, for deliberative, *to sympheron* and for epideictic discourse, *to kalon*. There has been little variation in the way translators have dealt with *to dikaion* and *to kalon*. In the case of *sympheron*, however, there has been a good deal of variation. It is often translated "the expedient" rather than "the advantageous." But "the advantageous" is more literal: *sympheron* usually means whatever brings with it advantage for the individual or the state (Latin, *utilitas*). For individuals, Hill takes it to be the equivalent of enlightened self-interest; for the state, it is equivalent to the national interest. These notions are better expressed by advantageous than by expedient. If one reads the text cynically, it would seem that Aristotle intends to divorce the concept from morality, but Hill thinks that when he postulates "the advantageous" as the end of deliberative speaking, as opposed to justice, the end of forensic speaking, he means that considerations of justice are subordinate to the advantageous in this kind of speaking. He does not mean that morality is not a factor to be considered, although Aristotle's simplified example seems to imply that position. The distinction between the just and the advantageous is well-expressed by the negative spokesman in the famous debate about capital punishment for the inhabitants of Mytilene, who had revolted from Athens in a time of her distress. "The question," he declaims, "is not so much whether they are guilty as whether we are making the right decision for ourselves. I might prove that they are the most guilty people in the world, but it does not follow that I shall propose the death penalty, unless that is in your interest; I might argue that they deserve to be forgiven but should not recommend forgiveness unless that seemed to me to be the best thing for the state." See Thucydides, *History*, bk. III, chap. 3 (tr. Rex Warner). This passage probably shows the influence of a pre-Aristotelian rhetorical handbook.

13  Reasoned choice is a translation of *proairesis*. In other contexts the term is translated as rational choice or moral choice, or even as intent or intention, as in the discussion of crime.

14  Edward M. Cope, *The Rhetoric of Aristotle with a Commentary*, 3 Vols. (Cambridge: Cambridge University Press, 1877), Vol. I, 159–160. The word translated here as capacity is *dynamis*, also used in the definition of rhetoric as "a *dynamis* for observing in regard to any subject the available persuasive factors." In this context it is often translated as faculty. Aristotle ordinarily uses the term in opposition to *energeia* or activity. A *dynamis* is a potential for an *energeia*. The art of rhetoric, presumably, is the potential for generating many rhetorical discourses, and in the *Rhetoric*, Aristotle uses the terms *dynamis* and *techne* as if they were synonyms. The question here is whether in Aristotelian thought a *hexis* (Latin: *habitus*) must be a fixed pattern of activity, or may also be seen as a fixed potential, a *dynamis*, which may (or may not) be actualized as habitual activity.

15 Larry Arnhart, *Aristotle on Political Reasoning* (De Kalb, IL: Northern Illinois University Press, 1981), 78–79.

16 Justice or *dikaiosyne* is, of course, the subject of Plato's dialogue in *The Republic*; manly courage, *andreia* is discussed in depth in the *Protagoras* (it does not seem to have occurred to Plato and Aristotle that there might be such a thing as womanly courage). Self-control, or *sophrosyne*, is sometimes translated temperance or prudence, but these words are misleading to the modern student. In connection with magnificence, or *megaloprepeia*, Kennedy cites the example of Lorenzo the Magnificent in a note to his translation. See George A. Kennedy, *Aristotle on Rhetoric: A Theory of Civic Discourse* (New York and Oxford: Oxford University Press, 1991), 80. The concept of magnificence seems at odds with the notion of humility as a virtue, a notion that seems to be foreign to Aristotle; it probably derives from Christianity. Magnanimity is the usual translation of *megalopsychia*; a literal rendering—great-souledness—is too awkward. The Greek for liberality, *eleutheriotes*, could as well or better be translated philanthropy or generosity, but Kennedy points out that *eleutherios* also means a free man for whom the humanitarian breadth of view that goes with a liberal education is possible. Keeping the translation "liberality" is intended to maintain this connection.

17 Phronesis, here translated good sense, is in this context translated prudence by Kennedy, 80. That translation well expresses one aspect of it, i.e., making choices conservatively. But in other contexts one might translate phronesis as shrewdness or common sense, or practical wisdom. We intuitively recognize a difference between this concept and sophia, or wisdom: not every theoretical physicist is shrewd in the management of his own affairs. A person with phronesis is a phronimos; that phronimoi are the target audience for the *Rhetoric* is the conclusion of Robert Olian "The Intended Uses of Aristotle's Rhetoric," *Speech Monographs* 35 (1968): 137–148. For an argument that the concept of phronesis is basic and even controlling for Aristotle's *Rhetoric*, see Self, op. cit.

18 Wrongdoing is the usual translation of *to adikein*, literally acting unjustly. Equating *to adikein* directly with the English word crime was the insight of Max Hamburger, *Morals and Law, the Growth of Aristotle's Legal Theory* (1st edn, New Haven: Yale University Press, 1951; 2nd edn, New York: Biblo and Tannen, 1965). Hamburger states that the *Rhetoric* contains the consummation of Aristotle's legal philosophy and theory.

19 A thorough treatment of the relation of *hedone* in the *Rhetoric* and the *Nicomachean Ethics* to Plato's *Philebus* is given by Godo Lieburg, *Die Lehre von der Lust in den Ethiken des Aristoteles* (Munich: Beck, 1958), 27–42; also see William Fortenbaugh, "Aristotle's *Rhetoric* on Emotions," *Archive für Geschichte der Philosophie* 52 (1970): 40–70; reprinted in Erickson, 205–234.

20 The translation of *epieikes* by fairness is justified by Kennedy, 105.

21 Arnhart, 103.

22 See comments of Arnhart, 109 and Kennedy, 115 and note. But the most negative phrase about such testimony may be an interpolation by a later writer.

23 The Greek words for the constituents of *ethos* are as follows: for good sense, *phronesis*; for good moral character, *arete* (all the moral excellences other than *phronesis*); for good will *eunoia*.

24 Fortenbaugh, op. cit.; William Fortenbaugh, *Aristotle on Emotion* (New York: Harper & Row, 1975), 12–18. Fortenbaugh cites E. Bradford, "Emotions," *Proceedings of the Aristotelian Society* (1956): 281–304, reprinted in D. Gustafson, ed., *Essays in Philosophical Psychology* (Garden City, NY: Doubleday, 1964). See also, Arnhart, 114–115 and note in which he cites Robert C. Solomon, *The Passions* (Garden City, NY: Doubleday Anchor Books, 1976).

25 Martin Heidegger, *Sein und Zeit*, 11th edn (Tübingen: Max Niemeyer, 1967), §29 p. 139.

26 A number of inferior manuscripts and the medieval Latin translation enumerate gentleness (*praotes*) among the *aretai* in I$_9$. This reading has been rejected by modern editors, see Rudolf Kassel, *Aristotelis Ars Rhetorica* (Berlin: De Gruyter, 1976).

27 The Greek here translated as "rational wish" is *boulesis*, from the verb *bouleumai*, to take counsel with oneself. Aristotle commonly uses this word to define a desire for which a reason can be given. Today, "boule" is the word for parliament, where elected representatives "take counsel" with one another.

28 *Thucydides: The History of the Peloponnesian War*, ed. M. I. Finley, tr. Rex Warner (London: Penguin, 1972).

29 This interpretation builds on an article by Frank Madden, "Aristotle's Treatment of Probability and Signs," *Philosophy of Science* (Chicago: University of Chicago Press, 1957), 167–172.

30 See Donovan J. Ochs, "Aristotle's Concept of Formal Topics," *Speech Monographs* 36 (1969): 418–425; reprinted in Erickson, op. cit., and the bibliographical notes given by Ochs.

31 Unless otherwise indicated all literal quotations from the *Rhetoric* in this section are taken from George A. Kennedy's translation of the work.

32 In Plato's defense of Socrates (and potentially also his historical defense), Socrates refutes the accusation against him that he did not believe in gods by reference to his "daimon" that had been recognized and that, if acknowledged, *by definition* meant that Socrates believed in the divine.

33 The precise meaning of this topos is unclear because Aristotle does not fully discuss it in the *Rhetoric* and provides no examples. Instead he refers to the *Topica*, either Top. I, 15 or Top. II, 3. Compare Rapp's commentary to this section in *Aristoteles: Rhetorik*, tr. and ed. C. Rapp, Vol. II (Berlin: Akademieverlag 2002), 761. Rapp's excellent German translation and commentary is the most exhaustive and reliable modern commentary to date.

34 This last of the non-fallacious *topoi* must appear strikingly weak if one thinks of a random first name given at birth as the archetype for the reasoning. Some of this weakness can be alleviated by names (e.g., nicknames or honorifics) that are either given to a person based on his/her achievements or character or that are an expression of the values that parents embedded in his/her education.

35 Georgiana Paine Palmer, in a dissertation, *The Topoi of Aristotle's* Rhetoric, *As Exemplified in* the Orators (University of Chicago, 1934), states that this *topos* is not used in any extant ancient Greek oration, though it frequently appears in extant dramas.

36 Friedrich Solmsen, "The Aristotelian Tradition in Ancient Rhetoric," *American Journal of Philology* 62 (1941): 35–50, 169–190. However, this system was to become a hallmark of Roman rhetoric, as can be seen in the following chapters.

37 Compare A. C. Braet, "Aristotle's Almost Unnoticed Contribution to the Doctrine of Stasis," *Mnemosyne* 52 (1999): 408–435; Y. Liu, "Aristotle and Stasis Theory," *Rhetoric Society Quarterly* 21 (1991): 53–59.

## 4 From Greek to "Roman" Rhetoric, with Synopses of Three Pragmatic Handbooks

1 We know that Aristotle studied early handbooks while preparing his own *Rhetoric* and discussed them in a lost work titled *Synagógé technon*. See Chaper 3 above. Robert Gaines discusses early "Roman Rhetorical Handbooks," in *A Companion to Roman Rhetoric*, ed. William Dominik and Jon Hall (Oxford: Blackwell Publishing, 2007), 163–180. Gaines' article is one of six in a book section titled "Systematizing Rhetoric."

2 Malcolm Heath, "Codifications of Rhetoric,'" in *The Cambridge Companion to Ancient Rhetoric*, ed. Erik Gunderson (Cambridge: Cambridge University Press, 2009), 63.

3 The main English translations of the *Rhetorica ad Alexandrum* are by E. S. Foster (Oxford: Oxford University Press, 1946) (The Works of Aristotle Vol. XI) and by H. Rackham (Cambridge, MA: Harvard University Press, 1937), Loeb Classical Library Vol. 317. Both also contain brief overviews and introductions. The journal *Rhetorica* has recently devoted a special issue (29 [2011]: 233–365) to the *Rhetorica ad Alexandrum*.

4 It had two medieval Latin translations, due solely to the supposed Aristotelian connection. See James J. Murphy, *Rhetoric in the Middle Ages* (Berkeley and Los Angeles: University of California Press, 1974), 7–8.

5 For a more complete discussion of the dating of the *Rhetorica ad Alexandrum* cf. Pierre Chiron, "Relative Dating of the *Rhetoric to Alexander* and Aristotle's *Rhetoric*: A Methodology and Hypothesis," *Rhetorica* 29 (2011): 236–262. Chiron also discusses the complex relationship between the *Rhetorica ad Alexandrum* and Aristotle's *Rhetoric*.

6  For a more detailed account of the background, see Chiron, "The Rhetoric to Alexander," in *A Companion to Greek Rhetoric*, ed. I. Worthington (Oxford: Blackwell, 2007), 90–106. And George A. Kennedy, *The Art of Persuasion in Greece* (Princeton: Princeton University Press, 1963), 114–124.

7  The division of certain genres or techniques into seven species is a heavily recurring phenomenon throughout the entire *Rhetorica ad Alexandrum*. For a list of some of the (rather odd) instances see Chiron, "Relative Dating," 245f.

8  This section of the *Rhetorica ad Alexandrum* clearly foreshadows the development of stasis theory.

9  For a more detailed analysis of this peculiar genre see G. Pasini, "The [exetastikon eidos] of the *Rh. Al.* and Parallels in Aeschines' *Against Timarchus* and Demosthenes' *On the False Embassy*," *Rhetorica* 29 (2011): 336–356.

10  For a more detailed explanation of the translation of these central terms see Manfred Kraus, "How to Classify Means of Persuasion," *Rhetorica* 19 (2011): 269. It is important to note that nearly all of the technical terms Anaximenes uses, such as *enthymeme, gnome*, or *tekmerion* can also be found in Aristotle's *Rhetoric*, where they mostly have a very different meaning. Most likely the meaning Anaximenes employs is the more common one in the rhetoric of the time. See also Kraus, p. 264f. and F. Piazza, "Pisteis in comparison," *Rhetorica* 29 (2011): 305–318. Kraus provides an excellent analysis of the structure of the proofs in Anaximenes.

11  This stylistic figure is more commonly treated separately as "preteritio" and not usually linked to the concept of irony.

12  David Mirhady provides a very detailed analysis of Anaximenes' speech structure in his "Aristotle and Anaximenes on Arrangement," *Rhetorica* 29 (2011): 293–304.

13  D. Matthes, "Hermagoras von Temnos," *Lustrum* 3 (1968): 58–214. *Hermagorae Temnitae testimonia et fragmenta* (Leipzig: Teubner, 1962). Also, see K. Barwick. "Augustins Schrift De Rhetorica und Hermagoras von Temnos," *Philologus* 105 (1961): 97–110. K. Barwick, "Zur Erklärung und Geschichte der Staseislehre des Hermagoras von Temnos," *Philologus* 108 (1964): 80–101. K. Barwick, "Zur Rekonstruktion der Rhetorik des Hermagoras von Temnos," *Philologus* 109 (1965): 186–218.

14  A. C. Braet, "Aristotle's Almost Unnoticed Contribution to the Doctrine of Stasis," *Mnemosyne* 52 (1999): 408–435; Y. Liu, "Aristotle and the Stasis Theory: A Re-examination," *Rhetoric Society Quarterly* 21 (1991): 53–59.

15  This theoretical background and terminology was not made explicit in the classical models, but must be assumed for a solid foundation of the theory.

16  Cicero and Quintilian also try to utilize it in other genres but ultimately fail to provide compelling proof of the applicability in these genres beyond a very trivial level of heuristics.

17  Cicero, *De Oratore*, tr. E. W. Sutton and H. Rackham (2 Vols., Cambridge, MA: Harvard University Press, 1959); see also Cicero, *Brutus*, tr. E. Jones (New York: AMS Press, 1976).

18  For a more complete description of the case and its background see George A. Kennedy, *The Art of Rhetoric in the Roman World* (Princeton: Princeton University Press, 1972), 84ff.

19  Quoted in Suetonius, *De grammatica et* rhetorica. 25, 2 and Aulus Gellius 15.11.2.

20  Quoted in Aubrey Gwynn, *Roman Education from Cicero to Quintilian* (Oxford: Clarendon Press, 1926), 61.

21  See Chapter 6 for a more detailed description of the transition to the new educational system, described by Marcus Fabius Quintilianus, which became the Roman standard for centuries.

22  Cicero, *De Inventione. De optimo genere oratorum. Topica*, tr. H. M. Hubbell (Cambridge, MA: Harvard University Press, 1968), xi–xii. He may have been 19 or 20 years of age.

23  *De oratore*, I. 5. (See the synopsis below.)

24  Friedrich Solmsen, "The Aristotelian Tradition in Ancient Rhetoric," *American Journal of Philology* 62 (1941): 170–171.

25  Cf. Hubbell (tr.), "Excursus," p. 346.
26  {Cicero}, *Ad C. Herennium De Ratione Dicendi (Rhetorica ad Herennium)*, tr. Harry Caplan (Cambridge, MA: Loeb Classical Library, 1964). The following synopsis is based largely on this text and translation, and on Harry Caplan's introductory analysis. Also, see *Cornifici Rhetorica ad Herennium*, Introduzione, Testo critico, commenta a cura Gualtievo Calboli. Secunda edizione (Bologna: Patron Editore, 1993).

## 5  The Rhetorical Theory of the Mature Cicero, with Synopses of His Major Rhetorical Works

1  Donovan Ochs, now deceased, is the original author of this chapter, and while it has been revised, his writing is still in evidence.
2  Unless otherwise indicated all dates in this chapter are BCE.
3  Accounts of Cicero's life and career are too numerous to list in a brief footnote. The reader may find two brief articles, however, that lay out basic information together with bibliographic suggestions for further study. They are James A. May, "Cicero as Rhetorician" and Christopher P. Craig, " Cicero as Orator," in *A Companion to Roman Rhetoric*, ed. William Dominik and Jon Hall (Oxford: Blackwell, 2007), 250–263 and 264–284 respectively. Also see James M. May, ed., *Brill's Companion to Cicero* (Leiden: Brill, 2002). Also useful is George A. Kennedy, *A New History of Classical Rhetoric* (Princeton: Princeton University Press, 1994).
4  J. W. H. Atkins, *Literary Criticism in Antiquity* (London: Methuen, 1952), II. 21ff. See also C. S. Baldwin, *Ancient Rhetoric and Poetic* (Gloucester, MA: Peter Smith, 1959), 37. An excellent book that demonstrates the interconnections between Cicero's rhetorical and compositional skills is Richard Leo Enos, *The Literate Mode of Cicero's Legal Rhetoric* (Carbondale, IL: Southern Illinois University Press, 1988). One must remember that Cicero delivered several hundred speeches (58 are extant). Also surviving are more than 800 letters he wrote. He published 25 books, not only the six on rhetoric but others on philosophical, political, and religious topics as well.
5  Cf. James J. Murphy, ed., *Demosthenes' On the Crown* (Davis, CA: Hermagoras Press, 1983).
6  Atkins, I1. 26. See also F. Solmsen, "Aristotle and Cicero on the Orator's Playing on the Feelings," *Classical Philology* 33 (1938): 401ff.
7  For a more detailed account of Roman law and the court system see: F. Schultz, *Classical Roman Law* (Oxford: Clarendon Press, 1951); A. H. J. Greenidge, *The Legal Procedure of Cicero's Time* (Oxford: Clarendon Press), and M. Alexander, *Trials in the Late Roman Republic: 149 BC. to 50 BC.* (Toronto: University of Toronto Press, 1990).
8  Cicero *Brutus* 306; Ad *Att.*, II. i. 9.
9  This was of course also the year of his *De Inventione*. A young man writes safe things— translations and summaries.
10  John C. Rolfe, *Cicero and His Influence* (New York: Cooper Square, 1963), 17.
11  *Brutus*, 91–93.
12  C. Habicht, *Cicero the Politician* (Baltimore: The Johns Hopkins University Press, 1990). For a penetrating analysis of the political machinations confronting Cicero see John T. Kirby, *The Rhetoric of Cicero's Pro Cluentio* (Amsterdam: J.C. Gieben, Publisher, 1990).
13  Cf. M. Tulli Ciceronis, *De Oratore*, ed. A. S. Wilkins (Amsterdam: Servio, 1962), 50–55, and Cicero, *De Oratore*, tr. E. W. Sutton and H. Rackham (Cambridge, MA: Harvard University Press, 1959), ix. Now see the new translation in *Cicero On the Ideal Orator (De oratore)*; tr. with Introduction, Notes, Appendices, Glossary and Notes by James M. May and Jakob Wisse (Oxford: Oxford University Press, 2001).
14  Cf. S. F. Bonner, "Roman Oratory," in *Fifty Years of Classical Scholarship*, ed. Maurice Platnauer (Oxford: Blackwell, 1954), 346, and Friedrich Solmsen, "Cicero's First Speeches: A Rhetorical Analysis," *Transactions of the American Philological Association* 69 (1938): 555–556.

15 P. MacKendrick, "Cicero's Ideal Orator," *Classical Journal* 43 (1947–1948): 345. See also *De Orat.*, I. 68, 128, 165–184, 256; III. 54; *Orator*, 113, 126.

16 Cf. Atkins, II. 23–24; D. L. Clark, *Rhetoric at Rome* (New York: Barnes and Noble, 1963), 51.

17 G. L. Hendrickson, "Cicero's Correspondence with Brutus and Calvus on Oratorical Style," *American Journal of Philology* 47 (1926): 239.

18 For an historical account of the political intrigue, see H. J. Haskell, *This Was Cicero* (New York: Knopf, 1964).

19 A more detailed treatment of this debate is available in Donovan J. Ochs, "Aeschines' Speech Against Ctesiphon (an abstract)" and "Demothenes' Use of Argument," in *Demosthenes' On the Crown*, 48–58, 157–174.

20 Cf. Rolfe, 33ff.; Hendrickson, 236.

21 Rolfe, 33. See also Wilkins, 48; and Bonner, 364.

22 Atkins, II. p. 27.

23 Atkins, II. p. 45. *Ibid.*, II. 45.

24 A proscription was a public announcement that no one would be prosecuted for killing a person named in the edict.

## 6 Quintilian's Place in Roman Rhetorical and Educational Theory, with a Synopsis of his *Institutio oratoria*

1 Malcom Heath, "Codifications of Rhetoric," in *The Cambridge Companion to Ancient Rhetoric*, ed. Erik Gunderson (Cambridge: Cambridge University Press, 2009), 73.

2 *Quintilian: The Orator's Education*, ed. and tr. Donald A. Russell (5 Vols., Loeb Classical Library. Cambridge, MA: Harvard University Press, 2001). This Russell translation provides a useful Introduction as well as extensive explanatory notes throughout.

3 See William Dominik, "Tacitus and Pliny on Oratory," in *A Companion to Roman Rhetoric*, ed. Willliam Dominik and Jon Hall (Oxford: Blackwell, 2007), 323–338.

4 For a useful treatment of the power of schools in the Roman empire, see Robert A. Kaster, *Guardians of Language: The Grammarian and Society in Late Antiquity* (Berkeley: University of California Press, 1988).

5 For an extended discussion of these teaching methods, see James J. Murphy, ed., *A Short History of Writing Instruction from Ancient Greece to Twentieth-Century America*, 3rd edn (New York: Routledge, 2012), 36–76.

## 7 Epilogue: What Happened Next?

1 Alex Novikoff describes the evolution of this new form in "Toward a Cultural History of Scholastic Disputation," *American Historical Review* 117 (2012): 331–364.

2 Traditional scholarship long assumed that Roman education and culture disintegrated after the barbarian invasions and the fall of Rome in 410, but recent studies show a far different picture. There is an intelligent summary of these findings in Ralph W. Mathisen, "Bishops, Barbarians, and the 'Dark Ages': The Fate of Late Roman Educational Institutions in Late Antique Gaul," in *Medieval Education*, ed. Ronald B. Begley and Joseph W. Koteriski, S.J. (New York: Fordham University Press, 2002), 3–19. Particularly important in his list of Works Cited are those by Haarhoff, Kaster, Marrou, Pirenne, Riché, and Roger. Also see Carol Dana Lanham, "Writing Instruction from Late Antiquity to the Twelfth Century," in *A Short History of Writing Instruction from Ancient Greece to Contemporary America*, ed. J. J. Murphy (New York: Routledge, 2012), 77–113.

3 The telling argument for the use of rhetoric in spreading Christianity was made by a converted teacher of rhetoric, Aurelius Augustinus (354–430 CE) in his *De doctrina Christiana* (*On the Dissemination of Christian Doctrine*) completed in 430 CE. See James J. Murphy, *Rhetoric in the Middle Ages* (Berkeley: University of California Press, 1974), 56–59.

4 Alcuin (c.735–804) wrote his Latin treatise in 794 CE. It is edited and translated by Wilbur S. Howell as *The Rhetoric of Alcuin and Charlemagne* (Princeton: Princeton University Press, 1941).

5 For an excellent description of the suppression of free speech under the emperors, see Chester G. Starr, *Civilization and the Caesars: The Intellectual Revolution in the Roman Empire* (Ithaca, NY: Cornell University Press, 1954).

6 See Simon Goldhill, "Rhetoric and the Second Sophistic," in *The Cambridge Companion to Ancient Rhetoric*, ed. Erik Gunderson (Cambridge: Cambridge University Press, 2009), 228–244. Another byproduct of this public interest in school exercises was the publication of collections of *progymnasmata*, by Hermogenes in the 2nd century and Aphthonius in the 4th. Apthonius had a considerable Renaissance influence, especially in England.

7 The complete history of Cicero's rhetoric has not yet been told, but see John O. Ward, *Ciceronian Rhetoric in Treatise, Scholion, and Commentary*. Typologie des sources de moyen âge occidental, fascicule 58 (Turnhout, Belgium: Brepols, 1995). Also see Peter Mack, *A History of Renaissance Rhetoric 1380–1620* (Oxford: Oxford University Press, 2011) as well as the standard histories of rhetoric by Conley, Kennedy, and Vickers listed in the bibliography later in this volume.

8 See John O. Ward, "Roman Rhetoric and Its Afterlife," in *A Companion to Roman Rhetoric*, ed. William Dominik and Jon Hall (Oxford: Blackwell, 2007), 362–363. The early printing history of these ancient rhetorical texts is described in Lawrence D. Green and James J. Murphy, *Renaissance Rhetoric Short-Title Catalogue 1460–1700* (Aldershot, England and Burlington, VT: Ashgate, 2006).

9 Again, as with Cicero, there is no complete history of Quintilian's influence. The best short survey, even after almost 90 years, is in the Introduction to F. H. Colson, *M. Fabii Quintiliani institutione oratoriae, Liber I* (Cambridge, 1924). It is interesting to note, though, that the *Institutio oratoria* was printed more than 90 times in various editions, commentaries, excerpts, and translations from the beginning of printing to 1700 CE. See Green and Murphy, *Short Title Catalogue*. Donald A. Russell provides a brief but significant account of "Quintilian's Influence" in his Introduction to *Quintilian The Orators' Education* (5 Vols., Cambridge, MA: Harvard University Press, 2001), Vol. I, 21–29.

10 See Murphy, *Rhetoric in the Middle Ages*, 90–102. The first printed Latin translation was published by George of Trebizond in 1475; the Greek text not until half a century later, in 1529.

### Six Classical Texts for Reading, Study, and Discussion

1 Charles D. Adams, ed., *Lysias: Selected Speeches* (New York: American Book Club, 1905), 233.

2 *Lysias*, tr. W. R. M. Lamb (London: William Heinemann, Ltd., 1957), 517. Speech text reprinted from *Lysias*, trans. W. R. M. Lamb (Cambridge, MA: Harvard University Press, 1957). First printed in 1930, reprinted in 1943 and 1957. Used with permission.

3 A poor man like the speaker was not the natural prey of a slander-monger, who would hope to be bought off by a wealthy defendant.

4 He means a slave who would learn the business and carry it on for him.

5 It would be natural for a cripple to ride about on a cheaply hired mule, if only he could afford it.

6 The archons were appointed by lot from all the citizens, rich or poor, except, apparently, those who were formally classed as infirm.

7 The speaker here solemnly appeals for himself as one of an unfortunate class. Speech text reprinted from *The Dialogues of Plato*, trans. Benjamin Jowett, 4th edn (Oxford: At the Clarendon Press, 1953). Used with permission.

8 Or, I am certain that I am right in taking this course.

9 Aristoph. *Clouds*, 225 foll.

10 George A. Kennedy, *Aristotle On Rhetoric: A Theory of Civic Discourse* (New York: Oxford University Press, 1991), 283.

11 Speech text reprinted from Appendix I of George A. Kennedy, *Aristotle On Rhetoric: A Theory of Civic Discourse* (New York: Oxford University Press, 1991), 284–288. Used with permission. Cf. Aeschvlus, *Agamennon 689*, a play on Helen's name: "Hell to ships, hell to men, hell to the city." Gorgias ignores the more favorable treatments of Helen in Stesichorus' *Palinode*, Herodotus' *Histories* (esp. 2.113–120), and Euripides' *Helen.*

12 Leda was thought to have conceived Helen when Zeus came to her in the form of a swan— cf., e.g., Yeats' poem "Leda."

13 Helen's many suitors swore to defend the rights of the one who gained her hand. This was Menelaus. When Helen was seduced, stolen, or raped by Paris, her former suitors went off to Troy to recover her in the war described in the *Iliad*.

14 The unnamed person is Alexander or Paris, son of Priam, king of Troy.

15 On this use of logos, cf. *Rhetoric 3.9.5.*

16 Helen thus is not to be blamed if she was promised to Paris by Aphrodite as a result of his judging that goddess more beautiful than Hera and Athene in the celebrated beauty contest on Mount Ida.

17 A view rejected by Aristotle, *Poetics* 1.10–12.

18 E.g., by demonstrating that the world is round.

19 John F. Dobson, *Greek Orators* (Freeport, NY: Books for Libraries Press, 1967), 202.

20 Cicero, *On Oratory and Orators*, tr. J. S. Watson (Carbondale, IL: Southern Illinois University Press, 1970), 270–271.

21 Dobson, 203.

22 Speech text reprinted from *Demosthenes Public Orations*, tr. A. W. Pickard-Cambridge (Oxford: reissued by arrangement with Clarendon Press. Original: New York: Dutton, 1916. Everyman Library No. 546). Used with permission.

23 G. Delayen, *Cicero* (New York: E. P. Dutton Co., 1931), 79.; Louis E. Lord, *Cicero, the Speeches* (Cambridge, MA: Harvard University Press), 3.

24 H. L. Havell, *Republican Rome* (London: George Harrop, Ltd., 1914), 477.

25 Speech text reprinted from *Cicero: The Speeches*, tr. Louis E. Lord (Cambridge, MA: Harvard University Press, 1953). First printing, 1937. Used with permission. To insure its safety the Senate was meeting in the temple of Jupiter Stator—at the upper end of the forum—not in the senate-house.

26 Publius Scipio Nasica, pontifex maximus in 133 BC. Not one of the civil administrative officers—like the consuls—nor a military functionary.

27 In a famine in 439 BC Maelius sold grain at a reduced price. He was suspected of doing so to win popular favour. When he did not appear promptly to answer charges preferred to Cincinnatus, the Dictator, he was murdered by Ahala.

28 The *senatus consultum ultimum*. See *Cicero: the Speeches*, 6.

29 121 BC.

30 100 BC.

31 For the chronology of the conspiracy see the Introduction, *Cicero: the Speeches.*

32 Catiline's charm for young men is described by Sallust, *Cat.* xiv. 5–7. The first day of the month (Kalends) and the thirteenth (or fifteenth) (Ides) were the regular days for paying— or failing to pay—bills.

33 66 BC.

34 It was unlawful for a citizen to carry arms within the city.
   The identity of this Metellus is uncertain. Perhaps the reading should be *Quintum Metellum, i.e.,* Quintus Metellus Nepos. See *Proceedings American Philological Association*, vol. lxv, p. 271. Quintilian quotes this passage as an example of irony.

35 A village about 50 miles north of Rome on the Aurelian Way in the direction of Faesulae where Manlius awaited Catiline.

36 To be the standard of his followers. In camp the eagles were kept in a shrine.

37 Cicero had been taunted with being an upstart, for he was the first of his family to achieve senatorial rank; he was a *novus homo*.

38 Satuninus, Tiberius and Gaius Gracchus were killed, the former by Marius in 100 and the Gracchi by mobs incited by the nobles in 133 and 121 on the charge that they were aiming

at unconstitutional power. The case of L. Valerius Flaccus is not so clear. He was consul with Marius in 100 and later with Cinna in 86. He was murdered by Fimbria in 86 when they were conducting a joint expedition against Sulla in the east.

39  The Roman army was being forced to retreat in a battle with the Sabines. Romulus vowed a temple to Jupiter if he would stay the flight. His prayer was answered and on the alleged spot a temple was built in 294 BC to Jupiter the Stayer of Flight. Cicero was speaking in this temple.

# A Basic Library for the Study of Classical Rhetoric

## A. Reference Works

Enos, Theresa, ed. *Encyclopedia of Rhetoric and Composition*. (New York: Garland Publishing, 1996).

Fix, Ulla, Andreas Gardt, and Joachim Knape, eds. *Rhetorik und Stilistik/Rhetoric and Stylistics. Handbücher zur Sprach- und Kommunikationswissenschaft, vol. 31*. (Berlin: De Gruyter, 2008–2009).

Haase, Wolfgang and Hildegard Temporini, eds. *Aufstieg und Niedergang der römischen Welt (ANRW)/Rise and Decline of the Roman World*. 41 vols. (Berlin: De Gruyter, 1972–).

Jasinski, James. *Sourcebook on Rhetoric*. (Thousand Oaks, CA: Sage, 2001).

Lausberg, Heinrich. *Handbook of Literary Rhetoric*. Trans. M. T.Bliss, A.Jansen, and D. E. Orton. (Leiden: Brill, 1998).

Lunsford, Andrea A., Kirt H. Wilson, and Rosa A. Eberly, eds. *The SAGE Handbook of Rhetorical Studies*. (Thousand Oaks, CA: Sage, 2009).

Pauly, August et al., eds. *Paulys Realencyclopädie der classischen Altertumswissenschaft*. (Stuttgart: Metzler, 1893–1978).

Sloane, Thomas O., ed. *Encyclopedia of Rhetoric*. (New York: Oxford University Press, 2001).

Ueding, Gert, ed. *Historisches Wörterbuch der Rhetorik*. (Tübingen: Niemeyer and Berlin: De Gruyter, 1992–2011).

## B. Histories

Ballif, Michelle and Michael G. Moran, eds. *Classical Rhetorics and Rhetoricians: Critical Studies and Sources*. (London: Greenwood, 2005).

Barner, Wilfried. *Barockrhetorik*. 2nd edn. (Tübingen: Niemeyer, 2002).

Clark, Donald L. *Rhetoric in Greco-Roman Education*. (Westport, CT: Greenwood Publishing, 1977).

Clarke, Martin. L. *Rhetoric at Rome: A Historical Survey*. (New York: Barnes & Noble, 1963).

Cole, Thomas. *The Origins of Rhetoric in Ancient Greece*. (Baltimore: Johns Hopkins University Press, 1991).

Conley, Thomas M. *Rhetoric in the European Tradition*. (Chicago: University of Chicago Press, 1994).

Dominik, William and Jon Hall, eds. *A Companion to Roman Rhetoric*. (Boston: Blackwell, 2010).

Fuhrmann, Manfred. *Die antike Rhetorik*. 5th edn. (Düsseldorf: Artemis & Winkler, 2003).

Fumaroli, Marc. *L'age de l'eloquence*. (Geneva: Droz, 2002).

Gunderson, Erik, ed. *The Cambridge Companion to Ancient Rhetoric*. (Cambridge: Cambridge University Press, 2009).

Howell, Wilbur S. *Eighteenth-Century British Logic and Rhetoric*. (Princeton, NJ: Princeton University Press, 1971).

———. *Logic and Rhetoric in England: 1500–1700.* (Princeton, NJ: Princeton University Press, 1956).

Kennedy, George A. *The Art of Persuasion in Greece.* (Princeton, NJ: Princeton University Press, 1963).

———. *The Art of Rhetoric in the Roman World.* (Princeton, NJ: Princeton University Press, 1967).

———. *Classical Rhetoric and Its Christian and Secular Traditions from Ancient to Modern Times.* (Chapel Hill: University of North Carolina Press, 1980).

———. *Greek Rhetoric under Christian Emperors.* (Princeton, NJ: Princeton University Press, 1983).

———. *A New History of Classical Rhetoric.* (Princeton, NJ: Princeton University Press, 1994).

Knape, Joachim. *Allgemeine Rhetorik.* (Stuttgart: Reclam, 2000).

Mack, Peter. *A History of Renaissance Rhetoric.* (New York: Oxford University Press, 2011).

Martin, Josef. *Antike Rhetorik.* (Munich: Beck, 1974).

Meerhoff, Kees. *Rhéorique et Poétique au XVIe Siècle en France.* (Leiden: Brill, 1886).

Murphy, James J. *Rhetoric in the Middle Ages: A History of Rhetorical Theory from Saint Augustine to the Renaissance.* (Berkeley: University of California Press, 1981).

Poulakos, John. *Sophistical Rhetoric in Classical Greece.* (Columbia: University of South Carolina Press, 1995).

Thiele, Georg. *Hermagoras. Ein Beitrag zur Geschichte der Rhetorik.* (Strasbourg: K. J. Trübner, 1893).

Vickers, Brian. *In Defense of Rhetoric.* (Oxford: Oxford University Press, 1988).

Volkmann, Richard. *Die Rhetorik der Griechen und Römer in systematischer Übersicht.* (Leipzig: Teubner, 1885).

Worthington, Ian, ed. *A Companion to Greek Rhetoric.* (Boston: Blackwell, 2010).

## I. General Readings in Classical Rhetoric

Atkins, J. W. H. *Literary Criticism in Antiquity.* (London: Methuen, 1952).

Baldwin, Charles Sears. *Ancient Rhetoric and Poetic.* (New York: Macmillan, 1924).

Barrett, Harold. *The Sophists: Rhetoric, Democracy, and Plato's Idea of Sophistry.* (Novato, CA: Chandler and Sharp, 1987).

Benoit, William. "Isocrates and Plato on Rhetoric and Rhetorical Education," *Rhetoric Society Quarterly* 21 (1991): 60–71.

Benson, Thomas W. and Michael H. Prosser, eds. *Readings in Classical Rhetoric.* (Davis, CA: Hermagoras Press, 1988).

Bernadette, Seth. "On Plato's Sophist," *The Review of Metaphysics* 46 (1993): 747–780.

Bizzell, Patricia and Bruce Herzberg, eds. *The Rhetorical Tradition: Readings from Classical Times to the Present.* (Boston: Bedford Books of St. Martin's, 1990).

Boedeker, Deborah and Kurt Raaflaub, eds. *Democracy, Empire and the Arts in Fifth-century Athens.* (Cambridge, MA: Harvard University Press, 1998).

Botsford, George W. *Hellenic History.* (New York: Macmillan, 1924).

Coby, Patrick. *Socrates and the Sophistic Enlightenment: A Commentary on Plato's Protagoras.* (Cranbury, NJ: Bucknell University Press, 1988).

Cole, Thomas. *The Origins of Rhetoric in Ancient Greece.* (Baltimore: Johns Hopkins University Press, 1991).

Combellack, Frederick M. "Speakers and scepters in Homer," *Classical Journal* 43 (1948): 209–217.

Connor, William. *Greek Orations, 4th Century* BC (Prospect Heights, IL: Waveland Press, 1966).

Cooper, Lane, ed. *Fifteen Greek Plays.* (New York: Oxford University Press, 1953).

Corbett, Edward P. J. *Classical Rhetoric for the Modern Student.* (New York: Oxford University Press, 1990).

Crowley, Sharon. *Ancient Rhetorics for Contemporary Students.* (New York: Macmillan, 1994).

DeRomilly, Jacqueline. *The Great Sophists in Periclean Athens*. (New York: Clarendon Press, 1991).

——. *Magic and Rhetoric in Ancient Greece*. (Cambridge, MA: Harvard University Press, 1975).

Dickinson, G. Lowes. *The Greek View of Life*. (Ann Arbor: University of Michigan Press, 1958).

Dobson, John. *The Greek Orators*. (Freeport, NY: Books for Libraries, 1971).

Enos, Richard Leo. "Ancient Greek Writing Instruction," in *A Short History of Writing*, ed. JamesJ.Murphy, 3rd edn. (New York: Erlbaum, 2012), 1–35.

——. *Greek Rhetoric before Aristotle*. (Prospect Heights, IL: Waveland Press, 1993).

Enos, Richard Leo and Margaret, Kantz. "A Selected Bibliography on Corax and Tisias," *Rhetoric Society Quarterly* 13 (1983, Winter): 71–74.

Farness, Jay. *Missing Socrates: Problems of Plato's Writing*. (University Park: Pennsylvania State University Press, 1991).

Fischer, Otto and Ann Öhrberg, eds. *Metamorphoses of Rhetoric. Classical Rhetoric in the 18th Century. Studia Rhetorica Upsaliensa*. (Uppsala: Avdelningen för retorik vid Litteraturvetenskapliga institutionen, 2011).

Fortenbaugh, William W. and David C. Mirhady, eds. *Peripatetic Rhetoric after Aristotle*. (New Brunswick, NJ: Transaction Publishers, 1994).

Fox, Matthew. "History and Rhetoric in Dionysius of Halicarnassus," *Journal of Roman Studies* 83 (1993): 31–47.

Freeman, Kathleen. *The Murder of Herodes*. (New York: W. W. Norton, 1963).

Fuller, B. A. G. *History of Greek Philosophy*. (New York: Greenwood Press, 1931).

Gaillet, Lynee Lewis and Winifred Bryan Horner, eds. *The Present State of Scholarship in the History of Rhetoric*. (Columbia: University of Missouri Press, 2010).

Gleason, Maud W. *Making Men: Sophists and Self-presentation in Ancient Rome*. (Princeton, NJ: Princeton University Press. 1995).

Gomperz, Theodore. *Greek Thinkers*. (London: John Murray, 1905).

Habinek, Thomas. *Ancient Rhetoric and Oratory*. (Malden, MA: Blackwell, 2005).

Hadas, Moses. *History of Greek Literature*. (New York: Columbia University Press, 1950).

Hinks, D. A. G. "Tisias and Corax and the Invention of Rhetoric," *Classical Quarterly* 34 (1940): 59–69.

Hubbell, Harry M. *The Influence of Isocrates on Cicero, Dionysius, and Aristides*. (New Haven, CT: Yale University Press, 1913).

Hunt, Everett L. "Plato and Aristotle on Rhetoric and the Rhetoricians," in *Studies in Rhetoric and Public Speaking in Honor of James A. Winans*, ed. Raymond F. Howes. (New York: Century, 1925).

Irwin, Terence. *Plato, Gorgias*. (Oxford: Clarendon Press, 1979).

Isocrates. *Isocrates*. 3 vols. Trans. George Norlin. (Cambridge, MA: Loeb Classical Library, 1954–1956).

Jarratt, Susan C. F. *Rereading the Sophists: Classical Rhetoric Refigured*. (Carbondale: Southern Illinois University Press, 1991).

Jebb, R. C. *The Attic Orators from Antiphon to Isaeos*. (New York: Russell, 1962).

Jensen, Minna S. *The Homeric Question and the Oral-formulaic Theory*. (Copenhagen: Museum Tusculanum Press, 1980).

Johnston, Christopher Lyle. *Listening to the Logos*. (Columbia: University of South Carolina Press. 2009).

Joyal, Mark, Iain MacDougall, and J. C. Yardley. *Greek and Roman Education*. (New York: Routledge, 2008).

Kagan, Donald. *The Peloponnesian War*. (New York: Viking Penguin Press, 2004).

Kastely, James L. "In Defense of Plato's *Gorgias*," *PMLA* 106 (1991): 96–109.

Kennedy, George A. "The Earliest Rhetorical Handbooks," *American Journal of Philology* 80 (1959): 167–178.

Kerford, G. B. "The First Greek Sophists," *Classical Review* 64 (1950): 8–10.

——, ed. *The Sophistic Movement*. (New York: Cambridge University Press, 1981).

——. *Sophists and Their Legacy: Proceedings of the Fourth International Colloquium on Ancient Philosophy, Homburg, 1979.* (Wiesbaden: Steiner, 1981).

Lysias. *Lysias.* Trans. W. R. M.Lamb. (London: William Heinemann, 1957).

——. *Lysias: Selected Speeches.* Ed. C. D.Adam. (New York: American Book Co., 1905).

——. *Selected Orations of Lysias*, 8th edn. Ed. William A. Stevens. (Chicago: S. C. Griggs and Co., 1891).

MacDowell, Douglas M. *Demosthenes the Orator.* (Oxford: Oxford University Press, 2010).

——. *The Law in Classical Athens.* (New York: Cornell University Press, 1978).

Marrou, H. I. *A History of Education in Antiquity.* Trans. G. Lamb. (New York: The New American Library, 1964).

Matsen, Patricia P., Philip Rollinson, and Marion Sousa, eds. *Readings from Classical Rhetoric.* (Carbondale: Southern Illinois University Press, 1990).

Meijering, Roos. *Literary and Rhetorical Theories in Greek Scholia.* (Groningen: E. Forsten, 1987).

Meyer, Michel. *Principia Rhetorica: Une théorie générale de l'argumentation.* (Paris: Fayard, 2008).

Morison, J. S. "An Introductory Chapter in the History of Greek Education," *Durham University Journal* 41 (1948): 55–63.

Murphy, James J., ed. *Demosthenes' On the Crown.* (Davis, CA: Hermagoras Press, 1983).

Naas, Michael. *Turning: From Persuasion to Philosophy.* (Atlantic Highlands, NJ: Humanities Press, 1993).

Nienkamp, Jean, ed. *Plato On Rhetoric and Language: Four Key Dialogues.* (Mahwah, NJ: Lawrence Erlbaum Associates, 1999).

Ochs, Donovan J. *Consolatory Rhetoric: Grief, Symbol, and Ritual in the Greco-Roman Era.* (Columbia: University of South Carolina Press, 1993).

Payne, David. "Rhetoric, Reality, and Knowledge: A Re-examination of Protagoras' Concept of Rhetoric," *Rhetoric Society Quarterly* 16 (1986, Summer): 167–179.

Pernot, Laurent. *Rhetoric in Antiquity.* Trans. W. E. Higgins. (Washington, DC: The Catholic University of America Press, 2005).

Plato. *The Dialogues of Plato.* 2 vols. Trans. Benjamin Jowett. (New York: Random House, 1937).

——. *Phaedrus.* Trans. C. J. Rowe. (Atlantic Highlands, NJ: Humanities Press, 1986).

——. *Plato on the Trial and Death of Socrates.* Trans. Lane Cooper. (Ithaca, NY: Cornell University Press, 1941).

——. *Symposium and Phaedrus.* Trans. Benjamin Jowett. (New York: Dover Publications, 1993).

Plutarch. "Lives of the Ten Orators," in *Plutarch's Morals*, vol. 5. Ed. William Watson Goodwin. Trans. Charles Barcroft. (Cambridge, MA: Press of John Wilson and Son, 1870).

Porter, James I. "The Seductions of Gorgias," *Classical Antiquity* 12 (1993): 267–299.

Porter, Stanley E., ed. *Handbook of Classical Rhetoric in the Hellenistic Period, 330 BC–AD 400.* (Leiden: Brill, 1997).

Raaflaub, Kurt and Deborah Boedeker, eds. *Democracy, Empire and the Arts in Fifth-century Athens.* (Cambridge, MA: Harvard University Press, 1998).

Rankin, H. D. *Sophists, Socrates, and Cynics.* (London: Croom Helm, 1983).

Sallis, John. *Being and Logos: The Way of Platonic Dialogue.* (Atlantic Highlands, NJ: Humanities Press International, 1986).

Sattler, William. "Socratic Dialogue and Modern Group Discussion," *Quarterly Journal of Speech* 29 (1943): 152–157.

Schiappa, Edward, ed. *Landmark Essays on Classical Greek Rhetoric.* (Davis, CA: Hermagoras Press, 1994).

——. *Protagoras and Logos.* (Columbia: University of South Carolina Press, 1991).

Shearer, Thomas D. "Gorgias' Theories of Art," *Classical Journal* 33 (1938): 402–415.

Smith, Bromley. "Protagoras of Abdera," *Quarterly Journal of Speech Education* 4 (1918): 196–215.

Smith, Morton. *The Ancient Greeks.* (Ithaca, NY: Cornell University Press, 1960).

Sprague, Rosamond Kent. *The Older Sophists.* (Columbia: University of South Carolina Press, 1972).

Stafford, Emma J. *Ancient Greece: Life, Myth, and Art.* (London: Duncan Baird Publishers, 2004).

Stone, Isidor Feinstein. *The Trial of Socrates.* (Boston: Little, Brown and Company, 1988).

Too, Yun Lee. *Education in Greek and Roman Antiquity.* (Leiden: Brill, 2001).

——, ed. *The Rhetoric of Identity in Isocrates: Text, Power, Pedagogy.* (New York: Cambridge University Press, 1995).

Toohy, Peter. *Reading Epic: An Introduction to the Ancient Narratives.* (New York: Routledge, 1992).

Untersteiner, Mario. *The Sophists.* Trans. Kathleen Freeman. (Oxford: Basil Blackwell, 1954).

Waterfield, Robin. *The First Philosophers: The Presocratics and the Sophists.* (London: Oxford University Press. 2000).

White, David A. *Rhetoric and Reality in Plato's* Phaedrus. (Albany: State University of New York Press, 1993).

Wilcox, Stanley. "The Scope of Early Rhetorical Instruction," *Harvard Studies in Classical Philology* 53 (1942): 121–155.

Williams, James D. *An Introduction to Classical Rhetoric: Essential Readings.* (Malden, MA: Blackwell, 2009).

Wilson, Thomas. *The Art of Rhetoric.* (University Park: Pennsylvania State University Press, 1994).

Wisse, Jakob. *Ethos and Pathos: From Aristotle to Cicero.* (Amsterdam: Hakkert, 1989).

Woodman, Anthony J. *Rhetoric in Classical Historiography: Four Studies.* (Portland, OR: Areopagitica Press, 1988).

Worthington, Ian, ed. *Demosthenes. Statesman and Orator.* (New York: Routledge, 2001).

——, ed. *A Historical Commentary on Dinarchus: Rhetoric and Conspiracy in Later Fourth-century Athens.* (Ann Arbor: University of Michigan Press, 1992).

——. *Persuasion: Greek Rhetoric in Action.* (London: Routledge, 1994).

Yunis, Harvey. *Taming Democracy: Models of Political Rhetoric in Classical Athens.* (Ithaca, NY: Cornell University Press, 1996).

## II. Aristotle

Adamik, Thomas. "Aristotle's Theory of the Period," *Philologus,* 128 (1984), 184–201.

Aristoteles. *Rhetorik.* Trans. Christof Rapp. 2 vols. (Berlin: Akademieverlag, 2002).

Aristotle. *On Rhetoric: A Theory of Civil Discourse.* 2nd edn. Trans. George A. Kennedy. (New York: Oxford University Press, 2006).

——. *Rhetoric.* Trans. William Robert Rhys. (New York: Modern Library, 1954).

——. *The Rhetoric of Aristotle. An Expanded Translation with Supplementary Examples for Students of Composition and Public Speaking.* Trans. Lane Cooper. (New York: Appleton-Century-Crofts, 1932).

——. *Rhetorica.* Trans. William Rhys Roberts. In *The Works of Aristotle Translated into English, vol. 2,* ed. W. D. Ross and J. A. Smith. (London: Clarendon Press, 1924).

Arnhart, Larry. *Aristotle on Political Reasoning: A Commentary on the* Rhetoric. (DeKalb: Northern Illinois University Press, 1981).

Barnes, Jonathan. *Aristotle: A Selected Bibliography.* (Oxford: Oxford University Press, 1977).

Bauman, Richard W. *Aristotle's Logic of Education.* (New York: Peter Lang, 1998).

Black, Edwin B. *Rhetorical Criticism: A Study in Method.* (New York: Macmillan, 1965).

Braet, Antoine Camillus. "Aristotle's Almost Unnoticed Contribution to the Doctrine of Stasis," *Mnemosyne* 52 (1999): 408–435.

Brandes, Paul D. *A History of Aristotle's* Rhetoric. (Metuchen, NJ: Scarecrow Press, 1989).

Brockriede, Wayne. "Toward a Contemporary Aristotelian Theory of Rhetoric," *Quarterly Journal of Speech* 52 (1966): 33–40.

Burnyeat, Myles F. "Enthymeme. Aristotle on the Logic of Persuasion," in *Aristotle's Rhetoric. Philosophical Essays*, ed. David J. Furley and A. Nehamas. (Princeton, NJ: Princeton University Press, 1994), 3–55.

Conley, Thomas. "The Enthymeme in Perspective," *Quarterly Journal of Speech* 70 (1984): 168–187.

——. "Pathe and Pisteis: Aristotle, *Rhetoric* II 2–11," *Hermes* 110 (1982): 300–315.

Cope, Edward M. *An Introduction to Aristotle's* Rhetoric *with Analysis, Notes and Appendices*. (Hildesheim: G. Olms, 1970).

——. Introduction to Aristotle's Rhetoric. 2nd edn. (Carbondale: Southern Illinois University Press, 1966).

Enos, Richard L. *Greek Rhetoric Before Aristotle*. 2nd edn. (Anderson, SC: Parlor Press, 2012).

Enos, Richard L. and Lois P. Agnew, eds. *Landmark Essays on Aristotelian Rhetoric*. (Mahwah, NJ: Hermagoras Press/Lawrence Erlbaum Associates, 1998).

Erickson, Keith V., ed. *Aristotle: The Classical Heritage of Rhetoric*. (Metuchen, NJ: Scarecrow Press, 1974).

——. *Aristotle's* Rhetoric: *Five Centuries of Philological Research*. (Metuchen, NJ: Scarecrow Press, 1974).

——. "The Lost Rhetorics of Aristotle," in *Landmark Essays on Aristotelian Rhetoric*, ed. RichardLeo Enos and Lois P. Agnew. (Mahwah, NJ and London: Lawrence Erlbaum Associates, 1998), 3–13.

Evans, J. D. *Aristotle's Concept of Dialectic*. (Cambridge: Cambridge University Press, 1977).

Fortenbaugh, William W. *Aristotle on Emotion: A Contribution to Philosophical Psychology, Rhetoric, Poetics, Politics, and Ethics*. (New York: Barnes and Noble, 1975).

——. "Aristotle's Rhetoric on Emotion," *Archiv fur Geschichte der Philosophie* 52 (1970): 40–70.

Freese, John H. *Aristotle: The "Art" of Rhetoric*. (London: Heinemann, 1926).

Furley, David J. and Alexander Nehamas, eds. *Aristotle's* Rhetoric: *Philosophical Essays*. (Princeton, NJ: Princeton University Press, 1994).

Garver, Eugene. *Aristotle's* Rhetoric: *An Art of Character*. (Chicago: University of Chicago Press, 1994).

Grimaldi, William M. *Studies in the Philosophy of Aristotle's* Rhetoric. (Wiesbaden: Steiner, 1975).

——. *Aristotle,* Rhetoric: *A Commentary*. 2 vols. (New York: Fordham University Press, 1980 and 1988).

Hauser, Gerald A. "Aristotle's Example Revisited," *Philosophy and Rhetoric*, 18 (1985): 171–179.

Hill, Forbes Iverson. "The Genetic Method in Recent Criticism on the *Rhetoric* of Aristotle." Diss. (Ithaca, NY: Cornell University, 1963).

——. "The Amorality of Aristotle's *Rhetoric*," *Greek, Roman and Byzantine Studies* 22 (1981): 133–147.

Hinks, D. A. G. "Tria Genera Causarum," *Classical Quarterly* 30 (1936): 170–182.

Hoppmann, Michael. "Rhetorik des Verstandes. Beweis- und Argumentationslehre," in *Handbuch der Sprach- und Kommunikationswissenschaft (HSK 31.1). Rhetorik und Stilistik*, ed. Ulla Fix, Andreas Gardt, and Joachim Knape. Vol. I. (Berlin: de Gruyter, 2008), 630–645.

Jebb, Richard Claverhouse. *The* Rhetoric *of Aristotle*. (Cambridge: Cambridge University Press, 1909).

Kennedy, George A., trans. *Aristotle On Rhetoric: A Theory of Civic Discourse*. (New York: Oxford University Press, 1991).

Knape, Joachim and Thomas Schirren, eds. *Aristotelische Rhetoriktradition*. (Stuttgart: Steiner, 2005).

Kraus, Manfred. "Enthymem," in *Historisches Wörterbuch der Rhetorik*. Vol. 2, ed. Gert Ueding. (Tübingen: Niemeyer, 1994), 1197–1222.

Liu, Yameng. "Aristotle and Stasis Theory," *Rhetoric Society Quarterly* 21 (1991): 53–59.

Long, H. S. "A Bibliographical Survey of Recent Work on Aristotle," *Classical World* 51 (1958): 96–98, 117–119, 160–162, 167–168, 193–194, 204–209.

Madden, Edward H. "Aristotle's Treatment of Probability and Signs," *Philosophy of Science* 24 (1957): 167–172.

——. "The Enthymeme: Crossroads of Logic, Rhetoric, and Metaphysics," *Philosophical Review* 61 (1952): 368–376.

McBurney, James A. "The Place of the Enthymeme in Rhetorical Theory," *Speech Monographs* 3 (1936): 49–74.

Mirhady, David. "Non-Technical *Pisteis* in Aristotle and Anaximenes," *American Journal of Philology* 112 (1991): 5–28.

Nehamas, Alexander and David J. Furley, eds. *Aristotle's* Rhetoric: *Philosophical Essays*. (Princeton, NJ: Princeton University Press, 1994).

Ochs, Donovan J. "Aristotle's Concept of Formal Topics," *Speech Monographs* 36 (1969): 419–425.

Palmer, Georgiana Paine. *The Topoi of Aristotle's* Rhetoric *as Exemplified in the Orators*. (Chicago: University of Chicago Press, 1934).

Rapp, Christoph. "Aristotle – Rhetoric," in *The Stanford Encyclopedia of Philosophy*, ed. E. N. Zalta. http://plato.stanford.edu.

Richards, H. "Notes on the Rhetoric of Aristotle," *Journal of Philology* 33 (1914): 172–181.

Ryan, Eugene E. *Aristotle's Theory of Argumentation*. (Montreal: Bellarmin, 1984).

Sandys, John E., ed. *The* Rhetoric *of Aristotle*. (Salem, NH: Ayer, 1988).

Schmitt, Charles. *A Critical Survey and Bibliography of Studies on Renaissance Aristotelianism, 1958–1969*. (Padova: Antenore, 1971).

Self, Lois S. "Rhetoric and *Phronesis*: The Aristotelian Ideal," *Philosophy and Rhetoric* 12 (1979): 130–145.

Solmsen, Friedrich. "The Aristotelian Tradition in Ancient Rhetoric," *American Journal of Philology* 62 (1941): 35–50, 169–190.

——. "Aristotle and Cicero on the Orator's Playing Upon the Feelings," *Classical Philology* 33 (1938): 390–404.

Warnick, Barbara. "Judgment, Probability, and Aristotle's *Rhetoric*," *The Quarterly Journal of Speech* 75 (1989): 299–311.

## III. From Greek to "Roman" Rhetoric

Adamietz, Joachim. *Ciceros de inventione und die Rhetorik ad Herennium*. Diss. (University of Marburg, 1960).

Anonymous. *Rhetorica ad Alexandrum*. Trans. E. S. Forster in *The Works of Aristotle Translated into English*, ed. W. D. Ross. Vol. 11. (Oxford: Oxford University Press, 1924–1955).

Aristotle. *Problems: Books 22–38. Rhetorica ad Alexandrum*. Trans. W. S. Hett and H. Rackham. (Cambridge, MA: Loeb Classical Library, 1937).

Aristotle. *Problems: Books 20–38. Rhetorica ad Alexandrum*. Trans. Robert Mayhew and David C. Mirhady. (Cambridge, MA: Loeb Classical Library, 2011).

Barwick, Karl. "Augustins Schrift De Rhetorica und Hermagoras von Temnos," *Philologus* 105 (1961): 97–110.

——. "Zur Erklärung und Geschichte der Staseislehre des Hermagoras von Temnos," *Philologus* 108 (1964): 80–101.

——. "Zur Rekonstruktion der Rhetorik des Hermagoras von Temnos," *Philologus* 109 (1965): 186–218.

Braet, Antoine Camillus. *De klassieke statusleer in modern perspectief. Een historisch-systematische bijdrage tot de argumentatieleer*. Diss. (Groningen, 1984).

Calboli Montefusco, Lucia. *La dottrina degli „status" nella retorica greca e romana*. (Hildesheim: Olms-Weidmann, 1986).

Cicero. *Ad c. Herennium de ratione dicendi*. Trans. Harry Caplan. (Cambridge, MA: Loeb Classical Library, 1964).

Cornificius. *Rhetorica ad C. Herennium*. Trans. and comm. Gualtiero Calboli. (Bologna: Pàtron, 1969).

Enos, Richard Leo. "Rhetorica ad Herennium," in *Classical Rhetorics and Rhetoricians: Critical Studies and Sources,* ed. Michelle Ballif and Michael G. Moran. (Westport, CT and London: Praeger, 2005), 331–338.

———. *Roman Rhetoric and the Greek Influence.* (Prospect Heights, IL: Waveland, 1995).

Heath, Malcolm. "The Substructure of *Stasis*-theory from Hermagoras to Hermogenes," *Classical Quarterly* 44 (1994): 114–129.

———. "Hermagoras: Transmission and Attribution," *Philologus* 146 (2002): 287–298.

Matthes, Dieter. "Hermagoras von Temnos," *Lustrum* 3 (1958): 58–214.

———. *Hermagorae Temnitae testimonia et fragmenta.* (Leipzig: Teubner, 1962).

Nadeau, Ray. "Hermogenes' *On Stases*: A Translation with an Introduction," *Speech Monographs* 31 (1964): 361–424.

O'Rourke, Sean Patrick. "Anaximenes, *Rhetorica ad Alexandrum,*" in *Classical Rhetorics and Rhetoricians: Critical Studies and Sources*, ed. Michelle Ballif and Michael G. Moran. (Westport, CT and London: Praeger, 2005), 19–23.

## IV. Cicero

Alexander, Michael Charles. *Trials in the Late Roman Republic: 149 BC to 50 BC* (Toronto: University of Toronto Press, 1990).

Anonymous. "A Survey of Selected Ciceronian Bibliography, 1939–1953," *Classical Weekly* 47 (1954): 129–139.

Bonner, Stanley Frederick. *Education in Ancient Rome.* (Berkeley: University of California Press, 1977).

———. *Roman Declamation.* (Liverpool: Liverpool University Press, 1949).

Canter, Howard Vernon. "*Digressio* in the Orations of Cicero," *American Journal of Philology* 52 (1931): 351–361.

———. "Irony in the Orations of Cicero," *American Journal of Philology* 57 (1936): 457–464.

Cicero. *Brutus.* Trans. E. Jones. (New York: AMS Press, 1976).

———. *Cicero on the Ideal Orator [De oratore].* With introduction, notes, appendixes, glossary, and indexes. Tr. James M. May and Jakob Wisse. (New York: Oxford University Press, 2001).

———. *De inventione. topica.* Trans. H. M. Hubbell. (Cambridge, MA: Harvard University Press, 1949).

———. *De natura deorum.* Trans. Francis Brooks. (London: Methuen, 1896).

———. *De Oratore.* Two vols. Trans. E. W. Sutton and H. Rackham. (Cambridge, MA: Harvard University Press, 1959).

———. *On Oratory and Orators.* Trans. J. S. Watson. (London: Bell and Daldy, 1871).

Ciceroni, M. Tulli. *De Oratore.* Ed. Augustus S. Wilkins. (Amsterdam: Servio, 1962).

Classen, Carl Joachim. "Cicero, the Laws and the Law Courts," *Latomus* 37 (1978): 597–619.

Cowell, F. R. *Cicero and the Roman Republic.* (Baltimore: Penguin, 1956).

Craig, Christopher P. *Form as Argument in Cicero's Speeches: A Study of Dilemma.* (Atlanta, GA: Scholars Press, 1993).

Delayen, G. *Cicero.* (New York: E. P. Dutton, 1931).

Dorey, Thomas Alan, ed. *Cicero.* (London: Routledge and Kegan Paul, 1964).

Enos, Richard Leo. *The Literate Mode of Cicero's Legal Rhetoric.* (Carbondale: Southern Illinois University Press, 1988).

———. *Roman Rhetoric: Revolution and the Greek Influence.* (Prospect Heights, IL: Waveland Press, 1995).

Fantham, Elaine. *The Roman World of Cicero's De Oratore.* (Oxford: Oxford University Press, 2004).

Forsyth, William. *Life of Marcus Tullius Cicero.* (New York: Charles Scribner's Sons, 1896).

Fortenbaugh, William W. "Cicero's Knowledge of the Rhetorical Treatises of Aristotle and Theophrastus," in *Cicero's Knowledge of the Peripatos*, ed. William W. Fortenbaugh and Peter Steinmetz. (New Brunswick, NJ and London: Transaction Publishers, 1989).

Fuhrmann, Manfred. *Cicero and the Roman Republic.* (Cambridge, MA: Blackwell Publishers, 1992).

Greenidge, Abel Hend Jones. *The Legal Procedure of Cicero's Time.* (Oxford: Clarendon Press, 1901).

Habicht, Christian. *Cicero the Politician.* (Baltimore: Johns Hopkins University Press, 1989).

Havell, H. L. *Republican Rome.* (London: George Harrop, 1914).

Hendrickson, G. I. "Cicero's Correspondence with Brutus and Calvus on Oratorical Style," *American Journal of Philology* 47 (1926): 239.

Kennedy, George A. *The Art of Rhetoric in the Roman World, 300 BC – AD 300.* (Princeton, NJ: Princeton University Press, 1972).

Kirby, John T. *The Rhetoric of Cicero's* Pro Cluentio. (Amsterdam: J. C. Gieben, 1990).

Leeman, Anton D., Harm Pinkster, Jakob Wisse et al. *M. Tullius Cicero: De oratore libri III. Kommentar.* 5 vols. (Heidelberg: Universitätsverlag Winter, 1981–2008).

MacKendrick, P. "Cicero's Ideal Orator," *Classical Journal* 43 (1947–1948): 345.

May, James. *Trials of Character: The Eloquence of Ciceronian Ethos.* (Chapel Hill: University of North Carolina Press, 1988).

May, J. M. *Brill's Companion to Cicero: Oratory and Rhetoric.* (Leiden: Brill, 2002).

Mitchell, Thomas N. *Cicero: The Ascending Years.* (New Haven, CT: Yale University Press, 1991).

——. *Cicero, the Senior Statesman.* (New Haven, CT: Yale University Press, 1991).

Peterson, Torsten. *Cicero: A Biography.* (Berkeley: University of California Press, 1920).

Richards, G. C. *Cicero.* (New York: Houghton Mifflin, 1935).

Rolfe, John C. *Cicero and His Influence.* (New York: Cooper Square, 1963).

Solmsen, Friedrich. "Aristotle and Cicero on the Orator's Playing on the Feelings," *Classical Philology* 33 (1938): 401.

Taylor, John H. "Political Motives in Cicero's *Defense of Archias*," *American Journal of Philology* 73 (1952): 62–70.

Tyler, Hannis. *Cicero: A Sketch of His Life and Works.* (Chicago: McClure, 1918).

Wood, Neal. *Cicero's Social and Political Thought.* (Berkeley: University of California Press, 1988).

Wooten, Cecil. *Cicero's Philippics and their Demosthenic Model.* (Chapel Hill: University of North Carolina Press, 1983).

# V. Quintilian

Adamietz, Joachim. "Quintilians Institutio oratoria," in *Aufstieg und Niedergang der römischen Welt.* Vol. II 32.4. Ed. Wolfgang Haase and Hildegard Temporini. (Berlin and New York: De Gruyter, 1986), 2226–2271.

Ahlheid, Fraus. *Quintilian, the Preface to Book VIII and Comparable Passages in the* Institutio oratoria. (Amsterdam: B. R. Gruner, 1983).

Albaladejo, T., E. Del Rio, and J. A. Caballero, eds. *Quintiliano: historia y actualidad de la retorica.* 3 vols. (Logrono: Ediciones Instituto de Estudios Riojanos, 1998).

Atkins, J. W. H. *Literary Criticism in Antiquity.* 2 vols. (Gloucester, MA: Peter Smith, 1961).

Bonner, S. F. *Roman Declamation in the Late Republic and Early Empire.* (Los Angeles: University of California Press, 1949).

Brandenburg, Earnest. "Quintilian and the Good Orator," *Quarterly Journal of Speech* 34 (1948): 23–29.

Calboli, Gualtiero. *Quintiliano y su escuela.* (Logrono: Gobiamo de la Rioja, Instituto de Estudios Riojanos. Ayuntiamento de Calahorra, 2001).

Caplan, Harry. "The Decay of Eloquence at Rome in the First Century," *Studies in Speech and Drama in Honor of A. M. Drummond.* (Ithaca, NY: Cornell University Press, 1944).

Classen, Carl Joachim. "Quintilian and the Revival of Learning in Italy," *Humanistica Lovaniensis* 43 (1994): 77–98.

Cranz, F. Edward. "Quintilian as an Ancient Thinker," *Rhetorica* 13 (1995): 219–230.

Erickson, Keith. "Quintilian's *Institutio oratorio* and *Pseudo-Declamations*" [A bibliography], *Rhetoric Society Quarterly* 11 (1981): 45–62.

Galand-Hallyn, P., F. Hallyn, C. Levy, and W. Verbaal, eds. *Quintilien, Ancien et moderne etudes reunies.* (Turnhout: Brepols, 2009).

Harding, H. F. "Quintilian's Witnesses," *Speech Monographs* 1 (1934): 1–20.

Katula, Richard A. "Quintilian on the Art of Emotional Appeal," *Rhetoric Review* 22 (2003): 5–15.

Kennedy, George A. "An Estimate of Quintilian," *American Journal of Philology* 83 (1962): 130–146.

Leff, Michael. "Commonplaces and Argumentation in Cicero and Quintilian," *Argumentation* 10 (1996): 445–452.

Lopez, Jorge Fernandez. "Quintilian as Teacher and Rhetorician," in *A Companion to Roman Rhetoric,* ed. William Dominik and Jon Hall. (Oxford: Blackwell, 2007), 307–322.

Meador, Prentice A. "Quintilian's *Vir Bonus*," *Western Speech* 34 (1970): 162–169.

——. "Speech Education at Rome," *Western Speech* 31 (1966): 9–15.

Mendelson, Michael. "Quintilian and the Pedagogy of Argument," *Argumentation* 15 (2001): 277–294.

Murphy, James J. "Grammar and Rhetoric in Roman Schools," in *Geschichte der Sprachwissenschaften/History of the Language Sciences.* Ed. Sylvain Auroux et al. (Berlin and New York: Walter der Gruyter, 2000), 484–503.

——. "The Key Role of Habit in Roman Education," in *A Short History of Writing Instruction from Ancient Greece to Modern America.* 2nd edn. Ed. James J. Murphy. (Mahwah, NJ: Hermagoras Press/Lawrence Erlbaum Associates, 2001), 35–78.

——. "The Key Role of Habit in Roman Rhetoric and Education as Described by Quintilian," in *Quintiliano. Historia y Actualidad de la Rhetorica.* 3 vols. Ed. Tomas Albaladejo Major, Emiliodel Rio, and Jose Antonio Cabalerro. (Logrono: Ediciones Instituto de Estudios Riojanos, 1998), 141–150.

——. "The Modern Value of Ancient Roman Methods of Teaching Writing, With Answers to Twelve Modern Fallacies," *Writing On the Edge* 1 (1989): 28–37.

——. "Quintilian," in *Encyclopedia of Rhetoric and Composition.* Ed. Theresa Enos. (New York: Garland, 1996), 581–585.

——, ed. *Quintilian on the Early Education of the Citizen-Orator. Library of Liberal Arts.* (New York: Bobbs Merrill, 1966).

——, ed. *Quintilian on the Teaching of Speaking and Writing: Translations from Books One, Two, and Ten of the* Institutio oratoria. (Carbondale: Southern Illinois University Press, 1987).

——. "Quintilian's Advice on the Continuing Self-Education of the Adult Orator: Book X of the *Institutio oratoria*," in *Quintilian and the Law: The Art of Persuasion in Law and Politics.* Ed. Olga Tellegen-Couperus. (Leuven: Leuven University Press, 2003), 247–252.

——. "Quintilian's Influence on the Teaching of Speaking of Teaching and Writing in the Middle Ages and Renaissance," in *Oral and Written Communication: Historical Approaches.* Ed. RichardLeo Enos. Written Communication Annual, No. 4. (Newbury Park, CA: Sage, 1990), 158–183.

——. "Roman Writing Instruction as Described by Quintilian," in *A Short History of Writing Instruction from Ancient Greece to Contemporary America.* 3rd edn. Ed. James J. Murphy. (New York: Routledge, 2012), 36–76.

Parks, Edilbert P. *The Roman Rhetorical Schools as Preparation for the Courts under the Early Empire.* (Baltimore: Johns Hopkins Press, 1945).

Pennacini, Adriano, ed. *Quintiliano. Institutio oratoria. Edizione con testo a fronte.* (Turin: Einaudi, 2001).

Pujante, David. *El hijo de la persuasion. Quintilian y el estatuto retorica.* 2nd edn. (Logrono: Instituto de Estudios Riojanos, 1999).

Quintilian. *The Institutio oratoria of Quintilian.* 4 vols. Tr. H. E. Butler. (Cambridge, MA: Harvard University Press, 1921).

——. *The Orator's Education. [Institutio oratoria].* Ed. and tr. Donald A. Russell. 5 vols. Loeb Classical Library. (Cambridge, MA: Harvard University Press, 2001).

Ramus, Petrus. *Arguments in Rhetoric against Quintilian.* Ed. J. J.Murphy. Trans. Carole Newlands. (De Kalb: Northern Illinois University Press, 1986).

Reinhardt, Tobias and Michael Winterbottom, eds. *Quintilian Book 2.* (Oxford: Oxford University Press, 2006).

Spence, Sarah. *Rhetorics of Reason and Desire: Vergil, Augustine, and the Troubadors.* (Ithaca, NY: Cornell University Press, 1988).

Sussman, Lewis A. *The Major Declamations Ascribed to Quintilian: A Translation.* (New York: Verlag P. Lang, 1987).

Tellegen-Couperus, Olga, ed. *Quintilian and the Law: The Art of Persuasion in Law and Politics.* (Leuven, Belgium: Leuven University Press, 2003).

Ward, John O. "Quintilian and the Rhetorical Revolution of the Middle Ages," *Rhetorica* 13 (1995): 231–284.

Winterbottom, Michael, ed. *The Minor Declamations Ascribed to Quintilian.* (New York: De Gruyter, 1984).

## VI. Epilogue

Abelson, Paul. *The Seven Liberal Arts.* (New York: Columbia University Press, 1906).

Anderson, Graham. *The Second Sophistic: A Cultural Phenomenon in the Roman Empire.* (New York: Routledge, 1993).

——. "Rhetoric and the Second Sophistic," in *A Companion to Roman Rhetoric.* Ed. WilliamDominik and Jon Hall. (Oxford, UK: Blackwell, 2007), 339–353.

Augustine. *Saint Augustine on Christian Doctrine.* Trans. D. W. Robertson. (New York: Library of Liberal Arts, 1958).

Flood, Emmet T. "The Narrative Structure of Augustine's *Confessions*: Time's Quest for Eternity," *International Philosophical Quarterly* 28 (1988): 141–162.

Lamb, Jonathan. "Longinus, the Dialectic, and the Practice of Mastery," *ELH* 60 (1993): 545–567.

Longinus. *On Great Writing (On the Sublime).* Trans. G. M. A. Grube. (New York: Library of Liberal Arts, 1957).

Macksey, Richard. "Longinus Reconsidered," *MLN* 108 (1993): 913–934.

Nadeau, Ray. "The *Progymnasmata* of Apthonius in Translation," *Speech Monographs* 19 (1952): 264–285.

Seneca the Elder. *The Suasoriae.* Trans. W. A. Edward. (Cambridge: Cambridge University Press, 1928).

Tacitus. *Dialogus, Agricola, Germania.* Trans. William Peterson. (Cambridge, MA: Loeb Classical Library, 1956).

Walsh, George B. "Sublime Method: Longinus on Language and Imitation," *Classical Antiquity* 7 (1988): 252–269.

Welch, Kathleen E. *The Contemporary Reception of Classical Rhetoric: Appropriations of Ancient Discourse.* (Hillsdale, NJ: Lawrence Erlbaum, 1990).

Whitmarsh, Tim. *The Second Sophistic.* (Oxford: Oxford University Press for the Classical Association, 2005).

# Index

Page numbers suffixed with *fig* or *tab* refer to figures or tables respectively.